THE SUNDAY TIMES
SPORTS BOOK

Power, grace, speed . . . Andrea Lynch drives from the starting blocks

Edited by
John Lovesey ● Nicholas Mason ● Edwin Taylor

THE SUNDAY TIMES
SPORTS BOOK

World's Work Ltd

Published by World's Work Ltd., The Windmill Press,
Kingswood, Tadworth, Surrey

© Times Newspapers Ltd (The Sunday Times) 1979
SBN 437 15445 9

Printed in Great Britain by
BAS Printers Limited,
Over Wallop,
Hampshire.

Contents

Foreword
by Sir Roger Bannister

Nothing is as dead as yesterday's newspaper and there is much ephemeral sports reporting, sensational prose littered with hyperbole that would be more suited to a cataclysmic earthquake than a football match. Yet the best sports writing is arguably the highest form of journalism, not despised by creative writers of Paul Gallico's calibre. Many readers have an avid command of detail which forces the writer into a more scrupulous regard for accuracy than other journalists need show. The sportswriter must also create a mood. Neville Cardus quoted here describes the bowling of Wilfred Rhodes as "lulling his victims into the tranced state in which he could work his will, and make them perform strokes contrary to their reason and intention". The writer must also set the occasion in the perspective of the year, the decade, the century. It is only to be expected that this book contains many treasures of sports writing. A bonus is the penetrating analysis of detail for which *The Sunday Times* is renowned. Serious commentaries are balanced by pungent comments on sport's foibles and follies.

Why does sport have such appeal? Sir Francis Chichester, already a pensioner when he circled the world, said simply: "Challenge makes living more intense." Sport provides one of the few chances to pit body and brain against a rival or against nature. Through millions of years we evolved as hunting animals and is it any surprise that when desk-bound or factory-constrained, we get depressed? If we cannot enjoy the cathartic release of sport ourselves, and I place this first, we can still identify with a team or hero that carries the magic of victory. Sport, like art as an attribute of civilisation, is to be nurtured and respected. It is one world of sport that spans the diverse feats by competitors from the agile gymnast Olga Korbut to the gentle giant shot putter Geoff Capes.

This book covers a decade of record breaking and prompts the question "When will it all end"? As more and more countries take part in sport, with China and India just about to enter the world stage, there is a greater chance of discovering many more athletes of exceptional physique and temperament. Sometimes an ingenious technical advance like the fibreglass vaulting pole or the Fosbury backwards high jump "flop" immediately reshapes the steady progress of the record curve. In running, many records have passed to the Kenyan descendants of Masai warriors who adapted to life at altitude so well that they can transport oxygen more efficiently from lung to muscle than any other runners.

Bannister the immortal—25 years ago the lung-bursting culmination to the first mile run in under four minutes made Roger Bannister a household name and launched a new era of athletic achievement. The photographs are unmistakable and unforgettable.

The contents of this book throw an interesting light on national character. Abroad the Englishman has a reputation of giving to sport the energy which should be devoted to life itself. If the English have an obsession with sport, the most gifted players are the Celts not the Anglo-Saxons. In this year's Football Association Cup Final between two "English" teams three-quarters of the players were from Scotland, Ireland and Wales.

More famous than our language or laws or parliamentary institutions, British sport has penetrated everywhere: from the leafy jungles of former colonies of the developing world, resounding with the crack of cricket ball driven to cover, to Europe, where our sport has made more impact than our trade or industrial skills.

It was the British "Club" conceived in the mid-19th Century that combined social and athletic activity and bridged the classes more often that it divided them, from cycling in the North to village cricket in the South. Later clubs joined together to reduce the muddle of rules and form a framework of governing bodies that exists today. The public school ethic of muscular christianity has led to *Le Comité Internationale pour le Fair Play*. Some of our professionals must be bewildered by the term as they perfect that modern device the professional foul!

Today's sport certainly has some dark areas. The sad story of oppressed political minorities, the slow progress away from apartheid and the dreary battle against drugs and anabolic steroids. Since the Sports Council pioneered tests that have resulted in suspensions, there has been progress. The hope is that athletes and their doctors will decide against stupidly risking disqualification and long-term ill health by such abuses. Commercialism and cost bedevil the international sporting scene, including the Olympics.

More heartening than the relentless pursuit of records is the change in recreational sport in the past decade. This book traces the trend from the middle-aged "guinea pigs" pursuing fitness schemes culminating in *The Sunday Times* National Fun Run in Hyde Park last October when 10,000 runners aged 4–80, men and women, fat and thin, good and bad, enjoyed themselves with no more serious mishaps than the odd sprained ankle and some blisters. Doubtless there are fitness bores and jogging bores and I would be the last to wish people to be dragged into the dreary fitness routines by fear of heart attacks. Rather we need a variety of recreation to suit every physique and personality, encouraged locally by our towns and nationally by the Sports Council. This should ensure that the habit of exercise should be carried from school into family life.

The *Sunday Times* team describes the world of human striving liberally mixed with human frailty. They have not been content to take an event at its face value but, in the reflective way that justifies Sunday newspapers, have probed more deeply. Why did we lose the World Cup? What is the logic of football tactics? How does altitude affect Olympic performance? What are the ingredients of East German supremacy in so many sports? The answers which emerge are diverse, sometimes shocking, never dull.

This is the sportsman's ultimate bedside book that will enthrall and educate—whetting his appetite for fresh sports. In the past few of our ancestors were rich enough to enjoy sport. Now we are being catapulted into a silicon chip age. Even the intellectuals who formerly curled their lips at sport can now see that it can produce happiness for many who still lead over-burdened lives. There has never been a better prospect of "Sport for All".

Roger Bannister

London, August 1979

Introduction

Each week the sports pages of *The Sunday Times* contain around 16,500 words, and a selection of photographs and other illustrations. If you account for the different match reports carried in various editions in one night the total number of words is actually higher. Many of these words are processed at great speed. For the first edition, which goes to press promptly at 5.30pm on Saturday, reports of matches are phoned or telexed into the office in small sections during the afternoon so that as the deadline draws close all that is left to handle is a relatively small amount of copy. Even for the paper's immediately subsequent edition, writers out in the field have to dictate their completed stories little more than 15 minutes after the final whistle. It is an operation that never fails to excite and it is one that intrigues even the least knowledgeable of outsiders.

Over the course of a year the sports pages thus carry approximately 900,000 words and hundreds of illustrations. Over the 12 years which this book encompasses, it adds up to approaching 11 million words and thousands of illustrations. Sifting this material to arrive at the selection in this book took more than two months of very concentrated work and, inevitably, it now seems just a drop in the ocean of more than a decade's coverage.

Why, readers might ask, did the book not stick to a decade of sports reporting, with boundaries traditionally accepted? The simple answer is that 1967 is the year Harold Evans became Editor of *The Sunday Times* and his influence on the conception of our current sports pages was paramount. Indeed, their origin goes back even further, to January 1966 when Evans joined *The Sunday Times* as Chief Assistant to Denis Hamilton, who was then Editor. One of Evans's first jobs was "to give a fresh slant to the sports pages."

The paper at that time gave sports a "blanket coverage", cramming in as many reports and results as space would allow. There is a lot to be said for blanket coverage of sports, particularly when you can change pages liberally through Saturday night and thereby cater very carefully to regional interests. However this policy did not fit the "new image" Sunday newspaper that was being created in the 1960s, and certainly did not make sense without sufficient page changes, which became increasingly difficult to provide as circulation and pagination increased.

Harold Evans's solution was to develop an attractive mixture of news and features, with fewer but longer and more carefully selected reports. It is a policy that has continued to be developed into an era of sports which is even more demanding of its journalists.

Before I joined the *The Sunday Times* from *Sports Illustrated* I discussed many times with Harold Evans the type of approach to sports journalism, particularly to features, which is amply illustrated in this book. After I joined the paper in 1967, initially as Sports Features Editor, before becoming Sports Editor in 1970, Edwin Taylor, the paper's Director of Design, became increasingly involved with me in the illustrations and graphic analysis that have become a characteristic of the sports coverage in *The Sunday Times*.

Sport, of course lends itself well to analysis by writers working closely with artists and photographers. But few laymen can comprehend the amount of work that goes into such features. Indeed, if a feeling is conveyed that a lot of effort has been involved in the production, the chances are that the illustrations have failed. The object of the exercise is to break the complex down into simple elements that are instantly understood, but to achieve this may involve the detailed study of photos and video tape recordings, hours of interviews, and countless amendments before it's right.

From 12 years of sports pages, many of the features that we have been most pleased with at the time, have regrettably not found their way into *The Sunday Times Sports Book*. None of our "instructional" series appear in total. There simply was not the space, just as there was not the space for some of our longer articles and series of articles, such as those written by Keith

PICTURE FILE: the gallery of photographs that introduces this book

● Ninety minutes from the World Cup. Brazil's footballers pose for a phalanx of photographers before the kick-off of the World Cup Final in Mexico City, 1970. They beat Italy 4–1 to win the Jules Rimet Trophy for the third time. Photo: Gerry Cranham.

● The last open ditch, King George VI Chase, Kempton Park, Boxing Day 1973. Richard Pitman and Pendil (No. 4), the eventual winners, follow hard on the heels of Inkslinger (Tommy Carberry, No. 3) and The Dikler (Ron Barry). Photo: Gerry Cranham.

● Near miss at sea. The British yacht Morning Cloud (with her owner and skipper Edward Heath in the stern) passes uncomfortably close to the Italian Levantades during Britain's triumphant passage to victory in the 1971 Admiral's Cup. Photo: Gerry Cranham.

● Trials of strength. A rugby ball's eye view (left) of the sixteen-man scrum. The final straw (right) for Wales's Jeff Bryce, whose failure here left him the bronze medal in the 56kg class at the 1978 Commonwealth Games. Photos: Gerry Cranham/Chris Smith.

Botsford and Brian Glanville on the Solti scandal in European football, which could fill a book by themselves and certainly deserve one.

Missing from this book, too, are several other investigatory articles which caused a considerable stir when they were published but have less general interest now. Time has simply blurred their impact. For the same reason only two match reports are included. The day after a game a first-class report can capture the imagination with its insight, but in a week's time, let alone a year or more, it can appear thoroughly stale through no fault of its own.

Though the editors of this book kept a constant eye on balance, we can only plead in any final analysis that ours is a subjective choice, and that is probably as it should be. The resulting book, mined from such a vast store, is an impression at least of a form of sports journalism and a reflection of a fascinating era in sport. It was a period within *The Sunday Times* which added significant new names to the renowned ones of writers like Henry Longhurst and Vivian Jenkins. It was a period dominated by one sportsman more than any other, Muhammad Ali. It was a period marked by changes in the appreciation of sport's connections to our social and political environment. And it was a period enhanced by a broadening interest in many more sports than used to be the case. *The Sunday Times* tried to reflect all this and itself encourage certain developments. The sports pages have been in the forefront from the beginning of the fight against apartheid and have campaigned for the acceptance of physical recreation facilities as a social right rather than a privilege.

Some of these subjects have been covered so extensively in the sports pages that it proved impossible to pick out one article to sum up our coverage adequately. This applied notably to our campaign for middle-age fitness, and here we have provided a summary by the main writer involved. In most cases in the book, however, the articles are printed as they ran originally in the paper; we have not changed the tense or cut out a single "yesterday" if we felt it would destroy the immediacy of the flavour. The criterion has been simple: Does the piece stand the test of time?

At the end of each piece, including the items from *The Sunday Times*'s Inside Track column, we have given the date of original publication in the paper. Where we have felt it necessary we have provided a brief postscript.

The breakdown of subjects suggested itself. In one original selection the compartments were numerous, but as the refining progressed the pieces settled into the six divisions we have in this book.

All the people who helped with the production in a remarkably short space of time are listed here. Only one other person deserves acknowledgment, apart from the Editor Harold Evans. This is Derrick Collier, now the Production Editor of *The Sunday Times*, who was Deputy Sports Editor of the paper until succeeded by Nick Mason in 1977. Until that year Collier had been a sports journalist most of his working life and the part he played in the reshaping of the sports pages of *The Sunday Times* was crucial. Without his hard work, encouragement and flair many of the articles that follow would never have made the sports pages of the paper, let alone the pages of *The Sunday Times Sports Book*.

J.L.

Production team

Editors: John Lovesey, Nicholas Mason, Edwin Taylor. **Text:** Bob Campbell, Norman Harris, Rob Hughes, Chris Oram, Peter Roberts. **Photographic research:** Ray Blumire, Bernard Neighbour. **Design:** Ros Newcomen, Peter Baistow, Gillian Crampton Smith, John Grimwade, Derek Alder, Duncan Mil. **Production:** Victor Shreeve, Peter Snowball, Michael Turner, Mandy Jessup. We are also most grateful for the help given by the staffs of the Library and the Darkroom at *The Sunday Times*.

● A place in the final. Berwyn Price (Wales, No. 414) trails behind Australia's Warren Parr (28) in the 110m hurdles semi-final at the Edmonton Games. In the final next day Price overcame his notoriously shaky start to take the gold medal. Photo: Chris Smith.

● A question of height. Rob Bishop (left), 15-year-old karate expert. Doug Walters (centre), Australian batsman, in a tangle against the fast men of South Africa, 1971. Nelli Kim (right), Russian gymnast, Wembley, 1977. Photos: Chris Smith/*Natal Mercury*/Chris Smith.

● Cup fever. In 1974 Newcastle were beaten by Liverpool in the F.A. Cup Final. Two years later their fans repeated the long journey to Wembley for the League Cup Final against Manchester City. Fanaticism was not enough— Newcastle lost 2–1. Photo: Jack Hickes.

● Runners and bathers (back endpaper). Ireland's last remaining official beach race-course at Laytown, some 40 miles from Dublin. Jockeys complain about flying sand and the puddles that have to be jumped, but the holidaymakers love it all. Photo: Chris Smith.

1

THE CONTEST

Confrontation in sport is the contest. Not merely team versus team, but one human being facing another – in the ring, on the track, even in the sky overhead – in a competition which is, at its best, a form of co-operation. It is also a test of oneself, striving to some new limit of performance or endurance. Thus the contest occurs

The world heavyweight championship encounter between George Foreman, the holder, and Muhammad Ali in Kinshasa, Zaire, in 1974, was a pinnacle of the decade, and the devastating right-hander from Ali which knocked out Foreman in the eighth round to regain him the title for the first time was the perfect finale. It was a big black extravaganza, President Mobutu's gift to his people. Black was the theme of the huge Festival of Zaire that year, and the moment that Mobutu's government put up the money to stage the *combat du siècle*, a global dimension was grafted on to a parochial celebration. There was one snag. In Foreman's final preparations in the week prior to the contest, he was cut over the right eye while sparring, and the fight was postponed for 30 days: a debilitating hiatus in the compelling drama.

A godly stalemate for two black knights

The accident to George Foreman's right eyelid happened on Monday afternoon in the hot auditorium of the N'Sele Presidential Domain. There, along the banks of the re-christened River Zaire, down whose mile-wide waters float hummocks of the green continent and marked by a mile-long road leading to nothing but an ornamental pagoda lodge, Ali, Foreman, some of the Press and worthy cadres of President Mobutu's Popular Revolutionary Movement come for reward or further indoctrination. There Foreman brought the curtain down on Act I of this drama with the heavy thud of anti-climax.

Foreman had been sparring with considerable ferocity. He'd got through one partner, and was coming at a second, Bill McMurray, a many-times loser, with such venom that trainer Dick Sadler tried to get him to lay off, ease back a bit.

Cornered against the ropes by the head-down, bullish onslaught of Foreman, McMurray did what any of us would do: he stuck his elbows up like chicken-wings to ward off the blows, and caught Foreman coming in; right across the eye. There was blood, most of it from McMurray's mouth, and Sadler—he of the lightweight porkpie hat and Step'n Fetchit manner—together with most of the Foreman camp, was in the ring in a trice and taking their man off for repairs.

A lot of people saw the cut: only the intimates got close enough to know how bad it was, and they are not talking. The scenery, as I write, is still in place, but Act II looks likely to be long, languid and short on dramatic action. It's all going to take place inside each fighter's mind and body. It's going to violate the classical unities, and be five hot weeks of speculation: what Ali calls "mental, physical, psychic battle."

Both men were approaching their

George Foreman: he has the bodily attributes of kingship Africans admire.

peak. Who now is going to be most let down? As Ali says: "It's hard to find the exaltation when you don't know the date of the fight." Now he knows it, how does he start the long grind back? I've been up at Trumanesque hours every morning since the fight was postponed, and I haven't seen Ali out running yet. And he needs it. He fights

by Keith Botsford

on his legs. It's the Dancer v. Explosion Inc., as the American publicity has it.

Or is it Foreman, less whole, less sure of himself, less outgoing, less people around, less bite into the world's apple, who is going to find his the lonelier, harder role?

Without keeping his legs in perfect shape, can Ali stay out of distance long enough to outlast Foreman, who hasn't had to go more than 11 minutes and 35 seconds in defence of his title? Can he rebuild his training so he can weave and turn Foreman's much harder punches into glances?

And what of Foreman? Now that he's been cut, is he scared? Ali is a cutter. I've sat inches out of range while he jabbed my way, with the twist

of the fist at the outermost point like the snap of a whip.

The answers await in Act III. Don't go away, folks, this is one fight that will not be allowed to die down.

For once it isn't just publicity and the media that will keep a fight going. Because it's in Zaire, this one happens to be that very rare thing, a real event in a real place. Confrontation, with a championship fight as its excuse, between four different versions of black; Ali's, full of ultimate Armageddons, Foreman's which is mostly indifference and only occasionally burning resentment, President Mobutu's, which tends to a new African world order, and the Zairois's, which has ramshackle connections to that new Africa, but far more to the old where gods and heroes still stalk the earth.

The fight and its protagonists really fit Africa, a place which is all about gods, and about ordinary lives that are as cheap as vegetation.

Instead of literature, which is something taught in schools, you have oral poetry that people make up and sing. No Zairois prefers fact to fiction, or biography to romance. He is a re-enactment of his ancestors, and his roots are as important as the gods that protect him. To be a hero or a god is what matters, being oversized, celebrated in song and dance. Your image, like the President's to float across the screen on a king-sized cloud, to appear from nowhere as if by magic, to be unable to walk the streets for the throngs that want to fondle the hem of your garment, or wear—as they do Ali's and Foreman's—as a sort of second best, your plastic image on their breasts.

Ali has Zaire by the tail because he understands this sort of thing by instinct. He not only plays the role of the paramount chief, he enjoys it. A poet himself, hyperbole is his natural idiom: he's so fast, he says, when he turns the

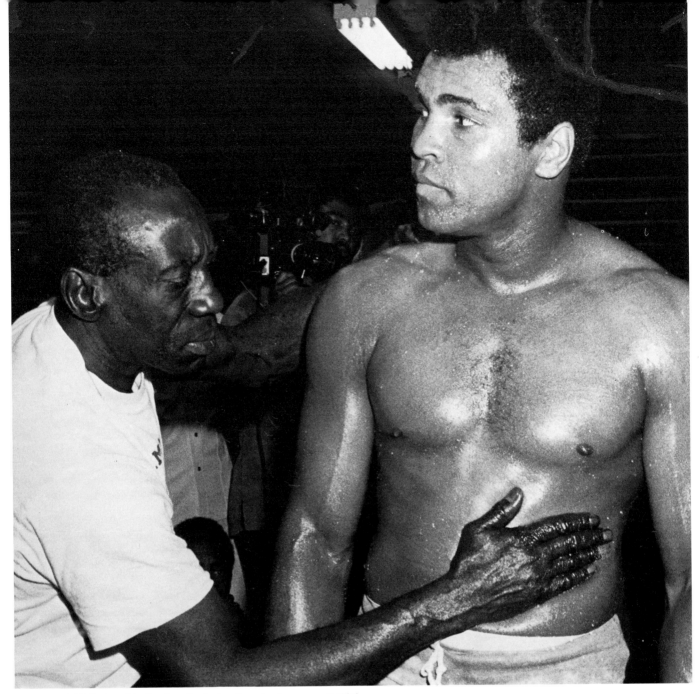

Muhammad Ali: he has Zaire by the tail, playing the role of paramount chief.

lights off he's in bed before they're out. It's his sort of place, in one way, because it is attuned to his sense of divinity: "My mission here is divine. Know the powers of God, and be a little god yourself."

Part hokum to him and to us, to the African it is very real. If they understood English, he could inflame them. Here, he said, in one remarkable flow of eloquence, there were no white shadows looking over his shoulder, no sheriff waiting to pull him in to the side of the road, no disagreeable looks, no white Press, no white Uncle Sam, the draft man: "Here," he says, "I can be myself." Meaning, here he could be, as nowhere else, much more than himself.

Alongside Ali, Foreman is poor material for Authenticity. "He never

would relate to Africa," Ali says. "He expects to shake an elephant's trunk when he gets off the plane. I told him, 'You've got a white Jesus on your wall, you don't belong here.'"

It isn't that Foreman doesn't feel his blackness—it just isn't that much of an issue with him. No more than Americanism is.

His blackness only comes out when he feels he's been done in: over money, or when something that should have been his falls by the wayside.

He became champion in Jamaica: two hours after the fight he was alone in his bedroom looking out the window and not quite able to believe it. No god, he, why should he believe it? No one has treated him like the champ; he has no nicknames, no following; he can't

even get his share of his own purses. Between performances, which are the only times he's got all his attributes about him, he's almost determinedly neuter, breeds dogs and dwells in Livermore, California.

But Foreman has his Africa, too: the sheen, the polish, the cool, the confidence that needs no words. The bodily attributes of kingship that Africans admire.

The gods Africans like best are either frightening and awesome, or sly, cunning, devious, self-ironic. Ali is the latter incarnation, Foreman the presence in nature, the fleshly element. Ali says: "What's missing most in the world is confidence." Foreman doesn't even need to say that much—it comes off his skin. Both men are stuck in Zaire for five more weeks. Foreman may make anodyne remarks. "He says a few things like, 'I'm glad to be here,'" says Ali. "I tell him, 'You turn your back on your people.'" But Ali himself admits he misses the America he carries around inside himself.

To both it seems a physical and spiritual prison. "I'm in prison here," says Ali. "Maybe I have to suffer two months. So I got to suffer. But this is a war, a war for the resurrection of the black man. I'm a link between America and Africa: I'm like Columbus."

For Foreman the terms are less grandiose. Trainer Dick Sadler asked for maximum security for his boy. And got it. His house on the hills behind N'Sele, one of a few forlorn villas, is a veritable armed encampment: fences, helmets, guns, walkie-talkies, the whole bit.

One night I drove the 50 kilometres back from Kinshasa behind a cortege of five cars, the front and back pair jammed with troops, emergency lights flashing. As it turned south up into the hills, you knew how hard it was for young George to ventilate his gilded cage.

They are miles apart, physically and mentally, and confined now in the diminishing returns of a publicity campaign that has temporarily abandoned them to a country that needs them for its own purpose, and uses them expensively.

The one is laconic, opaque, the other all quicksilver and froth. Ali receives at home, Foreman appears at Press conferences in a kind of Dogpatch L'il Abner outfit, trendily patched overalls with nothing underneath but rippling, glistening biceps the size of most men's thighs. Ali is everyone's friend, Foreman only his own. "I'm not the world's greatest fighter," he says. "I never will be, I'm just me."

And would the postponement hurt him? "I'm the most boring man you could know," he says. "I don't do nothing in life, anyway, just sit around most."

It's his own kind of black humour, as Ali's ready wit is his dancing self-defence. Till October 30 then—when President Mobutu makes his gift to his people and opens the stadium gates to 100,000 Zairois. It has to be the great clash of the black knights with different-coloured souls. In the dead of night, in the heart of Africa, it has to be the black happening of all time. It can't miss. *September 22 1974*

Portrait of a cup-winner: Charlie George, flat out after scoring the winning goal, attended by a posse of overjoyed Arsenal colleagues.

The day of the double: Arsenal snatch the Cup in an extra-time thriller

The F.A. Cup Final, always a high point of excitement in the English football season, was beset by more tensions than usual in 1971 as Arsenal clinched the elusive League and Cup double with a 2–1 victory.

by Brian Glanville

The double is Arsenal's. Where Herbert Chapman failed, Bertie Mee has succeeded. Yesterday, at Wembley, the North London club became the second to accomplish the feat this century, the first since Tottenham, 10 years ago.

If this side lacks the aggressive fluency of Blanchflower's team, if it has still to find its considerable peak, its achievement is nonetheless astonishing. It was an almost intolerably dramatic, pulsating, Cup Final. The mystery of it was that all the goals should come in extra time when Arsenal had been so markedly superior for most of the first 90 minutes. Yet it was Heighway who gave Liverpool the lead, in the second minute of the extra period; Arsenal who had to call on their vast reserves of morale to come back with an equaliser by Kelly and a winning goal by George.

What indeed, could be more appropriate than that it should be scored by a youngster born virtually on the club's doorstep. Though every credit must be given to Liverpool for a late revival, inspired by the mercurial Thompson, for an exciting first goal by Heighway, there was no gainsaying Arsenal's superiority over the distance.

They were better in midfield, they were better at the back, they were by and large better at the front. And if Kennedy had taken the two good chances which fell to him, if one of Graham's headers had gone in, there would have been no need for extra time.

Arsenal bestrode the field playing, in the sunshine, some of their most impressive football of the season. Liverpool's celebrated defence looked,

Portrait of a cup loser: Ray Clemence, the Liverpool goalkeeper.

in the wider spaces of Wembley, quite disorientated, like men with a defective sense of spatial relations.

It must be said that Arsenal's beginning hardly suggested their later dominance. In the opening minutes, they gave away four free-kicks, and were almost torn open by Hall. It was precisely then that the ball reached George, who, looking up with that remarkable, panoramic vision of his, saw Kennedy and sent him clear. The big inside left was in his own half, indisputably onside, and the field was set for the kind of goal Milburn got, exactly 20 years ago. But Kennedy, for all his virtues, is a stayer, not a sprinter. Liverpool's defenders forced him left and his eventual shot was no more than a trite gesture.

Yet Liverpool continued to live dangerously and they owed much to Clemence. He had to come off his line very quickly when Hall, with a silly backpass, gave Kennedy another chance. When Graham, receiving from McNab, split Liverpool's statuesque defence again and sent Radford in from the left, Clemence once more was out of goal in a flash.

It was high time, that Liverpool gave

their loyal, melodious fans behind the Arsenal goal a little encouragement; and they did. When a free-kick was given on the edge of the box, Smith leaped over the ball and Callaghan pushed it to Lindsay whose shot was a bullet to the right-hand corner. Wilson justified the applause with which the Kop had generously greeted him by turning the ball round the post.

After 63 minutes, Arsenal took off the highly-physical Storey and brought on the more creative Kelly, as they could well afford to. Five minutes later, Liverpool produced Thompson, and for a little while came genuinely into the game. Yet 12 minutes from time, Graham twice came within a fraction of heading Arsenal into the lead they deserved. First, he rose superbly to Radford's prodigious throw from the right, to beat Clemence but head on to the bar, Smith's acrobatic scissor-kick clearing for a corner. Armstrong took it, Graham got up once again, but this time Lindsay cleared off the line.

So we had extra-time and after a mere two minutes of it, Heighway's simple, splendid goal put Liverpool ahead. Hughes found Thompson, Thompson set Heighway free on the

left, and he, with the sort of burst we'd been waiting for all afternoon, cut in to shoot behind Wilson into the right-hand corner.

There could well have been a second Liverpool goal when Toshack headed back Thompson's right-wing corner, Hall volleyed, but Wilson made another gallant save.

Thus, in the 11th minute of extra time, Arsenal were able to equalise. Those two strong men, Kennedy and Radford, forced their passes through the thick of the Liverpool defence and Kelly fought sturdily to turn the ball over the line.

The pendulum had swung again. Six minutes into the final period, George deftly nodded the ball to Radford on his left, got it back from him again and struck a mighty, right-footed drive past Clemence.

It was a goal fully worthy to win the Cup and League double even though it had been an unconscionable time a-coming. *May 9 1971*

Arsenal: Wilson; Rice, McNab; Storey (Kelly), McLintock, Simpson; Armstrong, Graham, Radford, Kennedy, George.
Liverpool: Clemence; Lawler, Lindsay; Smith, Lloyd, Hughes; Callaghan, Evans (Thompson), Heighway, Toshack, Hall.
Referee: N. Burtenshaw (Gt. Yarmouth).

Inside track

In January 1969, Inside Track first appeared in *The Sunday Times* and the column has been there ever since, irreverent, opinionated, funny, curious, campaigning and exhibiting a nose for news. Though always written by one writer, it is anonymous because it has countless contributors and because, like a leader column, it represents the sports pages' view. Long ago called "the Private Eye of sportswriting," it has revealed scandals, verified gossip and the sheer absurdities thrown up week by week in the world of sport. A random selection from a decade of columns appears at intervals throughout this book.

Mouse Man

Best untold sports story of the year has to be the tale of Henry Cooper and The Mouse, at the otherwise moribund Sir Alf Ramsey "farewell" dinner in July.

A glittering array of personalities from the worlds of politics and sport were gathered at London's Café Royal to listen to a series of speeches extolling the career of the former England manager.

The climax of the studiedly formal evening was a televised speech by Harold Wilson, on whom, as Prime Minister, fell the burden of giving Sir Alf the collective thanks of the nation.

After some minutes, with the Prime Minister still perspiring under the heat of the television lights, guests were surprised to see Henry Cooper rise from his seat, and start advancing stealthily on the top table. As Cooper edged nearer, Mr Wilson started giving wary side glances away from the television cameras towards the approaching figure.

Then, as Henry arrived at the top table, out flashed the famous Cooper left hook . . . and he grabbed a mouse.

To astonished titters from the assembled dignitaries, Cooper then melted away towards the kitchen, the mouse dangling from the famous left fist.

"I believe this is yours," said Cooper to the Café Royal's head waiter, who was waiting in the wings for the ex-British champion.

"Thank you," said the head waiter, who promptly squelched the intruder underfoot. *December 22 1974*

● Quote of the week—by TV scriptwriter Johnny Speight during the Linda Lovelace obscenity trial: "There are people who still do not know how to copulate, what two things to put together. I think it is no use reading text books. I read text books on golf and I still cannot play it any better."
February 1 1976

An era when cricket almost became the killing game

A retrospective view of the hazards of bodyline, by one who faced the bowling of Harold Larwood in all its considerable fury.

by Jack Fingleton

The "Mods," I am afraid, so often find my generation boring when we dip into the past but you can't always ignore history when it has to do with the present.

At Lord's recently the International Cricket Conference issued some nebulous stuff asking all countries to ponder the curse of pad-play. At the same time, I was chatting with Harold Larwood at Trent Bridge and I couldn't help thinking that without Larwood there would not have been this prevalent pad-play.

Of necessity, it sends me back to 1932–33, a turbulent period that burst upon me as a youngster in his first Test series against England. And as one connects Larwood with pad-play, so it must be added that had there been no Bradman there would have been no bodyline. It was, in itself, a tribute to Bradman's greatness.

Bradman had made Test scores in England in 1930 of 131, 254, 334 and 232. There had been nothing like him before. He cut all bowlers to shreds. He was the greatest challenge English cricket had known and a dour, remorseless Scot named Douglas Jardine was given the job of bringing him to heel and, of all places, in Australia. Jardine was 130 years after his time. He should have gone to Australia in charge of a convict-hulk.

So many of that English team have told me subsequently that they abhorred bodyline and wanted nothing to do with it. But it was a deep plot which obviously had its genesis before the English team was chosen. In that side were four fast bowlers—Larwood, Voce, Bowes and Allen—and Bowes just previously had bowled bodyline against the great Jack Hobbs at The Oval. There was no sterner critic of this than Sir Pelham Warner who wrote that it prostituted the art of cricket and that if it were continued it would ruin

Bradman: cut down to comparative size.

the game. Warner said Bowes had to stop it immediately.

"Plum" Warner, as he was known, soon after was made manager of the team led by Jardine to Australia. There must have been many nights when he never slept a wink.

In simple terms bodyline was nothing more than playing the man and not the ball. It was conceived for Bradman and, with Larwood the perfect instrument, it cut Bradman down to comparative size. But, as Warner said, it wasn't cricket. The batsman's first thought, against the thunderbolts of Larwood and Voce at his ribs and around his head, was of self-preservation.

Oldfield had a fractured skull; Woodfull was hit a nasty blow over the heart as so many others of us were. I can still recall the whistle of a bouncer from Larwood past my temple: I almost moved into it. Some Australians showed up in poor colours. Several didn't want to play; one champion indeed asked to be dropped. The mutterings were intense. No Australian as the series drew on passed a word with an Englishman.

Riding the storm—and crowd riots

were often imminent with mounted police on call outside Adelaide Oval—was the imperious, unflappable Jardine. He saw his job and he did it, impervious to all, including Warner, who remained publicly mute on the tour.

But Warner was more worried even than the Australians. I saw a letter which he wrote subsequently in which he said, in a *cri de coeur*: "I could do nothing with Jardine. He hates the Australians. The mere sight of one upsets him. I pleaded with him to stop it, at least to ease it. He coldly ignored me."

G. O. (Gubby) Allen alone stood up to Jardine. The skipper told Allen he wanted him to bowl bodyline in the second Test. Allen, who was a very good fast bowler, refused. "Then," said Jardine, "You won't play." Fifteen minutes before the game began, Allen was still in his street clothes. "Why aren't you dressed, Gubby?" asked Jardine. It was the only time on the incredible tour that Jardine lost a point. But Allen was an amateur. Larwood, Voce and Bowes were pros who did as they were told.

In the fifth Test, Larwood broke a bone in his foot while bowling and Jardine wouldn't let him leave the field while Bradman was batting. When Bradman got out (to Verity), Jardine turned to his great fast bowler and said, "You can go off now, Larwood." And Bradman and Larwood, in silence, walked off the field together. Larwood never walked on to another Test field.

There was the day when Warner and Palairet, his assistant manager, came into our Adelaide dressing-room to commiserate with the stricken Woodfull. Woodfull, under medical attention, said to the two Englishmen: "I don't want to discuss it. There are two sides out there. One is playing cricket. The other isn't." Warner and Palairet left the Australian dressing room in acute distress.

Warner wrote in a book later, "Unfortunately, there was a member of the Australian team who was a journalist and next day the story was blazoned all over the front pages."

That was a hard one at me. I was the only journalist in the two teams and I knew stories of that tour to make a newspaperman's pen drip with ink. But I kept quiet. The reporter who got the story told me years afterwards of how he made a rendezvous with one of our team the night of the incident and he

Larwood: bodyline's perfect instrument.

was told all. The stigma stayed with me. I told Woodfull years later who the "culprit" was. "A pity," said Woodfull, "that cost you the 1934 tour of England."

It was, of course, a distressing business. It was immoral against Bradman but Jardine's mistake was in using the unrelenting bodyline attack of Larwood and Voce—Bowes lacked the intensity of the others—against all the Australians.

It took years to abate and some of the bruises never healed. Bradman and Jardine never made it up—as others of us did with both Jardine and Larwood. I sat in front of the two in the Leeds Press Box in 1953 where some odd person had seated them together. "Good morning, Mr Bradman," would say Jardine. "Good morning, Mr Jardine," would say Bradman, and that was it for the day until the evening farewells came along.

No Australian blamed Larwood, wonderful bowler that he was. As I talked with him it was beneath a graphic picture of him delivering the ball. It all came back again. The classical upright pose of the body, with every muscle and sinew coming into

the delivery. It is one of the immortal pictures of cricket.

It was odd that he should settle in Australia. In 1948, George Duckworth asked me if I would visit Larwood in his little Blackpool shop in which he sold sweets and cigarettes—with no name over the door. Larwood was suspicious. He thought I was after a story. We induced him to come for a "sup of ale" and from that flowed a warm friendship which finished in him emigrating to Australia.

One Saturday in 1950 in Canberra I received a cable from him: "Leaving tomorrow with wife, five daughters and eldest daughter's fiancé stop can you find jobs and accommodation."

It was, at a time of housing shortage, a tall order, and it was an Australian Prime Minister, Ben Chifley, who helped Larwood most to settle. "I think," said Chifley, "that Larwood was too good for you chaps."

I told Larwood when he arrived he should come to Canberra and thank Mr Chifley. He was delighted to do so. I took him in and Larwood, in his thick Notts accent, thanked Mr Chifley. Chif, as he was known, looked in some amazement at me. "What did he say, Jack?" he asked. I interpreted. Then Mr Chifley, in his nasal Australian tones, said some nice words about Larwood, who looked at me. "What did he say?" asked Larwood. Again I interpreted.

Somebody asked Larwood at Trent Bridge whether he would like to return to England. "No bloody fear," said Lol, "I'm a bloody Australian now."

You see, then, how boring an old-time cricketer can become: I really set out to draw a parallel between Larwood's return to his homeland and MCC's edict on pad-play. If there hadn't been a Larwood, there would not have been a revision of the lbw rule allowing a decision to a ball pitched outside the off-stump.

This was a sop from Australia to help bury bodyline, to draw concentration away from the leg-stump. It led to a flood of offspin and seam-bowlers and this, over the years, had led in turn to the batsmen negating these theories by prodding the front pad at the ball.

Larwood was a shy man, a modest man, a great bowler—but what an effect he had, even to this day, upon cricket! Maybe, soon, to cure the ill of pad-play, cricket will revert to the old lbw rule. It would be the final and fitting tribute to him. *July 28 1968*

The Welsh invasion: there'll be a welcome in the Follies

The community of Aberflyarff, created by the cartoonist Gren as the true fountainhead of Welsh rugby lunacy, has become something of a cult in the Valleys. This Celtic coach outing to Paris for the France-Wales international was organised for the benefit of *The Sunday Times*.

by Dan O'Neill

The Vikings had Valhalla. Aberflyarff belongs to Wales. A perpendicular paradise where collapse is what you get in the scrum, not the economy, and a national crisis is an injury to Retaliate First Rees, the tighthead groiner and ref-abuser, or a GBH sentence for Attila Groinstomper, first-choice provoker. Aberflyarff RFC, incidentally, is the only team in Britain with an official streaker, namely Dai-the-Dap, dap being Valley talk for plimsoll.

The creator of the sublimely loony world of Ponty and Pop, and the growing gallery of engaging eccentrics who illuminate it, is a self-confessed failed flanker called Grenfell Jones. He's married with two children, and lives above the town of Caerphilly.

Grenfell was drawing a daily newspaper topical cartoon when, six years ago, he realised that nothing in the Wales he knew was as relevant to everyday life as sport. Wales, to the people he grew up with, wasn't an area, it was a rugby team. Sport, especially rugby, evoked more passion than politics. So it was natural when he invented the village Aberflyarff, at the wrong end of the Scrumcap Valley, to satirise all aspects of Welsh life through sport.

Now, to his bewilderment, he finds that pubs have transformed themselves into duplicates of Aberflyarff's Golden Dap for celebration nights; fancy-dress parties throughout South Wales have been swamped with Pontys and Pops; a TV adaptation has been suggested, and Ponty and Pop beam from T-shirts. The first Ponty and Pop annual sold out instantly, and is now a collector's item.

Ponty is the archetypal Valley lad, the 38-year-old bachelor forever fes-

tooned with fixture lists and raffle tickets. Darts and domino teams decline without people like Ponty behind them. He is the eternal secretary, avid watcher of all games, one of nature's scorers. (Ponty is the taller of the two characters in the strip above.)

Pop is his father only, you assume, through some odd process of parthenogenesis; he is the perpetual pub philosopher, the man, Barry John observes, who can tell you how Bleddyn Williams laced his boots before his last international.

There is no Mrs Pop. She'd only be in the way. The sex angle in Aberflyarff is provided by Bromide Lil, tattooed barmaid of the Golden Dap.

Ponty himself once broke off an understanding with Lil even though he'd always been partial to the Derek Quinnell type of bird. "An' I was only unfaithful to him twice," sobbed Lil. "Once with the male-voice choir, and once with the Aberflyarff Seconds."

Her customers include Byline Hopkins, sports reporter; Dai-the-Spy, Rugby League scout licensed to poach; Paunch Pest, teenage idol; plus assorted notables like Carwyn James, Barry John or even such Englishmen as Nigel Starkers-Smith. Nigel applied to join the club several years ago, but fled when he discovered that the particulars the secretary wanted didn't involve permits or past clubs. He was inquiring

Grenfell Jones—Gren of the South Wales Echo—is presiding genius of Aberflyarff, a coal-dusted valley where the rate of exchange is geared to the price of a North Stand ticket and the sun shimmers through the smog like a pale yellow rugby ball.

about blood group and next of kin.

Perhaps at Cardiff this week there'll be an end to the genial contempt for all English rugby you find in Aberflyarff. But then, how can we admire an international team beaten over the years by such scratch sides as the Mothercare Seconds, or the Derby and Joan Kung Fu Class XV. Roll on Saturday so we can forget Paris and feel our old selves again.

Life's like that in Aberflyarff, and through it all thread Ponty and Pop, bewildered First and Second Voices in a community as uniquely dotty as Milk Wood itself.

There is Bleddyn, the Woodbine-puffing dog; Neville the Sheep, head groundsman; Deuteronomy Jones, Deacon; and Owen the Oracle, the mild-eyed sage who meditates in his coaltip cave above the weedline. Yet Aberflyarff itself is the real star of the strip. Between the Keith Murdoch Memorial Viaduct and the famous leaning bridge built by Isambard Kingdom Pugh you'll find every sad echo calculated to moisten the eyes of a Welshman or town planner, an anthology of everything hideous in the architecture and industrial development of the 19th-century South Wales.

In Aberflyarff on a clear day, you can see next door. The coaltip broods over sagging roofs, while chapels collapse gently, the choirs and deacons departed, the River Efflew flowing into a sewer so disgustingly dispirited that even the rubbish is reluctant to enter. The Aberflyarff clubhouse, a rusting Nissen hut on the edge of the Everest-angled pitch, creaks and rattles.

This is the substance of South Wales. Max Boyce, who sings such scenes, feels that Gren's Wales is the *real* Wales, and he is delighted to sell his albums inside Gren-illustrated covers, happy to have Gren drawings in the book of his poems and songs.

So there'll be no end to Aberflyarff, Gren said the other day, "just as long as I get the boys back from Paris." You can see, above, how he managed it.

February 13 1977

All the Queen's men on parade — and a new champion aloft in the Bisley chair

The figure seated aloft in the Ceremonial Chair, the winner of the Queen's Prize, is one of the best-known sporting images. Like Wimbledon and Lord's, Bisley is an institution.

by Norman Harris
Photographs by Chris Smith

Engraved on every clubhouse wall at Bisley for the last two weeks, and on the mind of every marksman, there has been the fact that this is the Queen's meeting. Queen Victoria opened the first of them, at Wimbledon in 1860, by pulling a silken cord attached to the trigger of a rifle so carefully mounted that the bullet struck the target within a quarter inch of the centre. Since 1860 little has changed.

The Whitworth muzzle-loaded rifle may now be a 7.62mm target rifle. And Bisley in Surrey may have replaced Wimbledon, in 1890, as the home of the National Rifle Association.

But, whatever the changes of detail, they all still come to Bisley for the same reasons. Not only for the prizes, but also for a fortnight's holiday in a beguiling world where the rows of clubhouses nestling under the sweet chestnut trees, the gunsmiths' shops and the military canvas once evoked the description of a "Victorian Western."

Here there are no divisions of class or politics between riflemen, and women, of clubs as diverse as West Midlands Police, Barclays Bank, and Trinity College, Dublin (or one called Ballista Ferculorum Reversans, said to be Latin for Reversed Sausage Machine, or another called Central Bankers, which is said to be rhyming slang. . .). As one competitor says: "Every day of the year I read a newspaper. Except when I'm here. Time passes you by."

As for the competitions, many of these are for the same trophies as in Queen Victoria's day, and under the same rules. The most famous of them, as famous as the Derby or Wimbledon, is the Queen's Prize. Twelve hundred competitors shot the qualifying stage on Wednesday last week. Three hundred went on yesterday morning to shoot at 300, 500 and 600 yards; and the best 100 of them—the Queen's Hundred—shot the final stage in the afternoon, at 900 and 1,000 yards. The clear winner, scoring 283 out of a possible 300, was David Friend, a 43-year-old Sussex leather merchant.

Then history was again repeated, as he was borne away in the Ceremonial Chair. Simultaneously, another formality was being rendered. They still send, by telephone, the traditional telegram to advise the Queen of the winner of her prize. "The telegram people are usually a bit sceptical when you give them the address," says a NRA official. "But when they get over the hoo-ha of that, and start on the text, they realise they're on to something. We say that if a reply comes back to telephone us. And it usually does the same night."

July 24 1977

The Queen's Hundred: on the firing point at 1,000 ya

Far left: George Garrett, 72, is the backbone of the British Commonwealth Club. "The sort of chap," says a friend, "who'll think to water the flower baskets outside the pavilion."

Bob Geddes of Brampton, Ontario (left), chooses for his first appearance at Bisley a canvas twill jacket and rain trousers. Denis Cantlay (right), of the elite North London club prefers shorts, and a hat which is ten years old. The main unwritten rule about attire is that it should be comfortable and consistent; and the underwritten principle is that the age of the clothes determines the pedigree of the shooter.

a few minutes away from hailing a new champion.

The clubhouse, the monarch, the post-mortem.

As a former winner says: "Once in your career you may have the perfect shoot. It might be in practise, it might be in a minor competition; and if you're very lucky it's in the Queen's Prize." For David Friend, such a shoot makes the moment of a lifetime.

How the old lady deals with her ardent admirers

Scotland is the home of golf, and the home of golf in Scotland, and indeed the world, is St Andrews, one of sport's great institutions. Apart from taking its turn in staging the British Open and other major tournaments, it is also used by the locals and visitors from all over the world. A veritable golfing Mecca.

by Dudley Doust

At dawn a boy and his dog crossed the Swilcan Burn and disappeared in the haze hanging over St Andrews. He was the first of 196 golfers who played last Thursday through the rising raw wind at the Old Course. "That would have been a laddie having a few holes afore school," the links superintendent John Campbell said a little later. "Ye'll never find these links empty in May."

Campbell, "Little John," is St Andrews cheerful, rosy-faced head greenskeeper, son of "Big John" Campbell, a former Scottish greenskeeper. Campbell roamed the world's most famous course, walkie-talkie in hand, keeping in touch with his 23-man staff who look after the town's four municipal courses. The rolling Old Course looked parched under the lowering sky, the heather lifeless, the yellow gorse bushes giving the one dash of colour. Campbell stopped by the dreaded Hell Bunker on the fifth hole. Strong spring winds from the south-west had flung out sand. "When we put 50 tons of sand in there, you still canna see it."

Campbell instinctively stepped aside as Tip Anderson, Arnold Palmer's regular caddie, came into sight up the fairway. Anderson and his mate, a quiet man with mutton chops and an overcoat, carried for two Californians, Hank and Lew, who make an annual 6,400-mile pilgrimage to St Andrews. Anderson reckoned that by the second shot into the third hole he had his man taped. He is 40 and all his life, player and caddie, has been spent virtually at St Andrews, yet he can't give the yardage of the holes. "Ye canna explain St Andrews in yards." he said, as though someone had insulted the old lady. "Ye got to be there at the *time*."

The traffic quickened: two more Americans came by, three Swedes, a man and his dog straight out of P. G. Wodehouse. The layout can't take it. "We're getting such heavy traffic," said Campbell, "we're going to play the course in reverse next winter to give it a rest. Spread out the wear. We used to do it before the war and, if I am not mistaken, this practice is unique at St Andrews. It's something golf architects ought to think about."

If Americans, with their colourful clothes and enormous golf bags, were conspicuous last week, so was the St Andrean in his manner of play. Stewart Lawson, a former R & A Rules Committee chairman, is a self-confessed St Andrews player.

He revealed himself on the ninth fairway when, faced with a 30-yard pitch to the green, he bobbled it on with a putter. "St Andreans can still play a proper running shot," he said, "which is due, I suppose, to the fact

that we weren't brought up on target golf. We don't particularly like these new heavy-headed irons because we have to manufacture more shots. In fact, some St Andreans still prefer the lightweight 'feel' of a club made by Laurie Auchterlonie. Also," he added, "we're good laggers of putts—which is obvious, judging from the size of our greens."

(Incidently, Laurie Auchterlonie, the last in the line of great clubmakers at St Andrews, was at that time sandpapering the spoon of a handmade set of clubs for a Japanese lady, Mrs Kashiwadani. He is making a set for a Canadian and, apart from these, turns out £25 wooden "conversational piece" putters. "There is a lot of stuff and hooey about 'sweet spots' these days." he said, "whereas all ye need to know is a golfer's height and weight to make a club.")

On the 10th tee, in the tutorial way of the local player, Stewart Lawson raised his arm to show his English companion the "correct line" from the tee to the green. He then struck a low, useful drive in that rather tight, lingering swing that characterises the St Andrean. "We don't have the full swing of the inland golfer," said Lawson. "We're brought up to steer a ball through the wind. Cheerio." With that he was gone.

A bottleneck occurs at the intersection of the seventh and 11th fairways at St Andrews and a Ranger, Dan Latto, stationed himself there. Latto wore a hard, peaked cap and, with his moped popping beside him, he looked for all the world like a traffic warden. "We've banned the caddie carts this spring," he said, "and, aye, it's a good thing. They add 45 minutes to a round of golf."

A chubby English duffer was bashing his way down the 11th fairway. Latto crossed to him. "Canna ye hurry along please," he asked, "ye are one full hole behind." The dumbfounded Englishman saluted Latto, sped through the green, teed off on the 12th and actually jogged down the fairway after his dubbed drive. "It's mostly the bluidy Yanks that take the time," said Latto, "they hae ta putt every ball into the can."

A Japanese gentleman, Zenya Hamada, meanwhile stayed in his room at the Old Course Hotel, overlooking the famous Road Hole. Hamada did not set foot on the course, but his presence was felt throughout the town. It is he, a wealthy businessman, who is recreating stone by stone, dyke by dyke, a replica of the St Andrews course beside the River Hooki in Japan. "I must use the river for St Andrews Bay," he said cheerfully. "To recreate the sea is impossible."

In his effort to recreate a precise St Andrews—which he is calling "The New St Andrews Golf Club"—Hamada last autumn had an aerial survey map, 40ft square, made of St Andrews. He is recreating the Swilcan Bridge, an early version of the R & A clubhouse, even an oil portrait of the legendary "Young" Tom Morris who won four successive Open Championships a century ago before dying, at 24, in grief over the death of his wife. "Also I hope to transplant your whin bushes," Hamada added, "and I am giving 1,000 cherry trees to St Andrews."

As darkness settled over St Andrews, rain began to fall and the course grew empty. John Campbell, at home, wrote about the spring weather to a greenskeeper in America. Tip Anderson played darts in a pub, while other caddies gathered in the 19th hole bar. "Did ye see the cross-country match this week between Sir Ian Stewart and Mr A. D. Cave?" asked one. It was a match between Sir Ian, the outgoing R & A captain, and Cave, an earlier captain. "Ye play from the first tee to the ninth hole, going over the New and the Jubilee courses if ye choose. Then back from the ninth tee to the 18th hole. Sir Ian won going out, 24 strokes to 21 and Mr Cave won coming home, 17 to 16."

The American, Hank, had played 36 holes and, exhausted, missed dinner at Rusack's Hotel. And at his hotel, Zenya Hamada slept soundly, happy in his dreams of Japan's St Andrews, hard by the River Hooki.   *May 6 1973*

The good life at Lord's in quite a different class

"Typically English" is a description applied to many attitudes and activities, but few fit it better than the Eton and Harrow match at the headquarters of cricket. It is as much a social as it is a sporting occasion, redolent of traditions that proved a singular experience to at least one New Zealand-born writer.

by Norman Harris

Poor uneducated fool that I am, I wasn't quite sure if the thing was a charabanc or a coach. However I was assured it was indeed a coach that was carefully in place by the Nursery sightscreen when play started at Lord's yesterday. The sort of coach that goes with a pair, apparently. But the pair seemed never to have been employed, the coach evidently having been towed there or transported by some other means and set up, like a museum piece on wooden planks with wheel chocks.

It seemed a bit odd. I thought the idea was that you came in the thing, parked it, then sat on it. Not so. Those who hired it only briefly experienced the novelty of sitting on top before turning to their trestle table and drinks at grass level.

Another perplexity was the sight of a young black man bowling for Eton, Kio Amachree from Nigeria—"known usually as Chief," said fine leg. "A great character."

And in front of the Tavern, while

Fours were noisily cheered and shouted.

half the young men wore dark suits and silk ties, others were Dylanesque, with hand-rolled cigarettes. Is this the fabric of our society fracturing before our very eyes?

For Harrow, P. D. M. Greig was constantly looking for that purest of strokes, the almost square cover drive, and against Kary he nicked to second slip where he was badly dropped. Otherwise the Harrow openers had everything present and correct. Life at Lord's was good.

Fours were noisily cheered and shouted all the way to the line, the cacophony reminding one of those recent parliamentary broadcasts.

"Are we doing well or not?" asked a slim figure in velvet pinstripe, as he sipped a cocktail. "I haven't particularly noticed either way."

There were not really two ways about it. Harrow's openers had brought up the 50 in 20 overs Compton, who had been playing the quicker bowlers most positively, was being overhauled by Greig, who came on wonderfully against the slower stuff.

"Mark," said someone's sister, "to sit there and talk about your girlfriends is awfully boring."

". . . So we went in with them on," murmured one pater to another, "and when the girls didn't come in, we took them off . . ."

Greig went at 64, splendidly caught and bowled as he drove. But Compton went on with a much pronounced left elbow—unlike his unrelated namesake, the great D.C.S.—and none the worse for it. On the stroke of lunchtime he drove two fours for his 50.

Eton's young team however, were already more seriously threatened by Harrow's star batsman, the left-handed M. K. Fosh, who is a prospective Essex player. Strongly built and a croucher, with his hands low on the handle, he proceeded to drive, punch from the back foot, and to swing at anything near leg stump.

At Fosh's hundred an elderly gentleman took out a white handkerchief and waved it. The feat impressed another man's wife sufficiently for her to ask which one was Fosh. Others paused in a discussion about Scimitars and Simcas. "I hope Michael's boy gets his hundred. I really do . . . Oh he's got it, has he?"

In 90 minutes after lunch Fosh had scored 122, and in the final over before the declaration he pulled front-foot sixes to the long midwicket boundary in a manner that would have done credit to a Kanhai. An announcement said that his 161 was the highest score by a Harrow batsman against Eton since 1913.

Then, with the ball, Harrow emphasised the imbalance of a contest which was seemingly played between young men on the one hand and boys on the other. Pigott tore in like a Lillee and in his first over took two wickets, with the Harrow supporters roaring throughout like—let it be said quietly—crazed West Indians.
                              July 13 1975

Non-swearing, balletic, ambassador farmers

What is the day-to-day reality of a rugby tour of the British Isles? The 1978 All Blacks were accompanied for three days by our rugby correspondent John Hopkins and by artist Philip Sutton, whose impressions of the New Zealanders in training appear above.

In room 327, Bryan Williams lay in bed reading The Crash of '79. Above his head was a photograph of his wife and their six-month-old daughter. As Williams alternately read and dozed, his room-mate, Bruce Robertson, was making his way upstairs. On the floor below, a porter arrived at Room 345. Over his arm he carried a blazer and a pair of trousers. "Are these the ones?" the porter asked. Bill Osborne examined them closely. "No," the curly-haired Maori replied finally. "they aren't mine."

Life with the All Blacks is fun, but quiet. "We worked very hard with this team," explained manager Russ Thomas, settling back on his heels, his hands stuck deep in his pockets, as he looked cheerily around the bar. "Mindful of other tours, we were determined to make this one a success, and we went into it in the most thorough detail. No one is allowed out in the evening unless he is wearing the standard-issue blue socks, and we even have two men whose job it is to supervise dress."

The eighth All Blacks are captained by Graham Mourie, a 26-year-old bachelor, a man as dedicated as his manager to the social duties that are part of this nine-week tour. When the team stop to visit Wells Cathedral, it is Mourie who bounds out of the coach to talk to the Dean, while others mingle

Sound the trumpets in acclamation of this triumph of the spirit!

No touring side ever has an easy tour of New Zealand, and the 1971 Lions had been badly buffeted—losing key players—in the run-up to the important first Test. The Lions, however, heroically fought for, and won, an emotional 9–3 victory.

by Vivian Jenkins

Hallelujah! Sound the trumpets, bang the drums, crash the cymbals, make any old noise you like! They did it. The Lions did it, They beat the All Blacks in this all-important first Test at Dunedin by two penalty goals and a try to a penalty goal.

If ever there was a wet rag walking it was your correspondent as he tottered out of the grandstand at the end to pay homage to the magnificent winners; and never before have I kissed a rugby manager, let alone a 17st one like Dr Doug Smith.

It was indeed a famous victory, in front of a record crowd for the ground of 48,000 with 10,000 more locked out and forced to watch the match from the "Scotsmen's Grandstands" on a nearby hill and railway line. The All Blacks began as though they were going to demolish the Lions before the latter had even taken breath, and for the first quarter of an hour it was as though a colossal pounding machine had gone into action, with the Lions on the receiving end.

But the Lions held magnificently while some of us averted our eyes. Then came the first, and vital, counter-thrust. Having won their way to the other end, an amazing little bull of a man from Scotland had a moment of glory that shall aye endure. Ian McLauchlan is only 5ft. 9in. tall and 14½st. in weight—almost a pygmy in the company he was keeping yesterday. But never once did the "Mighty Mouse" flinch. The Lions won the set-scrummage count 24–9, with the help of most of the put-in, and Pullin took the tight-heads 3–1.

This alone would have been a mighty feather in McLauchlan's cap, as it was equally for Sean Lynch on the tight-head side. But McLauchlan's contribution did not end there. In that 16th minute, when the Lions reached the other end, he got the try that broke the All Blacks' hold at last. It also gave the Lions hope again and altered the whole psychological tenor of the game.

Fergie McCormick, the All Blacks full-back, sent back a pass under pressure to his No. 8 forward, Sutherland, 10 yards from his own line. Sutherland attempted to kick for touch, but there was the "Mouse" up in a flash to throw up his arms, charge down the kick and race after the rebound, behind the line, to score. He looked back from the ground, almost unbelievingly, as the referee awarded the try, and then raced back to half-way festooned with enraptured Lions.

The touring team's battle was not yet over by a long chalk. McCormick equalised with a penalty just before half-time, but the All Black fullback was to miss further kickable penalties in a disastrous day. He was tantalised all through by some wonderful clearing touch-kicking by John.

with passers-by and take dozens of photographs.

Mourie has a rare feeling for saying and doing the right thing. In after-dinner speeches he rarely talks for more than five minutes, yet manages to blend the necessities of thanking officials with an occasional joke.

Mourie's forefathers were Italian on one side and Scottish on the other. He lives near New Plymouth in the North Island, where his parents were farmers before him. In peaceful moments in his room (as team captain he is the only player who does not have to share a room), he is reading Zen and the Art of Motor Cycle Maintenance.

During training, Mourie leads by example. "He moves so gracefully," notes Philip Sutton as he stands on the touchline sketching the players. "So many of them do. There is something almost balletic about them, despite their size." At Millfield School, Mourie shouts the orders, while coach Jack Gleeson quietly oversees his men.

Back in their hotel, some players head for the room of Brian McKenzie, a 40-year-old physiotherapist on his first tour with the All Blacks. He has two boxes of equipment, and twice each week these boxes, along with the All Blacks' luggage, are loaded by bag-gageman Graham Short into a small van to move to the next game.

The team travel in a 45-seat luxury coach adapted from a 53-seater, and driven by Bristolian Richard Smith. As they whoosh over the motorways, with senior players such as Bruce Robertson and Bryan Williams settled in the back seats, the All Blacks listen to cassettes. They are not a singing team. Instead, each player has contributed one cass-ette, and Osborne is music master. The popular cassettes are the Rolling Stones, Simon and Garfunkel, Pink Floyd. There is no Mozart and, in the week of the 150th anniversary of his death, no Schubert.

November 26 1978

A Union Jack is waved aloft, the All Blacks are beaten and the captain of the Lions calls for a handclap for the vanquished.

But the most wonderful part of the Lions performance in that endless second half was the heroic tackling by Gibson and Dawes in the centre and the covering work by the three loose forwards, Dixon, Mervyn Davies and Taylor. Then there was John Williams at full-back, playing the game of his life, catching towering up-and-unders, taking fearsome punishment from the All Blacks forwards and always coming up for more.

As Dr Smith said, with a sidelong smile, at the after-match reception: "You can say I am reasonably satis-fied." Then, to the Lions: "Training at nine-thirty in the morning!" The spirit in this side was something to wonder at even before the game started. Now it has soared to the firmament.

June 27 1971

New Zealand: W. P. McCormick; B. A. Hunter, B. G. Williams, W. D. Cottrell, K. R. Carrington, R. E. Burgess, S. M. Going: No. 8 A. R. Sutherland; Second Row: I. A. Kirkpatrick, C. E. Meads (captain) P. J. Whiting, A. M. McNaughton; Front Row: B. L. Muller, R. W. Norton, R. A. Guy.

British Isles: J. P. R. Williams; T. G. R. Davies, C. M. H. Gibson, S. J. Dawes (captain) J. C. Bevan, B. John, G. O. Edwards, No. 8 T. M. Davies; Second Row: P. J. Dixon, W. D. Thomas, W. J. McBride, J. Taylor; Front Row: J. F. Lynch, J. V. Pullin, J. McLauchlan; replacement: R. Hopkins for Edwards (10 min).

Referee: J. P. G. Pring (Auckland)

The Tour de France: progress through the longest street party in the world

The Tour is run for profit by L'Equipe, France's sporting daily, and Le Parisien Libéré, another national newspaper. It makes a mint. The logistics are staggering: a hundred cyclists at the heart of 200 cars and motorcycles and 400 journalists from all over the world. *(July 10 1977)*

by Keith Botsford. Photographs by Chris Smith

France is laid on for the tour, and the crowds which patiently line the route form a ready market for the snapshots and souvenirs before the all-too-brief climax. Commerce is near to the French heart, floats and hard-sell are part of the pageantry. One third of France is out on the streets, the rest get it for three weeks on the telly. The tour provides exposure. As for the actual competitors, there are only some ten potential winners, the team leaders. The rest are peons, whose job it is to help the big boys, who try no harder than they have to. In the morning they all pedal round village squares loosening up, team managers plot strategy in the biggest game of bike-chess, the single most exacting solo sporting event in the world.

Rolled out from their barracks in big blue paddy-waggons, unusually polite, the fuzz have blocked off the streets of Saint Emilion. Two hours before the first cyclist appears whole families wait, necks crane. Then in a silent whirr lasting five seconds the pack wheels by. Expectation, exaltation. Les voilà! They push off home, having witnessed, but not by leg-power. The legs belong to Pedro Torres, lying 34th, waiting a push-start for a sprint. Cyclists' legs are close-shaven to make it easier to treat their injuries. Their veins swell, a river-delta of fatigue.

The gendarmerie runs before clearing roads, runs behind protecting stragglers. Up mountains, down. Big towns, tiny hamlets. The tour is inexorable. Nothing stands in its way. Saint Emilion, stuffed

The publicity caravan goes an hour beforehand, meticulously scheduled. Bulls, up-ended bugs, giant oil cans and rice packets, yoghourt, stick-ices and Monsieur Michelin, panting in the heat with his head off. Hucksters in the hills play their part too, hustling Eddie Merckx autographed plates at three quid a time.

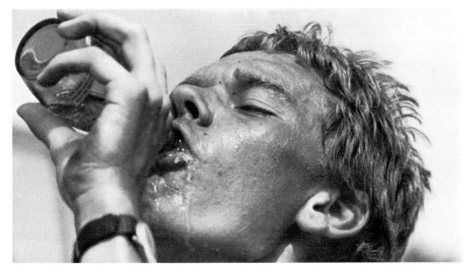

with its chateaux and wine, watches the pack through its mediaeval streets. Nothing in sport is so good-humoured, so familial. Picnics and festivity, kids on papa's shoulders. "When I was just a baby I saw Thurau on his first Tour." That's him there, riding a red Raleigh in the middle of the pack, yellow jersey on his back. He's keeping a watchful eye on his rivals and carrying a hope of millions in his heart.

Exhaustion is the end of each day's stage: before the giant fair-hall in Bordeaux, as in any of the 22 cities that bid for finishes. Last number of all, No. 100, Alex Van Linden of Belgium, placed 81st, almost 44 minutes behind, does what must seem like life-and-death to him after a 30 km time trial: he replaces what his body has consumed. For a few minutes after finishing the cyclists can't talk. Perhaps it's then they think how it's all got to be done again tomorrow. And tomorrow and tomorrow. Another 3,000 km, including a dozen Alpine passes, before the final ride up the Champs Elysées. And how it's never easy. And how there can be but one winner.

Inside track

Caber Capers

This summer, at least 20 stalwart athletes will make a decent, if strenuous, living by rushing about Scotland carrying 15ft logs. Tossing the caber can bring an expert up to £200 a week in prize money at the 100 or so meetings held each year under Scottish Games rules. In case any of our readers fancy their chances, here are a few pointers.

"The object is not to toss for distance," says Scottish Games secretary Tom Young. "The winner is the one who tosses the caber straightest." You have to make it turn over on its axis and fall in a straight line (see diagram). A long telegraph pole, weighing around 150lb, the caber is tapered at one end from 8 to 5 inches. You lock your fingers round the end if you want to copy experts like Yorkshireman Arthur Rowe (the ex-Olympic shot putter) or Bill Anderson you run like hell for 40 yards before releasing it.

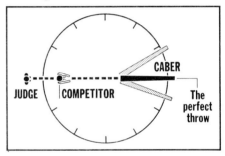

"The throw is akin to weightlifting," says coach David Webster, "a sudden stop, knees bend and an upwards thrust." A good thrower can "read" a caber, spinning it to the left or right to put it into the vital "twelve o'clock" position. The $17\frac{1}{2}$ stone Rowe worked for 18 months before mastering the technique. Each competitor has three tosses and if there is a tie (with both throws equally straight) they usually bring out a heavier caber.

Incidentally, while up in Scotland you might as well enter some of the other 10 heavy Highland sports, including putting a 16lb or 28lb stone, throwing three sizes of hammer, or tossing 56lb weights over a high bar. Between them, Rowe and Anderson hold records for all these heavy events.

Caber tossers, by the way, are clean living fellows, scorning betting, and anabolic steroids, not to mention trousers.

May 23 1971

● In case you thought we were getting a bit pushy about jogging: if you miss a Sunday with the Leningrad running club, they ring you up. Miss two Sundays and they write to you. Miss three Sundays, and they send you a questionnaire. We have no information on what happens if you miss four Sundays.

June 11 1978

A sad breakdown of communication: the diary of a grim tour

This account was written exactly ten years after Sir Alf Ramsey's first tour as the England team manager. At the end of that first triumphal journey pressmen threw a celebration party for him. There was not the slightest prospect of the gesture being repeated before England returned home in 1973. For that year's tour, first to Prague, then out again to Poland, Russia and Italy, had brought the relationship between Sir Alf and the Press to a new low level.

For some the antagonism was a personal thing; they resented his often abrupt attitude towards them. For some, it was a matter of sporting principles; they detested his sort of football. For most it was a mixture of the two.

Why this was important is that the antagonism coloured all that happened to Ramsey's England team. The players, bitterly resentful, were caught in the crossfire, and the public at home were conditioned by the writers' spleen.

by Brian James

PRAGUE

Friday: The tour begins for Ramsey when he eases his way through the ranks of gold teeth glittering in the Czech welcoming committee. The home championship had shown an upsurge in England's standing, but this first game is seen as the test of Ramsey's ability to shape a team to beat Poland in the World Cup. Few pressmen care for his pragmatic football, and have said so; but while he continues to win criticism remains muted.

He gives a brief conference to the Czech Press, who seem greatly perplexed that Keegan isn't in his squad ("Of course, Keegan is a very good player; but so are all these others"), before striding off to see how his players are managing. They are managing like players always do, grabbing their own suitcases, then standing about as patient as sheep while someone else deals with matters like passports, customs and currency forms.

At the hotel, smarter and more modern than most in Eastern Europe, they stand again in mute patience waiting to be allocated rooms, two by two. Sir Alf and his trainers decide the pairings, giving the matter a lot of thought. Known pals or club team-mates go in together automatically; the newcomer is put in with an old hand and the nervous is given a companion who will reassure him.

Alan Ball, as usual, is teamed with Bobby Moore, and goes upstairs chuckling. "Bob and I always share, but I think by the end of every tour he hates me. I'm a bit scruffy around the room, he's a nut on tidiness. You know something . . . he takes his money out every night and folds the notes on the corner of the table to get them even."

Their evening's entertainment is a reception at the British Embassy. "A duty," says Ramsey. "We were asked to go, so we went. For an hour. Actually we left after 55 minutes." Even that is a little too much for some of the players. "A right bloody drag," says Storey.

Saturday: Refreshed by 12 hours sleep the players are consumed with curiousity about the experiences of those of us who had been less wise: every breakfast conversation between player and pallid Pressman was an interrogation "Go out last night?" "Find any places?" "Anything about?" By tradition writers act as pathfinders for the one evening the players will be allowed out.

Apart from the man who kept insisting: "Honestly, she was going to do it for a lighter," the answers suggest the night life is more odd than satisfying.

Sunday: England scrape an uneasy draw and the reports correspondents telephone home tonight hint at a growing conviction that Ramsey is on the wrong lines; yet still the most violent critics are held muttering on the fringe, for it's the Poland game that will decide.

Ramsey, as is his custom, goes early to bed, leaving the players to begin a hotel-lounge party that lasts until dawn. On the surface the atmosphere is noisily calm but, conscious of the criticism they are sure to get, the players grow visibly edgy when the game is mentioned, and allow no remark aimed at their manager to go unchallenged.

Alan Ball tells another writer: "You blokes don't realise the power you've got. We are all human and we get hurt by what you say—never mind how we pretend it doesn't matter. None of you have played, know what it's really like. I wouldn't have the conscience of some of the writers for a million."

The arrival of the first English newspapers bring the players flocking and an attack on Norman Hunter by David Miller of the Sunday Telegraph brings a strong reaction. The most mild comes from Hunter himself: "Me and this bloke . . . we'll have to have a ball out between us somewhere, sometime."

It is the other players, Summerbee, Peters, Chivers, Hunter's rivals in league football, who seem most angry.

Monday (eight days later): Apart from a hand-picked crew ("You have to have a steward who knows a tactful way of refusing drinks to players if that is what the manager has ordered") there are 71 people on board BEA charter Trident BCH 482 which leaves Heathrow at noon.

Taking up all the first-class accommodation are the 20 players. In the seats behind the partition, forming a sort of cordon sanitaire, were the four team officials, manager, doctor and two trainers, the two paid FA officers, secretary Denis Follows and assistant Alan Odell, the FA chairman (Dr Andrew Stephen) and five members of the FA Council. The rest of the party at the back of the aircraft consists of 33 Press, TV and radio—writers, commentators, technicians and photographers; two travel agents. And four fans.

The finances are interesting. Hire of the plane is around £6,000 gross for the trip. But the journalists are being charged £150 each, and adding their contributions to that of the four fans makes £5,550. In this sense, the FA *needs* the Press.

KATOWICE

Tuesday: A very bad day for Sir Alf Ramsey and his relations with the Press. Disaffection begins when a chance remark by a travel agent discloses that both the FA party and the correspondents had been booked to stay in the modern Hotel Silesia—until the FA secretly arranged for the Press to be shifted to the vastly inferior Hotel Katowice.

Tempers of seething Pressmen are

Sir Alf Ramsey at bay: "Do I have to give reasons?"

Frank McGhee of the Daily Mirror asks with careful politeness: "Could you tell us why you are delaying the team—is it a matter of tactics, or are there practical reasons, like injuries?"

Ramsey stares back and snaps: "Do I have to give reasons? I have already told you what I am going to do." There is a long, dreadful, embarrassed silence; Englishmen stare down at their feet, acutely aware that the insulted McGhee has probably been Ramsey's greatest supporter over the past 10 years. The conference drags on for a further 10 minutes—time for Ramsey to complain about not being offered "even a glass of water" and about the Polish TV teams with their "hot and uncomfortable" lights. As he leaves a hostile silence is broken only by derisory handclaps from three Polish writers.

Wednesday: England play Poland and England lose. Now our place in the finals of the World Cup next year is in jeopardy, and for the critics this is the moment they had been awaiting. From their seats in the back of an open stand, surrounded by yelling Poles and handfuls of glum Englishmen, they pour into their telephones all the apparently now-justified doubts of recent months. Ramsey had picked the wrong players in the squad and from that squad chosen the wrong team. Ramsey had instructed the players badly, and failed to reinforce them with substitutes when he needed to do so. Ramsey had thrown away England's best chance.

They return to the Hotel Silesia to listen open-mouthed as the players proclaim they had played well but had been unlucky. Sir Alf edgily orders a supporter and his girlfriend to leave a group of players; then joins Moore, Ball and Clarke and sits quietly discussing the disaster into the small hours. Long before then the other players have gone moodily to their rooms.

Thursday: The man no one wants to change places with today is Nigel Clarke, of the Daily Mirror. His task on this tour is to "ghost" the weekly article under Bobby Moore's name, but from about 10 onwards Pressmen and players are in two very different camps. That is when, at Cracow Airport, the BEA cabin staff with bright unknowing smiles hand around the English newspapers brought from London.

In their reserved compartment up front, the players swap the papers, pausing only to throw glares of pure

not improved around noon when the first batch of England supporters arrive, and are ushered up to the 50 rooms in the team's hotel originally earmarked for them. A reporter said: "This is just bloody insulting—what it comes down to is that Alf would rather have his players surrounded by yobs in rosettes yelling for autographs, than us."

In the afternoon the Press party trail en masse to watch England train,

confident their stories for the day will be based on Sir Alf's Press conference at which he's expected to announce his team. More than 80 English and Polish Press and TV are waiting as he arrives, stonefaced. To the first question: "Can you give us the team?" he replies: "I will deal with this very quickly. The team will be announced tomorrow. Probably. Around lunchtime, probably." There's a grim silence, then

malice down the plane to where reporters sit, carefully absorbed in conversation with one another. Sir Alf does his share of reading, with not a flicker of expression as he notes headlines like "England Shamed" or "Ramsey's Plans Betray England."

All Nigel Clarke gets out of Moore in a brief and brave venture into the players' section is "Just say I'm sick," which was not much help to the Mirror in return for their £80 per article. Clarke gets a further brief word with Moore later, but has to fill in most of the other 996 words himself. He can't telephone the column until the England captain has read and approved it. It's mid-evening before Moore says: "Yes, OK, let it go," and Clarke stumbles back to his hotel.

MOSCOW

At Moscow Airport Jeff Powell of the Daily Mail is ill-advised enough to drift into the company of several players. He leaves, red-eared, a minute later after a player threatens to "stick one on you—and the rest of your bunch of blanks." Another pressman, Frank Clough of the Sun, is without a visa and is ordered to get back on the plane and fly home. 'Effing good job," calls a player, "And take the rest of these effers with you."

Friday: The busiest member of the party today is the doctor. Paul Madeley awoke with stomach cramps and vomiting, so room-mate Hunter has to be hurriedly evacuated, while the rest of the squad is checked for similar symptoms. Dr Neil Phillips is so much more than the team's physician. He's the morale officer, too. Players are nervy, superstitious, tense and often hypochondriacs. He goes up to Madeley's room every hour—so he doesn't lie brooding about his stomach. He finds time to chat reassuringly to Colin Bell, who's just heard his wife is ill after a miscarriage, news that later in the day sends him flying home.

Saturday: The day begins curiously for one FA official. He sits on a seat in the park opposite the team's hotel, ignoring the huddled presence of the unshaven "tramp" at the other end of the bench. He is a bit surprised when the tramp gets up, yawning, and is revealed to be England's captain, Bobby Moore. The explanation: Moore, around 5 am, had despaired of sleeping in a room as hot and sweaty as a sauna and had gone out for a stroll and fallen asleep.

Sir Alf meanwhile is mending some fences with the Press. After a hard-working training session for the players in the heat bowl of the Lenin Stadium, he gives reporters the names of 14 men from whom the team would come, hinting heavily that Hunter, certainly, would start the match.

Sunday: A long grim morning for Ramsey. The defeat by Poland is still bitterly in the atmosphere and at a time when he has never needed a victory more, it is a tired and morose squad that surrounds him as he waits for the coach to the Lenin Stadium, a place, surely, for only those great in spirit to perform with any success.

What happens in the next 90 minutes should be part of England football history. Ramsey's too dry to spit after five minutes; the players so blinded by sweat they call urgently for sweatbands after 10 minutes. They outrun, outplay and defeat the host side.

When it is over Ramsey comes out, unsmiling, to confess his astonishment at the recovery power of a team that had been "shattered, absolutely stunned" only four days ago. He cannot resist the barbed remark that he rated the performance nearly as good as that in Katowice; reporters swallow the rebuke wordlessly and go away to pack for tomorrow's flight to Italy.

TURIN

Tuesday: Although they wander the arcaded streets of Turin in twos and threes, the 70-plus members of the group are never more together than on this first free morning in a free city. Players join pressmen at pavement cafés for a coffee or mineral, officials stop in the streets to unwrap gifts to show what their lire bought.

Wednesday: There is another nasty dilemma for correspondents when a phone call from London reveals that the Evening News is front-paging a story that Martin Chivers's wife has left him and is to seek a divorce. Soon, reporters guess correctly, their offices come through asking for interviews and reaction from the England forward. Sir Alf even asks pressmen to pass the word that he doesn't want the player disturbed.

One reporter then approaches Chivers direct and tells him: "I am going to ask you about your wife and how you feel. You are then going to tell me you refuse to discuss it under any circumstances. And you are then going to give the same answer to every reporter who comes near you. Agreed?" Agreed.

Thursday: Literally a sore morning for the Press. Challenged to a football match with the Italian Press, the assumption was that 11 of the less paunchy writers would meet 11 of ours on a park somewhere, for an ambling affair amid a decent reticence. Not so. The match has been previewed on the front pages of the Turin newspapers and the English side captained by Billy Wright, is slaughtered 4–0 by a team of Turin sportswriters all of whom seem to have retired from active careers with Juventus or Torino only the day before.

In the international that evening, Ramsey has to sit and watch the discipline of the side disintegrate in the sun. His Press conference afterwards is predictable: he praises the players for their effort, complains—unusually—about the Italians' second goal, and then leads his team away knowing that the defeat has left him exposed once more to criticism.

Friday: The flight home is slightly hysterical; the players, many of whom show clear signs of a night of total freedom, are once again greeted on the plane by a shower of newspapers attacking their defeat if not, this time, their performance. They shrug and toss the papers aside.

In a different seat now, facing his players and with his back to the Press, Sir Alf sits as stonefaced as ever. Although the champagne flows steadily and voices get louder, he can't be unaware that here and there on the aircraft journalists are scribbling their wrap-up stories: and the message of most will be "Alf Must Go."

It is hard to say who has been right, for the problem is a total lack of understanding. The writers do not know what he trying to achieve with his teams, for he seldom theorises and never explains. Equally, he is so absorbed in his own function that he simply doesn't pretend to comprehend the pressmen's preoccupation with deadlines, communications or their nagging necessity to have something fresh to write about every day.

At Heathrow the party splits. Ramsey makes a point of going around thanking every player in turn. Only very few of the journalists shake his hand.

June 17 1973

Gentlemen, the toast is Tony Jacklin!

One of golf's most memorable moments since the war—when Britain hailed a home-grown champion.

by Henry Longhurst

What a day for British golf! What a shot in the arm! Tony Jacklin, the 25-year-old Potters Bar professional who has spent most of the year playing golf on the American circuit, brought the Open Championship back to Britain at Royal Lytham and St. Annes yesterday when with a final round of 72 and a four round total of 280 he took the trophy and first prize of £4,250. He is the first British player to win the championship for 18 years. Second was the New Zealand left-hander Bob Charles with a final round of 72 and a total of 282.

Not since Henry Cotton beat the full flower of the American Ryder Cup team at Carnoustie in 1937 has a home golfer defeated fairly and completely so many of the best Americans and the ovation that greeted Jacklin as he emerged through the masses who overran the 18th fairway must have warmed many thousands of hearts.

One knew already that of the many young players from this country who have braved the rigours of American professional golf, Jacklin was the only one not only to make any real impression, but also to feel at home there, and to say that he actually liked the life. Yesterday showed that he is now "hard" enough to take his place, and keep it, in any company. His future prospects are almost boundless.

This morning followed the pattern we have learned to expect during this championship—in other words a grey day, with a strong north-westerly wind but little apparent possibility of rain. This meant, for those who know Lytham, that the wind was blowing almost directly from the right at the first three holes—making it less easy to drive out of bounds on to the railway—and directly from the left at the 18th.

With a par of 71 or 213 for three rounds we started the day with only five players under par, ranging from five under to two under, with Nicklaus and Huggett level. This is a course with a

Jacklin: a burden of goodwill.

strong element of luck if you do not drive on to the narrow fairways. Only a few yards off the edge and you may be knee-deep in really thick stuff with the certain loss of a stroke or you may be lying perfectly well on a hump or on ground trodden down by spectators.

You have to take the rough with the smooth and trust to the luck to even itself out in the end. Easy enough to say but difficult to stomach if you find yourself almost unplayable a few yards off the fairway at the 71st hole.

One should not, of course, take sides but it is idle to deny that practically everyone's thoughts were on Jacklin and the prospect of a genuine true-blue British win at long last. Knowing this as of course he did, he was shouldering a tremendous responsibility and a bigger load of goodwill than any player in the world of golf for many a long year. His play so far had shown the stuff of which real winners are made and my own main hope for him was that he would add to his 68, 70, 70 at any rate a really good score and not something like a 77.

The first prize is £4,250, but Mark McCormack, his manager, reckoned before Jacklin started that a win would be worth $100,000 in America and, over a period of years, a few hundred thousand pounds over here.

Fairly early in the proceedings we noted that Peter Alliss had gone out in 30. "How much would you give, cash down," I asked McCormack, "for that score for Jacklin?" He replied: "A hundred thousand dollars."

A shaky start for Jacklin could have been fatal. There was no sign of any such thing. Lytham starts with a 208-yard short hole, played from the shelter of a large shrubbery, with the ball buffeted by the right-hand wind as it comes out into the open. Jacklin hit a beauty for his three, but Charles was short and took three more and this seemed to set the pattern.

Jacklin holed a very nasty four-footer at the second and then a magnificent one for a birdie 3 to go six under at the third. A few minutes later a huge cheer greeted an enormous putt, the best part of ten yards, as it popped into the hole at the fourth. What a start—3 4 3 3 against a par of 3 4 4 4! Just before this a neighbouring cheer was greeting O'Connor holding out for 2 at the short fifth, followed by de Vicenzo doing the same. Jacklin overshot this green, easy enough to do with a strong following wind, and took 4, so now only two shots separated him and O'Connor.

Soon after, alas, O'Connor began letting them slip away one by one, first to three under then two, and finally with a six at the 17th he was gone. Nicklaus got out in 33 to be two under, having said that he reckoned to have to do a 65 or 66 to win—which proved exactly right—but with 39 home he could do no better than 72.

I cannot say exactly when it was—perhaps at the 14th—but at some stage it came over me that we need not keep our fingers crossed for Jacklin any more and that he could do all that for himself, thank you very much. When Charles saw his younger opponent's armour, he began involuntary to relax the pressure. So it came that there was still three between them at the 17th, the hole where above all you can take 7 with a hooked drive. Jacklin hit a tremendous one and though he did take five he still had a two shot lead.

So now if he could avoid the masses of bunkers on the 18th he must surely be home. I saw the shot from just behind him and shall remember it to the end of my days. His swing never left him and this might have been on the practice ground. It might also have been fired from a rifle instead of a golf club—miles down the dead centre, veering neither to right nor left. He tossed the second up to within 10 feet and won with probably the shortest putt that ever won a championship—call it three eighths of an inch.

Gentlemen, the toast is Tony Jacklin! *July 13 1969*

Women's cricket: preparing for the invasion of Lord's

In the summer of '76, on a ground with 65-yard boundaries, and using a lighter ball (five ounces compared with the men's five and a half ounces) English and Australian women are pictured in battle during the second Test at Edgbaston, Birmingham. Women were first allowed to play at Edgbaston in 1930; Old Trafford fell in 1934; the Oval in 1935; but Lord's held out till August 1976. *(July 4 1976)*

Photographs by Ray Green and Patrick Eagar

With no trousers to protect their legs, players wind wool round pads' straps.

Overarm bowling, invented by a woman in 1805 because underarm the ball got tangled in her full skirts, was scoffed at by men for 50 years. Today English and Australian teams favour divided skirts, West Indian teams slacks, the Dutch shorts.

England wicketkeeper Shirley Hodges dives for the ball as a slip comes unstuck. Former hockey goalkeeper Hodges doesn't drink, smoke or chew gum. Captain Rachael Heyhoe-Flint's policy: "If you must chew gum for God's sake keep your mouth shut."

England's Chris Watmough thunders down the pitch towards Rachael Heyhoe-Flint.

Australia's Sharon Tredea, probably the world's fastest woman bowler, with a reputation for inflicting colourful bruises on her opponents.

Captain Anne Gordon's bra-strap repaired by Marie Lutschini, who feels: "You don't have to be butch to play for Australia."

Inside track

The Art of Cardus

Sir Neville Cardus is, with respect, a man who speaks with two tongues. In last Monday's Guardian he revealed all his extraordinary ability to span the work of music critic and cricket writer with outstanding authority.

In separate obituaries, on the arts and sports pages, Sir Neville was writing within hours of the deaths of Otto Klemperer and Wilfred Rhodes, men not only among the greatest in their sphere, but personal friends. Charged with anecdote and personal insight, Sir Neville's tributes offer a striking parallel manipulation of willpower.

On Yorkshire and England all-rounder Wilfred Rhodes: "The rhythm of his action was in its easy rotation, hypnotic, lulling his victims to the tranced state in which he could work his will, make them perform strokes contrary to their reason and intention."

On German conductor Otto Klemperer: "His eyes pierced the orchestra to the last of the back desks. The tympani were as much under the spell of his presence as the first violin situated immediately next to him."

Sir Neville was caught unawares by their deaths. "It is a curious paradox," he told our reporter, "that when people reach a certain age, say over 80, you don't think they are going to die at all. And when the news came through that they had died, one 95, the other 88 and myself 84, it was difficult to come to terms with my thoughts."

His thoughts on the blending over 54 years of music and cricket are, however, succinct. "Denis Compton," he says, "was able to provide just as artistic a form as any tenor. It is the art form I go to see, not a question of one team winning. That's not nearly so important." *July 15 1973*

Updike Down Hole

Golf is hard enough to understand without John Updike spinning his golden webs round the game. Here is the American novelist writing in his new book of essays, Picked-up Pieces, published by Andre Deutsch at £6.95:

"A non-chemical hallucinogen, golf breaks the human body into components so strangely elongated and so tenuously linked yet with anxious little bunches of hyperconsciousness and undue effort bulging here and there, along with rotating blind patches and a sort of cartilaginous euphoria—golf so transforms one's somatic sense, in short, that truth itself seems about to break through the exacerbated and as it were debunked fabric of mundane reality."

OK, John, what did you have at the last hole? *March 21 1976*

All alone at sea in the elegant care of her ladyship

After weathering a Force 10 storm, surfing 100 miles before an Atlantic wind, our man's entry for the Transatlantic single-handed race managed to qualify with less than 24 hours to spare.

by Murray Sayle

Entries closed last week of the 1972 Observer Single-handed Transatlantic Race with a record 56 yachts accepted and another two Italian and French awaiting confirmation. This is by far the most dazzling company yet assembled to contest the world's toughest ocean race, headed by the old master himself, Sir Francis Chichester in Gipsy Moth V and including almost every well known single-handed sailor in the world. New transatlantic records seem certain to be set by some of the monster yachts engaged—one French challenger, Vendredi Trieze, is a three-masted schooner 128 ft. long, a size considered impossible to single-hand only a year or two ago.

One entry, however, leaps out from the list of starters, at least in the affectionate gaze of this reporter. She is not the longest boat in the race, nor the widest, and in all this brave company, she and her skipper could hardly expect more than a good outside chance. But she is fast, sexy and seaworthy; she's called Lady of Fleet, because she is The Sunday Times entry for the race, marking our 150th anniversary as a newspaper with a friendly gesture towards our distinguished competitor and, to her bewitched skipper, she is entirely beautiful.

Lady of Fleet will be sailed by a Sunday Times journalist, an amateur sailor expressing a lifelong love of the sea, and of his trade, and paying a tribute to all the newspaper girls he has been in love/lust with down the years. In fact, by me. Lady of Fleet is a catamaran, one of two entered for the race. She is built of white fibre glass ("Tupperware!" some of them say at the yacht club, but it is the most durable yacht-building material yet developed) 41ft 3in long, which I thought was the biggest I could manage

alone, 17ft 9in wide, and displacing a trim 6.5 tons, which in sea-going terms is a figure like Twiggy's.

Apart from her Australian ensign she is all-British from keel to truck and is in a fact a production model Solaris 42, designed by Terry Compton and built by his firm, Solaris Marine of Southampton. She is modified from the standard production model only in minor respects, to lighten her; otherwise, in contrast to many of the one-off backyard racing specials which have been entered, Lady of Fleet is rather like a cosy London flat inside, with a huge saloon, four cabins with double berths, two toilets, a separate galley, bathroom, chart room, and radio room. Her one man crew hardly needs all this accommodation; but I'm setting out to demonstrate that the catamaran configuration offers a unique combination of space below and speed afloat and can still be safely handled by one man who is by no means the world's most experienced sailor.

Our 500 mile single-handed proving run, which I completed last week with less than 24 hours to spare before the deadline, has confirmed my choice of boat to my own satisfaction. Along with half a dozen last minute entries, we spent a nail biting fortnight waiting for the weather which would give us a sporting chance of completing our trial on time. There were warnings of south-westerly gales in the Western Approaches for 15 straight days in a row, and mournful news continually arriving in Plymouth.

I was going through agonies of indecision when the wind went round to the North, the gale warning was lifted, and I was off—the maiden voyage of Lady of Fleet, still not completed below decks, the first serious single-handed voyage of her skipper, and altogether a solemn moment for both of us.

Few honeymoons have gone off more happily. We had a few minor tiffs, inevitable with a new yacht: the compass repeating mechanism packed up and the boom fell off before I fully understood how the reefing system worked. But I was delighted with her speed, eight to ten knots to windward in a 24 knot apparent breeze, and happy that my system of watch keeping enabled me to get at least some sleep. (My secret weapon is a kitchen egg timer which is set for 20 minutes, doze off, jump up when it rings for a quick look round the horizon for steamers, re-set and doze off again.)

Lady of Fleet: "gorgeous creature."

I was, indeed, beginning to feel a bit guilty about getting good weather after the pounding which the other contestants had taken when I was unexpectedly hit by a screaming northerly, 100 miles south-west of the Scillies at 2 o'clock in the morning. The wind put my windspeed meter, which goes up to 50 knots, off the dial for half an hour. This is Force 10, a full storm on Admiral Beaufort's scale and an interesting moment in anyone's life.

I got Her Ladyship's genoa and mainsail off her in record time, and feeling that she wanted to head up into the seas, which were building up by the minute under the screaming wind, hoisted her small mizzen and engaged the self steering gear. Altogether, I was hove to and drifting slowly with the storm under this rig, and Lady of Fleet rode it out with elegant composure.

Next day we completed a memorable encounter with heavy weather by surfing 100 miles before the wind, far out in the Atlantic, doing 14 to 16 knots under a storm jib, skipping gaily past steamers rolling and splashing in 20ft waves.

The Western Approaches being what they are in April the storm was immediately followed by calm and sea fog as we ghosted back towards Plymouth, staring with tired eyes at the phantom fleet which always seems to be looming up at you out of the mist, so close you can almost make out their unbelievable names; Morning Clo . . . is it? or, surely not Torrey Can . . . or, good heavens, not Murray Say . . .?, before the grey goo swallows them up again.

I raised the Eddystone light at midnight and stole into Plymouth at 3am, with 586 miles on the log to tie up beside a surprised Polish trawler and crash exhausted for 20 minutes sleep (days later I still have trouble sleeping for more than an hour without looking round for steamers).

So we safely completed our trial, and for the moment, as in the early days of any love affair, I am enchanted by Lady of Fleet and still cannot quite believe the good fortune which has put me, even temporarily, in charge of such a gorgeous creature.   *April 23 1972*

PS. Murray Sayle had to withdraw from the race when he lost his main mast, sails and rigging during a storm at 2 am one morning. He estimated he was only 10 days off the finishing line. A US coastguard vessel, towed Lady of Fleet over 1,000 miles to Rhode Island. The race was won by Alain Colas. Sayle was not without distinguished company in his misfortune: Sir Francis Chichester didn't finish either.

How the most wanted and cherished of gift horses proved to have his teething problems

Preoccupations, priorities and even relationships can be affected by the acquisition of an equine member of the family.

by Philip Norman

To look at mother you would not think that she owned a racehorse. She is a smallish woman, not so very old, with light-coloured hair, exquisite hands and a nose which was once altered under the National Health. These characteristics stem from the 20 years which my mother spent applying cold creams and removing facial hair in the employment of a well-known cosmetics company. Now retired, she lives in a downstairs flat in London's Bayswater, and drives a Mini fitted with a basket-work device that gives added support to her back.

It is unnecessary to give an account of my mother's marriage to my late father, or explain how little likely her life once seemed to provide her with anything like a racehorse. Suffice it to say that she emerged from her difficulties, and met a man who grows vegetables in East Anglia who proved an altogether more suitable companion. It was this amiable farmer, late in 1975, who perceived my mother's wish to own a yearling colt, purchased at the Doncaster Sales.

The naming of the colt occupied my mother for many nights. I would discover her in her small kitchenette, with its tall glass column for storing uncooked pasta, surrounded by racing textbooks, cuttings from The Sporting Life and forms for the colt's registration with Wetherby's.

A typewritten pedigree, which my mother repeatedly showed me revealed his antecedents to be exceptional. His mother had been Harissa, and his grandmother Tudor Melody. His father, Levmoss, a descendant of the great Ballymoss, won both the Prix de l'Arc de Triomphe and the Ascot Gold Cup.

My attitude at this stage was, I fear, rather flippant. I asked if my mother's farming friend would next consider buying me a Formula One racing-car team.

A glance at any race-card will give proof of the incontinent haste with which most racehorses are baptised. So it was in my mother's kitchenette, with its carved wooden key-shaped key-holder, as she strove to think of names permutated from the colt's ancestry which might also possess the euphony of a Derby winner. From Levmoss my mother thought of Levinsky.

"I've got it!" she exclaimed on another occasion. "What about the French Connection!" It was here that I suggested the colt should be called Prince Myshkin. When my mother looked sceptical, I drew her attention to a copy of Dostoevski's The Idiot in a decorative but unread edition on her very own shelves. I explained that Prince Myshkin had not really been an idiot, but a high-minded, noble and tractable creature. My mother, pulling one of her faces, acceded.

Some months passed before I was able to make Prince Myshkin's acquaintance. He had been put into training with Neville Callaghan at Newmarket, with board and lodging subsidised by the favourable caprice of the Brussels sprouts industry. My mother, who visited him often, kept me up-to-date with reports of his elegance, his marked cleverness, the length of his eyelashes and his great fondness for Polo mints. He was, so my mother said, "just like a great big dog." I doubted the accuracy of this description.

The trainer's advice was that he should run as a two-year-old in the 1976 Flat season. Being a January foal, he would enjoy an advantage in size and strength over his fellow two-year-olds born later in the year. It was arranged that he should make his debut at York in June, in the Guy Fawkes Stakes.

The jockey assigned to him was Kipper Lynch, so named not for fishiness but for sleepiness. His colours were chosen to resemble those of my mother's friend's old school, Uppingham. My mother's colours, no less carefully selected, were a dress of yellow cotton voile and a yellow straw hat with a brim. No resemblance to Queen Elizabeth the Queen Mother was intended, I think.

The day Prince Myshkin ran at York, I fear that I forgot all about it. The mind takes time to accustom itself to a racehorse-owning mother. I spent the afternoon writing and re-writing a five-line paragraph which by six o'clock was unusable. At seven my mother telephoned, announcing without preamble—as is her habit—that Prince Myshkin had been unplaced, but that he had made a good showing among two-year-olds of parentage even more powerful than his. She added that her farming friend had mistakenly driven them both back from York to Cambridgeshire by way of Burton-on-Trent.

It was the same when Prince Myshkin ran his second race, at Sandown in the Paddock Maiden Stakes. Once more, the matter slipped my mind. I spent the afternoon in drafting and re-drafting a seven-line paragraph which, by evening, remained still incomplete. My mother telephoned me at about eight o'clock. Her words, as I recall, were: "He's only gone and won, hasn't he?"

At times of high excitement, my mother's Elizabeth Arden voice is apt to disappear. She told me that Prince Myshkin had led the field all the way, and had received a purse of £1,200. My mother had brought him into the winners' enclosure, her yellow cotton voile soaked by froth from his neck where she had hugged him.

I am sorry not to have seen this moment in my mother's life, since I believed that it now rivals in significance the moment of my own birth.

We drove out to Newmarket to see Prince Myshkin early one morning last summer. Potatoes were doing well, and my mother's farming friend sang little hymns of praise to them all the way, beating time against the steering wheel.

The stable was a plain concrete building, surrounded—such was the heat then—by withering flowers. We walked along a corridor of monastic cleanliness, perfumed with horses like a faint, expensive liqueur. Some, I noticed, lay on white shavings instead of straw, giving them the appearance of prizes fresh from the bran tub. Their names were posted on a bulletin board, together with their itineraries for the day.

I noticed that Prince Myshkin was the neighbour of an animal named Mr Playbirds, whose owner is the publisher of widely-read magazine. My mother had gone ahead, into an end stall, where I discovered her embracing a tall, thin, liquorice-coloured horse. He had a face as amiable as a Labrador retriever's, and legs that resembled two

Prince Myshkin: a tall, liquorice-coloured horse, with owner.

pairs of slim black evening trousers, independently posing. He was, as my mother had said, extremely fond of Polo mints.

When he ran his next race, at Newbury, I positioned myself in plenty of time before my television set, subduing all qualms of decadence and guilt. They were dispelled when Prince Myshkin's name appeared on the screen, on a racecard superimposed against the crowd. I confess to having been filled with a gaseous conceit. And Peter O'Sullevan called him "a nice colt".

He did not win. My mother explained afterwards that he had not liked the way the railings curved. He ran once more that season, in the Prince of Wales Nursery Handicap Stakes at Doncaster. Again, he did not win. My mother's explanation was that he preferred to lead the field all the way. I

passed this on to two of my colleagues who had, at my suggestion, bet £1 on Prince Myshkin each way. From me, I fancy, it sounded less convincing.

Prince Myshkin has spent the winter boisterously, tossing stable lads off his back. Formerly, it was on his way to exercise that he threw them off. Now he waits until they are returning, then he throws the stable lad off. This, according to my mother, presages a formidable career as a three-year-old. A slight scare, concerning warts on his mouth, fortunately came to nothing. According to my mother, his eyelashes have grown longer than ever.

Around my mother's sitting-room there are three photographs of Prince Myshkin, as against one each of Ivor Novello and of me. And my mother's farming friend? He thrives. He has now bought her two more racehorses.

February 20 1977

Inside track

Jones the Hoax

BBC Television Sport, which has given us the wit of Kenneth Wolstenholme and the discreet charm of David Coleman, presented us last Wednesday with a new interlocutor on Sportsnight: Tony Gubba. Significantly or not, Gubba's first words were lost beyond recall; the mouth opened but emitted no sounds.

Gubba, though, appears to thrive on the odd traumatic experience. Four years ago, a Young Turk with Southern Television after a spell as a sub-editor in the Manchester office of the Daily Mirror, he was sent to Norway to cover a Fairs' Cup match played in Trondheim by Southampton.

Ken Jones, the Daily Mirror football correspondent, heard to his surprise that Gubba appeared to know him well, but walked past him quite unrecognised, and a practical joke was born. The Daily Express reporter, Norman Giller, whimsically told Gubba that Jones was, in fact, Helenio Herrera, the famous Argentinian manager, come to look at the Southampton centre-forward, Ron Davies, on behalf of Roma.

Jones is small, sturdy, rubicund, and Welsh, Herrera swarthy, brooding and very Latin. Nevertheless, Jones-Herrera maintained the deception through an "interview" with Gubba, which he confined to gestures and monosyllables. Gubba, as a loyal ex-Mirror man, then rang the London office to acquaint them with the story. The joke foundered at last on the verge of Jones-Herrera's Press conference in Giller's hotel room. Jones felt he could hardly sustain it.

October 7 1973

A Fixtion

The next time our football writers face that hoary old chestnut—being accused of not attending matches they have reported—they'll be able to quote back the footballers who never went to the match they played.

It happened in the York and District League, where Heslington and Moor Lane Youth Club had such a fixture congestion that they decided to scrub one match and submit a fake 0–0 scoreline. They even gave the "referee" his obligatory marks out of 10 for his handling of the game. Sadly, they were found out, fined and relegated.

June 11 1978

● The Amateur Boxing Association has clamped down on long hair. Hereafter, beards are out and so are locks that fall below the earlobes or eyebrows. The reasons are logical: free-flying hair, if trapped by a glove, can (and has) damaged a boxer's eye. "I suppose," admits ABA secretary Bill Lovett, "a boxer's all right if he wears a bow in his hair." *October 31 1971*

John Disley (above), now 48, was once one of the world's leading 3,000 metres steeplechase runners. He, like Chris Brasher and Gordon Pirie, took to orienteering "because we loved running." The man who once won the men's over-43 "JK" title finished 16th yesterday.

In the starting pens, with countdown in progress, competitors get a first look at the map. In another minute, they get the final whistle and are released into the forest with a map that has been overprinted with their own course.

A day out in the woods with 2,000 people...

The sylvan folds of Leith Hill, Surrey, are a far cry from the more traditional kind of sports stadium, and the name of the Jan Kjellstrom trophy has a distinctly foreign ring. Yet these are the venue and title of Britain's biggest Easter sporting event.

by Norman Harris
Photographs by Chris Smith

Jan Kjellstrom was a young Swede who was sent to England by his father in order to learn English. But he also, during his stay, taught the art of orienteering to the British. Orienteering involves running through the forest with the aid of a map and checking in at a succession of control points; and it was the Kjellstrom family's development of a special compass which, in the mid-1960s, helped to turn the activity into a competitive international sport.

Young Jan got so enthusiastically involved in teaching orienteering to schools and clubs that his father sent him back for a second visit. He astounded the British with the speed and navigational skill of his own running, and indeed influenced the sport to such a degree that he was regarded as a sort of missionary. His death, at the age of 27 in a car accident in Sweden, was deeply felt in Britain. But in due course the sport was to mushroom.

The first event held in his memory, the Jan Kjellstrom Trophy of 1967, attracted 60 men and seven women competitors. Yesterday's 'JK' individual titles were contested by some 2,000 competitors, divided into 18 different age classes for men and women, boys and girls. The youngest age class was for those aged 10 or under, the oldest for the over-56s.

Today, Sunday, the same 2,000 go back into another forest for the "JK" relays. And tomorrow they're off to yet another forest for a "relaxation" event!

April 10 1977

Geoff Peck (above), 27, is Britain's No.1 — a pilot who gets navigation practice through flying low-level sorties. Yesterday he made a rare mistake, losing three minutes in a rhododendron patch. But he still won the elite event by six minutes.

...But keep a sharp lookout for the prams

A beginner's baptism in the sport "where rabbits can compete with Olympians"

by Michael Green

The trouble with orienteering is Chris Brasher.

As one who admires the Olympic gold medallist I'd better explain that. I mean the sport suffers from an image given by tough runners like Brasher who've taken it up. In the public mind it has become identified with the limit-of-endurance brigade, the sort who want everybody to carry lead weights to make it more difficult.

But it isn't like that at all. It's the finest family sport ever invented and almost the only one where rabbits can compete with the Olympians.

I was initiated recently by a colleague and apprehensively arrived at a remote wood in Buckinghamshire to go through the formalities of buying a map and entering for a middle range course. There was a choice of a dozen, from easy to impossible.

Now I am not the best of map-readers and in the Army I once guided a troop of tanks over a small precipice. As a yachtsman, I keep hitting the Isle of Wight every time I go to France. Even so, it was rather a surprise when I actually got lost on the start line.

You line up and, when a whistle is blown, run 150 yards to the master maps, from which you copy the location of the course control points on to your own map, and then rush off to find the first. Unfortunately, I dashed off in the opposite direction to everybody else and collided with the next lot of starters coming up, one of whom pointed out that my map was upside down.

However, my embarrassment was lessened by the presence of others who were not much more efficient, including schoolchildren, mums and dads, pensioners and at least one child-in-arms with the father carrying a push-chair. Some events allow prams.

They were clad in an astonishing variety of clothing. The only formality is that the competitors must be covered, a rule introduced ever since

someone suffering from hepatitis distributed the disease generously via the brambles. I was wearing a selection from the different sports at which I have failed in my life—rugby boots and socks; sailing trousers; cricket shirt; golf sweater. That's rather symbolic of orienteering. It's something like car rallying on foot, yachting through undergrowth or playing golf without knowing where the greens are. The golfing analogy persists—one thinks of each leg as "a hole."

The first control was 600 yards away. It took me an hour to find it and I wasn't the slowest. Control is a misnomer—it's just a small sign on a tree with a clipper to punch your card and prove you've been there. After that I got better. The next leg took a mere five minutes. Soon I was even being asked for advice by two schoolboys who were darting in all directions, uttering shrill yelps like lost dogs. I fear I may have misdirected them. They suddenly vanished over the edge of a deep gulley with howls of dismay.

Running was soon abandoned but I plodded steadily round the course with only a few minor errors, such as when I found control No. 8 before No. 6 and had to work backwards, followed by a young woman who was plainly lost, but whose presence merely led to excruciating discomfort, as I urgently wished to be alone to relieve myself (a problem in winter orienteering).

And so to the finish. In the euphoria of finishing I wobbled the last 50 yards, then pretended to collapse with cramp like Jim Peters in the marathon, and tottered in clawing the air and crying "Don't help me over the line!" They must have thought I was bonkers. I'd taken almost three hours to do just over five kilometres. Don't sneer, the winner took 53 minutes.

My girlfriend rushed out with coffee. She'd done the beginners' course, but she kept going round in circles and punched her card at the same control point three times.

The St John Ambulance people departed (only one customer, a sprained foot, although they once had a case of hypothermia). Then they presented the prizes, all home-made. A vote of thanks for the landowner. Applause for the winning team. An appeal for someone to give a lift to a student. And then we all went home to tea. It seemed a long way from the crooked world of the Olympics. But this was sport, just the same. *January 30 1977*

For the family, as for the elite, the day ends with countless post-mortems. "How did you do? What was your time?" As the provisional results are carded and studied, some still hope for honours. Others simply had a good time.

A seat with the Big Yin at the big game

That biennnial tribal rite by which the Scottish clans invade Wembley for the England v Scotland football international was celebrated in 1977 by a 2–1 victory over the old enemy and a visit of The Big Yin, the central character in a now defunct comic strip drawn by Malky McCormick (below, right) and based on the humour of the popular Scottish comedian Bill Connolly (left).

by Bob Campbell

The origins of the Big Yin strip go back some years to the time when Malky McCormick, working as a commercial artist and graphic designer, met Billy Connolly through a shared interest and involvement in the folk-music scene in Scotland—McCormick plays in a group called The Vindscreen Vipers. Increasingly, as Connolly capitalised on his biggest asset, a sense of humour that borders on the surreal, he and McCormick frequently discussed the possibilities of a cartoon strip.

McCormick gives particular credit to the now defunct Scottish Daily News, which pressured and cajoled him into finally producing a rough outline, at which point the SDN folded. Immediately the Sunday Mail stepped in with an offer and, with Connolly's blessing, the Big Yin was off on his travels, accompanied by his perfect foil, McCormick in the role of The Wee Yin, lampooning on the way anybody from Jock Stein to the Queen.

Apart from the strip's intrinsic merit and its connection with Connolly, it is unerringly topical. When the Queen toured Scotland, for example, she made a guest appearance in the strip, speaking of course, in a Glaswegian dialect. The difference was that her words were in copperplate handwriting to indicate that she's posh. Also, Con-

nolly and McCormick typify Glasgow humour, and when it comes to that there are no sacred cows: anyone or anything is a potential target.

That is why Connolly has often been compared with the late Lenny Bruce, America's tragic satirist. "Ah'm intae outrage," Connolly said last week over one of many drinks.

There are some Glaswegians who begrudge Connolly his success. They may even claim to be the originators of parts of his material. But, although some of Connolly's stories are public domain, the fact remains that he was

the first Scottish funnyman to get up on the stage and tell it like it is at street level.

There is a particular Glasgow penchant for running words together, as in "Urryizafftiragemme," which roughly translated means: "Are you going to the football match." That's some of McCormick's stock-in-trade for the strip. Or, similarly, "Giezzasooki-yirorange," which is: "May I please have a suck of your orange."

So basically, The Big Yin cartoon, like Connolly's stage act, is a celebration of the absurd. And although

anyone over about 5ft 8in in Glasgow can qualify for the title Big Yin, Connolly made it his very own when he produced a sketch about the crucifixion and resurrection of Jesus Christ. It was set in Glasgow, all the characters spoke in dialect and Christ is called The Big Yin, as in: "Hey, Big Yin, gie us wan o' thae stories," or "So The Big Yin's up on a cloud wi' his faither."

When the real-life Big Yin descended from the skies at Heathrow yesterday week, accompanied by his visual biographer and a host of apostles headed for Wembley, London had already been softened up for some days by advance parties, all in town for the England-Scotland match, known simply as "the gemme." Everywhere Connolly went, he added a special dimension to what is, for Scots, always an exhilarating occasion: "We are now approaching Belfast airport. Please extinguish your cigarettes, fasten your seat belts, and turn your watches back 300 years."

When he arrived at the home of English football, it actually looked more like the capital of Scotland. At the top of the stairs leading to the turn-stiles, Connolly, sporting an enormous Glengarry "bunnet," swung round and raised an exultant fist to the crowd, producing the first great roar of the afternoon. And with the number of flags around stating "Remember 1314—The Battle of Bannockburn," Connolly at that moment was for all the world like Robert the Bruce urging on his troops to victory over the English invaders.

The Wizard of Scots had come to preside over the Wembley passion play. Scotland was celebrating its religion, football.

June 12 1977

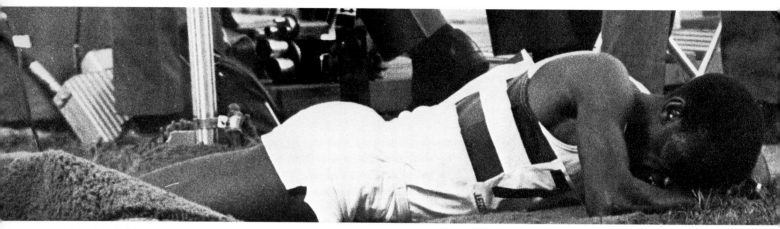

A victim of altitude, another dose of oxygen . . . were these really competitive races?

The mockery in Mexico — how altitude destroyed an essential Olympic ideal

The 1968 Olympics, held 7,350ft above sea level in Mexico City, produced an occasion that was, according to the man who first ran a four-minute mile, not sport, not a fiesta but a giant Wellsian farce of disproportionate performances. These included a long jump that over a decade later appeared to border on the apocalyptic.

by Roger Bannister

The distance events in Mexico City this week have been just as expected by most people except the International Olympic Committee—more of a fiasco than a fiesta.

As athletes have collapsed on the finishing line, white-coated medical attendants have rushed to their aid with oxygen masks, while television cameras have hovered over the prostrate figures like vultures. It has been a farce of almost Wellsian proportions instead of sport. Ron Clarke, the greatest distance runner in the world and one of the bravest too, said after his collapse in the 10,000 metres: "This isn't the Olympics; it's a triangular match between Kenya, Ethiopia and Mexico."

That he and many others should have been put in this ridiculous position leaves me practically speechless with anger. For an important minority the games have been an embittering and painful experience. And I can speak for this minority because but for an accident of birth and age I might have run under these conditions myself.

We watched the tiny country Kenya flower as the greatest producer of distance runners in the world as their rivals collapsed at the tape. The Kenyans just continued running up the ramp which led out of the stadium with an almost contemptuous ease. They seem able to suck oxygen into the muscle from the blood at a lower oxygen pressure. In physique they have long legs in proportion to trunk length, producing great stride length and power in proportion to their weight. Their chests, hearts and lungs are not strikingly larger.

There have been lessons to be learnt about the best way to run at altitude. The first part of the race must be run slowly to avoid an early oxygen debt that can never be cleared. The sea-level athlete cannot tolerate an increase in pace even later in the race. Clarke's collapse at the end of the 10,000 metres had all the features of circulatory failure and lack of oxygen to the brain. He was ashen grey and did not recover normal consciousness until he had been given oxygen for 10 minutes. His physical recovery was then remarkably rapid.

His psychological recovery owes a lot to Franz Stampfl, who was his original coach when, as an eighteen-year-old chosen to carry the Olympic torch in Melbourne, Clarke had already run the fastest mile in the world for a boy of his age. Stampfl, my own coach in the last year of my running, can inspire an athlete better than anyone I know. He told Clarke before he ran two days later in the 5,000 metres here: "No one can predict what will happen in the next race, but you have been through the worst in the 10,000 metres. To stand a chance you must accelerate three laps from home and try to keep it up."

Clarke did just this, knowing that if he left it to the last lap the Kenyans would outsprint him. He reached the final where the 10,000-metre story was repeated. Four out of the first six runners were born at altitude.

The winner, Mohamed Gammoudi, a Tunisian, has been "on leave" from the Tunisian army for two years and has spent much of this time at altitude. We know now from his performance, if anyone previously doubted it, that up to two years of altitude training improves performance at altitude and presumably also at sea level. His victory over those born at altitude was, however, achieved only because of a tactical blunder by the Kenyans. Keino has run at 7,000 feet in Kenya far faster over

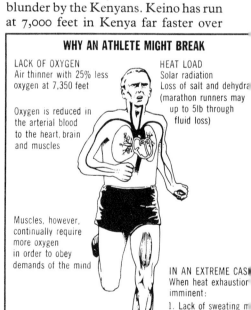

WHY AN ATHLETE MIGHT BREAK

LACK OF OXYGEN
Air thinner with 25% less oxygen at 7,350 feet

Oxygen is reduced in the arterial blood to the heart, brain and muscles

Muscles, however, continually require more oxygen in order to obey demands of the mind

IN AN EXTREME CASE
1. Brain may falter
2. Eyes may fail to respond to colour
3. Heart may lose natural rhythm of contraction

HEAT LOAD
Solar radiation
Loss of salt and dehydra (marathon runners may up to 5lb through fluid loss)

IN AN EXTREME CAS
When heat exhaustior imminent:
1. Lack of sweating m lead to the body temperature rising 105 degrees Fahren
2. Skin temperature approaches the temperature of the surroundings

5,000 metres than Gammoudi's winning time in these Games.

The Kenyans should have collaborated to share a fast pace in the early part of the race, aiming at a final time of about 14 minutes 45 seconds. Instead they meandered about at the back of the field like a pair of novices while the average speed per kilometre at 4,000m was 2 minutes 50 seconds.

Clarke, as in the heat, tried to increase the pace three laps from home but a lap of 66 seconds exhausted his frail reserves. It was a vain but gallant attempt to salvage something from his disastrous week. The Kenyans still waited but when Gammoudi unleashed a sprint over a last lap of 55 seconds—neither could catch him. But for me the rather heavy sad figure of Clarke dominated the race. He has a compulsion to run but will he ever want to run again?

The steeplechase was almost monotonously the same story. This time the most serious collapse was Herriott, the gallant Briton who was running about seven seconds a lap slower than in England. I can only explain this on the basis of the slight oxygen debt incurred by the extra effort of clearing each hurdle or water jump which destroys the body's rhythm.

Herriott had not recovered until two hours after the race when he said: "All I can remember of the last four laps is vaguely seeing some black spots on the hurdles." The next day he was still very weak and needed help in walking. Herriott, the Tokyo silver medallist for the steeplechase, has waited four years for this mockery of a second chance and now he will never run again. What an end to a career! People do matter, International Olympic Committee please note.

By contrast, the winner of the event was a tall ungainly Kenyan, Biwott, who is thought to be 23 but has no record to prove it, and is tactically naïve in the extreme. In the heat he sprinted crazily for the first two laps and opened a 70-yard lead. In the final, he was sixth, 20 yards back, at the bell and then overtook the field including fellow-Kenyan Kogo.

I am happy that Kenya should win as many medals as she can for winning will be an immense spur for sport there. I simply want to make it clear that a novice without adequate training, technique or judgment has won an Olympic title because of the chance of his birthplace. And I think this is utterly wrong.   *October 20 1968*

The day it came together for ever

by John Lovesey

Since Bob Beamon long jumped 29ft $2\frac{1}{2}$in in the 1968 Olympics to win the gold medal and set a new world record in the event, no other athlete has exceeded 28, let alone 29 feet.

His feat totally defied any logical progression in world records: while in the 33 years before Beamon's record, $8\frac{3}{4}$ inches had been added to Jesse Owens's distance of 26ft $8\frac{1}{4}$in, Beamon tacked 1ft $9\frac{1}{2}$in on to Ralph Boston's 27ft 5in, jumped in 1965. It was an 84-year advance at the previous rate. So how did it occur?

Dr Ernest Jokl, a professor at the University of Kentucky in the USA, a neurologist, has published detailed studies in an attempt to provide an answer. He calls Beamon's jump a "mutation performance," and has compiled factors that together could have contributed to the structuring of the feat. They range from the run-up, the following wind, to the longer legs that Beamon was endowed with.

There is, in addition, evidence that borders on the apocalyptic. In the first case, the altitude in Mexico City probably lowered everyone's reflex thresholds. This, in Beamon's case, may in turn have been combined with increased sensitivity of the system of the brain that controls consciousness as well as muscle tone in the antigravity muscles of the legs, a deduction that Jokl bases on Beamon's cataleptic collapse on being told the distance he had jumped.

But the more Beamon's jump is examined, the more mysterious it remains. "In one sense," admits Jokl, "it is entirely inexplicable. Nothing justifies the assumption that we're going to see another 29-foot jump." It is this that gives the picture above of Beamon in the midst of his jump, taken by the British photographer Ed Lacey, who died in a car crash last week, its impact and beauty.   *November 21 1976*

Barrington (foreground) and Hunt: both men argue with the referee, no-one smiles at all.

Squash at the top: cruel and vicious and noisy and subtle

Insight into a rivalry of the most intense competitiveness, which culminated later in the Irishman beating the Australian in the longest British Open squash final on record.

by Tony Clifton

Geoff Hunt is the greatest squash player in the world. He was leaning against the mirror in the dressing room at Northwood Squash Club. The only chair was full of Jonah Barrington, who was slumped against the wash basin, suicidally depressed and trying to make a joke with a reporter. "Why don't you write: 'Barrington is struggling,'" he suggested.

Both of them were suffering from the fallout of the match Hunt had just won 9–6 in the fifth game after two hours.

Squash played by the world champion and his nearest rival isn't the game played by good old Nigel and Tim at the Lansdowne Club every Tuesday after work. It is cruel and vicious and noisy and subtle and after two hours even the world champion is so weary he can just lean against the mirror and say "yeah . . . yeah . . . yeah" when some fruity-voiced sportsman in an old school cravat is telling him how he really ought to pay more attention to his drop shots.

The game at the Northwood Club last weekend was the third in a 15-match series the two are playing to prove who is the greatest. The games are being played because Barrington is so obsessive about proving he is the best that he actually paid Hunt's expenses to come to Britain to play him. The matches are jokingly called "exhibitions," which seems to mean that Hunt and Barrington stop just short of bursting their hearts to win. The real thing apparently will be the British Open this week when the two should meet in the final and one will damn near die before the other wins.

Geoff Hunt hits it so fast it would land somewhere near Cumberland if the back wall wasn't there to stop it. He's the typically aggressive Australian, thrashing it back again and again, eventually forcing Barrington into error. Barrington hates every minute of it because he knows he isn't at top form yet and here he is being beaten by this boy who is only 23 and world champion on an English court with a partisan crowd behind him.

Barrington hits a drop shot into the tin. "Discipline," he shouts at his right leg and smashes it with his racket. "You idiot, you fool ... come on Jonah, let's have a game of squash ... what are you doing here?"

Hunt is quieter. "Silly," he shouts when he hits a drop shot into the tin. Most of the abuse he directs at himself is brief. "Silly," "Stupid," "No" are the main cries. Both men argue with the referee. No one smiles at all and each one gets unhappier as the night goes on and the walls and floor get slippery as the warm air generated by players and spectators condenses on the cold surfaces. At 6–5 in the vital fifth game the nadir is reached when the lights go out because some fool hasn't put enough two-bobs in the meter. Amazingly

Hunt: aggression.

neither of these tense men attack the club officials.

Hunt went on to his 9–6 victory. Afterwards he talked about himself and the game, and began by criticising the English ball which he says has ruined squash in Britain.

"The trouble is that you use this very soft ball over here. The harder you hit it, the softer it comes back. It just splats against the wall, then rebounds slowly into play. This slow return means that a top level player knows he will never be beaten by power or speed. He knows he will always be able to get it back into play, so he plays this waiting game, playing these enormously long rallies hoping that his opponent will either make a mistake or lose through sheer exhaustion."

Hunt talks and plays with such authority that it is hard to believe he is

just 23, nearly five years younger than Barrington. Yet he is a squash veteran and has been playing at championship level for eight years ... he won the Victorian senior championship at 15.

He got very little formal coaching. One man, Alan McCausland, taught him ball control at 13 ("his strokes were terrible but his length was brilliant") and another, Brian Boys, a former Australian champion, got him for ten weeks when he was about 15 and gave him some unorthodox advice which he says enormously improved his game. Hunt for example hits his backhands when leading with his left foot. The classical way is to lean forward on the right but Hunt says this leaves you badly balanced to turn back to the centre of the court, whereas you pivot from the left with the minimum of leg and body movement.

"When I train for the world championships, I train for one hour a day, maybe five or six days a week, I do stomach exercises, some sprinting and

Barrington: dedication.

that's about all. I could never train like Jonah. Weights nearly killed me when I tried them. The reason I don't turn pro is that I think a professional's life is short and uncertain, and I'm not sure I could stand the game if I had to play it all the time. I have nothing but admiration for Jonah's dedication but I reckon I would last two months if I went at it like he does."

If Hunt admires Barrington, so the feeling is mutual. "We still persist with this attitude that it is not gentlemanly to appear to work at a game so the Australians come and bury us.

"Geoff Hunt is now the greatest Australian of them all. I think he will always hold this place, like Nurmi or Elliott or the other great champions, a man who will be remembered as remarkable as long as the game is played."

December 7 1969

Flea Power

Bob Beamon's long jump and Pat Matzdorf's high jump—world records at 29ft 2½in and 7ft 6¼in respectively—are fairly feeble feats when compared to a flea. If a flea were a man, we discover in the British journal Nature, he could leap clear out of a stadium. In fact, size for size, an Oriental rat flea can high jump 275ft and long jump 450ft.

"Although fleas," write Nature's flea-watchers, "have lost their ability to fly, they have retained and modified several important features associated with a winged mode of locomotion and incorporated them into the jump mechanism." Which is to say, the flea doesn't rely on muscular strength at all, but cocks and locks itself back on a store of springlike energy in its jumping legs before it lets fly. And then, oh man, does it let fly: its peak acceleration is 140 times the force of gravity, which is 14 times the acceleration that would cause a man to black out.

That rules out the application of flea power to athletics. In fact, if Nature magazine had scratched deeper they might have discovered, as a subsequent issue of New Scientist did, that another bug is a few jumps ahead of the flea. The click beetle, it seems, accelerates at 380 times the force of gravity when it has to flip over from flat on its back. *September 24 1972*

● Quote of the week. Peter Jones during his BBC radio commentary on last Wednesday's Liverpool-Red Star game: ... "Vladimir Petrovic. He has the same name as the goalkeeper. Don't get confused by it. Certainly Liverpool are not confused by it." *November 11 1973*

A racegoer's dream: those days of wine and horses

Racing across the Channel—a day out studying form in the sun at Deauville.

by Brough Scott

If you have ever promised yourself a blow out when one of those dud bits of information actually gives you a winner, you must, just once (twice might break the bank), go across to Deauville.

Not just for what the local paper calls its "snobbisme superbe" but for what we could only describe as its "sensualité formidable"—and at the races, too.

The sensual thing is in the whole feel, l'ambiance (why not?) of the place. Of course it is in part due to the sun and the wine. Alder, creator of the masterwork with this article, is not a teetotaller either. It is also due to the holiday spirit . . . people "en vacances" have far less reserve about them the world over and everyone appeared to be "en vacances" except racing men and restaurateurs.

But I think it also comes from the whole idea that you are at the races to look at the form and the movement of an animal in both a critical and a pleasurable sense, and if your eye is getting as personal as that with the horses it will automatically do the same thing with the humans.

If you think that is far-fetched go out to Deauville and see, and if you are a hardened racing worthy look deep into your heart and see if there is not some connection—I know one "lady of the track" who could lay you better ante post odds than any bookmaker.

Even the selling race at Deauville, yes "le selling," is worth 25,000 francs, and today's big race, named after the old Duc de Mornay, who started the whole of Deauville as a "summer station" in 1861 and the racecourse three years later, is worth 10 times as much.

This ensures that the real aristocrats of the horse world, two-legged as well as four, are there for your delight, and no stager of "beautiful people" adverts could ever choreograph them better.

We sat under the parasols and took the first demi of Sancerre with the paté

Welcome to Liverpool's mighty Kop

A plain man's guide to the pride of Liverpool, the heaving hillside of humanity that inspires the home team and overawes the opposition.

by Stanley Reynolds

Liverpool is one of the world's story-book cities, a maker of myths and legends just like Dublin or New Orleans, a place of magic where the unexpected is taken as a matter of course. How else do you explain the Beatles, the public house poets, the dockers' wit, and the mighty Kop of Anfield Road. It is magic.

The giant Kop on a Saturday afternoon is the quintessence of Liverpool, full of song, wit, vulgarity, and poetry. There are other Kops on other grounds, but they are mere imitations, pale fire, reflections only of the bright sun of Anfield Road.

Exiles come home to Liverpool, grown men, hard of eye and steady of hand in business deals, and yet they will admit that a tear or two rolled down their cheeks when they returned to Anfield and heard again the swelling roar, inexorable as the Western Ocean itself, coming from the red-lined Kop.

"You have not been to Liverpool," a Scouse philosopher said, "until you've had your leg urinated on in the Kop."

Perhaps chanting, banner-waving fans came first out of Italy, but the Spion Kop of Liverpool is the first, the only true, begetter of England's Kops. Like all things in Liverpool, the Kop was named half in jest and half in heart-felt sentiment. Liverpool men, along with men from Dublin and Manchester, had fought that terrible battle against the Boers up Spion Kop in the South African War, and when they returned home they named the bank where they stood at the match after the bloody mountain in Natal.

The Anfield Kop is now famous. Newspapers send reporters to cover the Kop rather than the match, the BBC did a documentary about it and at least six gramophone records have been made of the Kop singing; and what Anfield sings today, other Kops will be singing tomorrow.

It makes Liverpool Kopites smile in a superior way to hear other fans singing their songs. There is a reason for the Anfield Kop to sing certain songs, but the fans on other grounds presumably sing them because they lack the wit to think of their own. For example, it was to honour Ian St John that the Kop would roar When the

de foie, which is the first course of the standard 60-franc meal in the paddock restaurant.

It is pretty steep, our expenses are still awaiting payment, but for one day in this Lotus Land I think it is well worth it. You can get a menu for about 20 francs in the town, but quite apart from being tempted by shops like Hermès who move in here for the kill during the summer season, you miss the whole point of being able to sit and watch the world go by.

First you get hustling trainers flown down on the shuttle from Chantilly, or more relaxed, having spent some days here already. That first bottle seems to have got very empty, the service is snail-like, but you have arrived early and take your time. You are not here to sell encyclopaedias after all. Omar Sharif strolls in, all expert discussion . . . and in the sort of simple suit that you know you would never be quite able to manage.

Then there are the two grand ladies of this world, Baronne Helen de Rothschild, looking about 30, and the astonishing tawny-eyed silk-suited Mexican Maria Felix Berger, looking about 35. It is noised abroad that both beauties are a little older than that.

There are many, many more, looking at each other. A great observer of horses and humans pads up in a blue T-shirt and white sneakers, those crinkled eyes hooded in wrap around blue sunglasses and the cigar in the hand. He can move freely here, and only three years ago was top jockey of the whole meeting. He mutters out one of his best but unprintable stories—and helps himself to your ice cream.

Piggott did not take the big race that day, but Les Anglais did not go undefended, for the perfect grey-suited and panamaed figure of Bernard van Cutsem was present with Ksar and with the sort of victory sang-froid that movie actors could spend a lifetime trying to emulate.

By the end of the day we only appeared to be trying to emulate pats of melted butter, so get a cooler suit, and just once visit the land where everyone is beautiful. If you are also rich you can stay there, if not journey back through the skies . . . then it will all seem like a dream . . . perhaps it will always remain so, but just for once make this dream the stuff that life is made of.

August 19 1973

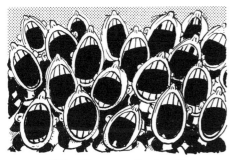

"You'll never walk alone."

Saints Go Marching In. And You'll Never Walk Alone joined the repertory of the Kop because it was near the top of the charts, and was sung by Liverpool's Gerry Marsden.

Much of the humour of the Kop is unprintable, and 22,000 voices singing "The referee is a bastard" while 44,000 fingers give the V-sign may be the bane of all progressively-minded men who see football as family entertainment, but it doesn't half put the wind up the opposing side.

Basically the Kop is hostile to opposition. Any teacher of modern European history, who wanted to give his pupils some idea of what the mobs of the French Revolution must have looked like, could do no better than take his class into the Kop.

Bill Shankly, that arch practitioner of psychological warfare, has placed a sign at the mouth of the tunnel which the opposing team takes to get on to the field, saying: "This is Anfield, home of Liverpool Football Club." The opposing players pass by this piece of bravado, and then come face to face with the Kop.

Liverpool have lost only three home games in the last four years, and there can be no doubt that the fanatical Kop has had something to do with this. Jack Bennett, the City of Liverpool's building surveyor, has done a study of Anfield, and he claims the wind whips down from the sloping roof of the Kop, and deflects the ball in flight.

"That's rubbish," a Kopite said. "What it is, is we all blow together."

There are plans afoot to modernise the Kop. The tremendous ebb and flow there is reckoned to be dangerous. There is a very funny report by two policeman who were sent into the Kop to give their professional view of the crowd movement. Written in classic police report style, it tells that "while standing in the north-west corner of the Kop I suddenly found myself in a horizontal position. I had difficulty in keeping my feet owing to the liquid nature underfoot."

"A quarter of a million pounds to modernise the Kop!" a Liverpool supporter said. "That's £11 a head. They could go to Dunlops and buy us all a couple of pairs of wellies for that."

April 14 1974

Wales in waiting: at work with the Saturday men

The perennial appeal of Welsh rugby: men who bring Cardiff Arms Park to its feet one day are back in the pit, the schoolroom or the steelworks the next. (*January 30 1977*).

by John Hopkins
Photographs by Chris Smith

The Duke to rugby people, Bobby Windsor (above) is just plain Bobby to the men at the British Steel Corporation's Whitehead steel works where he clears up muck that gathers beneath a bar mill. And though christened Glyn Shaw, the 6ft 2½in 15½ stone miner (top centre) is nicknamed Iron Man Shaw for his ability to wrest out heavy mining machinery from worked out coal seams one mile below ground. Dr J. P. R. Williams (right) should be able to hide among the 5,000 who work at the University Hospital of Wales in Cardiff; but before an international the senior house officer cannot walk five yards without people wishing him luck.

Friends at the Institute of Science and Technology at the University of Wales sometimes call Graham Price (above) the Jockstrap Gladiator, a mixture of admiration for his rugby and of university humour. The demands of Price's club, Pontypool, and of Wales have limited the 25-year-old prop in his appearances for UWIST since he began his four-year degree course last autumn, but even so his influence is considerable. So, too, is Steve Fenwick's at St Cenydd's comprehensive school in Caerphilly. P.E. with the fair-haired centre (left) is full of banter from him and his pupils. "He won't let us sit in his seat on the bus," chirps one muddy-faced youngster.

PICTURE FILE

Our photograph of 17-year-old Avis Willington performing the butterfly stroke makes even hard work in the training pool seem attractive. The idea that sport is primarily a matter of movement and self-expression is further suggested by more pictures selected from our files for this book's first photo collection.

The confidence and self-assertion of Jimmy Connors has frequently seemed provoking. But no one could deny the young American his talent, energy and courage: the greatest of triers, no matter the score or his form, he always seems to play like a winner.

"I love diving," said Alan Knott, the most agile and entertaining of all cricket's wicketkeepers. For practise he would position himself between two widespread stumps and dive like a goalkeeper to "save" balls thrown either side of him.

Very competitive, very difficult to beat in a close finish, Alan Pascoe was one of the most successful British athletes in the history of the sport. Despite the fact that he suffered more injury than most, he remained unbeaten at the 400m hurdles in international matches for Great Britain.

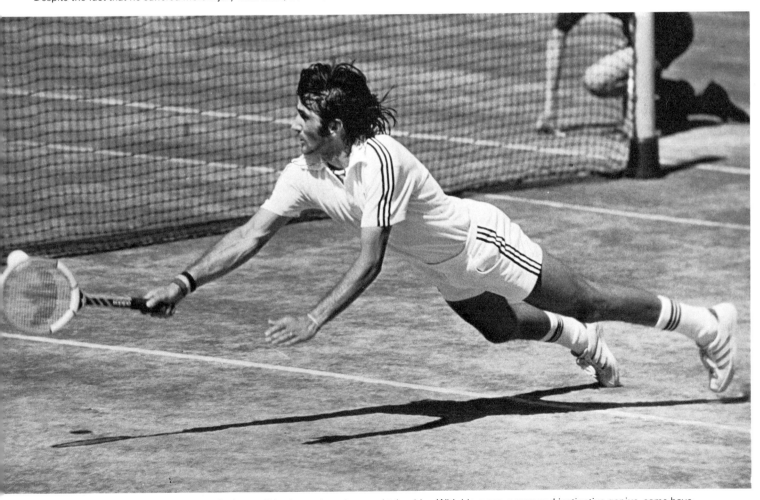

Ilie Nastase has always been able to make impossible shots when the mood takes him. With his grace, power and instinctive genius, some have seen him as a Nureyev of his art: perhaps not really a tennis champion but, at his best, a star.

The loneliness—and the contentment—of the long-distance runner. This one's going well as he clears a hedge, up with the leaders, in a 10-mile hound trail across the Cumberland Fells.

For most of the 1,000 runners who take part each year, this is the reality of the Southern cross-country championships at London's Hampstead Heath: but in the middle of the pack, contributing to a sea of scudding legs and bobbing vests, they're all athletes running their own private, fiercely individual races.

Eyes on the bar: Daley Thompson, on his way to pole-vaulting 15ft 9in and a Commonwealth Games decathlon victory.

Eyes on the batsman: Dennis Lillee, consistently the most attacking and dangerous fast bowler of his decade.

Eyes on the water: The backstroke racing start of John Naber, the American who won four gold medals and broke four world records at the Montreal Olympics. The eyes of the swimmer, fast bowler and pole-vaulter all demonstrate the mental composure of the athlete at peak physical effort.

Sabotage of an athlete. An Italian footballer falls, out of control, and Brazil's Pele suffers one of the many fouls which frequently seemed to threaten a brilliant career. An incident from the World Cup Final of 1970.

Horse and rider harnessed in common purpose, and control harnessed to power: the keynote of all sublime athletic effort. A riding stables in the homely fields of Surrey yielded this expressive moment to the camera.

2

SOCIETY

Sport holds up a mirror to our society in which good and bad alike are reflected. Football in Britain, for example, cannot be blamed for football hooliganism; it could, perhaps, do more to alleviate the problem, but hooliganism is essentially the fault of society. So too are many other aspects of life that affect sport – apartheid, terrorism, deprivation. The injection of sport with a razzamatazz once reserved for show business is also simply an extension of where we have arrived elsewhere – the PR man reigns supreme. But just as our society has its redeeming features, so the wholesome image of sport struggles through, bolstering a belief in virtues that no amount of violence, destruction or disaffection can diminish.

The ugly face of football – the victim of a knife at a match in Scotland

Throughout the past decade, the most enduring, inflammatory and intractable problem has been race relations. The dilemma facing the sportsman who wishes to compete against athletes from a country whose political ideology is anathema to him runs it a close second. The two questions combine and conflict most distressingly in South Africa: it was the Afrikaaners who endowed our language with the word apartheid. In 1969, as the Springboks rugby team toured Britain, the following piece described in convincing detail the attitudes current in South Africa towards rugby, and by implication towards race. The picture, taken at the Christopher Wren Comprehensive School, London, ironically situated off South Africa Road, shows a scene impossible to reproduce in a South African school.

The inescapable black and white facts

by John Morgan

Rugby is the mirror of the South African soul. "Victory," as the Afrikaaner intellectual Dr Kreuger put it to me, "is a vindication of the system": the system is apartheid. At Pretoria on a cold, sunlit winter's day last year, for any visitor who cared to recognise it, that mirror exhibited all the desperate, sour romanticism of the Afrikaaner's world. That memory—and the general character of South African rugby—is relevant to the uproar about the present Springboks tour.

The British Lions touring team were playing against Northern Transvaal, against representatives of the Afrikaaner heartland, the exemplars of the true faith. The natives—if they will excuse the phrase—were expected to win. The crowd was the largest ever at a midweek game in the history of South African rugby; 60,000, many perched high and trembling in the wind against the skyline on temporary stands.

I had travelled to the match with a crowd of farmers from a small town called Britts, few of them able to speak English, all convinced they were kind to their workers and between whom and their workers existed a feudal relationship; all believing their workers loved them, would fight, even, to defend them from attack from the black North. And until 10 minutes from the end of the match this astonishingly kindly false view of themselves endured. At which point the British Lions team took the lead.

In thirty years of watching rugby I have never known any experience comparable to the chilling transformation of spirit among that multitude. The silence was that of a people witnessing a tragedy rather than the normal disappointment of a home crowd. The referee, infected, rushed about the British half giving penalties for no reason at all in order to correct the score. The Transvaal full-back missed them. The match lasted six minutes longer than it should have but still the British won.

When the game was lost and over the crowd did not cheer, or groan. Without a word or a sound of any kind they shuffled out into the dusk and away back to the farmlands and their enchanted dreams and unspoken fears.

In the course of the next few weeks, I talked to the high priest, the ideologue of the South African game, Dr Craven, to old and present Springboks, to schoolteachers at a rugby fest, but was always unable to forget the remarkable experience at Pretoria, the experience of a crowd shocked as if betrayed, as if some element of faith had been called in question. As indeed it had. It was not like the natural discontent of supporters cross at a poor performance by their team. Not even like the tribal discontents of the Welsh when we fail to defeat England. It appeared to be a genuine comment on the embattled society and its philosophies. When Dr Craven talked about the spirit of South African rugby he talked in the language of a sociological rather than a sporting view:

"Being a young country we have to prove ourselves, and we try to do that. It's a big world and we are a small country. If you are weak then nobody takes any notice of you. You have to be strong."

When he gave an account of the kind of speech he used to make to the Springbok side in the dressing room before the Test match the emphasis was on the importance of living, eating and drinking rugby—which although odd in an amateur sport is not an attitude unknown elsewhere—but always in the interest of "not letting the country down." This is a nationalist intensity of a rare order in sport.

Even Dr Craven's drastic methods of training players have an ideological overtone. At Stellenbosch University where he presides over 80 rugby teams—now there's evidence of national obsession—efforts are made to reproduce the toughness of the voortrekker life. Young men groan as, like oxen, they yoke themselves to apparatus. Boulders are hung around their necks. No penal or military colony could be more exacting. One British Lion player told me it almost put him off rugby for life seeing these South Africans train, so that they could be as fit as the men who first set out across the veldt in search of the distant horizons. The Afrikaaner faith or mythology dominates the game at the expense of the more amateurish English spirit.

But by the time they begin intensive training at the university the young men have already had 10 years or so of experience of the game. They begin, so schoolteachers at Bloemfontein told me, at seven years of age and within three years are playing in competitive rugby. Once a year the senior schoolboys gather for Craven Week, a festival of humourless intensity named, suitably, after the dominant figure in the sport. "We try," as the teacher said, "to imbue our boys with the spirit of true sportsmanship."

Be that as it may, I cannot recall matches in which there was consistently more late tackling, more "running interference" for colleagues with the ball, more absurd refereeing than that practised by the South African sides against the British Lions. In the ideological battle between "sportsmanship" and victory, victory won. It may be that the present South African side in Britain will not do too well because they are nervous of playing in their natural style, inhibited by the political atmosphere, by a different interpretation of the rugby laws and, perhaps, by a fear of antagonising the rugby elements at British grounds.

This playing-field is in South Africa Road: it is miles—and years—away from Johannesburg.

But of all the curious experiences in observing South African rugby and talking to its leaders and followers, none was more astonishing than that none of them raised the question of African or Coloured players. The matter did not appear to exist in their mind. The African and Coloured rugby federations might have been in another physical continent, not merely a separate continent of the spirit. Old Springbok players would talk earnestly, even with passion, about the virtue of rugby in "uniting the races . . . religions." But for them the races were Afrikaaner and English, the religions Dutch Reformed and Anglican. The blankness with which they responded to the idea that rugby might bring other races together with white would be a useful spectacle for those to contemplate who believe that tours "build bridges."

These were men who had played in Britain and New Zealand and might have been expected to be familiar with anti-apartheid feeling. They might never have been outside the veldt. I find it hard to believe that many, if any, members of the present Springbok side in Britain will return to South Africa and begin to proselytise against apartheid. Can anyone conceive of the prospect of these ambassadors of the master race returning to Pretoria and arguing that Africans and Coloureds should play in the next Springbok side?

Their ideology must be that of Dr Kreuger and the Afrikaaner intelligentsia: "Apartheid is necessary or we will be swamped." Sport, and above all rugby, is an integral and necessary part of the system, and while the Springboks are received, the system will appear respectable.

November 16 1969

1. Establish on well-known sporting personality, such as young racing driver, pull out to see him nudging his wife in excitement.

SOUND: Where do you find the stars when they've got a day off?

2. Cut to see they are watching a cricket match. Batsman swings at ball.

SOUND: At a new cricket game!

3. Cut to wicketkeeper Alan Knott as he whips off the bails.

SOUND: New cricket is exciting!

4. Cut to the sporting personality applauding.

SOUND: Applause. The game really moves!

5. Wipe to another match. Barry Richards faces the bowling.

SOUND: Watch fantastic young Barry Richards.

6. He smashes the ball to the boundary.

SOUND: World's number one batsman.

Selling it the hard way: sport undergoes the baked bean treatment

In the winter of 1973 *The Sunday Times* cheered up the muddy January gloom by asking the advertising agency, Saatchi & Saatchi, to devise a campaign for promoting football. In the spring we turned our attention to cricket, enlisting the help of Hobson Bates and Partners, who came up with a TV commercial; and our cricket correspondent, who suggested worldly ways of streamlining the game.

Saatchi and Saatchi is a fast-moving ad agency handling such accounts as the Government's contraception campaign (the famous "pregnant man" ad was theirs), the corporate image of British Leyland and Cosmopolitan magazine. We gave them a day to show us how they thought a typical ad agency would look at the football business. The sample ads and reasoning (the text is theirs not ours) are what they produced:

"Taking the product as it stands, the target market can be defined on a sliding scale—from those people who are highly interested in football, and visit matches regularly to those people who are totally disinterested, and hardly ever go.

The job is basically to move people along this scale towards greater "favourableness" to the game, and therefore towards greater frequency of attendance.

Within this overall target audience the prime prospect group can be defined as the group who are interested in football, but are satisfied to follow the game via TV and Press coverage.

Their frequency of actual attendance *should be increased by highlighting* the incomparable drama, excitement, and atmosphere of being at the match itself."* *January 7 1973*

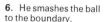

A

(A) Exploit the spectator's vicarious identification with the combat on the field and the resulting cathartic release of the latent aggressive tendencies and frustrations caused by the anomy and alienation of a competitive urban society. This should include the stressing of nationalistic prejudices (Britain v Germany) and regional prejudices (North v South) and ought to result in a greater fighting spirit among fans and more crowd support at away matches, etcetera.

B

Things happen after a football match.

The sparkle, the ambiance, the magic atmosphere of football... it could bring you closer to someone...

C

The family that plays together stays together.

Mum! Take the family to fabulous Molineux this weekend. Good wholesome outdoor fun for everyone.

Plus this free badge!

7. Cut to Charlie George watching Richards. He turns to speak to camera as we see Richards running in background.

SOUND: Charlie: When he plays in Australia, he gets a dollar a run, think what he earns!

8. Cut to another match. John Snow bowling flat out.

SOUND: Powerful John Snow. The world's fastest bowler.

9. Cut to Robin Nedwell of TV's Doctor at Large, watching and commenting to camera.

SOUND: Robin: Now he's angry: You'll see the stumps fly!

10. Cut to another match. Gary Sobers batting.

SOUND: And the greatest all-rounder you could ever hope to see: The incredible Gary Sobers.

11. Cut to Mick Jagger commenting to camera.

SOUND: Mick: He's the only fellow ever to hit six sixes off six successive balls . . .

12. Cut to triple split screen with action shots of Sobers, Richards, Snow. Super: New Cricket.

SOUND: Exciting! Streamlined! Drop in this weekend on New Cricket.

(B) Indicate the positive promise that being in a crowd of 40,000 people naturally offers, like meeting new people and making friends . . . including the possibility of some sexual contact after the game. In addition to these broad basic approaches, specific weak segments of the market should be identified for particular attention:

(C) **Women:** A key group because they are a distinct weakness in the profile of frequent attenders. Also because they are a highly negative influence on potential male supporters.

(D) **Upper Income Groups:** Important both for their contribution to ticket receipts and for the enhanced image and status they can bring to the game. More peer group pressure should be applied by the adoption of testimonials from famous people.

● In addition to the above, it would also be valuable to incentivise directly the infrequent attenders. For example:

Self-liquidating premium offers should be available on sending in, say, six ticket stubs—the offers geared to appeal to men and women.

On-ground betting on the results.

Football supporters' credit card for loyal fans—giving them discounts at local shops.

Season tickets available on credit with no-deposit terms available; etcetera.

D (With apologies to John Betjeman)

On Saturdays I take my air in Upton Park,
Upon the stand I stand while above a lark
Watches twenty or so worthies who, for all they're worth,
Kick to and fro a ball upon that lush green earth.

Suddenly, the roof is lifted by a terrible roar,
As thirty thousand voices announce a 'Hammers' score,
Come with me to the Park next Saturday, and enter in,
In all the world there's nothing sweeter than to taste
a West Ham win.

Cricket needs its managers — to hell with committees

by Robin Marlar

At the heart of the game, in the pavilions of the land where the business of cricket is done, committee members reign supreme. That magical cricket-club target for the finger of scorn, MCC, may have given way to the International Cricket Conference and the Test and County Cricket Board, but the method of government remains stubbornly the same.

What a pity! As with the players, so the administration needs personalising. You don't often hear players heaping compliments on members of their committees either singly or collectively.

Instead of dynamic leadership many men, some more awake than others, spend long winter evenings round a table facing acres of minutes and miles of agenda. When they see a chance to ride a hobby-horse they are liable to take breath and give tongue. The resolution-and-amendment game is played when a daily telephone call is what is needed.

Sport is abysmally ignorant about itself. It has only threadbare statistics. Trends cannot be followed. Jim Dunbar, the permanent administrative member of the National Cricket Association, is more switched-on than most. He knows, thanks to a Ministry of Housing and Local Government report, that 400,000 adults play cricket—only 200,000 fewer than play soccer.

Then there's the selling of cricket to the media. Only in the last five years has cricket learned the language of audiences and ratings. Before then it was being screwed unmercifully by television. Then help arrived in the form of experts, and up, up and away went the income.

There are research programmes too, vital seed corn for the future. Occasionally there is a controlled experiment. Some years ago players were issued with a smaller ball for practice. What did they think of it? "Give us back our big balls," wrote Sussex. Even cricket needs its Barnes Wallises, even if few inventions see the light of day: four stumps, a three-pound bat, 10 fielders. There is no data. Small wonder cricket was at death's door before the one-day injection revived it.

If management at national level is a job for specialists, county clubs need generalists. The success of two—Kent under Leslie Ames, a record-breaking cricketer and later a prosperous sports-shop director, and Leicestershire under Michael Turner, a young ex-player whose contribution has been punchier in the office than at the crease—has encouraged others to think about organisational change.

Even though such a business may have a distressingly low turnover figure, and an erratic profit record, it has to be run by men worth their salt, not by monkeys who will perform for peanuts.

It can be done. One county does not allow any committee member—not even the chairman—any authority outside the committee room. And inside it, the committee is merely a policy-making body. Would that all 17 counties were so sensible!

Management is not an injection, a once-off. It goes on and on and on. Whatever is best administered is best. Without a doubt, cricket is better run than it was, but in too many areas it lives a miserable existence in a dark age. Enlightenment and prosperity will come only if individuals are given responsibility and authority. To hell with committees! *May 20 1973*

The philosophy of hooliganism ends with a kick in the face

Violence perpetrated before, at, and after football matches in Britain by a rowdy element amongst the supporters became a significant social problem in the late 1960s and during the 1970s. A plethora of reasons for it (mostly liberal analyses) and remedies (largely punitive and vengeful) were advanced. But who were these hostile young outsiders? Here is the Glasgow epitome.

by Dudley Doust

Scotland's defeat in Czechoslovakia last week was reason enough to get drunk, and Bobby McTear didn't rouse himself until noon the next day. Gazing idly at the Ulster Volunteer Force's poster and the King Billy portrait on the bedroom wall, he dressed and then drifted down to the local pub near Bridgeton Cross in Glasgow. It was Bobby's first day back since he was jailed and fined £40 for assault and breach of the peace at the Aston Villa-Rangers match in Birmingham.

"Pleasure? No pleasure in throwing a bottle, mon. Revenge is the word for it. When you throw the bottle you hope you'll hit some bastard, a polis, or a Catholic, a guy who's given you some shit about the Orange or Rangers or Glasgow." His accent was as thick as porridge. "There's always going to be fighting at Rangers matches. Aye, it's a good feeling to kick some guy in the baws. He's down and he's useless, and so you kick him in the face after that. That ends it."

Bobby McTear is not the lad's real name, but his story is true. He is 17 years old. He looks younger. He has a spray of facial pimples and wears a scab, much like a signet ring, on his left little knuckle. He has also a knife-wound which, in the quiet of a nearby library reading room, he later pulled off his shirt to display: an ugly red welt under the shoulder blade.

"Parkhead," he said. "I didn't know what happened to me until I got home and was changing my shirt. Then I saw all this blood, and I went to the Royal Infirmary and got seven stitches. A

The hooligan apprehended, an all-too typical tableau of the last decade.

week later we played the Celtic bastards again, and 16 of us got two guys on the London Road and we done 'em in. I took an open razor and did a guy's jaw. Seventeen stitches."

In two seasons Bobby has been convicted on 11 charges of assault or breach of the peace following football matches. He has served two short spells in prison. "I had my first football fight when I was 13," he said. "I was standing in the railway station after the Rangers-Aberdeen game, and a guy went like this to my dad, and told him to get out of the road. So my dad starts fighting him, and I hit the guy over the head with a bottle. Out cold. Thirteen stitches." Stitch-count is important in the language of violence.

Bobby was born in Bridgeton Cross, one of Glasgow's gloomy Victorian slums. His mother was born a Catholic in Northern Ireland, and down the years her husband, who is sometimes a long-distance lorry driver, has fought with her Catholic brothers. "We all go to the Orange Order," said Bobby. "I'm a Protestant, and I'll always live up to my religion. I'll live up to it until

the day I die."

Rangers hooligans—indeed, even most of their orderly fans—have found comfort in the unblinking, bigoted policy of the Rangers Football Club. During it's 103-year history, the club's proud tradition has been not to sign or play a Catholic in the side. That suits Bobby. Further, it is unlikely that he was shaken later when the club announced it was to drop it's sectarian bias.

"A Catholic playing for Rangers?" he laughed. "You gotta be joking. You'll never see a Catholic in the side and if you do you won't see me supporting Rangers." He sensed the irony of this ultimatum. "Maybe that would be a good thing. Maybe if they brought in a Catholic on the side there'd be a lot less trouble because we guys, the troublemakers, would be finished with Rangers."

Bobby, however, foresaw a closer surveillance of alcoholic liquor at Ibrox, perhaps identity cards, cages for fans and even a lock-out for himself and his hooligan friends. He would like to see lounges and proper seating, he said, and then in the way of a Glaswegian, he delivered a sudden, soft, piercing throw-away line, ". . . and give us more respect."

Bobby left school abruptly at 15. "If I'd finished school I might have been in some better place than this one," he said with neither self-pity or remorse. "I got expelled. I hit the teacher with a case of books." He trained briefly as a bricklayer but, he says, due to his many criminal convictions he has been unable to get work. He drifts, steals, does a bit of house-breaking and, best of all, fights at football matches.

"I'm doing it because there's nothing else to do. There's not even a cinema or a dance hall down here at the Cross. Things might be a wee bit different if I had a job." He smiled. "But I'd still go to games and have a battle."

The Villa battle followed a familiar pattern. Bobby and his mates, joined by three girls and half-a-dozen Rangers supporters from Belfast, boarded a chartered coach (£6 return) at Bridgeton Cross, at seven o'clock on Saturday morning. They had their standard battle gear: razors, screw-top bottles of beer, bottles of sweet Old England wine, blue-and-white Rangers scarves and, scattered across the occasional breast, the badge of the Red Hand of Ulster. "If you don't have your gear ready, they'll be ready before you."

On the coach, Bobby slept much of the way down the M6, and now and then joined in the songs exalting the beautiful Rangers and blaspheming the Pope. He was spoiling for the inevitable fight: "If we get beat, we'll look for trouble. If we *don't* get beat, somebody else will look for trouble and we'll battle them back."

The coach arrived at Villa Park just before noon. Bobby and his mates sent their girls into a pub with the purpose of enticing young Villa fans to the coach. The waiting Scots ambushed and "mangled" the luckless English. Bobby stole £1.50 from one victim. "You got to be half-drunk when this happens. If we weren't drunk? That's a hard question. I'll tell you, I wouldn't do it alone unless I had a bottle of wine in me."

At the turnstiles, Bobby says, a young Villa fan taunted him: "Go back to Glasgow, you yellow Orange bastards," Bobby swung, missed and hit a brick wall. Trouble later broke out when Rangers went two down. Bobby and his mates swept into the passages under the stands. They smashed open a kiosk, went for the beer when "this big polis started waving a stick at us. Then he dropped his stick, and we jumped in and gave him a battering."

Bobby was arrested outside the ground, and after appearing in court on Monday ("fined £3 a week and I'm not paying it"), he wandered the Birmingham streets that night, stealing £20 from a newsagent and finally jumping on a train back to Glasgow without paying the fare. He slept under the seats to avoid the guard. What did his parents think of all this? "They don't know. They don't know anything. My father just says, if you do daft things it's your own fault."

Bobby one day may kill somebody. Would he be *happy* to kill anybody? "No," he said, "I don't want to kill anybody. I want to hurt him bad, really mark the bastard, but I don't want to kill him. He has to go home to his mother and father. Same as me."

Bobby was restless. He wanted to leave the library. But it was past 2.30 in the afternoon, and the pub would be closed. So he went to a nearby snooker hall. One look at his face, and the attendant stopped the turnstile. The boy wasn't wanted. Bored and barred, Bobby walked back towards the street, pausing to urinate against the big oak door. *October 17 1976*

Cup Final fever or how to sell a load of old rope

An alternative to say-for-pay footballer interviews.

by Michael Parkinson *

We've received a letter which will be of interest to anyone who believes in paying money for old rope. It is from Mr Bobby Moncur, the captain of Newcastle United Football Club, setting out a scale of charges for any newspaper wanting to interview himself or members of his team between now and the Cup final.

The letter requests the Sunday papers to pay £75 each to the players' pool for what is described as "the co-operation so far provided by the players and their continued help preceding and after the final in normal news-gathering and day-to-day matters, including after-the-match interviews."

In other words, any inquiries as to Mr Bobby Moncur's bowel movements before the final will cost £75 as will his after-the-match comments which, if Newcastle lose, may well be unprintable.

I wouldn't mind if we got something original for the money, but it is always the same dreary, predictable pap. Chewing-gum for the mind. It is so predictable that I am going into business with my All-Purpose Pre-Wembley Kit for Newspapers. For a small fee to be donated to my favourite charity—the Bob Lord Early Retirement Fund—editors can purchase one of these kits and save a lot of time and trouble.

The kit consists of what I call the Pre-Match Dignified Skipper's Statement, which starts: "I have the greatest regard for Emlyn Hughes/Bobby Moncur and his lads. Liverpool / Newcastle are a good team. You have to be good to get to Wembley . . .," and so on.

This article ends: "It will be a close game, but at 4.40 tomorrow it will be the black-and-white stripes of Newcastle/the red shirts of Liverpool that will climb the steps to receive the Cup. Wembley will be drowned by the noise of our wonderful fans singing the Blaydon Races / You'll Never Walk Alone. And I, Bobby Moncur / Emlyn Hughes will be the proudest man in Britain."

Then there is the Aggressive Striker's Statement, which goes: "Liverpool / Newcastle will win by two clear goals. Who says so? I do. And who am I to talk? I'm Malcolm Macdonald / John Toshack, and I'm going to score both of them. Call me big-headed if you like, but I'm the man with the big-match temperament and dynamite in my boots, etc."

No kit would be complete without a Soccer Star's Superstition interview, which goes: "When I go out into the white-hot cauldron which will be Wembley tomorrow, I shall not have picked my nose for 10 days/I shall be wearing two left-boots / I shall be carrying my wife's lucky handbag/I shall be wearing my grandfather's vest. It is my lucky charm. It might seem silly, but it is going to put Liverpool/Newcastle out of the Cup."

For after the game, there is the Diabolical Decision Interview which comes complete with headline: Shankly/Harvey Fumes As Tyneside/Merseyside Goes Mad.

It continues: "'It was diabolical. I've never seen a decision like it.' said Newcastle / Liverpool manager Joe Harvey / Bill Shankly. He was lashing out at the penalty / offside decision which gave Liverpool / Newcastle the Cup. 'The referee / linesman must be blind,' the irate manager said. The Newcastle / Liverpool supporters thought so too. The referee had to be protected from angry fans as he left the ground, and a black-and-white / red-and-white paving stone was hurled through the windscreen of his car."

I know my all-purpose kit is bound to be unpopular with the players, who will accuse me of taking the bread from their mouths. As a journalist, I can only reply that this is infinitely preferable to their habit of lifting the bread from our wallets. *April 28 1974*
*As told to Himself.

A Leander coxed four in training on the Thames. A growing number of oarsmen are members of both this club and the Thames Tradesmen, although the clubs remain basically very different in origin, tradition and facilities as well as membership.

'The Best in the West' — an alliance where above and below stairs all pull together

It would be hard to find two rowing clubs less alike than these two, one nestling on the banks of the rural Thames, one next to the rubbish dump at Chiswick.

by Richard Burnell
Photographs by Chris Smith

Leander, based in the Thames Valley, and Thames Tradesmen, in Chiswick— are the cornerstones on which British rowing became "the best in the West" last year.

The alliance would have been impossible prior to 1937 because of the infamous amateur status law, repealed by the Amateur Rowing Association in that year, which classed "artisans" as professionals—Henley went one better and described them as "menials". Today there are no such distinctions and even Henley has bowed to the pressures of social change. Nevertheless Tradesmen and Leander remain very different types of club, but with mutual respect and a growing number of dual members.

Leander claims to be the world's premier rowing club, and during the Victorian era unquestionably was. A fairer claim today would be that it is the world's premier social club for distinguished oarsmen. The Henley clubhouse, sometimes irreverently referred to as the Pink Palace, was completed in 1896. Founded in 1818, at Stangate, the club moved to Putney in 1860, and built its first boathouse there in 1866.

Thames Tradesmen, on the other hand, were in a position twenty years ago of having no clubhouse. Originally (1897) Brentford Town Rowing Club, then Brentford Conservative RC, and finally Thames Tradesmen RC, the club lost its premises so often that it became known as "the club which refused to die". In 1963 the Council provided the present site and building—bare shell and services. The members did the rest.

In the long term, Tradesmen's greatest contribution to British rowing may be in demonstrating that a small club can reach the top, whilst Leander's may be in showing that a large and intensely traditional organisation can successfully adapt to change.

June 25 1978

Leander's Five Star loo (left) boasts marble topped vanity basins, redolent of more gracious days. But there are no longer individual hand towels, nor hair brushes. They used to get "taken away"—by visitors, of course. There is corresponding Five Star service in the riverside Dining Room (right) too. Leander welcomes social members, who share the honour of wearing the club's City tie, but not the famous pink tie reserved for full Rowing Members. Some members, later in life than Oxbridge undergraduates, are elected for services to rowing, usually as coaches or administrators, as also are a small number of foreign oarsmen. British internationals are usually, but not invariably, elected while still active. In all, there are some 2,000 members of Leander, many resident abroad, particularly in the US and Australia.

Thames Tradesmen welcome beginners. "We send them out sculling," says club captain, Tony James. "If they keep at it for two or three weeks we start to take a serious interest in them—and then the sky's the limit." Above is a Senior "C" eight on a Sunday morning outing. There are now more than 80 members on the club's books, including the world coxless pairs silver medallists John Roberts and Jim Clark, and several members of the national team eight. An impressive record for such a young club.

No waitress service (left), but more than 80 hours per week voluntary help from members and wives keeps the club solvent. Henry Cooper used to be a regular, appreciating the fact that he was "just one of the blokes." Tradesmen have only one luxury—the best boats money can buy. Thames Tradesmen's plumbing (above) may be more DIY than Five Star, but it works, even though currently somewhat exposed. Roy Lendrum, in charge of renovation, says: "There is always someone around with the necessary skills." He press-gangs workers from the crews.

Out where the Dinka dance in feathered skirts Isaac sees tennis courts and high jumps

Early in 1978 a delegation, including a full FA coach and a professor of sports medicine, visited the Southern Sudan to study the problems of sport in the underdeveloped country. They found the distance between the Nile and Wembley more difficult to bridge than they had at first imagined.

by Keith Botsford

The director of physical education for the high schools of Juba, in southern Sudan, is short, squat, shiny and black. Everyone else we meet is very tall, between 6ft. 6in. and 7ft. 3in. The following dialogue between our delegation and Mr Antony ensued:

"How many secondary schools are there in Juba?"

"Three."

"Does each of them have a physical education programme?"

"Oh yes, all except two."

That is Juba: optimism in conflict with dusty reality.

We are an odd bunch. The Vice-President of the Sudan has invited us down, a cautious, sleek man who has survived a 17-year civil war in which the south Sudanese, who are Christian or pagan, fought off the Arab north. The Vice-President was one of their leaders, and Juba contains a fair number of such survivors, each with his own atrocity story to tell. There is no war so ugly as civil war.

The Sudanese President, General Nimeri, is a keen footballer. If he were a philatelist, our delegation might have consisted of stamp dealers instead of sports specialists.

A football game was specially staged in our honour. Or thrown together. A team had to be imported from Wau, a mere few hundred miles of scrub and desert away. The locals were the police team. The final score was 0-0. The pitch was patchy and hard. The Dinka solve the problem of ball control by raising their long legs with ease to the 6ft. level, and bringing the high bounce down that way. The spectators several thousand of them, are entranced by incident, as though at a stage play. Personal challenges and encounters really get them. A shot at goal is clearly understood as assault, and brings up a great cheer.

The chief incident of the game, however, was the incursion of a dog on to the pitch. At Wembley it would not have happened, but the referee took a commonsense view. Which provided the following exchange with our FA coach, Keith Wright.

"How do you rate the referee?" I asked after the match.

"Oh, very strict," he answered. "All the dog did was run on the field, and he killed it."

The regional Minister for Sport is Isaac Eli. He is also the Vice-President's nephew. He was trained at Loughborough by Don Anthony, a broad, hairy, genial ex-hammer thrower who is in charge of our delegation. Isaac's filial piety is great, and like many an ex-colonial, he clings to his vision of the distant green playing fields of his young manhood. Out where the Dinka dance in feathered skirts and painted legs, while carrying sticks as symbolic spears, he see a sports complex rich with tennis courts and high jumps.

That is our problem: no developing country will leave well enough alone, but must have what the developed have. If we said to Isaac Eli, "Do you want Adidas, hooligans, Mark McCormack, Marlboro and Don Revie?" he would refuse the sporting future he so wants. But that's not the way he sees sport.

The ministry holds it staff meetings under a tree by the one local tennis court. We have brought six tennis balls. Juba has not seen a new tennis ball in six months.

Peter Ate, a local who spent 17 years in Uganda as a refugee (he belongs to a tribe that borders Southern Sudan and Uganda), has a more direct approach than the courteous, smiling Isaac Eli. He wants to develop and perfect the indigenous games. For instance, a spear game, not unlike skeet shooting, with a target tossed in the air by the opposing side. Originally, it was how the young were trained to kill game on the move. Peter sees a way of standardising its rules. Which is the way all sports began: done for fun, acquiring skill along the way, and anarchic without rules of some kind.

Peter took us to the Dinka dances.

Where Isaac sees the playing fields of Loughborough. There are several hundred dancers, the young men gathering well away from the dance's centre to daub themselves, and their feathered skirts, in ash. In small bands, they then run to join the dance, which is in a wide but packed circle. Four leaps with the feet together, a hop and then four running steps forward. The boys signal the girls by waving fingers to indicate how many cattle each of them has. The girls join the dance, but remain impassive, expressionless.

On an evening walk over the ramshackle bridge which spans the Nile, which here is some 150 yards wide, and only a few hundred miles from its source. In the twilight, a figure marches up the middle of the dusty road. It is an immensely tall Dinka, naked and covered with ash. He carries a spear, and is off to hunt lion come to water at nightfall. Is it right that he should become an Olympic basketball player?

Women cover themselves when we approach. Says Peter: "We had no shame about it until about 25 years ago. Everybody knows what a man is hiding, or what a woman is hiding."

The heat is intense. Our delegation collapses, one by one. Juba's only swimming pool is in the United Nations enclave. As usual, the international civil service, supposedly aiding the benighted locals, has created an island of privilege for itself.

Civilisation—with a whistle

Isaac described his daily boyhood swim to get to school. The Nile is infested with crocodiles. He was caught by one, and a schoolmate jumped in to save him. Isaac got away to the river bank, but the other boy was taken away in his stead. For Isaac it was matter of record. There were no tears or dramatics, no moral dilemma at being saved at another's expense. If caught by a crocodile, he says, you must let it carry you away. Don't fight. Wait until it releases you to start chewing, and then stab it in the eyes. Olympic swimming training: a mile upstream with a crocodile in pursuit.

Sports problem: organise the arrival in Juba of a gross of football boots. By ship, overland from the Red Sea to the capital at Khartoum, still a thousand miles away. Will they not wind up on the more prosperous Arab feet of the north?

By the Nile, a sports day. Volleyball, basketball, boxing. As natural athletes, they are superb. Economy of motion, instinct in action, co-ordination and reflex perfect. The refereee with his whistle represents civilisation. Their fathers were cattle herdsmen. Training in the sun in heat of seldom less than 100 degrees Fahrenheit, a diet of beef and maize meal.

It is physical activity for them, but is it intelligible to them? They can be trained to our notion of sport, a game raised to competition between adversaries, between teams, one of whom must win, but centuries lie between the banks of the Nile and Wembley Stadium. In games, they are more disciplined than we; before and after, more relaxed. We think of sport as a game, as taking us away from our inner disciplines and constraints. They behave like schoolchildren wrestling with a problem in mathematics. The childhood of their adult lives lies outside sport.

Our delegation confers on their needs: professional instructors to make sure they get their football right (after all, when the Sudan meet Argentina in the 1990 World Cup, what referee will permit a leg raised over an opponent's head?), equipment, proper physical training in the high schools, dissemination of news about sport, results and instructional manuals, cartoon strips, films made available.

All this bounty, our delegation can assure. Isaac Eli promises the budget will be made available. A sports-minded nation is a healthy nation.

Meanwhile, young Bob Price, who is a specialist in sports for the handicapped, has been trying to raise a local doctor to explain to him how the crippled can play sports. But the people of Juba have no concept of the handicapped. In desperation, Bob visits the hospital on his own. The operating room makes him feel ill and he has to return to his sickbed. The patients are stacked on the floor like logs. Flies are everywhere. Sports?

The new university at Juba wants a sports programme. It has 18 students, and offers a passport to individual upwards mobility: a graduate is a person of substance. The assistant vice-chancellor is a nutritionist, and he

The Dinka is very tall but "is it right he should become an Olympic basketball player?"

sets out the principles of the university: severe practicality, husbandry, stock-raising, teacher training. What, I asked, would happen if a genuine intellectual appeared among the Dinka with advanced notions of mathematics?

"He would have to wait," said the assistant vice-chancellor. "There is nothing in the budget for that."

But sport grinds on. Our delegation is determined that Juba shall be sports-minded, though questions are beginning to arise in our minds. Maybe we are more alien than we know, and our games are foolish games. Aren't the locals happy with their ritualised wrestling, their spear-throwing and their dancing?

Throw a football in the market place, and kids kick it about. Because it's there. Because it rolls. There are no goals in the brick-red dust. No one has a rag to spare to mark the spot, nor a shoe to serve as a corner-flag.

A sceptic among us says: "I wonder if the noble savage is as happy as we make out? Illness is endemic, life expectancy short, mere subsistence the rule. Your Dinka faces a life of exploitation by Arabs, just as 100 years ago he was hauled across the sea and sold into slavery."

"Yes," says James Platt, whose benevolent international swap-shop (the Central Bureau for Educational Visits and Exchanges) has arranged our visit, "but the Kuwaitis have just contributed several million pounds, look what they have done with sport." What have they done, indeed?

But as I write, some months later, £90,000 of sports equipment is on its way to Juba, their local tennis star (a northerner) is training at Loughborough, the university is to get two sports specialists attached to its staff, further visits are planned.

It is called development. The British invented football and cricket and most other sports and exported them, just as they clad natives in Lancashire cotton, and their souls in pious Methodism. They go on doing it out of colonial reflex: that what is good for us must be good for them.

Meanwhile, the young people will continue to foregather in the lesser heat of the evening on the edge of Juba, and dance their immemorial dance. Until, that is, Isaac Eli has built his sports centre, and ministers can play golf where once the noble savage trod.

May 28 1978

THE SUNDAY TIMES
presents the
all-round sportsman

VAVASOUR

An outstanding cricketer, squash and tennis player who represented the Navy at all three. Sir Geoffrey Vavasour was denied a chance to play for England at rugger by World War II. He was a reserve stand-off for an England trial by the time he was 25, on September 5, 1939. Five days later war broke out. A keen golfer, he now plays to nine

THE SUNDAY TIMES
presents the
all-round sportsman

KAYUM

Donald Kayum, 19, is rare in being outstanding at both athletics and ball games. Of the latter he is best at cricket, having played for the England Schools 19 group. At athletics he has run a 50sec 400 metres and represented Surrey at cross country. Between 1970 and 1972 he was registered as a schoolboy with Fulham FC. He has also played rugger for the London Counties 19 group

Great Wilson! Still alive and well and living in Britain

When *The Sunday Times* launched the Great Wilson! contest, it was hoping to find one to rival the amateur super-sportsman of the Wizard comic. Six people were outstanding but it was Mike Corby who most mirrored the old ideal.

by John Hopkins

In a large and varied postbag, the funniest entry was William Browning, a thin-legged, pallid man of 28 who has sporting dreams at night but in reality is so unco-ordinated that he can't kick or catch a ball, faints at the sight of blood and is unable to run faster than his own father, who is 66 and has a heart condition.

Inevitably we had to make some arbitrary decisions to exclude a few obvious candidates. Jim Fox, the modern pentathlete, for example, who is a world class all-round sportsman. In view of the encouragement and time for training the Army gave him we ruled him ineligible.

Yet even after eliminating the jokesters, the ineligibles and those who just weren't quite good enough, we were left with an extraordinarily varied list to choose from. The amateur ideal as personified by C. B. Fry and the Corinthians football team at the turn of the century is far from dead in our present age of professionalism. Indeed the vigour of our entries confirm the ideal to be alive and thriving in 1974.

Had we tried, we could not have expressed the ideal better than it was done by a man who signed himself simply Lofty, when he nominated an officer in his old regiment. "Frank Reynolds was a born ball player, an

A catalogue of some of the lesser-known achievements of our hero – from a well-wisher

The haunting effect of Wilson's spirit unsettled the minds of some of our readers. One familiar name was moved to respond, more in sorrow than in anger, in authoritative prose.

by Michael Parkinson

Dear Sir,

In spite of my protestations, you have gone ahead with your Great Wilson competition and, as president of the Great Wilson Appreciation Society, I must register a severe protest at the casual way you treat the memory of an extraordinary man.

In case any of your readers are unfamiliar with his feats, perhaps you will allow me the space to complete their education, by listing the feats of *The* Great Wilson in order that people might judge the folly of your comparison. In chronological sequence, Wilson's feats were:

1. First man to run 300 yards while the church bell struck thrice.

2. First man to jump seven feet (from a standing position).

3. First man to run a sub-four-minute mile (into a gale).

4. Only Caucasian to become pyramid-climbing champion of Egypt.

5. Only man to run 100 yards in nine seconds dead.

6. Only man to run 220 yards in 21 secs and 440 yards in 42 secs (on the same day).

7. First and only paleface to hold the Shawnee Totem Pole Throwing Contest (a totem pole being twice the size and weight of a caber).

8. The oldest competitor in any Olympic Games. In London in 1948 when he retained his world records for 100, 220 and 440 yards, high jump, long jump and marathon, he was 153 years old. Indeed, when he volunteered for the RAF in 1939 he was 144, and passed a medical A1, ending his career

as Squadron Leader W. Wilson, DSO, DFC and Bar with 25 Boche to his credit.

What is not generally known is that the Great Wilson is a Yorkshireman, born in fact near the brewery at Barnsley. All his adult life he lived in a simple abode in the Pennines, existing on a diet of berries and coming to Barnsley market only to get a new uniform of black vest and matching woollen combinations. Thus attired, he achieved athletic feats that staggered the world, and have never been surpassed.

Long before Sir Edmund Hillary climbed Everest, Wilson had already been there and made the final ascent running backwards. Shortly after, in darkest Africa, he broke the world long jump record by leaping across a pit containing sharpened spears, carrying two buckets of cement. Had he failed, he would most certainly not have been able to achieve his most spectacular feat, which was to carry the Olympic torch all the way from Mount Olympus to London for the first post-war games. On arriving at the French coastline, he swam the Channel with one hand

THE SUNDAY TIMES
presents the
all-round sportsman
BALDING

Winner of the National Hunt
Chase (the amateur Grand
National) and the top amateur
flat race, the Thursby Amateur
Stakes over the Derby course
at Epsom. Ian Balding also
trained the great racehorse
Mill Reef. He has played county
squash for Somerset, toured
Barbados with a good class
cricket team and, like Vavasour,
was once reserve for an
England rugger trial—at
full-back

THE SUNDAY TIMES
presents the
all-round sportswoman
LAUDER

Mrs Phyllis Lauder played
table tennis for England in one
world championship and hockey
for the Anglo-Scottish touring
team to Australia in 1938.
She still keeps active at 64,
competing regularly in league
table tennis and just last
month she won the Romford
League women's doubles title.
Like Vavasour, she was deprived
of reaching her full sporting
potential by the last World War

THE SUNDAY TIMES
presents the
all-round sportsman
CORBY

Our choice for Britain's
greatest all-round amateur
sportsman. Corby holds 88 caps
at hockey for England and
Britain, has also played and
captained Britain at squash.
His tennis is good enough to
have won the Junior
Wimbledon doubles and his
natural speed sufficient to
earn him a time of 59 seconds
for the 400 metres hurdles.
At cricket he is a hard-hitting
batsman and a brilliant fielder

individual to whom a poor standard of play was more acceptable than a highly skilled player with no sense of sportsmanship."

In reaching our final decision we were influenced most of all by those who had represented Britain. Five of the most interesting entrants are pictured here, as is the man we nominate the most outstanding of them all—Michael Corby.

Corby is probably best known in hockey and squash circles. At both these games he has played for Britain. No other nominee is a double British international. Any doubts about Corby that lingered in our minds were dispel-led when we remembered what happened the other night at the Royal Automobile Club, London. There, 10 of the best British amateur squash players were matched against each other in an event to open a new season. Corby, after defeating his Scottish international opponent in three games, raced into the dressing room. "Where," he was asked, "are you going in such a hurry?"

"Got to dash," he replied. "I have to play hockey for the Roses." The Roses is another name for the England indoor hockey team.

That's our man. A Corinthian to the end. *October 20 1974*

Inside track

Beyond the Pail

Astonishing is the story of "Systematic Lung Expansion" outlined to us by its innovator, Mr Cyril Greenhill of Torquay, for the possible benefit of all get-fit enthusiasts. Mr Greenhill's programme literally consists of putting his head in a bucket. Of water.

The idea came to him when, suffering the effects of World War One phosgene gas (with increasing bouts of coughing), he was advised to swim. But, he says, because the nearest pool was too distant and because he couldn't swim anyway, he decided instead to exercise the lungs without swimming—with a pail of water.

He took a deep breath, plunged his head in, and let his air escape in short, separate puffs, counting as he did so. The first time he managed 10 puffs in emptying his lungs. in two weeks he had got up to 16, in a month 32. Eventually 100. By this time, the coughing had stopped. Now, Mr Greenhill is 77, and says he owes it all to his Systematic Lung Expansion. The message is quite obvious. Don't kick the bucket. *February 29 1976*

holding the torch aloft, and such was his speed of foot that he arrived early for the opening ceremony, and for three days had to kill time by running up and down the A4.

The above feats are but a sample of what the Great Wilson achieved. I have not even bothered to remind you that he also won the light-heavyweight boxing championship of the world, and was the only man to jump the Pit of Fire to defeat the tribes of the wily Sheik Ibn Kader.

In view of the present strained relationship between the Arab states and the Old Country, it is also worth reminding ourselves that The Great Wilson gallantly refused the fabulous bejewelled statuette of an Arab stallion which was his of right when he jumped the Pit of Fire. Sheik Ibn Kader and his tribes instead swore undying loyalty to The Great Wilson and the Crown. They would now do well to reciprocate Wilson's fine and generous gesture, and remember their oath by cutting oil prices and giving us back the London Clinic.

One other disturbing feature of your Wilson competition is that it provokes an inordinate amount of correspondence casting doubt on his very existence.

Such letters fill me with sorrow, expressing as they do the ignorance in some quarters of a man who is most inadequately described as a silver thread running through the rich tapestry of British life.

And that is not all. As W. S. K. Webb, the great man's official biographer, wrote in his enthralling book, The Truth About Wilson: "He upheld the prestige of Britain in peace and war. Perfection was his aim, and he did not count the cost. He was the greatest man I have ever met."

Any fair-minded reader comparing The Great Wilson's record with that of your competition winner will understand my anger at having my hero's reputation stained in this way. Wilson was a giant among pygmies, and it is our duty to honour his memory.

I remain sir, your humble servant.

Watkinson

October 20 1974

Tony Greig abandons the England ship and goes over to the big bad pirate

The summer of 1977 was the most devastating in the history of world cricket. In its midst arrived Australian media magnate Kerry Packer who announced his intention to create a professional cricket circus, living off most of the world's top players. England captain Tony Greig was to recruit them. The establishment was stung into action.

by Robin Marlar

No one should be singing anthems following the suicide of cricket's King Tony. The week has been hard to bear and especially so for one who campaigned hard for his accession. Yet the main fear has been that the reply of the cricket world to Mr Kerry Packer would be as diffuse as the organisation he has chosen to confront. Cricket is a natural prey to a well-organised pirate whose objectives are limited to the aggrandisement of himself and his gang, just as world trade used to be. Bullying? Only pirate Packer is the bully.

There was no need to worry. Cricket in England is having an above average decade in the pavilion if not on the field. The decisiveness of the Cricket Council's response and indeed its language prove the point.

The statement made it clear that Greig's crime has been the same as John Profumo's in that he betrayed trust. To say in one breath, as Greig did on an ITV interview yesterday, that the Test and County Cricket Board had not earned his trust, while emphasising the greatness of the honour conferred on him when he was entrusted with the England captaincy, is the reflection of a muddled mind. It is, incidentally, a fact that not only did he not tell those who were helping him build an England team of his plans, but he also had nothing to say about them to Sussex, his adopted county.

Clearly it was a matter of concern to them. If Greig, whose statements remain splendidly articulate but increasingly intransigent, continues to act as Packer's agent then the TCCB, doubtless supported by the Cricket Council, are entitled to ban him from the English game. If they were to issue Sussex

with an instruction to that effect then I have reason to believe the Sussex Committee would be prepared to carry it out.

Yesterday in a radio interview Greig committed himself to war with the cricketing authorities and thus gave further grounds for action against him by referring to the circus as "we" and by referring to Greg Chappell and other Australians as his "colleagues".

Greig also revealed that Dennis Lillee's absence was so that he could rest for his forthcoming appearances in the Packer circus. This must indicate to the Australian Board just how far the conspiracy under their noses was allowed to fester even whilst the Centenary Test was being played.

In all Greig's appearances and statements he has indicated, to those who know him well, an awareness that he has no defence to the charge that he has betrayed trust, hence all the patent double talk. He knows this, because those closest to him advised him not to go ahead with his plan.

Kerry Packer: "Giving up is not a possibility."

As far as English cricket is concerned, his loss will be great. And loss it must be, for unless he tears up his contract with Packer there can be no place for him even as a player in the England team. This is sad, though his superb performance as captain in India was more decisive in that series than it was likely to be again. It is also true that, ignoring Snow's involvement as irrelevant, the principal concern of the TCCB has been Alan Knott and Derek Underwood.

It would be a tragedy if mistaken loyalty to Greig were to drag these two magnificent cricketers out of the England XI in whose cause they have laboured so mightily. Doubtless there

are many cricketers in England who will on the face of it be beguiled by Greig's arguments and only positive action by the counties and the TCCB can put the record straight.

Why, it may be reasonably argued, should Greig have taken the advice to ignore the circus, when by joining it he is trying to achieve the praiseworthy objectives of securing a better future for his family and a better lot for the world's best cricketers? At 31, surely he should be allowed to bat and bowl for gold (not that he is short of it after his lucrative winters in Australia)?

If the TCCB, or any other cricketing body, was dedicated to levelling down the top players there would be more in this argument. But the game's administrators—at least in the UK—have recognised the value of star quality and have left the big names free to earn what they can. Although team games players do not do as well as golfers, tennis players, show jumpers or boxers, they have been earning more and must do better still. But not by disembowelling world cricket.

Had Greig talked openly to the TCCB he would have found a receptive audience.

Of the two contenders for the vacant throne, Boycott seems to have learned nothing, if the reports of his negotiations with Packer are true, from his previous attempts to dictate who should be his captain. But as an ex-England player at the moment he could hardly be blamed for listening to offers. Brearley has earned his chance to succeed by his captaincy of Middlesex and his efforts in India.

Packer thinks he will win, and that eventually world cricket will have to treat with him. "The fact of giving it up is not a possibility," he told me. But in the end he will lose and if we are to avoid blood he would do well to recognise the validity of what that wise old bird Jeffrey Stollmeyer, the chairman of the West Indian board, had to say about it all. Stollmeyer, like most others in cricket, knows how short a career in cricket can be and how necessary it is to improve the earnings of all cricketers, especially the stars. But he also commented that a cricket circus "is never likely to be as popular as Test cricket."

He might have added: Either in the flesh or on TV. In my judgment, the case for world cricket as it now is can rest on that essential wisdom.

May 15 1977

Will Packer's Howzat succeed? Fielding, from left: Greig, Procter, Knott, Snow and Underwood.

Packer talks to the judge as if an ogre has begun to read a bed time story

Cricket goes to the High Court and receives a lesson in timing.

by Philip Norman

It is doubtful if Tony Greig has ever faced a more testing adversary than Michael Kempster, that mild and velvety QC. The witness stand is half the trouble, contorting the cricketer's dangling frame into an uneasy, elevated crouch. His large hands pendent, he leans earnestly forward, sometimes tracing the syllables of a question with his lips.

A High Court action before Mr Justice Slade marks the latest inroad by Kerry Packer, the Australian TV tycoon, into English cricket. Greig and two fellow players, John Snow and Mike Procter, are contesting the right of the cricket authorities to ban them from Test and county matches if they appear in Packer's so-called World Series Tests in Australia this winter.

Mr Justice Slade must decide the matter upon which few Englishmen can pronounce without emotion. In signing with the Packer circus, are Greig and the others likely to damage a hallowed game whose mysticism depends largely on its remaining untouched by commerce? Or does the ban, imposed by the Test and County Cricket Board and the International Cricket Conference, constitute a "restraint of trade" against already downtrodden members of the last unliberated professional sport?

Enough half-familiar faces have filled the public seats to provide endless prattle between the overs. Snow and Procter, Greig's co-plaintiffs, sit close to Richie Benaud and far from their putative masters in the TCCB. Older heroes, their history told in tie-stripes, watch with spellbound revulsion behind the crooks of polished walking sticks.

Their ogre is himself sporadically visible. Kerry Packer's style is to sit in court for long periods and then vanish with an abruptness that may give disquiet to his opponents. Now he is back again, arms neatly folded, trainer-like on a front bench among his solicitors.

Greig's halting voice and tortured vocabulary are peculiarly suited to totting up what he regards as long-standing wrongs. Modest are the emoluments he claims to have received as captain of Sussex and England; Sussex paid him £5,000 a season, for a life continuously on the move between matches; for each Test payment was fixed at £210 for five days' play; during his captaincy his views were never sought on the appropriateness of this payment.

Then there were the winter tours from November to March: the ceaseless travel, the play in gruelling heat, the MCC's strict paternalism. Wives were allowed to join their husbands on tour for only 21 conjugal nights. On the fateful tour of India, Sri Lanka and Australia, Greig almost lost Alan Knott as wicketkeeper because Knott wished to see his wife on nights other than those prescribed.

For that highly successful tour, Greig was paid £3,000 with a £300 captain's bonus—a sum "absolutely, totally ridiculous" in view of the attendances. He felt fortunate compared with those who had not been selected and who, unpaid by their clubs in winter, took work in pubs or signed on to the dole.

Greig had approached Kerry Packer in Australia after the Centenary Test, in the hope of obtaining winter employment himself, on one of the tycoon's television stations. Instead he found himself offered leadership of the "Supertest" squad, already under recruitment in Australia, whose matches would be televised on Packer's Channel 9 network.

Greig's allusions to Packer have been fond. He is indebted to Packer already for sending him on holiday to the West Indies. For the first time since he sacrificed a university degree to professional cricket, he can look forward to the future with confidence: beyond his three-year playing contract, worth £25,000 a year, he has been promised a desk job with Packer after he retires and a loan, if he needs one, to buy a house in Australia. He trusts Mr Packer's word.

Somewhat apologetically, Michael Kempster, for the defendant cricketing bodies, inquired if an English county cricketer could not make a large tax-free sum when his club awarded him a benefit year. He might, Greig answered, but at personal cost. In his benefit year, the player had to go around to pubs, soliciting donations. It was often "a cap-in-hand situation."

Was it not true that Amiss's benefit earned £35,000? And Underwood's £24,000?

Those were record figures, Greig replied. "Can you tell me a figure higher than £35,000?"

Cross-examining counsel, on this occasion, did not exhibit the usual frigid rage at being questioned by a witness.

"You're not really supposed to ask *me*," he said benignly, "but I'm told that d'Oliveira's was £45,000."

The witness-stand, so uncongenial to Tony Greig, fits Kerry Packer like one of his suits. In no time at all, the oath administered, he is leaning back, telling the judge man to man how he rescued Australian golf a few years ago. It is as if an ogre has suddenly begun to read a bedtime story.

He is quiet, fluent, perfectly composed, a little vexed, a little wounded by the outcry that has always greeted his philanthropic gestures. One waits in vain for the bruising argot of his native land. The highest term of Packer approbation is revealed to be "gentlemanly." The cricket boards have been "not gentlemanly" in their dealings with him over Channel 9 and the Supertest.

And if he gets his way as a television tycoon and is allowed to show the existing Tests exclusively on Channel 9, will he then, as some suggest, abandon the Supertests and the players contracted to him?

"If the Test and County Cricket Board say that, then all I can say is . . . they're being dishonest."

Kerry Packer has a sense of timing.
October 2 1977

PS: Mr Justice Slade found in favour of the three Packer cricketers.

The haves: why South Wales schools rule ok!

Urban deprivation is a burning issue in Britain. One of the problems is how best to utilise existing recreational facilities; especially, to achieve a qualitative increase in access to school sports halls, gyms and pools, all too often locked when the community needs them most.

by Bob Campbell
Photographs by Chris Smith

In order to illustrate the problem and its solution we picked probably the best and the worst situations in Britain, 1977—the county of Gwent and the city of Liverpool. Gwent represents those forward thinking authorities who killed two birds with one stone: as they were building new schools, they went into partnership with district councils to provide recreational facilities which are used by the pupils and the public on a 365-days-a-year basis. Urged on by what one official described as "a hand-

ful of individuals imbued with unbridled fanatical enthusiasm," Gwent County Council went full steam ahead when money was plentiful. Over the last 12 years they have built school-based leisure centres to the point where the area might be over-provided! The pictures of The Haves are from Fairwater Comprehensive School, in a district of Cwmbran new Town in the Borough of Torfaen, and serving a population of 12,000. Last year some 180,000 used it facilities.

Behind these boys is a derelict church: £60,000 would convert it to a sports hall.

The have-nots: how the kids suffer Liverpool's lock-out

Liverpool is the least well provided urban area in Britain for indoor recreational facilities—and one of the cities which most badly needs them. Last week a spokesman for the City Council said that the priority—on the face of it a worthy one—in its urban renewal programme had been house-building. But what do residents do when you've built houses? There is one community school at Netherley, a barrack-like new estate on the edge of the city. There are 14 further education establishments, and 21 evening institutes, but none of these is open on a 365-day basis and you have to be a member of a course or programme.

In two square miles of the Everton district, there are nine junior and secondary schools, none of which is open to kids, let alone the adult public, at evenings and weekends and holidays. This is a barren inner-city environment bisected by Scotland Road. It has

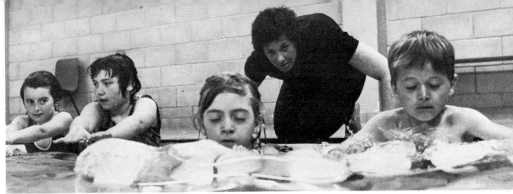

Fairwater Comprehensive School is a multi-purpose facility. Pupils have PE sessions outside in the playing fields in which the school is set. But even during school hours sections of the local community can use it for activities such as mothers and toddlers' swimming clubs. The main sports hall is in almost continuous use seven days a week, 12 hours a day. The school uses it in daytime for basketball practice, five-a-side football and so on. It is turned over to the community in the evening, and one night a week one portion is allotted to the indoor bowling club. In general, kids tend to return in the evening with their parents: a comprehensive family affair.

to be said that there are a couple of gravel football pitches and a large patch of grass nearby. But the kids in the locality prefer, in the main, to play in their own streets.

One child told us last week (anonymity to spare the rod) that his headmaster had told him and his mates that they'd be prosecuted if they used the school to play football after school.

Liverpool may have the worst record in the country for indoor leisure provision, but the rest of our conurbations are almost as bad. At least possibilities of dual use of school facilities are being discussed in Liverpool. The question is: are communities getting use of educational facilities commensurate with the investment? The answer is a resounding no. *May 29 1977*

One price that Liverpool pays for failing to fashion a community key to its school doors is an annual vandalism bill of £4 million. The childen pictured here live in Jason Street, the heart of a harsh housing estate in Everton. It is a cruel irony that in a city boasting the best football team in Britain, the children on its doorstep have to rely on squeezing through the school railings illicitly in the evening to find a decent playing surface.

A guided (if shaky) tour of sport's vast gin and crisps reception circuit

Public relations in the world of sport in Britain tends to rely almost entirely on pressing large quantities of alchohol on journalists to encourage them to extol the bizarre, the obscure and the downright uninteresting.

by Michael Green

"Thus spake the brewer's PRO.
A man who really ought to know
For he is paid for saying so."
John Betjeman

Probably the people who have benefited most from sponsorship in sport are the manufacturers of gin. These days it seems impossible for a sponsor to tell the Press the simplest fact without floating it in gallons of spirit, or burying it under potato crisps. During the year, a newspaper sports department receives about 250 invitations of this sort. The majority go into the wastepaper bin. But recently we decided to see what would happen if we accepted every one in a week.

For a pipe-opener, I choose a macabre champagne breakfast in the gloom of a Penthouse club tastefully decorated with illuminated photographs of female loins. This is to launch the Penthouse-Rizla-BAF 1977 grand prix racing car. I sit at a table with two journalists just there for the grub. "I don't know why they invite us to these things," complains one as he washes down marmalade with champagne. "We never print anything. Typical British PR."

An aide appeals for questions.

"How much will it cost?"

They refuse to say. Pressed, a spokesman says: "Considerably more than last year."

"How much did it cost last year?"

"Considerably less than this year," booms a drunken voice. Laughter.

There are no more questions. The champagne ceases suddenly as the Penthouse girls go outside for the real business of the day, a photograph of the car draped with females.

This is followed by Horror Day—three receptions in one lunchtime. The gin flows freely at the Lawn Tennis Association as they tell us about the ATP Grand Prix qualifying singles

but I've only time for seven or eight before I dash to the Football Association HQ for a reception by the Women's FA, who apparently just want to make the Press happy. This is sponsored by Pony, the drink with a kick, who have thoughtfully left bottles of the stuff all over the place. I drain a couple. It does indeed have a kick.

Outside, Lancaster Gate is rocking gently in the sunlight, and the pavement sways up and down as I hail a taxi by the simple process of staggering in front of it. From somewhere near the bumper I call imperiously to the driver: "Take me immediately to the Havoy Sotel!" He does so.

At the Savoy, the Colgate-Palmolive freestyle skiing championships are holding an intimate lunch for reporters to meet four beautiful American girl skiers, and good fortune and Colgate-Palmolive place me next to the lovely Suzy Chaffee, who was once pictured nude on skis in *The Sunday Times*, and preaches the philosophy of Love Your Body and Let It All Hang Out, Man.

The gins and the Ponys are joined by a couple of large Camparis and a quart or so of Chateauneuf du Pape. The fumes rise to where the brain would be in a non-journalist. Miss Chaffee looks unutterably desirable in her tight-fitting light blue romper-suit. Sud-

denly she squeezes my arm affectionately and says: "When was the last time you gave someone you love a massage all over?"

The headline fantasies weave around my Chateauneuf du Pape-sodden brain.
BEAUTIFUL GIRL SKIER TELLS OF AFFAIR WITH SPORTS WRITER
Incredible Potency
Like an Animal in Bed
Massaged all over
My head sinks drunkenly over the tablecloth until it is about three inches from Miss Chaffee's beautiful bosom. There is a gentle tinkling noise, as of ice dropping into a glass. Miss Chaffee is talking.

"Michael," she says. "Do you know I have been to a doctor, and taken one

"A macabre champagne breakfast in the gloom of a Penthouse club tastefully decorated with illuminated photographs of female loins"

of those tests they do in Sweden, and they tell me I have a biological age of only 15."

"You could have fooled me," I mutter into the tablecloth, and then reluctantly pull myself together. Miss Chaffee may have a biological age of 15, but mine at the moment feels like 75.

Giving the Olympic Games a sporting chance of survival

When our rowing correspondent won an Olympic gold medal in the double sculls at Henley in 1948, he was "breaking" the Olympic eligibility rules. This true-life confession was a prologue to an examination of shamateurism in the Olympic movement.

by Richard Burnell

It seems that the International Olympic Committee may at last be about to make an honest man of me. No longer will the midnight knock at the door herald the possibility that Mr Brun-

dage has called to collect the gold medal I won 25 years ago. Under Lord Killanin's benign rule I can even make my confession without fear of retribution.

So be it. When I won my Olympic medal I was already *The Times* rowing correspondent, albeit part-time and anonymous. My only concession to Olympic proprieties was to hand over my duties, during the period of competition, to the late T. D. Richardson, then *The Times* skating correspondent, who conveniently happened to be a rowing man.

To make matters worse I was also employed by the British Council, who allowed me all the training time I wanted on full pay. And, when it was all over, I quickly wrote a book about it. If this was not a particularly profitable venture it was not for the want of trying.

In fact, my hangover is so powerful it lasts until the next day, which is unfortunate, as I have been invited to take gin with Eley Ammunition at some damp meadow in Rickmansworth that morning, and to blaze away freely. I wake with a head that feels as if a Press reception were being held inside it, and

"My head sinks drunkenly over the tablecloth. There is a gentle tinkling noise, as of ice dropping into a glass. Miss Chaffee is talking"

an apprehension that it is rather dangerous to hand out shotguns to 30 gin-sodden journalists ("I tell you what, ol' man, you put your gin and tonic on your head, and I'll shoot it off.") Every bang goes through my head like a spike, but I return whole, having hit two clay pigeons out of 12, and even they gave themselves up. I lunch on gin, brandy and crisps.

By next day I have developed a terrible heartburn. A potato crisp must have become permanently lodged in the gullet, so I don't care that I have a diary entry for 11am which I can't read. Somewhere they are swilling gin and eating crisps, and I am not there, and I am glad glad glad.

Thus I arrive for the Ford Motor reception in a bad temper, but the affair proves quite informative. Smooth and professional, it includes a phone link with driver Roger Clark in Nairobi. A delicious lunch, however, is wrecked by the crisp in my gullet, which now appears to have burst into flames. What shall it profit a man if he gain a whole free lunch and a duodenal ulcer?

I've been prejudiced against horses ever since I served as a trooper in the 7th Hussars, so I attend the British Show Jumping Association lunch in a vile mood, but they are utterly charming. Over steak and burgundy in the cloistered atmosphere of the Anglo-Belgian Club, Belgrave Square, Col. Harry Llewellyn frankly answers questions on sponsorship, breeding and the next Olympics and launches a spirited defence of Princess Anne's performance in the Montreal Games. It is all so charming that even the representative of the *Sun* is overcome by the good humour and promises not to report a rash remark with a cry of "Don't worry Harry, I've put my pen away," a concession to good manners which will probably earn him the sack. By the fourth glass of port my heartburn is numbed and I stagger forth at 3.30 and return to the office where I fall asleep in the lift.

However, by six o'clock I am in the Tom Cribb public house, near Haymarket, to meet Alan Lloyd, author of The Great Prize Fight. It's an unusual reception, just three or four people including the author and Henry Cooper jammed in a public bar while Cassells pay for the drinks. By nine o'clock I am awash, and catch my Tube train. But I have to get out two stations early, as I feel sick.

I determine not to drink anything at the All-England Badminton Championships at Wembley, but on arrival, behold! there are the free gins all lined up winking at me, and it is all too much. I see no badminton.

And so it all ends. I gain seven pounds in weight during the week, which is just about equal to the weight of paper I collect, most of it bearing useless information such as the fact that

"Suddenly she squeezes my arm affectionately and says: 'When was the last time you gave someone you love a massage all over?'"

Rizla cigarette papers were founded in 1799. I also have 40 cigarettes, three badges, a notebook and a thing to stop your car smelling. I shall need an operation to remove the burning pain in my gullet.

I should like to suggest yet another Writer of the Year award. It would go to a journalist who had survived the most Press receptions. It would be sponsored by a gin company. And I would be the first winner.

March 27 1977

The proposal at the Olympic Congress in Varna that a competitor shall be eligible provided only that "he has not derived personal profit from competing in his sport", may not be perfect. But it is a practical solution today, and one which has been overdue ever since the skater Sonja Henie became the first amateur sporting millionairess.

It is not simply a problem of shamateurism, though that may be serious in sports where opportunities exist for personal gain. More important, I believe, are the different social *mores* which obtain in different countries. Some, including Mr Brundage's during the relevant period, have habitually offered university scholarships in order to produce their athletes. Others offer jobs or sponsorship in varying forms. Some offer employment in the armed forces or police.

In communist countries, where the Welfare State has been carried to its logical—or illogical, according to your point of view—conclusion, so that everyone is employed or supported by the State, the Western conception of amateur and professional is meaningless.

And the problem varies in different sports as well as in different countries. In rowing, for example, there are few significant professional openings. In boxing, amateur success opens the door to a profitable career. In equestrianism, amateurs compete alongside others who, to the ignorant layman at least, have all the appearances of being totally professional until they actually enter the Olympic arena. In football, we have had the anomaly that one country has been able to field the same team for the Olympic Games and the World Cup, while another cannot use a single player in both competitions although this is now about to be corrected.

Amid such confusion there can be no "amateur definition" which is meaningful and enforceable in sports in all countries. Lord Exeter may claim that "there is something special about amateurism."

He is probably right, except in his choice of tense. But today not one athlete in 10,000 could be Lord Exeter's sort of amateur and still be competitive at Olympic level.

The only speciality of Olympic amateurism during the past 25 years has been the ingenuity of its double talk. If we wish the Olympics to continue in anything like their present form, it is time to forget the double talk. If the international governing bodies of the various Olympic sports believe that they can solve the problem, let us invite them to try.

October 7 1973

A hooded Arab terrorist . . .

Four years after the Munich tragedy: guilt about being alive

Those who were there and those who watched on television retain vivid memories of the 1972 Munich Olympics, a terrorist on a balcony, the overhead thrash of helicopters on their fatal flights and, later, in the main stadium the bowed skull caps and the Munich Philharmonic Orchestra playing the haunting movement of Beethoven's Eroica Symphony. The nightmare, though diminishing, was still being experienced in Tel Aviv four years later.

by Dudley Doust

The mouth of the Kalashnikov sub-machine gun that was shoved into his side, just above the hipbone, stays in his mind. Gad Tzabari, the little Israeli linotype operator, drifts from job to job, sits sipping beer through the night, and often drives down the coast in search of the flowers. He is most at ease when he is coaching youngsters, or the deaf and dumb wrestlers at the Helen Keller House in Tel Aviv. Tzabari nips round the mats, his brown eyes aglow, fully absorbed in his sport. "I coach

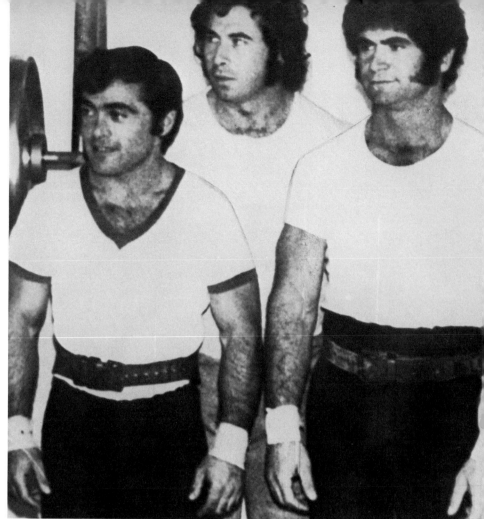

Nightmare memories of an Olympics: . . . three Israeli weightlifters who were killed . . .

because I am alive," he said last week. "Only when I am coaching can I forget about Munich."

Tzabari is the Israeli who made the run for it. He's the little wrestler who broke free from his terrorist captors and, under a hail of gunfire, zigzagged to safety. He still is light on his feet, tiny at 7st 8lb and, at 32, still apparently fit enough to fight in Greco-Roman wrestling competitions, He isn't, alas, fit. The Israeli defence forces have a "fitness profile" made up of both physical and psychological factors: the top grade is 97, and the lowest 21. Tzabari is now rated 24. "I went for one day in the army after Munich," he said, "and they told me to go home."

Tzabari was a bachelor those first years after Munich and once, at his parents' home, he awoke to a sharp clatter of metal. He jumped from his bed, ran across the room and awoke with a crash against the wall. "It was my father who had made the noise," Tzabari recalled with a wan smile. "He had got up early for synagogue and, in the bathroom, he dropped something into the bath-tub."

Tzabari's wife, seven months preg-

nant, brought coffee, cakes and nuts. She sat, smiled and folded her hands over the baby. Sun flooded into the sitting room, and all seemed peaceful until an idle question cast a shadow: Tzabari's block of flats is built on a site in Tel Aviv which, before the 1948 war, was an old Arab village. There is no trace now of that culture. By instinct, I asked if Tzabari, somehow or somewhere, had received a gesture of sympathy or regret from an Arab since Munich. His eyes went hard: "I wouldn't accept such a thing. They killed my friends."

After Munich, when he could neither eat nor work nor sleep, Tzabari visited a psychiatrist once a week. In six months it was down to once a fortnight and, phasing out, he now only pays desperate calls: "We talk about Munich." He recounted for me that murderous dawn of September 5. By the next morning 11 Israeli sportsmen and six Arab terrorists were dead. He slowly took a pad of paper and drew a sketch of Compound 31, Connollystrasse, in the Olympic Village. "I was upstairs with David Berger, from America. Romano and Friedman were here, and here were Slavin and Halfin."

... American Air Force officers carrying the coffin of one of eleven dead Israeli sportsmen. Gad Tzabari (left) was a survivor. He escaped by zigzagging to safety under a hail of gunfire.

He gently slapped down the pen: "All those boys are dead."

Berger, a scholarly boy from Ohio, suddenly shouted in Hebrew for his mates to fight the Arabs. "One of the terrorists understood Hebrew," recalled Tzabari, "and the terrorist put the gun in my side and said 'Go!'—and I went first." The four terrorists then led the eight sportsmen to another apartment.

There Tzabari saw a staircase guarded by another terrorist. "He wore a stocking mask, and he said nothing, just moved his gun." Tzabari rushed him, knocked his gun aside and dashed down a staircase. His zigzag for freedom was on, and he now has no real idea how many bullets were fired: "It was the worst moment of my life. Whatever happens to me now is a game."

Tzabari rarely sees other survivors of Munich. He has not once seen Tuvia Sokolsky, the other sportsman who escaped from the clutches of the terrorists. Sokolsky, a weightlifting coach, had a bed beside a French window in the first beseiged apartment. As a teammate fought to hold back the Arabs, and rammed a bed against the door, Sokolsky jumped through the window to safety.

The walker Dr Shaul Ladany, who at the age of eight had been confined in Bergen-Belsen concentration camp, is now a professor of industrial engineering at the Ben Gurion University. He was one of the six Israelis in Apartment Two of the compound who all survived. Ladany still talks, still thinks of Munich. He brings an academic distance to the tragedy. He was, for instance, watching a televised news programme of Yassar Arafat's visit to the United Nations last year and, among the crowd of pro-Palestinian demonstrators, he spotted a face that looked like one of the terrorists: "I have reported it to the authorities, but have heard no more about it."

Ladany also ponders the Arabs' decision to pass over Apartment Two, his apartment, and strike the ones on either side. It is commonly thought that the wrestling coach, Moshe Weinberg, now dead, led them from the first to the third apartment in hopes that the sturdy wrestlers and weightlifters there might put up a fight. "One year later another thought came to my mind," says Ladany. "The Arabs were well prepared, and they might have known we were armed in our apartment. We had two marksmen with ammunition."

The marksman Henry Herscovici, however, had no intention of using his .22 rifle. He had finished 23rd of 106 competitors in the small-bore prone position competition and, he supposed, the last shot was fired for him in the Olympics. "I later offered to fire on the terrorists from another compound," recalled Herscovici, now a jeweller in Tel Aviv, "but at the time of the attack I didn't know the number of terrorists, where they were or how many hostages they held. I could have killed one of them, but I couldn't take the responsibility for reprisals."

Herscovici watched from his apartment window as the terrorist leader, only a few feet away, handed over his ransom demand for the release of 200 Arab prisoners by the Israelis to a German security guard. "I will always remember his hands, the terrorist's hands. I don't gesture like an Arab, and it struck me as strange."

He escaped with the others in his apartment, and today in his tiny shop on Ben-Yehuda Street, Herscovici now displays a proud memento of Munich: a Haitian commemoration stamp stuck in a showcase of watches. It depicts the Israeli delegation marching in the Olympic opening ceremony. Their flagbearer is Herscovici.

So, the nightmares are slowly receding. The survivors are left with their memories. Mrs Hiriya Romano, the slain weightlifter's mother, died with hers. She had been acutely depressed since the tragedy, and last March, on a fine day, she set fire to herself. Her death, while barely remarked upon in the Israeli newspapers, did not go unnoticed among the survivors.

What little Gad Tzabari's wife says of her husband applies, in various depths, to all those who returned with the coffins: "Gad sometimes feels guilty that he lived and others died."

February 22 1976

Snouts in the port as MCC dithers on a decision about apartheid

Apartheid in sport generally, and Britain's sporting links with South Africa in particular, became a cause for public concern in the 1960s. The MCC's procrastination over the d'Oliveira affair brought the issue to the attention of non-sporting sections of the community like the church. In the 1970s racism at home had become a recognisable social disease, and at least one leading black sportsman was moved to speak out against it.

by Michael Parkinson

The MCC which has had many nasty things said about it, and most of them true, this week squared up to the problem of the colour bar in cricket and then turned its back on the fight. In doing so it surprised none of us who over the years have watched it build up an unenviable reputation for evasions, shilly-shallying and downright barminess.

But whereas in the past the sight of this shambles in action has been confined to the few of us who love cricket, today, because of the nature of the current problem, MCC stands in all its pot-bellied impotence for everyone to see.

MCC has, for many years now, conveniently shoved aside the problem of South Africa's ban on blacks and whites playing together. And it would have continued to do so had it not been for the arrival of Basil d'Oliveira, a Cape Coloured, who six years ago came to Britain to make his living in the leagues, qualified for Worcestershire and last season was capped for England.

He is a fine cricketer, possibly the best all-rounder in the land. As soon as d'Oliveira proved himself in the England team it became apparent that providing he didn't suffer a drastic loss of form, he would be an automatic choice for the tour of South Africa in 1968–69.

For some time now journalists have been posing the basic question to MCC: what happens if South Africa formally declares that d'Oliveira would not be allowed to tour because of their racial discrimination laws? And for some time now MCC has buried its snout in the port and said "We'll wait and see."

They have now been shaken from their cosy attitude by an announcement from South Africa. Mr Pieter le Roux, the South African Minister of the Interior, stated emphatically that d'Oliveira would not be allowed to tour if picked for England. It was at this point that cricket's problem became the concern of the nation, a fact borne out by the number of MPs who signed a petition demanding that the MCC cancel the tour immediately.

MCC was now being watched by a new and demanding audience and under such scrutiny it struggled to its feet and said, "No comment." Later it enlarged on this first fine thought and said: "The MCC committee will consider this as and when it arises."

It would be wrong, of course, to condemn MCC outright for what on the face of it is an act of outrageous folly. It might be that their wait and see policy is a deliberate diplomatic tactic which in the end will see them shining bright and triumphant. This being the case it is perhaps worth examining some of the things that MCC hopes might happen between now and 1968 to let them off the hook.

The simplest thing would be for d'Oliveira to lose his form and therefore not become a candidate for the tour. That apart, he might fall under a bus, change colour overnight or give up the game to become a crooner.

It could be, of course, that none of these things happen and that in 1968 Basil d'Oliveira will stand as an automatic choice for the tour. In that case the MCC tactic of playing a waiting game will succeed only if Mr Vorster turns out to be a secret Liberal and if pigs might fly.

Whatever happens there will come a point in time when MCC will have to commit itself one way or another. The time is surely now. It should, of course, have been before now.

Leicester   Chester   Wakefield

The cricket tour: a church divided in its attitude

by Dudley Doust and Robin Knight

A *Sunday Times* sports poll, conducted over the past eleven days, reveals that the diocesan Bishops of the Church of England are divided on the question of whether the South African cricket team should tour Britain this summer. Twenty of the thirty-four available Bishops replied to our questionnaire, a gratifying number in the light of a confidential letter sent to the Bishops by the Archbishop of Canterbury last week suggesting that the clergy should not reply. Moreover, wrote one anonymously, "episcopal opinions are no more likely to be right than that of others who may well be closer to the situation." That may be. But let's listen to the Bishops.

Question: Do you feel that the South African cricket team should tour Britain this summer?

Yes	7
No	13
Declined to comment	14

While the Bishop of Wakefield, Dr Eric Treacy (for tour), said "no one

The fact of the matter is that many people in this country have waited too long and seen too much to tolerate any longer the sight of MCC evading an important human principle. The sad figure in this sordid mess is Basil d'Oliveira. It is painful and degrading for him to be used this way. What makes it worse is that he is paying the price for MCC being such a weak-kneed lot of boobies in the past.

Any more deliberation on this issue is futile. The mood of the people as expressed by their MPs cannot be ignored by the MCC.

They should tell the South Africans without more ado that not only will England refuse to tour unless d'Oliveira is accepted but that she will not tour at all as long as the laws of the country prevent a white man and a black man playing together. *January 29 1967*

PS: Basil d'Oliveira was indeed selected for the 1968–9 tour of South Africa, but Premier Vorster denounced his inclusion as "political", and the tour was cancelled.

Clive Lloyd clobbers Powell's racist attack

by Bob Campbell

Clive Lloyd is very obviously black, and equally obviously one of Britain's sporting idols. When he captained West Indies to victory over England last summer, black and white rose as one to applaud, illustrating that sport—with the exception of South Africa—is colour blind. A pity, then, that this picture is not mirrored in society at large; frightening when Enoch Powell shrieks "civil war"; of vital importance when a sportsman of Lloyd's stature speaks out, which he did yesterday.

"This latest speech shows again that Enoch Powell is a racialist. We've known this for years, it's nothing new. It's like his rivers of blood he was talking about a long time ago now. Since then a lot of people have tried to make things better, and he seems to be trying to harm that

work. Mind you, he's one of those publicity-seeking people."

A number of people have already approached the Attorney General, demanding that action be taken against Powell. How did Lloyd feel? "It's up to the Race Relations Board, surely, to see that something is done to prosecute him, to ask the Government to do something about these racialist statements." At the same time Lloyd refuses to be rattled by the Powellites. "Things have got better in this country, and I don't think Powell can change that."

Prior to Powell's latest hysteria, I asked Lloyd if he would serve on the Race Relations Board if appointed. "Obviously I would be very happy to perform some service to the community in return for what has been done for me. I think I have the advantage of being respected by both sections of the population in England, black and white, and I would like to help in drawing people together."

Authorities please note.

January 23 1977

Southwark (AGAINST)

Peterborough (FOR)

Oxford (AGAINST)

seems to object to our playing chess or football with Communists," the Bishop of Southwark, Dr Mervyn Stockwood (against tour), replied: "The answer is that the Russians have little opportunity to protest against their government. If they do they probably end up in a concentration camp. The South African cricketers not only voted for apartheid but they decided for themselves to become members of the team."

And the Bishop of Portsmouth, Dr John Phillips, in favour of the tour, and the Bishop of Ipswich, Dr Leslie Brown, opposed to it, both find moral reason in their views. "I cannot reconcile discrimination against white South Africans with what I believe in as a

Christian," said Dr Phillips, while his East Anglian colleague, Dr Brown, replied: "The tour has become a symbol of a racial policy which Christians reject."

Question: What is your view of demonstrations against apartheid?

| In favour | 16 |
| Against | 4 |

"I think the demonstrations are stupid and do more harm than good to the cause they try to promote," wrote the Bishop of Peterborough, the Rt. Rev Cyril Eastaugh (for tour). "Reasonable discussion is the only satisfactory way of settling differences." The Bishop of Wakefield concurred: "Many demonstrators are activated more by hatred than love, and hatred

achieves nothing."

All of the sixteen who favoured demonstrations stressed that they must be peaceful. The Bishop of Chester, Dr Gerald Ellison, and the Bishop of Gloucester, the Rt. Rev Basil Guy, agreed, nearly verbatim, with the Bishop of Durham, Dr Ian Ramsey, who thought "the Springboks (rugby) demonstrations have shown that non-violent demonstrations are not only possible, but effective." The three opposed the tour.

On sporting relations generally, the Boat Race umpire and former Oxford rowing Blue, the Bishop of Chester, wrote: "We should encourage the governing bodies of sport to accept the Olympic standards and refuse to welcome nationally representative teams which are selected on any grounds other than merit."

Finally, from the Bishop of Southwell, the Rt. Rev Gordon Savage (against tour), came this novel suggestion: "Let the South Africans tour Britain as 'The Apartheid Team'."

February 1 1970

PS: The tour was called off by the cricket authorities, ostensibly at the behest of the Government, and because security at grounds was an insuperable problem.

On and off court — the battles fought for the liberation of women's tennis

"The only thing a woman is allowed to sell in public is her body. If you are a chorus girl, model, or prostitute, that's OK, that's feminine. Use your athletic skill to make a living and suddenly you're hard or masculine"
US tennis star Julie Heldman, 1971.

by Vincent Hanna

Wimbledon 1971 has become the backdrop for a new conflict, violent and strange in the strawberries-and-cream atmosphere of British tennis. The march of Women's Lib.

It makes the prospect of a Court v King final a nail-biting one, for each represents the opposite extreme in a battle that has drifted from the realms of sport and has become social, even political.

On September 27, 1970, in Julie Heldman's bedroom in Houston, Texas, eating left-over spaghetti like a bunch of St Trinian's girls having a secret dorm feast, nine young professional ladies cocked a collective snook at the US Lawn Tennis Association and formed the first all-women's tennis tour.

In 14 tournaments over $200,000 has gone into female purses and has been spent on clothes, cars, political polemics, and at least one garbage disposal unit. To a group of 16 girls it has meant financial independence, but to the male-dominated tennis world it has assumed the sinister proportions of an epidemic of bubonic plague.

"A woman should stay home and have babies," says Stan Smith, "that's what she's for. I mean this women's lib thing could go too far." "If you worry too much about money," says Margaret Court, "you become hard, like a man. It's a bad thing."

That midnight feast in Houston happened ironically as the direct result of a flash of male chauvinism. Jack Kramer runs the Pacific South West Tournament in Los Angeles every August. In 1970 the prize money was split in a 12:1 ratio between the men and women; the women received $7,500 and had to get to the quarter-finals to win anything. Billie Jean King and Rosie Casals wanted to organise a boycott of the Kramer event, but

eventually eight top lady players arrived in Houston for an alternative tournament sponsored by Virginia Slims cigarettes and organised by Gladys Heldman, owner of World Tennis magazine and mother of Julie.

The details of the row between Mrs Heldman, Kramer, and the USLTA have become a little blurred around the edges, but there is no doubt that Kramer promised not to cause the girls any trouble. He then sought to achieve this worthy aim by refusing to agree to the USLTA granting the girls a sanction for the Houston tournament unless, strangely, they agreed to play for nothing. Billie Jean and friends formed the breakaway tour and all got suspended by the USLTA for their pains. In February after much toing and froing with Gladys Heldman they were reinstated.

"Let's face it," says Billie Jean "The

Julie Heldman: a mind like a honed razor.

scene for women last year in tennis was pretty sick, unless you were a champion and could demand appearance money." It's a point which I could find no-one to dispute, even among the game's administrators. "Of course, women are discriminated against," says Basil Reay, Secretary of the International Lawn Tennis Federation, "they have no proper representation on any important committee in the game. Neither here nor in the US are they allowed to play their full part. I deplore it."

Take Ann Jones. She is current captain of the Wightman Cup team. But she will not be allowed to select her team, or even vote on it. That job is

traditionally reserved for an all-male amateur committee.

Ann Jones is very much a part of the women's lib group, a fact that has somehow been forgotten in the public bitching of the past month. She is expecting a baby in December and doesn't play now, but took part in most of the tour, winning the largest tournament in Las Vegas. Her husband, Pip, acts as official tour manager, escorting the girls round the world.

There are now 24 girls in the lib lobby, but the deal is still the same as was worked out at that famous dormitory feast in Houston. They won't play unless the tournament guarantees a minimum prize money of $7,500 for eight girls and $18,000 for 32. That way even first-round losers get enough to cover expenses. As part of the deal the players must give free clinics to local youngsters and do their own publicity.

They are as diverse a bunch as is possible to meet. Rosie Casals was born in San Francisco and talks very tough. "The LTAs don't care if women tennis players drop dead. They want to develop only men."

Mary-Ann Curtis is the ultimate all-American girl, living in a cocoon of instant America, and looking for a hamburger and coke five minutes after landing in Rome. "If I hadn't joined, I would have been without a tourney between September and February, and that would have been disastrous. I got an expensive apartment and my dog to support."

There are exotic ladies like Tory Fretz, who had all her bras stolen last January in Milwaukee and can't be bothered to replace them. Or Kristy Pigeon, who at 20 feels that men are unnecessary. "You should be able to get babies out of test tubes." Or Francoise Durr, who is the best doubles player in the world and swears with aplomb—and skill—in the language of the country in which she is playing.

Some are clearly motivated by the politics of women's rights, but most are not, they just want to make a decent living playing tennis.

Julie Heldman, who is 25, is a Stanford history honours graduate whose playful exterior hides a mind like a honed razor. She wears a dress on court with "women's lib" around the waist, and means it. You could hardly call Ann Jones a militant, yet she will argue strongly in favour of collective action as a means of achieving even the

From the top: Billie Jean King, the breakaway leader; Margaret Court, the oppositionist; Rosie Casals, the tough talker.

limited aim of better prize money.

Ironically, the most antipathetic reaction to the girls tends to come from American housewives. "They ask me every day when I am going to settle down and have babies," says Billie Jean." "We seem to be a threat to the life they have been moulded into. But anyone who has a tennis-playing daughter should get on his knees and thank us."

Although a lot of publicity has been given to alleged conflict between the group and two other players (Virginia Wade and Evonne Goolagong) such stories are mostly rubbish. The Australian girl is still very much under the personal supervision of Vic Edwards, her coach, and would not be ready for a prolonged winter American tour. As for Virginia; she is rightly described by Ann Jones as "the last of the true amateurs," playing as and where she wishes without commitment. There is no ill-feeling between her and the rest of the girls . . . apart from tennis rivalry that is. She is expected to enter for the next Houston tournament.

But whatever way you look at women in tennis you have to return to one issue, and one great match . . . Margaret Court v Billie Jean King. There is no love lost between the two (and that is putting it mildly), and Margaret doesn't hold with women's lib: "I don't think women should be paid the same as men, even outside tennis," she says. "We aren't equal."

She angered the lib group by refusing to join their circuit. "I'm all in favour of better prize money for women," she says, "it helps the younger girls a lot. But I can make just as much on my own. Besides I would hate to play the same women week after week."

There have been violent words, too, from some of the women's lib girls about Margaret's enthusiasm for playing to segregated audiences in South Africa. "There are special enclosures for the blacks," she says. "They were always packed when I played."

Billie Jean, then, sees herself as the symbol and leader of a movement which has an arch enemy in Margaret Court. She also has a burning passion to avenge her defeat in last year's final. If she wins it will be a remarkable effort for she has thrown herself life and soul into the women's pro tour, doing two children's clinics, two television broadcasts and playing two matches most days for six months. Within the past year she has had two knee operations and a serious illness, so it is little wonder she is keyed up to win.

"I am fighting for a movement this year," she declares. "Before I came to England I would have liked to have had Margaret on the tour. But her attitude towards the girls has made me angry. The Centre Court isn't big enough for both of us."

June 27 1971

Jolly Boating

Tim Crooks and Pat Delafield, Britain's brilliant double scullers, may have a reputation as incompatible oarsmen but listen to the story of the Danish doubles, Niels Secher, a medical student, and Jorgen Engelbrecht, an auto mechanic. They really irritated each other. Rowing in the final of the European championship last year in Copenhagen, they grew so angry at each other's blade work that, in mutual pique, they pulled up and stopped rowing before reaching the finish.

They then switched to single sculling and, as with Crooks and Delafield, set out through the winter to win separate places as single scullers in the Danish Olympic team. They both failed. Secher had second thoughts: to go or not to go, that was the question, and finally he swallowed his pride. He went down to the garage where Englebrecht works in Copenhagen. "Jorgen," he said, "should we try again as a doubles team?" Engelbrecht wiped his greasy hands on a rag and in a moment replied: "Go outside and give me 30 minutes to think about it." In half an hour the mechanic came out and the two were reconciled. In the space of four days the two had rigged their boat, taken a few practice swipes at the water and were second by less than a length to the Norwegians at the international regatta in Oslo on July 30. Two days later they were selected for Munich.

As we always said: a couple that rows together rows together.

September 3 1972

● Cruel quote of the week. Muhammad Ali's medic, Dr Ferdie Pacheco, on the sale of video-cassettes of the two Ali-Spinks fights for $89.95: "Hell, for that money, Spinks will come to the house."

October 29 1978

When the odds are uneven elsewhere, war games on ice can settle an old score

Nationalism, however unwelcome in the sporting arena, has sometimes, perversely, added an almost unbearable dimension of excitement and anticipation. That was the situation when, after the Russian invasion of Czechoslovakia, the two countries confronted each other at ice hockey.

by John Lovesey

Seldom can a sporting event have been so drenched in politics as the extraordinary ice hockey matches between Russia and Czechoslovakia, which led directly to last week's rioting in Prague and the new crisis there. The games themselves, during the world championships in Stockholm, contained moments of emotion which those who watched will never forget.

When the first dramatic match, which Czechoslovakia won, was over, Josef Golonka, the heroic Czech captain, and one of his players both fainted. All his team cried. Big, tough men, they broke down and the tears streamed down their faces.

Just as moved were some three to four hundred Czechs in the audience, whom Russia's young Communist newspaper, Komsomolskaja Pravda, called "counter-revolutionary scum." They carried round their necks signs written in Russian:

"Now it's March—not August." "Russians—your tanks won't help you this time." "Freedom to Czechoslovakia."

For those who know the place ice hockey holds in Czechoslovakia's affections, the ensuing reaction there was not surprising either. First played in Czechoslovakia 60 years ago, top ice hockey players' names are household words and the game ranks equal with football, the top summer sport, for attention. The national team patterns its play on football. They shoot with power and precision and stop, start and change direction with bewildering speed.

If the Czechs are the supreme artists of amateur ice hockey, the Russians are the heavies. Ironically, they first learnt the game from the Czechs. Then, as in other sports, they built up to their present domination by spending money and countless hours on intensive study and preparation. In Stockholm, the Russians finished the tournament with the same number of points as Sweden (second) and Czechoslovakia (third) but won their seventh successive world title with a superior goal average.

"Our thanks to you for the bronze medal with two diamonds," read one of 2,000 telegrams the Czech team received. "It's worth more to us than the gold." Two cables, one from Dubcek and the other from Cernik, arrived after the team had left for home and a tumultuous welcome in Prague.

For the first Russia-Czechoslovakia match, extra police were brought into the stadium. Fireworks were set off behind the Russian goal and the police had to break up one fight. The cheers of 300 Russians, whose dormitory was a tourist boat in Stockholm harbour, were drowned by whistles.

Russia lost 2-0, its usually well-drilled players thrown into a state of panic when, with two of their team in the penalty box, Czechoslovakia's brilliant Jan Suchy, chosen as one of the tournament's top three players, scored the first goal. The second came in the last 20 minute period when the puck sliced through the Russian defence to Josef Cerny, who skated round an opponent and beat the Russian goalkeeper with an angled backshot.

It was enough to send the Soviet coach, Anatoly Tarasov (who looks like Krushchev and writes furiously in a small notebook during matches), into a Stockholm hospital for a cardiogram check-up on his weak heart.

It was Russia's first defeat in over a year; the last time they were beaten was at the Grenoble Winter Olympics, where they also fell to the Czechs. More than that, it was the first time since 1955 that the Russians had failed to score in a match. In Czechoslovakia, this was excuse enough for the party paper, Rude Pravo, to elevate their country's goalkeeper Vladimir Dzurila heavenwards: "It was almost as if St. Wenceslas was helping him to keep goal."

Countrywide demonstrations and tough Russian countermeasures did not come, however, until after the all-important second game, which took place just over a week ago. If it was not sparkling ice hockey, the atmosphere was even more charged. The Russians were like men trying to put up a tent in a storm; as fast as they pegged down one corner, another blew up.

The final result, a 4-3 victory for the Czechs, reflected the respective merits of the goalkeepers as much, if not more so, than their teammates.

And after this match, as the first, the Russians stood on the ice, heads bowed, as the Czech national anthem was played and the Czech flag was raised. As the last strains died away, the Czech players, instead of shaking hands with their opponents, turned and skated away. *April 6 1969*

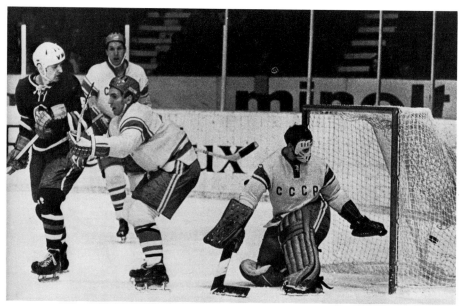

The Czechs score against the USSR . . . sport drenched in politics.

Failure to secure peace of mind: the lesson from the Montreal Olympics

Four years after the murder of Israeli competitors at the 1972 Munich Olympics, the ungainly, vulnerable Goliath that the Games had become lumbered into Montreal, whose city administration had mortgaged its citizens to the hilt to stage them. The need to render the 21st Olympiad terrorist-proof meant security obtruded to the point of farce.

by Norman Harris

"The Soviet Union" read the note stuck under my door, "are holding a Press conference to announce they will pull out of the Games unless Canada hands back their high diver, Sergi Nemtsanov, who has defected."

Only briefly did one consider the possibility that this was a hoax. We might as easily have been reading a scenario by a satirical playwright instead of watching a real Olympics. The Games which opened with the African boycott, ended with Russia shouting back angrily at her detractors—and with athletes' accusations that the body-building steroid drugs are being superseded by the new wonder preparation of blood retransfusion. Nothing is real any more.

Sometimes we have had the feeling of wondering where on earth we were. It was such a moment the other night outside the weightlifting arena, which was too full "for security." The steel gates were shut and defended against us by an orange-suited "security" attendant and by soldiers.

Suddenly the night was pierced by flashing lights and sirens, and within a few bewildering seconds we had been pushed back—evidently too rapidly for a victim to be sighted or a hand-grenade unpinned—as in swept a half-dozen black limousines bearing a few Very Important People and squads of secret service men.

The gates were again shut against us—rifles again barred the way, and on the pavement of this residential suburb three small boys with bikes, and a man walking his dog were curtly ordered to "move it along." They moved, and we had by now stopped arguing against the soldiers who were stopping our "unrestricted access" demanded in the Olympic Charter. I am not really playing by the rules here. The idea is that we journalists are not meant to belabour you with our difficulties, and certainly not supposed to let on that we didn't even see the event. But I must do that, because a night like this was symptomatic of a Games not so much of Franz Kafka but according to George Orwell's 1984.

At any rate, this night had a happy ending. Gaining at last a security clearance to the emptying stadium where the superheavyweight, weightlifting contest had just finished, we met an extraordinary champion with the stature and the humour to defeat the system which ironically is so like that which, in our Western eyes, exists in his own country.

Vasily Alexeyev, of the Soviet Union, now twice the Olympic champion is an enormous man. His 24½st so hangs from his breast and bulges from the belly that when I had seen him earlier on the TV screen I thought I was looking at the most gross figure in the world. But now, as he walked across the platform to talk to us, he seemed an avuncular giant.

Soon, he accommodatingly pulled a chair right up to the edge of the platform, placed his hands on his knees, and regarded us like so many infants at the feet of the most popular teacher in the school. Behind him, the electronic scoreboard showed that he had made utter nonsense of what was supposed to be the most keenly-contested event in the Olympics, setting a world record with his second clean and jerk (225 kilograms) and not even bothering to take his third as he won by 440 to 405 kg.

I asked Alexeyev if he thought he was a typical Russian. He put his fists on his hips and declared: "I am typical of Rayazan" (his home town). So what is the characteristic of Rayazans? "They are true-blooded Russians." So he *was* a typical Russian? "I am," he said, spelling it out, "the best example of a typical Russian."

Later, outside, as he approached the team coach amid shouts and cheers, he recognised an American couple from a weightlifting visit last year. Then, they gave him the hospitality of an ordinary American home, canned beer, and a visit to the supermarket. Now, they had photographs to give him, and a new baby for him to see. As a sea of ordinary faces crowded around him, and the big man held up the baby to his cheek, the soldiers shuffled uneasily, helplessly, in the throng. They could scarcely have been more incongruous if they were standing there in pyjamas.

Real concern for security has become confused with the everyday handling of people. The soldiers and the armed police were all too ready to back up the orange-suited boys who were really only attendants who have been indoctrinated with the word SECURITY and with the instruction: "Don't let anyone push you around." This was not the spirit of other Olympics.

I end with an image from the Sunday of the rowing final:

The last, the classic, race had been rowed, and all the eights swung through together in a grand row-past. The music, of celebration and farewell, was affecting. Then, the New Zealand crew halted its progress back to the boat-sheds and instead turned back to the far bank and the astonishing number of their supporters who had grouped at that point. The crew had rowed an attacking, desperate race to try and defend their Olympic title, and in the end had held on for bronze.

That bronze had cost them and their supporters £13,000, a bank overdraft which they now have to return home and try to clear off. As the crew rowed in close to the bank and their supporters clambered down into the water, there was a sort of communion that needs no description. Then, the inevitable official dinghy came buzzing over the water to stop the infraction.

I walked away from the main stand, upset, to come face to face with SECURITY. Along a paved pathway which was bordered by orange-suited attendants. They were stationed there to stop people leaving the path and crossing the grass encircled in the middle. After being twice stopped by grabbing hands, I broke through and deliberately walked across that 50 yards of very ordinary, rather rough grass—like some others were doing. And then I stood and stared back, unable to think about the rowing or anything else; only the sight of 20 orange-uniformed figures, regularly spaced, watching the passing crowd like policemen facing demonstrators, as they defended a patch of grass. *August 1 1976*

The unwritten laws of a man's game — and the rogue elephants

Much of the character of rugby football is rooted in physical conflict, and within a "man's game" the use of boot and fist has not always earned instant condemnation. But as early as 1967 our rugby correspondent challenged the "win-at-all-costs mentality" in an amateur game, and so did his youthful successor in 1978.

by Vivian Jenkins

Boots, fists, biting, butting—the annual chorus has begun again. Every year, as regularly as falling leaves, the cry of "too much dirty play in Rugby" is raised to the skies. Yet the game still soldiers on, in spite of it. This time, though, the trouble has started sooner than usual. Cardiff has cancelled fixtures with Neath, and the critics, ever alive to this particular bandwagon, have jumped in with typewriters a-flail.

The game has always had its rogue elephants, and I can recall Neath and Aberavon, my home town, having fixture troubles more than 30 years ago. The biggest fuss of all occurred even earlier, in 1925, when Cyril Brownlie, the All Black forward, was sent off the field in the match against England at Twickenham—in the presence of the then Prince of Wales.

But rough play and dirty play are two different things, and there is an "unwritten law," among forwards themselves, about what is admissible, and what is not.

If a player falls on the ball in front of attacking forwards and decides to lie there, he knows what to expect—the boot, and plenty of it. But he takes it—if the referee will let him—because it is in the interests of his side. No doubt it is all wrong, in law, but this happens.

It is not so much the rough play, but the feeling behind it, that counts. Big men, it seems, like a scrap, provided they know one another well enough! Most people too would excuse a blow struck in anger when an opponent is committing an offence, such as jersey-grabbing. What really irks, however, is foul play committed for its own sake, in cold blood. This, of late years, has certainly been on the increase. Only

Brawling on the veldt, as the 1962 Lions meet the South African Combined Services.

once in the whole of my playing days was I deliberately kicked in the face, and I have not forgotten the man who did it.

Nowadays, however, kicks on the head are far too common and the Welsh fly-half, David Watkins, for one, has a scar under his right eye to prove it. It needed seven stitches. A kick on the head, of course, could kill a man, in an extreme case. A kick on the rump is another matter, and most rugby men would regard it as one of the hazards.

"I don't mind being kicked," says Denzil Williams, the 16 stone Welsh and British Lions' prop. "You get used to that. It's this gouging that gets me down. It's dangerous." Some understatement.

Biting, of course, was given a full airing last season, in the case of the Australian hooker, Cullen. Such an offence is incomprehensible to anyone who played 30 years ago.

Why all this mayhem should have crept into the game is a moot question. Perhaps it is just the violence of the times, and the absence of real wars, promoting strange psychological twists in the young. Others might put it down to the "spread of the game," involving new social elements. But the ethos of the public schools, in any case, was always far removed from that of the Welsh miner. Perhaps the "win-at-all-costs" mentality so prevalent nowadays, could also be held responsible. Losing has become the ultimate disgrace. Yet someone has to lose, and to an amateur, whose real work in life is his job, not his rugby, it should not mean the end of the world.

Whatever the cause of the trouble, it is up to the powers-that-be, in this season of all seasons, when the All Blacks are here, to put an end to it all. Referees can do much, but not everything. I wish, though, that they had

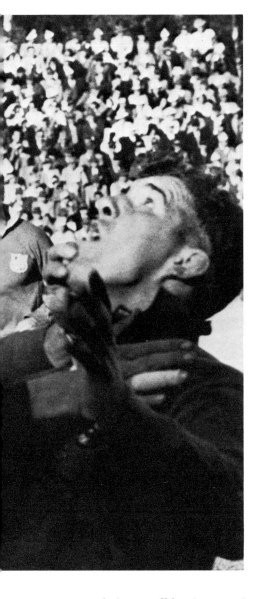

The bravado of rugby, and schoolboys in the hospital spinal units

by John Hopkins

A *Sunday Times* survey of spinal units at hospitals in England, Wales and Northern Ireland shows that nearly three-quarters of the past and present injured rugby players treated at these units were forwards. Furthermore, 72 per cent of the injuries, to both forwards and backs, were from set scrums, including the horrible collapsed scrum, and mauls. "I'm not surprised to hear that so many forwards are injured," says Dr J. P. R. Williams, Wales and British Lions full-back. "Scrummaging is the one phase of the game where the neck is under greatest pressure. You are likely to have your head kicked in in a ruck, but not to have your neck broken. Something must be done about the collapsed scrum. You must penalise one side."

Too few people in rugby accept how desperate the situation is. Some confuse it with irrelevant bravado about how much softer the game is today than it used to be, and thus show themselves oblivious to the strength of feeling against the game by those on the fringes of it—mothers, wives, etc. Too few share the perception of the president, of the French Rugby Federation, Albert Ferrasse, who recently warned: "Rugby must not become a game to which you bring your knife and revolver."

"I'm terrified for my two young sons," a doctor told me. "I love the game; I played it until I was 30, and I don't want to stop them from playing it. But I am scared for them."

Some progress has been made. The Scots have continued to act firmly, recently suspending one player for 30 weeks. RFU president Stanley Couchman has openly and honestly discussed rough and dirty play, a subject some of his colleagues have been reluctant to talk about, too keen to cover up. The French have announced they will never again select their second-row forward, Michel Palmié, who was convicted by a court of maliciously injuring an opponent. But the game *is* rough today. Too many players are being injured by deliberately dirty tactics—the punching of a hooker and gouging at his eyes in a set scrum, trampling and deliberate kicking of a player trapped on the ground, punching, the stiff arm tackle, and the collapsing of a scrum.

One of the most dangerous of these is the collapsing of a scrum. "Five years ago, I can hardly remember it happening," says Charlie Faulkner, loosehead prop for Pontypool and Wales. "Now it has become almost the only counter to an eight-man shove and drive."

Our survey reveals that the number of players admitted to spinal units is growing—slowly in some parts, more quickly in others. Professor Brian McKibbin, who conducted an investigation in South Wales with Dr J. P. R. Williams, and will soon publish their findings in the British Medical Journal, says categorically it is worse now.

Their investigations show that between 1968 and 1974 they did not find a single case of a player being paralysed as a result of a rugby injury. Since 1974 there has been an average of one each season, and this season there have already been two.

The Sunday Times survey also reveals another disturbing fact—the number of schoolboys who have been injured. At Stoke Mandeville earlier this month there were three casualties in the spinal-ward unit—two schoolboys and a 22-year-old. Of four cases J. P. R. Williams interviewed at the Cardiff Royal Infirmary, three were schoolboys. Two of the four currently at Rookwood Hospital, outside Cardiff, are schoolboys.

Clearly the dirty practices of senior rugby have seeped down to schoolboy games. Schoolmaster Mike Davis, formerly coach of the England under-19 schoolboy team, believes so. Another schoolmaster says: "It's the frequency of fouling that is so noticeable now." A third even admits he has taught his boys how to collapse the scrum.

"The boys aren't to blame," says Ron Tenninck, secretary of the Rugby Football Schools' Union. "There is too much psyching-up by Sir. They take their teams two, three or four days each week. Before the game, Sir is banging the table in the changing room shouting, 'Come on boys, you've got to win.' Now winning has become the most important thing in schools. That's down to Sir."

November 19 1978

---

power to send players off for the rest of the game, or part of it, without all the ensuing rigmarole of written reports and attending "courts martial."

They might then send players off more often, and the clubs would suffer, through having to play a man short. The offending player, then, might be dropped by his club, which is always being advocated by presidents of the Rugby Union, not always with success. A penalty "try at goal" for foul play, involving three points certain, and two more if the kick is successful, making five points in all, would have a similar deterrent effect.

These things, however, are matters for the International Board, which has never yet done anything new, or really imaginative, about them. Forty years ago, to my knowledge, people were complaining about "too much dirty play in rugby." They still are!

October 1 1967

A death in the Family but the show goes on

Death in sport is a cruel paradox, but one perhaps demanded, even required, in a cathartic sense by modern man. Seen by some as the ultimate exercise in futility, by others as a final glorious sacrifice, such deaths are never commonplace. But in the compulsive sports of motor racing and mountaineering they are an ever present risk.

by Keith Botsford

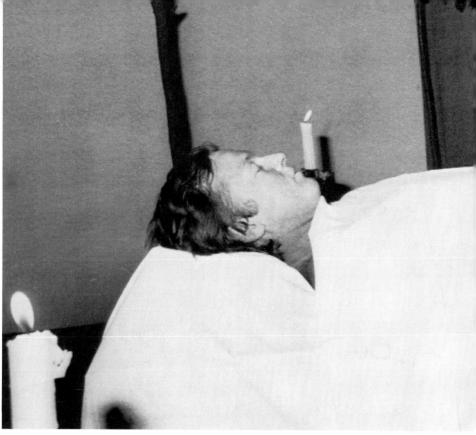

The body of Ronnie Peterson awaits burial—the logical conclusion for an eager volunteer in Formula C

They buried Ronnie Peterson in Sweden on Friday afternoon, and the Family was present; wife and the extended Formula One Family in which Ronnie, with his bland, whey-like face, his childlike and puckish smile, and his body, smooth as baby-fat, had figured so prominently for over a decade. And that other old-timer, Vittorio Brambilla, coming up to 40, lies inert, unconscious and perhaps a total write-off, in a Milan hospital.

To be sure, the Trade Descriptions Act's correct labelling for motor racing would say it was hazardous, might be injurious and can be fatal. In that sense, all FI drivers are knowing volunteers and the Family will soldier on. In another sense, the fatal accident at the Italian Grand Prix at Monza last Sunday was running against the tide, for certainly no lethal vehicle or potential victim is as cosseted and protected against accident as a Formula One car and driver.

In the old days, fatality was a by-product of disregard for safety; it was part of derring-do. Modern motor racing is a much more controlled business, yet it still suffers from three basic types of accident, mechanical failure, an accident on the track and driver error. In all three cases, the fatalities are unnecessary: are they avoidable? Not really—not always.

From the very beginning last Sunday, there had been something wrong with Monza, a subdued sense of crisis, heavy weather, rumour. The crowd was restless, murmuring, hissing. Down where I watched the start of the race, at the first chicane, some 500 metres down from the start-line, a gentle slope away from disaster, there was the usual unease among the Monza Apes, the fans who cluster on scaffolding among the trees.

Ronnie had already had one accident in practice—a high speed crash that wrecked his Lotus 79. He had come out of that unscathed, but relatively poorly placed (for Ronnie) on the grid. Tension was high. He alone of all the drivers had some chance of wresting the championship from Mario Andretti: if he so wished, if Colin Chapman, the team boss of both of them, agreed, if Mario let him. An unlikely combination, but still always on the cards, especially after he had broken with Lotus for next season. A lesser eagerness, no extra hype, his usual car, a row or two further up and Ronnie would be alive today.

The warm-up lap is designed to get cars ready for the start. It is not a way to gain advantage, but to check all systems one last time. It also provides the final burst of adrenaline coursing into the bloodstream and cortex. The machines come in roaring, the men concentrated on a lonely high. What happened at Monza will be blamed on starter Gianni Rastelli, but blame the game, blame the hype. Rastelli's part was only contributory to the final fiasco.

For a proper start, all cars must come to a complete halt. In reality, however, there is always a little crawling forward from the back of the grid: the second division has to find some way to compete with the first. And among that lot was Vittorio Brambilla.

Excitement? Inattention? Inexperience? Only the first few rows were fully stopped at the start of the race, and when the green light went on, some drivers in the middle of the grid were still coming down into neutral before revving up their engines for the start. And others, at the back, simply approached the grid in second, at 60 to 80mph; when they saw the front take off, they followed suit. With their extra velocity, it was like pouring a bagful of Dinky-Toy cars down a funnel: at some point they bunch and collide.

That it had such disastrous results was due to two more factors: the topography of Monza, and the mental spiritual configuration of Ricardo Patrese, the young Arrows driver. For the first, let it be said that Monza is wide at the start—in front of the pits and stand—and becomes a narrow tunnel as the cars hurtle down the slope towards the first chicane: a place where a driver *has* to get through first, or else bluff and bravado have no further meaning. Only first is safe.

As for Patrese, he is far from being a bad driver. On the contrary, he is a very strong, very brave, very quick. But like many young drivers he lacks judgment. And experience. He is a deliberately hairy driver, and what he did at Monza—going up on the inside of the track and then cutting right across

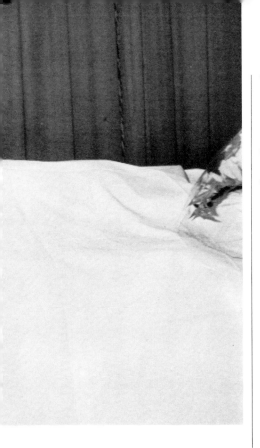

To climb or not to climb: the question posed by a rare but tragic accident

by Peter Gillman

At five in the evening on August 13 two British climbers, Dave Condict, 26, a London lecturer, and David Charity, 26, a solicitor, were one hundred feet from the summit of the Aiguille du Peigne, one of the thrusting granite needles above Chamonix in the Range of Mont Blanc.

They had already climbed 1,900 feet of the Aiguille's North Ridge, a route graded as "Très Difficile," the second most difficult of the French Alpine Club's six categories of difficulty.

But now, according to their guide book, the difficulties had "eased," and there was just one short 50ft. pitch to climb before they reached a chimney that led easily to the summit. It was Condict's turn to lead. With slight difficulty he negotiated a minor overhang at the foot of the pitch and disappeared from Charity's view.

The rope snaked steadily up through Charity's hands for some minutes— but then abruptly stopped. Charity assumed that Condict had paused to work out a move. But then he heard Condict yell the chilling words: "Dave, get ready for a fall."

"About five seconds later Dave fell past me a few feet to my left," says Charity. "I remember seeing the rope go slack and I braced myself for the jerk. I don't remember seeing him falling so I think I must have closed my eyes. Then there was a terrific blow but I managed to hold him."

Condict was now hanging on the rope about 40 feet below. As Charity could not see him, he called down: "Shall I lower you, Dave?" But Condict called back: "There's nowhere to lower me to." He was, it turned out, swinging free in the air below another overhang, unable to reach the rock face to find a foothold, the rope round his waist a lethal, suffocating force.

In this situation only one solution remained for Condict: to climb back up the rope on slings tied in special "prusnik knots" (devised so that they can be pushed up the rope without slipping down again). Charity asked if he should slide a pair down the rope. "It's no good," Condict called back. "I'm too tired." They were the last words he ever spoke. "He moaned a few times," says Charity, "and then he stopped." Condict lost consciousness within five minutes of his fall, and died of suffocation probably not more than 15 minutes later.

Charity himself was now in an appalling predicament, alone, with night and bad weather approaching, near the top of a 12,000-foot peak. He sat on a ledge for 36 hours and then, having failed to attract anyone's attention, climbed alone the now snow-plastered pitch on which Condict had fallen.

The descent from the summit should normally have taken two or three hours; it took Charity, equipped only with a 40-foot length of rope and a dozen slings for abseiling from (a method of descending), 10 hours.

Condict's body was recovered by guides from Chamonix, a week after his fall, and flown home. At his funeral on September 2, I spoke a tribute to his memory.

For Dave Condict was my own climbing partner, and one of my closest friends. The first time I went climbing, four years ago in Snowdonia, was with him; and so was the last time, last summer, again in North Wales.

In 1967, I wrote in an article in *The Sunday Times*: "There *is* danger in climbing, and it has to be faced." I had already seen one man die, the American, John Harlin, as he tumbled through the frame of my telescope as I peered at the North Face of the Eiger during the siege of the Direct Route in March, 1966.

Climbers, I wrote, accept that they are putting themselves at risk, but balance this against climbing's varied, complex pleasures. They do, and I did.

It isn't worth it. I would foreswear now the intense exhilaration climbing has given me in Snowdonia, in the snow-covered Cairngorms, in Switzerland, if Dave could be alive still. Real friends are too precious.

Will I ever go climbing again myself? Climbing in Britain is certainly far less dangerous that in the Alps—but how do I explain that to my wife, when confronted with an accident as rare and as unlucky as Dave's? And what did Dave die for? Why did he die? Why, why, why.

If only I knew. *November 10 1968*

---

the middle just when the front rows were beginning to brake—is nothing new. Patrese expects others to yield.

This was one occasion when they did not. And could not, for in their rear-view mirrors they could see the back of the grid bearing down on them. Thus Patrese's "opening," his way back into the right line for the chicane, was cut off. As Hunt didn't yield, he nudged Hunt, who caught Ronnie. The Swede's car slewed around into the Armco barrier, sheering off the front of the car and bursting into flames as the fuel-lines were split. And someone—no one can say for sure whom—hit Ronnie sideways, finishing what the Armco had begun.

The Milan prosecutor may rail and Bernie Ecclestone, backed by drivers like Fittipaldi and Lauda, may claim Monza is intrinsically accident-prone, but the fact is that the safety-techniques of the sport broke down, and a driver, incautious, unthinking, seeking the edge all drivers seek, committed a fatal error. The Family went to Orebro for the obsequies, and will race again for the thrills, the cash and the glory.

The cash and the glory. The difference between the animal world and the mechanical is that the former can learn, and should, and that the latter cannot, and goes on doing what it is programmed to do—kill. All Ronnie did was get in its way. Being mere flesh.

September 17 1978

Rugby in the Shetlands: where a ball in touch means having to row out to bring it back

Rugby isn't all Twickenham, Lansdowne Road and international matches. It's also tiny clubs in far-flung places. Our rugby correspondent, and artist John Thirsk, visited one such place.

by John Hopkins

It was windy, but not enough to bend the 20-ton girders that thrust vertically from the jetties where the oil tankers will soon berth to load up with crude oil, but enough to create ripples on the pools of water that stood on the pitch. Underfoot, the mud squelched. On the touchline, spectators huddled together. Both cross-bars were broken and hung down disconsolately.

It was the last rugby game of the season on the Shetlands, and Sullom Voe Wanderers were playing LJK Mushrooms at Ollaberry, a few miles from the most north-easterly extremity of the British Isles. "You wanna know about LJK Mushrooms?" Archie had asked. "Och well, we're the champions. We're the Triple Crown holders. We've beaten the other three teams up here." He grinned and walked off.

Geoff Savage, a Sullom Voe Wanderer, smiled and then said in his thick Liverpool accent: "They're called the Mushrooms because they sprang up overnight, and everybody throws abuse over them."

Rugby in the Shetlands is a triumph against the odds, like the oil terminal itself, hewn in three years out of a bleak mountainside at Sullom Voe. There are three civilian teams, all made up from the 5,000 men who work at the oil terminal. The fourth team is from RAF Saxavord. There are six rugby balls, two referees and three pitches. Sullom Voe Wanderers, who wear the black jerseys of the New Zealanders and thus call themselves the Oil Blacks, play at Brae on a muddy pitch on the edge of a large inlet.

Savage and several others founded the Wanderers three years ago. It was the first rugby club on the Shetlands. Savage, who played for Warrington before moving north, gazed fondly down at the Brae pitch: "At first it was word of mouth around the construction village. I had to go into the canteen and ask if anyone had ever played rugby. If they had, then I picked them.

"The first game we ever played was on that pitch and was in the worst conditions I have ever played in. There were six inches of mud, and once the ball was blown out into the Voe, and we had to row a boat out to get it back.

By tradition, team secretaries are the most long-suffering of officials, coping with one excuse after another with good-natured humour, but those in the Shetlands face unusual problems.

Almost all the men at the terminal have left wives and families behind in a single-minded attempt to earn money as quickly as possible. Working an average of 80 hours, they can clear £150 a week. But their life is so hard and solitary that they work four weeks on and one week off, returning home in charter aircraft. Even when Savage knows a player is not on leave, he has no guarantee that the man will turn up.

But those who do, show an enthusiasm that can be measured in the amount of money they lose from their wage packets. Tony Rogers, a curly-haired Welshman who drives an excavator, loses £36 when he plays a game; Andy Hall, a tall young civil engineer who is the Wanderers' leading goal-kicker, not much less.

Wednesday evenings, a keep fit class is held at the new gymnasium in one of the two villages where the men are housed. Denis Tarrant, a former Parachute Regiment PTI with broad shoulders and distinguished silver hair, takes the class. Soon he has John Christi, Gordon Mories and Colin Munt dripping with sweat.

After doing their exercises, Steve Fogg and Andy Hall head back to the changing room. "Our team is different," says Hall. "The younger ones are more interested in money, and the older ones want a bit of exercise. We have to balance the two." Adds scrum-half Jeff Lunt: "What you end up with are young, unfit three-quarters and elderly, wise forwards." The match between Wanderers and Mushrooms ended the season in typical fashion. Wanderers led 6–0 for most of the game, only to concede a penalty and a late try that was converted. "Never mind," said Savage, "we'll get them next year." *November 5 1978*

Colin.

Passion for sport

Barbara Cartland had just finished a book about men and their passion for sport. It seemed an excellent time to ask her about women and sport.

by Rob Hughes

● *What do you think of the willingness of many women to become sports widows?*

Women are silly asses if they become sports widows. If you've got a husband who's a terrific football fan, the sooner you learn about football the better. A woman's job in life is to inspire men.

● *Do you still take part in any sports?*

Oh dear! I don't actually wave my legs around my head if that's what you mean, because I simply haven't time. If you live with men as I've always done, because I have two brothers as well as two sons, you soon find that nobody actually *wants* a woman to show off. They want to show off to you.

Steve.　Geoff　Andy Tony　John.　Jeff

● *What sports have you tried?*

I played tennis, rather feebly; I used to swim, badly, but I must admit I do *fish* rather well—salmon fishing. My daughter (Lady Dartmouth) has been terribly athletic and my mother, who's now 95, played cricket. She was a very good bowler, but I think women look fools playing cricket and football. Women's *real* sport is chasing men.

● *Can a woman athlete protect her femininity?*

I think you can be feminine. It is a mental thing. Olga Korbut is feminine, but that is pure ballet. And the little girl tennis player with ribbons in her hair (Evonne Goolagong), she's frightfully feminine too. But women slow up tennis. And it's unbecoming, all that sweating. Ann Jones did nothing for herself as a woman, and Virginia Wade— she tries her best, doesn't she?

● *You once said the two best exercises are making love and dancing. . .*

Quite true. You can't find another exercise which uses every muscle in your body. Dancing is marvellous, particularly if taken out of doors, and I suppose you could say the same for making love. Making love exercises simply everything . . . the mind, the body and the soul and the heart, so it's a jolly good idea.

● *Should one indulge in sex before sport?*

The old-fashioned idea that you refrain is exploded. It was Goethe who said he couldn't write after he'd made love, and it's a lot of nonsense. Sex should be invigorating unless there's something wrong with you.

● *Can sport ruin a woman's sex life?*

It's well known that athletes in strenuous sports are not usually such good lovers because they channel their energy into sport so much.

● *Does it turn you on to see a muscular male athlete in action?*

Absolutely not. I think if a man is very beautiful and looks like Michelangelo's David one admires him. But women aren't excited by naked men. I once asked women if in erotic dreams their lovers were dressed

"Making love exercises everything."

or undressed. Every single one said dressed, in full regimental boots if possible.

● *How then do you explain sales of pin-up pictures of Mark Spitz in swimming trunks?*

The only people I can imagine looking at them are men.　*May 6 1973*

A celebration of the past: nourishment from the grassroots

During the closing months of 1975, *The Sunday Times* Sporting Ballad competition attracted more than 500 entries. The art of ballad-making, though, demanded more skill than at first appeared, and some of the earlier entries did not conform to the conventions—the most important being that you should have a tune in mind while writing to ensure that the verse retains a regular rhythm. Many chose to embroider round themes of the great figures, like Ali, Arkle or Tom Finney, but the best celebrated an unsung hero: Joe Ackroyd, the everyman of dignified sporting endeavour. A luncheon was held at the Savoy to fete the winner, Derek Foster. He revealed that Joe Ackroyd was modelled, with fond respect, on Bobby Robson, the manager of Ipswich Town, who was brought up, like Foster, in the Durham village of Langley Park. After the presentation of £100 and a silver salver, the judges, including Scottish comedian Billy Connolly, joined Geordie pop composer Alan Price, who had set the lyric to music as part of the prize, and assembled round a handy piano where a rousing rendition of the Ballad of Joe Ackroyd shook the chandeliers.   Music © Jarrow Music Ltd.

Verse 2

I once knew a man called Joe Ackroyd
There was Joe with a bat in his hand
If he played a good shot he'd be clapped like as not
By the other side's Joes in the stand
And this Joe never ripped up a Test pitch
Nor slashed carriage seats for the hell
If he did he got thrashed, but the once was his last
Now I know you remember him well

Verse 3

I once knew a man called Joe Ackroyd
There was Joe who played hard on the wing
Though he wasn't George Best but like all of the rest
He would play for the love of the thing
He could play any place from eleven
The idol of each breathless fan
For he'd not take the man with the ball at his feet
But the ball from the feet of the man

An investment in the future: sowing seeds of sportsmanship

Terry Delahunty, headmaster of Long Lane Junior School in Warrington, fights a campaign against victory being considered more important than playing the game. Most of the children understand this philosophy of sportsmanship, some are slower to believe. Eight-year-old Ian Chatters confronts Debbie Williams, a year older and already a guardian of the ideology.

Ian: "I play to win. Sometimes I get mad and tell t'ref off. Teacher, Mrs Clarke, says: 'Shut up and get on with t' game.'"

Debbie: "Arguing is stupid! If you don't think it's right, well you can try again!"

Ian: "Not if it's last match."

Debbie: "You can win the cup next year."

Ian: "Not if it's a better team the next year you can't."

Debbie: "Yes you can. Your team might be better itself. Anyway you can't win by blaming the ref."

Ian: "Sometimes you can. If the ref's one of our players, you get him to let you score. If he's one of theirs, they do the same."

Debbie: "That's just cheating!"

Ian: "It's not."

Debbie: "That's just cheating!"

Ian: "What about rounders, then? There are no referees in that, so you can cheat if you want."

Debbie: "We don't . . . Cheats shouldn't play." *May 25 1975*

Inside track

The Shrinks

Two California psychologists have driven a plough through the "playing fields of Eton" theory that sport builds character. The pair, known as The Shrinks to their subjects, are Professors Bruce Ogilvie and Thomas Tutko of San Diego State College, who surveyed some 15,000 sportsmen over eight year before publishing their results in the current issue of Psychology Today. It makes grim reading, chaps.

"The personality of the ideal sportsman is not the result of any moulding process," they begin, "but comes out of the ruthless selection process that occurs at all levels of sport." The Shrinks go on to debunk the myth that sportsmen are natural leaders. On the contrary, they claim, sportsmen have a "low need to take care of others."

The pair claim, furthermore, that "competition doesn't seem to build character, and it is possible that competition doesn't even *require* much more than a minimally integrated personality." From this, The Shrinks' conclusion flows naturally. "Sports competition has no more beneficial effects (on character-building) than intense endeavour in any other fields."

It comes as no surprise to read elsewhere that The Shrinks were turned down when they applied to become psychology consultants to the US Olympic team.

October 10 1971

PICTURE FILE

Given that the British love to queue, many would still say that this was ridiculous. The fact that Charlie George on the right has been first to head the ball away, while teammate George Graham and opponent John Hollins must make do with *almost* being "in the right place at the right time." The players, intensely involved at this moment, will also, later, have relished viewing this photograph. All sport is something of a stage performance, whether public or private, professional or amateur, and as the pictures on the following pages show, it can evoke pleasure and humour even without resort to the so-called lighter moments.

Yachtsman Edward Heath on top of the world: at least, on top of Morning Cloud. The skipper will find that the brand-new ocean racing yacht, with below-deck accommodation, adds a new dimension to his previous hobby of dinghy racing.

Lacrosse goalkeeper Barbara Dobson on top of her job and ready for anything, including inactivity. Her ''shut out'' of Scotland in England's 13–0 win means that a cold winter's afternoon in 1975, not conducive to standing still, is made even colder.

Stan Mellor is not talking to his horse, nor is he addressing the riders in front of him: he's just demonstrating that in order to achieve anything, including success as a steeplechase jockey, it all depends how you hold your mouth.

Whatever Julie Heldman may have been saying to herself, the dialogue is almost at an end: for the New York girl, a centre court appearance at Wimbledon is ending in defeat.

Intensely silent thoughts by England bowler Jill Cruwys as she contemplates her Australian adversaries, and works on a plan for spinning them out at Old Trafford.

It's easier in the air—as the young Gareth Edwards, one of rugby's great scrum halves, demonstrates with his dive pass.

It's prettier in the air—as an Arabian Cartwheel is performed by Canadian figure skater Karen Magnussen.

Above: It's more impressive to get the feet up in the air—as golfer Gary Player demonstrates in the Wentworth clubhouse.

Left: Sometimes the only way is to go by air—but even so, Graham Stilwell can't make this return against Arthur Ashe.

London Irish and Richmond forwards attempt to fashion something from a line-out. Even the players do not always claim that rugby is the most orderly of team games. Indeed, when the struggle is later recollected—in the bar—such moments may be remembered with affection.

The race may indeed be to the swift, but whether the best beast will win is another matter. Uncle Bing and Brown Lad have to carry J. Francome and T. Carberry respectively. The swan carries no weight and, furthermore, doesn't have to jump Kempton Park's open ditch.

With any luck, this may be the perfect partnership. Gordon Jackson, a Kent farmer, blasts away at a hill in a Trials contest, while passenger Peggy, his "bouncer", works away manfully to concentrate weight on the spinning rear wheels.

3

SUPERSTARS

It is a modern idiom but not a new idea – the sporting superstar, the hero with an extra dimension which totally transcends his activity and communicates itself to the spectator. An electrifying quality, it is part intelligence, part arrogance of a lesser or greater degree, part a feeling for humanity that is not necessarily even expressed in words, and only partly related to the performance. Thus a superstar retains his fervent following even when he is on the wane or retired. There have been few female superstars, Billie Jean King springing most readily to mind, but as the times become more liberated, the prospects are enhanced. Meanwhile, here is a small band who have particularly impressed The Sunday Times over the years.

Muhammad Ali, the living legend at work

Henry Cooper's initials could stand for honesty and character, and those are certainly the attributes which have endeared him to the British people. He established himself as British, Commonwealth and **European heavyweight boxing champion, and had a superb left hook in 'Enery's 'Ammer which all but demolished Muhammad Ali, The Greatest. He was, in fact, the acceptable face of British boxing.**

The way Henry Cooper was made

In his fighting days, Henry Cooper used to struggle out of bed at 3.45 in the morning and jog through the dawn, but now, aged 43 and retired from the ring, he sleeps till a reasonable hour. At his home in Hendon, North London, one morning last week, he got up at 7.30, had tea, toast and orange juice, drove his two young sons to school and returned to look at his post. It included nine fan letters—about average for the day—all of which he will answer with an autographed photograph. "I got one of them signature stamps," he said, "but people like you to sign your autographs by hand."

Cooper, six years an ex-boxer, is a modest man, and finds it hard to explain his enduring popularity as probably the most beloved British sports figure since the war. "The public either takes to a person or they don't and, thank God, they took to me," he said. "I don't know why, perhaps it was because if I had a bad fight I used to admit I stunk the joint out. If you put on airs and graces, you'll come unstuck. I once seen a footballer, I won't name him, who told a little kid to f—— off. Blimey, that geezer not only lost a fan but, by the time the story got around, I bet he lost a *neighbourhood* of fans."

Over the next couple of days Henry Cooper, OBE, will visit several children's Jubilee parties. That is nicely appropriate, because this year Cooper himself celebrates his own sort of Silver Jubilee. In 1952 he won his first boxing title, the Amateur Boxing Association's light-heavyweight crown. "I beat Joe Maclean, a big raw Scots guy, in the final," he recalled. "He didn't have a lot of finesse, and I knew I could beat him. I stayed clear, and knocked him silly with the old trombone left hand—boom, boom, boom."

Cooper smiled. He drove his blue Opel towards Central London. He was dressed impeccably in a blue check suit, a regally red-white-and-blue tie, a small gold watch and black Italian shoes. The air tingled with the smell of men's cologne. At 14st 5lb, about 11

Henry Cooper: "I look back at me life and I always say whatever I done I would do it again. I don't think I made any big mistakes. I think we done it right."

pounds more than he weighed in 1971, when he fought his last fight (against Joe Bugner). "I'm a burner, I can eat and drink what I like, and burn it all up. When I was in training it used to come off too quickly."

by Dudley Doust

At a traffic light, a motorist gazed over, nudged his wife. Those famous craggy eyebrows, a legacy of his raw-boned mother, also showed signs of countless amateur and 55 professional fights, despite the efforts of his peerless "cut man" Danny Holland. "Blimey, the advice we used to get about them scar tissues! Take a jar of pickled onions, take the onions out, and use the vinegar. Piddle in a bottle, let it cool down and use your own urine. All sorts of herbs. Crank tips—but people meant well."

We were on our way to a cosmetic trade show at the Royal Lancaster Hotel and, providentially, a billboard appeared at Swiss Cottage. It depicted Henry Cooper and Barry Sheene, the motorcycle star, plugging a men's

cologne. "I used to use a cheap spirit-rub to tone myself up, and close up the pores after a fight," said Cooper. "So these cologne people, who was looking for a guy who could be stripped to the waist legitimate, got on to me. Pretty soon they put me in a bathroom, and I'm splashing the stuff all about and telling people how good it is."

Cooper is a regular BBC fight commentator and a sports-quiz panellist, a Lloyd's underwriter, a director of an insurance brokerage firm, and indefatigable fete-opener, but Fabergé takes the lion's share of his time. "Since we've had Henry, things have been lovely," says a company official. "He's the man who knocked Ali on the seat of his pants."

That fabled blow, a left hook, is the high point of post-war British boxing. It came on June 18, 1963, in the fourth round at Wembley. In his autobiography, The Greatest, Ali claims he was distracted at that instant by Elizabeth Taylor screaming at the ringside. Down, Ali was saved by the bell at the count of four. "Back in my corner, Angelo (Dundee, his trainer) discovered that the seam of my boxing glove was busted," writes Ali. "The cushion was coming out, and the rules and regulations in boxing are strict—the gloves must be in good condition. It took nearly a minute to make the replacement."

That minute, in Cooper's view was the crucial minute of the fight "It gave Ali another minute to recover which, to a hurt fighter, is a lifetime," he said.

Cooper shrugged. "In our second fight, at Arsenal Stadium in 1966, Ali had learned so much off the first fight that when I got him close, to go to work on him, oh boy, it was like being in a vice. The first three rounds I was falling just short with my left and, in the last rounds, when I was beginning to get the distance, my bleedin' eye slit open. The referee had to stop the fight in the sixth. So what can you do? It was a physical thing. If I had had negroid features, all round and smooth, maybe I'd have been the champion."

Mild, gentle and likeable outside the

GREAT MINDS THIN

Fabergé on Cooper: "Since we've had Henry, things have been lovely."

ring, Cooper was known to be hard on his sparring partners, vicious in battle. He agrees. "The real thrill in boxing is when you hit the other geezer on the whiskers and you see that look in his eyes, that blank, dead look. Some people say, 'Watch the legs, the knees.' That's rubbish. The eyes tell you everything and in a split second you know he's gone and he'll never get up and its marvellous."

We were driving to Ealing Golf Club, Cooper's club, and the only sports moment he could compare to a knock-out blow, at least for pure exhilaration, was to hit a drive "right out of

the screws." And 280 yards. He plays to a handicap of 12, and like most left-handers, probably *all* left-handed boxers, he plays a big, roundhouse slice. He duck-hooked one that day, when a passing schoolboy shouted while he was on his backswing.

"He put me off, yeah, but not for the rest of the day," he said. "I've always said that there was more tension in boxing than in golf because golfers bring it on themselves. After all, that golf ball is never coming up and belting you in the whiskers, is it?"

There was no arguing and, besides, we had a session booked with the

photographer. Cooper, helpful as ever, endured the afternoon and returned home for tea. His wife, Italian-born Albina, fixed him a plate of prosciutto and a glass of red wine, and then he collected the boys, Henry Marco, aged 14 and John Pietro, nine, from school. Cooper returned for more Fabergé meeting and greeting in the evening before dining at home with his wife on grilled sole and a green salad. "I look back at me life and I always say whatever I done I would do it again," said Henry Cooper, a contented man. "I don't think I made any big mistakes. I think we done it right." *June 5 1977*

Inside track

Milburn's Injury

It must have occurred to all of us: could a transplanted eye replace the one that cricketer Colin Milburn lost last weekend in a motor accident?

"Not in the foreseeable future," says physiologist Michael Gaze, dismissing the exaggerated eye transplant claims recently made by an American in Houston. "Eyes have been replanted in newts and frog tadpoles, but not yet in mammals."

Dr Gaze leads a team engaged in the world's most ambitious eye-brain connection research, now being done at Edinburgh University. "There are two reasons the transplant doesn't work in mammals," he says, "one is immunological rejection and the other, more basic, is that in a mammal the fibres of a severed optic nerve do not regenerate and re-attach themselves to the brain."

Astonishingly, in newts and tadpoles they do. A Swiss zoologist cut the optic nerve of a newt 45 years ago and found that the thousands of fibres grew back again in a seemingly hopeless tangle, only to sort themselves out. Each fixed itself into its proper place in the brain. Vision returned.

Later, an American established that the regenerating fibres used a "shotgun approach" towards the mating with their appropriate brain cell partners. "What we're trying to do now with newts and tadpoles," says Dr Gaze, "is to discover how these fibres get back to their proper places. The selection appears to be both a chemical and a hereditary process. We haven't even begun work on mammals."

On a simpler level, Dr Robert Weale of London's Institute of Ophthalmology explains that Milburn's loss of three-dimensional vision reduces his effective depth perception about tenfold. Are there visual compensations? "His one eye will learn to read the other clues to distance," says Dr Weale, "the intensities of colours for instance and shadow delineations and he'll probably develop a sharpening sense of size. A cricket batsman is so familiar with an approaching ball that he relates its distance to its size. That will help Milburn."

June 11 1969

● Brian Chorley is a wing-forward for Old Windsorians RFC with a good tale to tell at the club bar. Playing against Camberley, his head and an opponent's face hit so violently that Brian was taken away to be stitched up and the other man left minus three teeth. Even after the stitches had been removed the Chorley cranium was left with a bump. One day he scratched his head over a tactical problem and dislodged an enemy tooth.   *February 27 1972*

The steam-fitter's apprentice who went seven up on the wide world of golf

Tony Jacklin's solo flight at the end of the 1960s saved British, and perhaps European, golf from drowning in its own sorrows. Just when it seemed that the US had ensured a complete monopoly, the working-class boy from Scunthorpe upped and matched the might of America, winning the Open championships on each side of the Atlantic in successive years.

by Henry Longhurst

Contrary to what all the commentators, including myself, have written and said, our golfing hero of last week is not the third but the *first* Englishman to win the US Open championship. The other two, Vardon and Ray, as a pained reader from that island points out, were Jerseymen. British, yes! . . . English, never! Whatever the nationality, however, Jacklin's victory was the most remarkable single episode I have seen in golf and still has an air of unreality about it.

For an outsider to win the US Open is unlikely enough. To win it by seven shots in a field containing every one of the world's best golfers is like the conjurer's final trick—not only extremely difficult, ladies and gentlemen, but actually impossible.

Jacklin's win was set up on the first day when blasts of up to 40 mph swept treacherously through the trees and blew away the rest of the field, great and small, like chaff. He led with a 71, the quality of which may be judged by the fact that no-one managed 72 and only four managed 73. He followed it with a 70, itself beaten by only five players.

This meant that he went out last at 2.30 and here the pressure really did begin to build up. But in the end it was Jacklin's putter that did it. In the third round, he holed one after the other from eight feet or less and what might have been 76 became another 70.

You have to have a bit of luck somewhere to win at golf and on the last day Jacklin had it on the ninth. He had missed a short one on the sixth, which at last did seem to unsettle him; he dropped shots on each of the next two holes and the gap between him and America's Dave Hill, playing just in front, narrowed ominously.

What saved the day, a turning point if ever there was one, was his putt on the ninth, perhaps 25ft or more. The ball raced towards the hole and one just had time to think, "Oh, Lord, here comes three putts and the beginning of the end," when it hit the back of the hole, jumped six inches in the air and disappeared.

Thereafter victory was a certainty and I do hope you sat up to watch the

Pieces of Jacklin's puzzle to try out on your own

Your swing telegraphs your eventual shot, and top pros suggest that the swing comprises parts of a puzzle which must be progressively solved. Here is artist Paul Trevillion's interpretation of the Jacklin swing.

 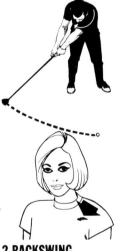   

1 ADDRESS
Tony Jacklin makes a point of moving his hips back into a semi-sitting position at address. Getting the hips out of the way in this manner allows a free passage for the arms through the hitting area. It also places your body weight in a position evenly balanced between the balls of your feet and the heels. These are two vital factors which eliminate the possible fault of falling into the shot at impact.

2 BACKSWING
In the backswing, the correct shoulder turn as executed by Tony Jacklin should start with the left shoulder coming down until it is eventually under the chin. Unfortunately many golfers, especially women, have the bad habit of turning on too flat a plane. One tip, ladies, is to look at your left shoulder. If there are lipstick marks, your shoulder is not going under your chin.

3 TOP OF BACKSWING
With his right elbow pointing to the ground. Tony Jacklin takes the copybook position at the top of his backswing. To check if you do this, try swinging without a club and stopping at the top of your backswing. Now see if you can hold a tray in the right hand. You will only be able to do this if your elbow is pointing correctly to the ground.

4 IMPACT
By keeping his head still and in position behind the ball, Jacklin increases the whipping action of the clubhead at impact. This principle applies when a vehicle brakes suddenly. The person who stands still receives a powerful forward jolt, whereas moving in unison lessens the impact. So it is with golf. If your head moves forward into the shot, you will lose a lot of power.

5 FOLLOW THROUGH
At the completion of his swing, Tony Jacklin's belt buckle faces the target. If, at the completion of your follow through, your belt position points to the right of the target, you have restricted your hips during the hitting area. Correspondingly, if it points left of target, you have swung through with too loose an action. To hit straight ahead your body must point straight ahead.

triumphant finish via the satellite and to note the tremendous hand our British champion was given by the American gallery.

Jacklin is wiry and tough, both mentally and physically, and he will need to be with what faces him! Flying home on the night plane, you arrive at about 3 a.m. and put the clock on five hours, so that instead of bedtime it is 8 a.m. and the start of a bright new day. Younger men than I find that it takes at least two days to recover.

Jacklin's plane arrived at Heathrow, London, about half an hour before mine and he had had, said the porter, as we threaded our way between the massed Indians and Pakistanis and their worldly goods, a wonderful reception. After all this, he got into a fast car and drove all the way to Scunthorpe.

From now on he will be like an election candidate, "giving" and "giving" till there is nothing left in the battery, not for three hectic weeks but for months, maybe years, as Palmer has done.

By no means unfortunate in Jacklin's success has been Mark McCormack, who undertook to manage him long before he won the British Open, let alone the American.

McCormack now has on his hands the hottest commercial property in golf and we may expect to see Jacklin endorsing anything from jet aeroplanes to liquorice allsorts.

I shall not, I am sure, be queering the pitch if I marvel at people with figures like mine rushing to buy, say, trousers that look well on Jacklin or Player or Palmer. But the fact is that they do, in tens of thousands, otherwise the manufacturers would not ante-up.

Jacklin said in America that the British Open had made him financially independent for life. Now money no longer means anything. Indeed, like royalty and the late Lord Castlerosse, Jacklin now need never deign to carry any. If he wants six Aston Martins, let them be sent round—and so it will go on. No taxes to worry about. Everything will have been taken care of by McCormack's offices, all over the world.

All this at 25 years of age—and only 10 years ago a steam-fitter's apprentice in a steelworks at Scunthorpe! Let me say simply that it could not have happened to a better man, nor to one more likely to take the same size in hats in 10 years' time.   *June 28 1970*

What happened when Mammon met up with a tiring Tony

The aftermath of Jacklin's elevation to golfing greatness was testing to say the least. Commercial off-course commitments bore down on him at the same time as a critical public perused his progress, or lack of it, through a crowded tournament programme.

by Henry Longhurst

Returning after more than three weeks in the States, exhausted as usual, I am distressed to find myself the target of hostile comment on account of the headline of my last despatch from Tulsa, Oklahoma. "Jacklin," this read, "should be immune from rounds of 79." Reasons of space naturally enough caused the omission of my original words "on this course"—i.e. the par-70 Southern Hills.

The fact was that in his first two appearances in America after winning their Open he had failed to make the cut, in other words to finish in the first 60 after two rounds.

The contracts continue to pour in via the ubiquitous Mark McCormack, who is absolutely ruthless, and so he should be, in securing the maximum for his client. The client, however, has to give of himself in return—dinners, personal appearances, photographic sessions, approving numerous articles and instructional strips (if indeed he

"The only hope for Jacklin, if he is not to become a puppet golfer dangled incessantly and ineffectually from one tournament to another, is to separate entirely the businessman and the golfer."

ever sees them), making TV commercials, and heaven knows what else.

I do not myself think it made any difference to the Open at St. Andrews, but he had also contracted to play an 18-hole television match two days after the Open and by the time this was finished—in a very strong wind—he really had "had" golf. He was going to Henry Cotton's resort course in the Algarve he said, and was simply going to lie in the sun for 10 days.

I could almost swear that he said he

would not even take his clubs, but now I see in an article by Cotton that they "played together a number of times" and that Jacklin insisted on playing off the very back tees, scarcely ever used and making a course of 7,500 yards. This is not "lying in the sun."

So he returned to America on August 2 to New York, where the stink of exhaust gases is rapidly rendering life intolerable and where on the clearest, brightest day the sky is still grey and children are growing up who decline to believe the fairy-tale about it once being blue.

In this atmosphere he spent August 3 on business and at a prestige cocktail party given by one of his sponsors. Next day he flew to Akron, Ohio, and on the following day played in the preliminary "pro-am", one of the most tedious trials for a well-known professional, partnering three amateurs, being affable with them all and taking five and a half hours. Next day he played in the 150,000 dollar tournament and failed to make the cut.

Off he flew to Tulsa and after one day's practice played in the PGA championship and again failed to make the cut, taking the 79 about which I appear to have given such unwitting offence. So off to Sutton, Massachusetts, one day's rest, another pro-am, and, starting last Thursday, another 160,000 dollar tournament—and as I write this very sentence we learn that once again for the third time the US Open champion has failed to make the cut, this time with a round of 78.

So off he goes this weekend to New York for more business and television commercials, then a practice day for the Dow-Jones tournament with a record 300,000 dollars in prize money, then a pro-am, then the tournament. After which he flies home for the John Player tournament at Nottingham, flies back to Akron, Ohio, for the world series (a four-man affair, first prize 50,000 dollars, for the winners of the British and US Opens, the Masters and the PGA—Nicklaus, Jacklin, Casper and Stockton), then back to Britain for two more tournaments, then, believe it or not, away to Australia for two more, and thence, via San Francisco, to Buenos Aires for what used to be the Canada Cup and is now, since becoming a sponsored event, known as the World Cup.

This just cannot go on for ever and, though the millions may be assured in the end, some of the contracts are only

A fan wrote to Jacklin: "It's not your fault. It's the ball's."

for a year or so and will not survive constant oblivion at golf. Is it humanly possible to carry out the schedules arranged by McCormack and still play golf like a champion?

The only hope I can see for Jacklin, if he is not to become a puppet golfer dangled incessantly and ineffectually from one tournament and one business meeting to another, is to separate entirely, both in mind and body, Jacklin the businessman and Jacklin the golfer.

That is to say, he should arrive four days before the tournament and immediately in his mind *turn pro* again. No business, no calls from the Cleveland office, no adulation, no official parties—only business in the sense of being a professional golfer. It might work. The present life threatens to kill his golfing image stone dead.

August 23 1970

Why the faithful keep on following

"Follow that", they say in the theatre, and Tony Jacklin couldn't. But his supporters remained utterly loyal.

by Dudley Doust

The Jacklin fan, wearing close-cropped hair and a faded cotton pullover, had taken the day off and drifted over to Walton Heath last week for a look at the European Open. "The guv'nor knows I'm here," he said. "He knows I'm a Jacklin fanatic."

The fan now stood in the crowded gallery and gloomily watched his man line up a short putt. "Look at him, sweating like a pig," he whispered.

"What I'd like to do is put my hand on his shoulder and say, 'Look, old son, forget the bloody ball. Just hit it, it'll go down'."

Finally Jacklin hit it. It didn't go down. The fan swore through his teeth at the ball and jockeyed towards the next tee. There is an element of Jacklin followers who blame the ball. Jacklin himself is touched and amused by them. "I had a letter from this bloke in Scotland the other day," he said. "'Don't worry,' he wrote, 'it's not your fault. It's the ball's.' He went on for 10 pages explaining that no two golf balls had the same centre of gravity and that's why my putts veer away."

Jacklin's current miseries are the subject of intense study among the learned, of whom there are many, in his galleries. Over a stretch of only a few holes last week you found two former assistant professionals, both of whom oddly had quit the game, and a local teaching professional. Both erstwhile assistants noticed Jacklin walks slowly on to a green while the old pro, skipping the psycho-analysis, insisted that all mental faults stem from technical faults. He was looking for these.

Looking for nothing special, but wise and aware, the evergreen Argentine Roberto de Vicenzo played the two opening rounds with Jacklin. When pressed, he too took a view. "Tony is striking the ball as good now as ever I see him," he said, "but he no longer the optimist. He the pessimist."

The fan in the faded pullover, now beside the tee, waited for de Vicenzo and Jacklin's other partner, John Mahaffey, to drive. Meanwhile, he defined the undeniable magic that cements Tony Jacklin to his amazingly loyal followers: "He's one of us. His parents didn't have the money that Oosterhuis's did and, I dunno, I just can't *feel* for Faldo." It seemed even Jacklin's suffering served the purpose: All Human Life Was There.

Jacklin now teed up. He gritted his teeth and, attacking as he has done down the years, he sent his drive whistling down the fairway. The fan grabbed your shoulders and wrenched you round to follow the flight of the ball. "Look at that! From tee to green he's still the best in the world. It's you Press lads wot put him off. You wait, once he gets sorted out on the greens, Tony'll win us another Open."

With that the fan was away, tramping hopefully through the heather.

October 22 1978

Men whose memories shall live on when all else withers

Even amongst stars there are the few who stand alone. On this page, Robin Marlar comments on Geoffrey Boycott's dismissal by Yorkshire; opposite, Dudley Doust records Arnold Palmer in reflective mood, and Rob Hughes bids farewell to the incomparable Pele.

● Et tu Yorkshire? This weekend England's greatest cricketer may be forgiven for wishing he was as dead as Rome's most famous Emperor. Instead, he is holed up in a dark corner of his proud county trying to staunch a bleeding heart and still a tormented mind.

Poor Geoffrey. Was it for this that he exiled himself from England's dressing room? Was it because of his responsibilities to this institution, the Yorkshire County Cricket Club, that he handed back the Packer contract?

For all his ambition he is not one of nature's leaders and so the absence of Cups these past seven years is at least understandable. Not that it is solely Boycott's fault that the Yorks team has been sub-standard. The policy not to import players, a longstanding aloofness from the grassroots, only recently cured, and an inability to find adequate fast bowlers, are as much to blame.

A talk with John Temple, Yorkshire's chairman of committee, is to see the captain's agony mirrored in that of the wider group. "That it should come in the week when he has lost his mother is a dreadful second blow but then this is the meeting at which the club has always considered the captaincy and we felt we had to make a change. We sincerely want him to stay with us."

Consider now the new man Hampshire. As a player with most of his career behind him he is not a batsman, in my opinion, fit to step into the boots of a Boycott. Equipped with far more natural talent Hampshire has to look back over many seasons of wasted potential; to Boycott's supporters he must look like Claudius after Hamlet.

Boycott will prove himself a big and forgiving man indeed if he can eventually cure his disappointment and stay with Yorkshire. *October 1 1978*

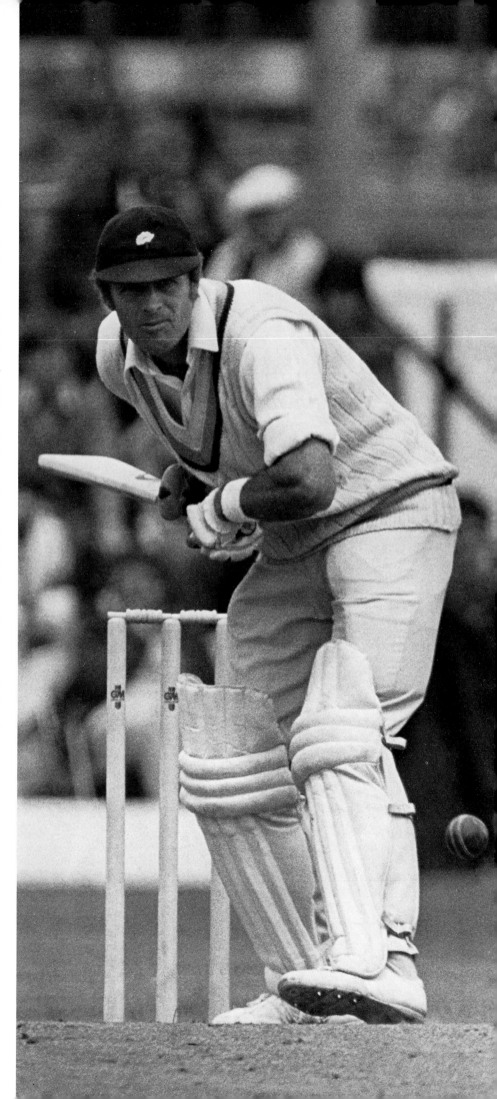

Boycott: getting into line.

• At 42, Palmer is a step slower than he was when he first came to Europe. His face has turned leathery under too many suns. His back creaks and he is 1½ stones heavier. His concentration tends sometimes to falter. "Maybe for a while in the late Sixties my will to win wasn't as strong." He smiles. Yet in 1971 Palmer already has won four major tournaments and, among the Americans, only Trevino can sing such a song.

"I guess I finally got tired of not playing well," Palmer said. He was re-wrapping the leather grip of his pitching wedge. "This year I am trying to analyse my game, emotionally and technically. What I'm trying to do is get ready for the Masters next spring."

"What did I do in '62 when I won it? I played well. I drove well. But am I driving as well now?" Palmer simply wasn't certain of this. "Is it bothering me subconsciously, because I'm not hitting the ball as far? Or is it a matter of somebody hitting it farther. The driver doesn't always feel right."

Palmer feels he could have been the governor of Pennsylvania today. "I could have got the Republican nomination two years ago and, almost certainly, I would have been elected." He laughed.   *October 17 1971*

• Pele as the world remembers him: soaring salmon-like above every skill and tension football has known. Was there ever a sportsman who exuded pure joy, or communicated enthusiasm so often and so lastingly? Throughout 22 years the thrill of scoring, the right-fist salute, raised him off his feet after 1,280 goals in 1,362 games.

"The ability to make something out of nothing," is how Pele—born Edson Arantes do Nascimento—describes his gift. From now on, memory and film are all we shall have to recapture what Pele did better than all the rest. Superlatives won't embellish that.

He left the game with that mixture of tears and happiness which comes naturally to him. Today the ache of withdrawal will begin to seep through to a man who it seemed forever had a ball, and thus the world, at his feet.

Football became the language of his life. Now he must come out into the real world, and it is perhaps the supreme paradox that whereas Pele grew into very much a man, the truly sustaining quality has been that of a child to invent; to believe in fantasy, and make it happen before our eyes.

October 2 1977

Pele: man-child who moved the world.

Inside track

Aaaa — hh!

Tarzan, aged 68, recently swung down out of the past to bellow about swimming. "I was better than Mark Spitz," said Johnny Weismuller, the former film star who now runs a swimming pool business in Florida. "I never lost an event in my life. Even when I was swimming at the YMCA."

At the Paris Games in 1924 and in Amsterdam in 1928, freestyler Weismuller competed in only five events. He won them all. His Olympic record: five gold medals in the 12 swimming events open to him. All-rounder Spitz, on the other hand, won seven out of a possible 15 gold medals last summer to bring his grand total at Munich and Mexico City to nine golds, a silver and a bronze in 30 possible events. In medal production, then, we'd rate the two great swimmers about a dead heat.

"But," Tarzan continued, "it's easier to go faster now. You don't have to touch with your hand on a turn now and that's worth a fraction of a second. The pools are deeper, the starting blocks higher, so you gain a couple of strokes entering the water." Weismuller's best-ever 100m time, 58.6 secs., nevertheless, is far in the wake of Spitz's 51.2 secs. Tarzans fans can look elsewhere for comfort: Jane's beau held a world record—100 yards in 51 secs—for 17 years and all of Spitz's records surely will sink before this.

Besides, Tarzan won an Olympic bronze medal in water polo and, in our book, that's even more scary than wrestling with alligators.   *December 10 1972*

• Two hot-blooded Italian footballers, playing in the Canadian National League, were recently disciplined for spitting at a referee. One was suspended for 18 months. The other was suspended for four years which, was more than he expectorated. Why such a stiff sentence? "One spit missed," explained a league official, "the other spit hit."   *February 6 1972*

Keegan — the keen kid who got lucky in Liverpool

If ever a footballer achieved stardom through outright honest endeavour, it is Kevin Keegan. His dashing performances on the field won over the men on the terraces, and the hearts of their wives and daughters were claimed by his winsome personality.

by Dudley Doust

Len's Junk Shop, just off Lilley Road in Liverpool, seemed an odd place to look for an idol but there he was in his office at the end of the passage. "Here, take the electric fire," Kevin Keegan said, swinging it over, "your legs may get cold."

Keegan, himself, is pretty hot property. He is Britain's most electrifying player, Liverpool's jumping jack forward, an enchanting little elf who not only enjoys football but can be *seen* to enjoy it. Keegan has literally and figuratively stepped into George Best's boots. The other day he took over many of Best's contracts for footwear.

In Keegan's office there are no windows and the light burns in the daytime. The walls are yellow, the carpet purple. It all seems weird. "This is a dream world," Keegan said of his fame. "This

Bobby Jones, the courteous conqueror of the fairways

They made Bobby Jones a Freeman of St Andrews, whose Old Course became his favourite stamping ground in golf. And the popularity and esteem in which this American was held long outlived his active playing career, in which he won everything there was to win in his era.

by Henry Longhurst

The death of Bobby Jones will have come as a relief not only to his family and the many friends who knew of his final condition, but to himself. If ever

there was a case of the Lord giving with one hand and taking away with another, it was Bobby Jones. He conquered not only everything in the world of golf but the hearts of golfers wherever he played.

His record, including the "impregnable quadrilateral" as his biographer O.B. Keeler called it—the Open and Amateur championships of Britain and the United States in the same year, 1930—together with innumerable other titles, would seem to make him the greatest golfer in the game's history but he himself had the last word on this age-old controversy. "All you can do," he wrote, "is to beat those who are around when you are around. You cannot beat those who came before or those who follow after."

With nothing left to conquer, Jones retired and became a "businessman golfer", thereafter playing wholly for

the pleasure of himself and his friends, but not, alas, for long. Something went wrong with his spine and he underwent an operation, and then another. He went from bad to worse, but until a few years ago was still able to receive his old friends, with a brave heart but in an ever more pitiable condition, during the Masters at Augusta, which, of course, he helped to found. Now at last has come the merciful release.

Though he kept completely up to date with modern golf and methods, Jones was at heart a traditionalist in that he liked foursome play, now unknown in America, and too heavily watered greens, and the Old St Andrews, with which he had what he described in print as a "love story." On his first appearance he tore up his card but thereafter it is a fact that he never lost a tournament or a match thereon.

A particularly moving occasion at St

is a world where everybody sees me as an image, not as a person. Sometimes it's hard to keep in touch with yourself." All that fan mail in the corner? Keegan laughed. "You ought to see some of it. Whooo, is it sexy. You know, 'My measurements are so-and-so, please come to tea.' My girl, Jean, won't answer that stuff. She tells me to answer it myself."

Keegan has a strong, photogenic face: brown eyes, a rebellious stubble of beard, a full helmet of hair. Admirers often try to wipe away the smudgy scar under his eye. "Once I had a little girlfriend. She was fatter than me and when our see-saw broke, the plank went up in my eye." He fingered the scar. "It's like a miner's scar that's never been cleaned. My Dad's back is covered with them."

Keegan, the son of a coal miner, was born in Armthorpe, Yorkshire, and judging by his current mailbag, appropriately on St Valentine's Day. At four, the family soon moved to the centre of Doncaster, "a slum," where Kevin lived in a smell of dubbed leather. "If I couldn't find a friend, a wall was my friend. Head-knee, side-of-the-foot, Head-knee, side-of-the-foot. I'd keep it up until I drove Old Gibby crazy next door."

At primary school, where Kevin's picture now hangs among the crucifixes, Sister Mary Oliver wrote in his report: "Encourage his football." At secondary school, where his photograph hangs under the Pope's, Kevin's headmaster remembered "he was good. He never stole the blackboard duster. If he hadn't taken up football, he had a university intellect." Keegan mustered O levels in history and art.

Keegan tried out for Coventry City, failed, and at 15 played reserve football for Pegler's Brassworks in Doncaster. "I thought I was destined to be a good Sunday League player. That was my ambition." At 16, and 5ft 2in tall, a scout found Keegan for Scunthorpe United. "Kev was so keen," recalled Scunthorpe's trainer, Jack Brownsword, "that two days a week we had to send him home from training." He was happy. Perched on a director's knee, he acted a ventriloquist's dummy on the team bus. "But over the next couple of seasons Kev grew frustrated," Brownsword said. "None of our players could read him fast enough."

Arsenal, Millwall and other clubs showed interest. But nobody fetched Keegan up from the darkness. "I finally told Jack I was quitting," Keegan recalled, "and he said 'wait.' Liverpool was after me." In March 1971, Bill Shankly paid £35,000 for Keegan.

Keegan begged out of dinner. He had an award to bestow. "The more you do," Keegan said, "the more you get asked to do. I'm not complaining. I like most of it. I just wish they'd ask some of the other lads." Keegan in recent days has played Father Christmas at an Approved School, attended a Barmitzvah and visited a boy in hospital who is doomed with leukemia.

During that visit, Keegan took over a draughts game between a Sister and another bedridden boy. "I could see that the Sister was trying to lose it," he recalled in his office. "But I can't let *anybody* win. I really tanked the kid good and felt rotten afterwards. Trying to win, that can't be that bad, can it?"

Later that day, Keegan, his young hometown girlfriend Jean Woodhouse, his agent Vic Huglin and I went to a nightclub where Keegan signed autographs for a succession of crouching grown men. Jean and he drank Coca-Cola. Kevin laughed. "If I'm in a bad mood, Jean will say 'get yourself half a bitter' and it cheers me up."

Huglin, a carpet merchant, handles only Keegan's "literary affairs." The heavy commercial artillery such as mail order house modelling, boot and clothing contracts and perhaps foodstuff commercials are now left to a Leeds agent called Paul Ziff who hopes to make Keegan the biggest name in the history of football. Kevin, I am told, could earn over £30,000 in 1973.

After midnight Keegan dropped me off at my hotel, called out "Merry Christmas" and climbed back into his car. As he drove off towards his digs, something his Scunthorpe manager, Ron Ashman, had said came to mind. "It would hurt me for someone to take Kevin for a ride," he had said. "It would hurt him bad."

December 24 1972

Andrews was the time in 1936 when, already six years retired, he came over to watch the Berlin Olympic Games and on the way home for old times sake played a private and unpublicised round on the Old Course. You cannot, however, keep these things secret in such a place and when he arrived on the first tee he found at least 2,000 people waiting to walk round with him. Unpolished as his game had become, he did the first 10 holes in 35.

"I shall never forget that round," he later wrote. "It was not anything like a serious golf match, but it was a wonderful experience. There was a sort of holiday mood in the crowd. It seemed, or they made it appear at least, that they were just glad to see me back, and however I chose to play was all right with them only they wanted to see it... I could take out of my life everything except my experiences at St Andrews and I'd still have a rich, full life."

Let me close this brief tribute by quoting a friend of mine who was once partnered with Jones in the Open. "If I had had sons," he said, "I should have sent them out to see him—as much for his behaviour as for his play." Jones was probably the greatest and certainly the best-loved golfer of them all.

December 19 1971

Bobby Jones driving at Hoylake in 1930 on the way to winning his third British Open.

A question of loyalties: the trials of Manchester United's prodigal son

The early 1970s were punctuated continually by the comings, goings and not-turning-ups of George Best, unquestionably the most exciting footballer, and most frustrating employee, of the day. The pro and anti cudgels were taken up in *The Sunday Times* by Hunter Davies (above, right) and Brian James.

Hunter Davies calls for more

It's been a great week for George Best fans. I've bought every newspaper, listened to every news bulletin and been distraught if an hour passed without a new development. I can't get enough of Mr Best. I'm just so grateful that he exists. I know only too well that if he didn't exist, nobody would have created him.

First, I'm grateful as a football fan. Would you believe that in this day and age an adult could be told by his employer to move out of his own house and into digs? It's positively feudal, which of course football is. The clubs get away with murder, treating their players like serfs, convincing them it's how it should be, choosing them in the beginning because they'll conform and toe the line.

Naturally, they end up producing deformed human beings with stunted personalities. If their charges get to the top and, even worse, start freaking out in any way, the coaches become contorted with jealousy. They're stuck with their ridiculous 1930s rules and conventions and can't cope with players on £200 a week who can have as many girls as they can eat. In their day, it was a pint and pie and, boy, were they grateful. What they want is players who are *scared* of the masters. On the whole, they've achieved it. Players are now so scared to lose that they get little enjoyment out of the act of playing—which means less enjoyment for those in the act of watching.

Suddenly, along comes Mr Best who goes against the system, who dares to ignore authority, who has the effrontery not to turn up for training, who openly enjoys girls and night-clubs, who openly puts his fingers up at footballers' sacred conventions. They don't know what to do. If they change the system for one person, it makes a mockery of it all. If the system *was* good, which it isn't, they could take exceptions like George Best in their stride. For football's sake, football needs *more* George Bests.

Secondly, I'm glad that he exists if only to upset the world at large. All week they've been tut-tutting in their pubs and offices, saying he should be whipped, he's spoiled, United will be well shot of him. I know that my father-in-law, sitting in his working men's club in Carlisle, has been working himself into a fury all week, saying Best is a bighead, they should send him to the moon. If you'd worked in a factory for a hundred years, clocking your life in and out, keeping your nose clean, then it's an affront to all your values if a young whipper-snapper, one who's so obviously got everything you never had, should then bite the hand that feeds him. That's what I love.

Unfortunately, George Best isn't a rebel. I know I'm romanticising his motives. He's not doing it on a point of principle, would that he were. He's

Supergoal — the private sporting fantasy that excites even a footballing genius

Shortly before he announced his plan to quit football, George Best revealed his own sporting dream to the American magazine Sports Illustrated. He imagined himself in a Cup Final at Wembley before the Queen, with millions watching on television. Manchester United were leading by two goals with 20 minutes left. The team is invincible, so he says: "It is time to show off." And he proceeds to score the dream goal of all time.

A 'First a long kick from the goalkeeper balloons down the field, and I trap it against the turf with my backside.'

B 'I sweep past the left flank of the defence bouncing the ball on my thighs and never letting it touch the ground.'

C 'I centre across the face of the opposition goal.'

D 'Forget about the laws of balance, I fly into a handstand and volley the ball into the foot of the net with my feet.'

Drawn by PAUL TREVILLION

doing it because he's doing it. He's simply the retarded adolescent which football has made him. He's the ultimate victim, the ultimate football fodder. He'll probably end up saying "I'm sorry I've been silly, I'll now be a good boy."

George Best has got away with being George Best simply because of his football talent. As human beings go, my father-in-law has more charisma. But just wait till a George Best with a sense of purpose comes along. That'll really make football sit up.

Over to you, Bri . . . .

Brian James calls for a halt

Given a choice, one would have soon as entered an argument with a spokesman for the Flat Earth Society. It is not that Hunter Davies's defence of George Best is startling; indeed one had heard similar mutterings before, except that previously it had been possible to smile soothingly while moving smartly to the other end of the bar.

My purpose is not to attack Best (with the friends that he has it becomes hard to find sufficiently more devastating weapons to be seen as an enemy) but rather to point out the consequences of accepting such a ludicrous defence. Davies mocks Manchester United's attempts to discipline George, including the order to move back into digs; but forgets that for nearly 10 years his club had allowed him to play it his way. Discipline, in effect, finally became the only present United could offer to A Man Who Had Got Rid Of Everything. Davies claims football wanted to turn Best into yet another robot, again ignoring the fact that it was precisely because he was not made to play and perform as a robot that the game encouraged him to become rich.

Davies, moreover, finds it ridiculous that Best was required to report with others for training, or that he should be expected to attend and play matches for which he had been chosen. One can too easily visualise a fixture list if the game became as "free" as Best appears to wish and Davies now advocates: Division One—A Number of Arsenal Players v Manchester United (or anyone else who turns up) at Highbury Stadium (unless anyone comes up with a more trendy venue), K.O. 3.15 (or, at any rate, sometime before Xmas). If wet, at Tramps after the floorshow.

The game, of course, would be played according to the Laws. Except on those occasions when someone, anyone, wants to do something different. Why should some fascist pig of a referee disallow George's marvellous 123rd goal just because he carried the ball into the net?

The point Davies misses is that no one wants to tie Best down, so long as he returns to keeping his half of the bargain. My own favourite footballer is scarcely less famous, and has a social life scarcely less lurid. Many a weekend, when the party breaks up after dawn and his friends go on shrieking "to Fiona's for brekkers" he "goes on," wincing, to his club for training. And there, morosely dripping 90 proof sweat, he grinds on among teammates he can scarcely recognise until, once again, he is fit enough to play. Now there's a man it is possible to envy and respect.

The point about Best was hit neatly this week by a teammate who declared: "He thinks he's James Bond." And all the evidence is that Best does attempt to live in that fantasy world in which the hero never needs an income because he's never presented with a bill; where drinks are ordered and left untouched on the bar, where men never have need of parking meters, can cross frontiers without queuing or customs, and whose girlfriends never have a period.

A world, in fact, I recently heard described thus: "One day I'll be rich an' everyone will do what I say an' I'll ride horses an' I'll take my cat to bed when I like an' Daddy will get well an' all the nasty people will die an' then I'll be Queen and have icecream for supper an' I'll order the rain to stop an' I won't let Angela come to *my* party either. . ."

If it saddens me that I could not go out and provide my daughter, then aged five, with *her* dream world, then it saddens me no less that Hunter Davies still encourages George Best to believe he will one day discover *his*. Davies, of all people, should know better. Researching his marvellous book on Spurs he lived with the players, virtually, for a year and discovered that few of them were monks and none of the 11 would qualify for the Temperance Seven. What finally emerged from his book was the evidence that no matter how wildly the players may, in midweek, dally . . . on Saturday they still manage to deliver. And that is all anyone has ever asked of Best.

December 10 1972

Genius in disgrace: Best sent off in Northern Ireland's 1970 match with Scotland.

Welcome back to the boxing skills of Muhammad Ali

Boxing at the end of the 1960s denied itself its greatest asset—Muhammad Ali. Because he refused to fight in the Vietnam war, and was denounced by the US Government, he was stripped of his world heavyweight title. In 1970 he was allowed back in the ring, and the world waited to see if Ali could still work the oracle.

by Neil Allen
Drawings by Paul Trevillion

Muhammad Ali's easy victory over Jerry Quarry in Atlanta, Georgia, answered the question as to whether he is as good now as he was three and a half years ago: within another six months he may have attained new heights as world heavyweight champion.

Those who praised Quarry are probably suffering from a basic sense of frustration that the traditional manly school of slugging is becoming emasculated by Ali's demonstration of new dimensions of the sport. An analysis of the three rounds Ali boxed, before his opponent suffered a split eyebrow, indicate some of these skills.

Certainly Ali, now 28, is right to believe that he is hitting harder and is stronger (there are plenty of examples of athletes increasing in strength after their thirtieth birthday). And though speed is more likely to disappear with the coming of age, those concerned that Ali became a little flat-footed in the third round overlook the basic boxing law that a man settled firmly on his feet can deliver more powerful blows.

It is still a matter of opinion as to whether the cut by Quarry's left eye, which needed 11 stitches, was caused by a right cross in the third round as Ali was driven back towards the ropes. Ali himself said he could not recall any vital punch at that stage but added significantly: "Anyone who is going to be hit by a consistent stream of left jabs with 213lb behind them is going to risk getting cut."

Quarry himself fought a lamentably inadequate fight. He said that he would have won by a knockout in another two or three rounds if he had not been cut,

The left jab, which speared Quarry so many times during the first round, strikes home and Ali gives it an additional cutting edge by turning the wrist to the right at the moment of impact. This was the powerful blow which initially softened the skin round Quarry's left eyebrow.

Ali holds Quarry with open glove using advantage in both height (2½in) and reach (3in) as he stands imperiously above his frustrated opponent. Ali used this stance successfully whenever Quarry tried to bull his way in close, invariably keeping his chin well out of range.

but cuts, except through a clash of heads, are not caused by accident. Quarry seemed to have forgotten that he was halted by Joe Frazier in 1969 through an eye injury and that only last March he suffered a cut needing 36 stitches from George Johnson.

Quarry took more than 50 punishing left jabs to the face during the first round as the Atlanta audience whooped their hero back from exile.

It was obvious that Quarry's best chance lay in landing his left hook to Ali's mid-section because it was suspect after a crash programme of training. But Quarry found his hooks to the head solidly blocked and only once, in the second round, landed a really hurtful punch to the body.

"Ali's timing was off. Look how he missed with combinations," said some ringsiders, and Ali admitted that his opponent was evasive. But Quarry, in trying to get away from the fearsome left jab, was ducking well below the

waistline and rarely in position to counter from his turtle-like crouch.

The future and greater Muhammad Ali will continue to use the whole ring, but he will not go in for so much swaying back or palpable dropping of the hands. He will prefer blocking or parrying from an upright stance so that he is better poised to strike back.

Those who reflect wistfully on Quarry's chances should recall the gesture of frustration by Jack Dempsey in 1927 when he beckoned the skilful Gene Tunney to come to him. Or think further back to the time when Jim Jeffries unsuccessfully challenged Jack Johnson to a fist fight in a locked room at the back of a bar.

One writer said then: "Johnson at work has the grace of a dancing master. He knows he could dance away from Jeffries in a dance that would end with Jeffries on the floor. But a locked small room is no place for dancing." Nor for Muhammad Ali.   *November 1 1970*

The kind of slashing right cross which opened the cut by Quarry's left eyebrow. Ali was being backed up against the ropes but managed to get sufficient leverage for the blow even though for once his own ground had been substantially invaded by Quarry.

Why Quarry failed

Quarry's best punch, the left hook, was blocked by Ali's forearm (above). If he had shifted to a body attack he would, because he is shorter, have stood more chance and also tested Ali's stamina. Quarry did make Ali miss by ducking and weaving beneath the waistline (below), but it is an impossible position from which to strike back.

Inside track

Monkey Punch

Muhammad Ali's swivel punch, which we once cynically thought of as a weapon to cut his opponent, takes on new significance under the microscope of engineering science. "In boxing, a straight shot to the jaw isn't as effective as a blow that twists the opponent's head," says Professor Sunder Advani, whose studies at West Virginia University relate to the effect of force on the brain.

His main work is the development of car safety devices such as air bags, but related to boxing it poses this theory; that brain tissue is more vulnerable to rotation. This is because the brain's soft tissue, suspended inside the skull like a bubble in a carpenter's level, will, if hit by direct impact, attempt to expand but cannot because of the skull. However, if a glanced blow or multiple blows are landed and the brain is caused to rotate, even fractionally, it will suffer damage and induce unconsciousness.

A boxing fan, Professor Advani reasons that his work could explain why the "soft, innocuous" blow nobody sees often produces a k.o. We wrote asking him which boxers were concerned in tests. "No tests on boxers were performed," he writes back.

"I did, however, conduct tests on monkeys and guinea pigs at Northrop Space Laboratories, California, to successfully demonstrate the rotation hypothesis."

August 5 1973

Images of Muhammad, and the day they played the rushes and cried

The motion picture industry finally cornered Muhammad Ali at the ripe old age of 35, to film the Richard Durham biography, The Greatest, and it was love at first sight.

by Dudley Doust

He had been in Miami, Houston, Atlanta and Louisville and now Muhammad Ali is filming scene 60 of the picture at Caesars Palace hotel in Las Vegas. He sits above the sunken casino floor, head down, solemn as a boxer waiting for the bell to ring. He wears baggy trousers and a make-up girl sprays away the grey hairs on his head. In this scene, which actually happened in 1963, he is only 21 years old and still called Cassius Clay.

The director, Tom Gries, nods. The cameras whir. Ali rises to his feet and suddenly the great, chocolate voice explodes across the crowded casino. "All right, you big ugly bear. . . ! This town isn't big enough for two fast hands. . . ! One of us has gotta leave. . . ! He walks down the steps and

---

"Even when he's not looking at the other actor, he gives the appearance of listening to him. This is something it takes some actors years to learn. Ali's a natural actor."

---

across the casino floor, trailing his raggle-taggle entourage. "You'd better saddle up and ride out of town by high noon tomorrow. Hear? Hear me, sucker? I'm the greatest fighter of all time."

Ali has now reached the gambling table where the actor Roger E. Mosley, who plays the role of the late Sonny Liston, continues to roll the dice. He finally tires of the berating from the upstart and, getting slowly to his feet, pulls out a pistol. Ali freezes, pleads that he's joking, panics and flees among his followers. Four pistol shots ring out. The crowd screams and scatters. Chairs tumble. Actor Mosley then dramatically puts the pistol to his temple and fires. He laughs. The bullets are blanks.

"Cut! Cut!" shouts Gries. He is

pleased but he will shoot the scene another time and, most importantly, from several cut-away angles. "These scenes are easy for Ali. He can turn them on like a tap."

Gries, sadly, is now gone from The Greatest. He died, aged 53, of a heart attack while playing tennis last week, scarcely a fortnight after shooting the last scene of the film. He was an especially nice man, bald as Kojak, one of those tough-tender Americans with a real gut feeling for sport. His most recent pictures were Breakout and Breakheart Pass, starring Charles Bronson.

Preparing for the film, Gries got to know the champion well. "If I hadn't got to know Ali, judging from his behaviour as portrayed by the media I would have thought 'My God, he's going to be a terrible ham, he'll blow up the camera'," Gries said. "On the contrary, he's a quiet man by nature and from time to time I'll have to lift him up from a whisper. Sometimes he gets tired. You've got to remember, he's spent all of his fighting career getting up at 4.30 in the morning and doing roadwork. He's used to having a nap in the morning and he occasionally gets sleepy."

Gries said he gave only one acting tip to the ebullient Ali: "Listen, *listen* to what the other actor is saying, and that's what he does. Even when he's not looking at the other actor, he gives the appearance of listening to him. This is something it takes some actors years to learn. Ali's a natural actor."

Gries seemed genuinely enthusiastic (and surprised) over other acting skills Ali brought before the film camera. If another actor went off the track, for instance, or blew a line, Ali could guide him back on course through an improvised line. Gries was not alone among the crew who remember the first scene shot in production, scene 75—for film scenes are never shot in script sequence—which took place in Miami. A white promoter called Bill McDonald, played by Robert Duvall, is trying to set up the first title fight between the then Cassius Clay and Liston which subsequently took place in February 1964 in Miami. Clay had begun trafficking with Malcolm X and the Muslims which was thought to be

courting dangerous publicity. In the script Bundini Brown, Clay's close colleague who plays himself in the film, tells Clay that McDonald is unhappy and could Clay step into his office. Clay's manager, Angelo Dundee, played by Ernest Borgnine, tells Cassius to keep cool. "Remember, there's such a thing as compromise, for Chrissake!"

In the script, Ali is meant to smile knowingly, say nothing. In the film, however, Ali breaks away from the script and ad libs with furious feeling: "What do I care if he doesn't love me any more. I'm just another nigger to him. If I win the fight I'm his nigger. If Liston wins the fight *Liston's* his nigger. Whoever makes money for him's his nigger."

Gries shrugged, recollecting the scene. "He just took that scene and took it on a trip. We were wide-eyed. You bet it's going to stay in the film," he said. "That was the moment we knew we were home free with Ali as an actor." That piece of improvisation suggests the looseness writer Ring Lardner jr. had to bring to the script. Instinctively good or not, Ali is not a professional, and to follow lines verbatim would have brought a stilted, crippled performance.

The major problem in writing the script, Lardner feels, was to escape the imprisonment of truth. "We decided not to be inhibited by the facts, to change them, if necessary, to adhere to the truth." Lardner wanted poetic truth but, as in all drama, needed sharp, heightened motivations. Thus, Cassius Clay's repudiation of the white world by dropping his Olympic gold medal into the Ohio River (which actually happened in life) is dramatised in the script by an even more humiliating ban from a white Louisville restaurant than the one

---

"I can't say Ali's face is naturally very expressive but when he gets in front of a camera, that's something different."

---

described in Richard Durham's The Greatest, the book on which the film is based.

Lardner was impressed, too, by Ali's almost total emotional recall. In the spring of 1973, for instance, Ali suffered his worst and most painful ring defeat. That was the fight in which his jaw was broken by Ken Norton. His

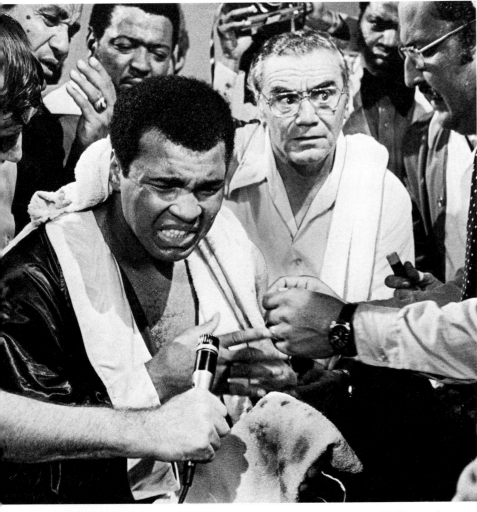

say Ali's face is naturally very expressive but when he gets in front of a camera, that's a different thing. Something happens. He's got what all great film actors need: wonderfully expressive eyes."

In make-up terms, the Ali job has been easy. "He's got a wonderful bone structure and very good skin. For this scene, when he's 21 years old, I've cleaned up a few wrinkles round his eyes. We all have irregularities in our skin colouring. Ali's got a light streak just above his eyebrows, which may be from frowning so much, and it's darker up by his hairline. So I've cleared up

---

"Ali is tired. He yawns like a lion but, true to form, soon is talking in that harsh whisper of wonder."

---

these irregularities, which automatically makes him look younger. Also, when you eliminate the beard-line on a man you make him look younger."

The casino again is in action, on camera and off. Ali's bellowing and Liston's pistol shots thread like a *leitmotiv* across the floor as Vegas life goes on round the film unit. Ali's real mother, with her son's round face, plays the wheel of fortune. Ali's real father, oddly small but with the same secret smile, cranks the one-arm bandits. The unit publicist says: "Mr Clay, I'd like you to meet a newspaperman from London."

"I'll be in my office on Monday."

"But he'll make you famous."

"I'm already famous." Coins clatter down, as though to confirm it.

A few minutes of film have been achieved by the end of the afternoon. Ali goes to his hotel room where he holds court for a Los Angeles television crew, a German show business writer and myself. There is only one more day of shooting on The Greatest and Ali is tired. He yawns like a lion but, true to form, soon is talking in that harsh whisper of wonder.

"Did you ever hear of a man, not yet 35 years old, making his own life story, playing his own self in a movie picture?" he says. "I tell you, I'm so good it's hard to believe. People will laugh, people will weep, people will cheer when they watch Muhammad Ali—the world's greatest movie actor in the history of all time." Ali stares at us as his words hang and fade in the air.

January 9 1977

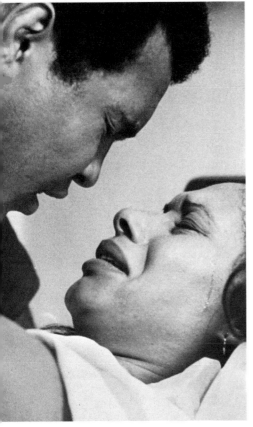

wife at the time, Belinda, became hysterical at the ringside and was taken to hospital. She thought her husband was dead. Ali himself was under surgical care at the time, having had his jaw wired shut, but hearing of her condition he quickly went to her.

Ali re-creates this confrontation in the film, right down to the emotional scene where, realising she is unaware of his broken jaw, he calls himself Dracula and tenderly buries his teeth against her neck. "The consultant physician who was there in 1973 was then on the set," says the film's producer, John Marshall, "and he said it was eerie the way Ali recalled it. We played the rushes of that scene the other day and, I swear, people were crying."

If Ali's is the world's most famous face, the make-up director, Bill Tuttle, has made a professional study of it. He has been round Hollywood since 1934, dealt with such celebrated faces as Clark Gable and Spencer Tracy, and is the only make-up man ever to win an Academy Award. Tuttle is a face-watcher, a face-fixer by trade. "I can't

Two scenes from The Greatest: Ali's almost total emotional recall was particularly impressive.

Original man meets Smith and Son's spiritual suckling

For the third time in his tenure of the world heavyweight title, Ali faced a British challenger, Joe Bugner, in Kuala Lumpur. The bout in prospect looked lacklustre but the colossal contrast in the character of the protagonists was fascinating nonetheless.

by Keith Botsford

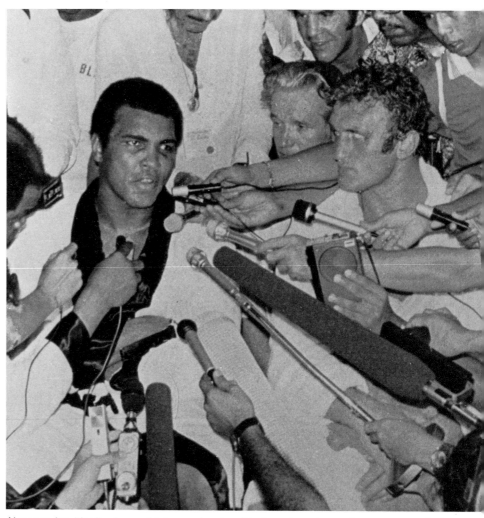

Alas poor Joe, it's all mikes on Muhammad, a showbiz champion who needs to consume a fresh audience a day just to stay alive.

Well, it's all over bar the fighting, which is on Tuesday morning when the sun will be beating down hot from the gentian hills and the humid haze over the valley of Kuala Lumpur will be lifting: if, that is, the ringside spells of the witch doctor (a most respectable man in a business suit) work. Then enter Muhammad Ali for his 15th championship fight and Joe Bugner, a local 6-1 underdog, for his first crack at the title.

On one side of the ring, on plush armchairs with his retinue, will sit H. M. The Yang di-Pertuan Agong, Duli Yang Maha Mulia Seri Paduka Baginda Tuanku Abdul Halim Mu'Adzam Shah ibni Al-Marhum Sultan Badlishah; around the rest, the Press. Around them the security, which is fierce and efficient.

Then £200, £100 and £50 seats (a monthly unskilled wage is between £10 and £20) and banked about the baking, gleaming 38,000 capacity Merdeka Stadium the seats that remain largely unsold as the Malaysian public awaits a decision on local television.

The weigh-in went off with ceremony, flourish and the usual nonsense. The fighters entered accompanied by a Bunga Gumbang, a ceremonial escort of drummers preceded by young men in demi-sarongs bearing aloft miniature trees of blue, white and yellow feathers. For Bugner who came in first, the drummers played the Kuda Kepang and for Ali, the Berteh Ranchak. Promoter Don King with his electrocuted head towered over Datuk Harun, his local counterpart, while the Ali mob crowded the ring pushing aside patient Malays.

It was all as it ever is, down to the ritualised punch-up between Ali

(225lb) and Bugner (230lb) which induced tiny Scot Andy Smith, Bugner's manager, into flailing at that arch-Calabrian Angelo Dundee. In short we saw another round in the phoney war that now precedes every title fight.

What else can they do? Their bodies are in shape; Bugner, as Ali says, "was already in too good shape when he arrived." And the Ali we saw on Friday going through 15 rounds of sparring without a break in the 95 degree heat may be a little lax about roadwork, but not in his element, which is the ring. So it is only each man's soul that is vulnerable. Each stalks the other's dark spots: Ali to terrify Bugner, Joe to sow doubt in Ali's mind by ignoring threat, taunt and terror.

Life before a fight is time on one's hands. It is living in air-conditioned paradises that are really skyscraper prison cells, sneaking out in the dead of night to run round the Turf Club's track, stoking the body (Ali with a mix of "soul food," fish and citrus and

Bugner with more traditional fare) and then sweating off the weight.

It is relaxing the mind over much-thumbed magazines and listening to endless talk, receiving the Press and the glad hands. It is honing nerve and body by work and letting it down by sleep. It is becoming a huge animal, half asleep. It is PR, Joe addressing 1,200 schoolchildren at a prize day and Ali crowning Malaysia's unhappily-named Miss Heavyweight. It is contracts and squabbles and fear.

But the most significant and revealing event of this last week took place on the 16th floor of the Equatorial Hotel where Bugner's relatively modest camp ("Ali can still afford 50 men," said Joe quietly) consists of Andy Smith, Danny Holland, the cuts man, and friend-cum-bodyguard Simon Ince (who looked on in horror).

Nobody likes to see a man unzip his mental fly, but when Andy ran out of the room whining hysterically how he couldn't "stand this crap," we were seeing one of the reasons why nobody

has much faith in the gentle giant with the candied blue eyes and golden hair. There were no little steel balls, but Smith was captain Queeg in full manic battle-dress.

And what was wrong? It was just Joe talking about hard times and old times; life as it was before his manager and he put together this emotional investment portfolio which binds one to being Baby Bunting and the other to take the place of Bugner's real and missing daddy ("they're divorced, we don't talk about that in the family"). Joe was left unmanned and holding the bag.

Not for the first time. A displaced person at six, is he any less displaced at 25? The athlete-schoolboy who wins everything in sight, discus, javelin, shot put, is refused coaching by the usual officious officials. Other kids got it, he remembers, kids from ritzy schools; but he is deprived. Who does battle for him? Did he really want to go into boxing? It's doubtful. You throw against yourself, it's a loner's sport. But they won't help you, you're a big boy, you go into boxing. With Joe's temperament it must have seemed a giant and potentially unpleasant step.

But he dreams of strong men; the movies fill him with James Bond; real men aren't heroes, but Samson and Hercules: "I was infatuated with supreme strength." Strength he's got, but anger? If he's angry he'll go into the back garden and break a spade in two ("and what's the spade's name?" one wit asks). Or get into his car, only on straight roads, mind you, and drive like hell. He reads autobiographies, he says. Instead he should be considering his own. And why he's still a spiritual suckling. And why it comes off both men, Andy and Joe, or Smith and Son, that in their hearts they'd rather not win this fight. Knowing what that would entail. Not least, killing Daddy.

Andy Smith fancies himself a teacher of boxing. Joe is an intelligent boy: why hasn't he learned rhythm, how to follow a left with a right, how to put together simple sequences? It must be that he hasn't been taught. Has the wee man, who said some time back, "If I could turn Joe Bugner into an animal I wouldn't do it," a proper understanding of where Joe's gone. Bugner the beast? No, only a rush of adrenaline once in a while.

Of course Joe's got a lot on his back. He started out fighting for Andy by getting k.o'd. Then Ulric Regis died after fighting Joe. True, Joe wasn't responsible, but it's not a nice thought in the small hours. Then he beat Cooper, the national hero, and no one liked that. His high points are lasting out, coming back after an early knockdown against Joe Frazier, staying the distance with Ali in Las Vegas. His mind doesn't dwell, in retrospect, on how he might have won.

Here is a man of no style, born an irresolute loser, facing a thirty-three-year-old (that apt age) whose spirit is not always willing and whose flesh is sometimes weak. And the fear of losing is a worse enemy than a fear of winning.

Ali too has a lot on his back. Not least his hangers-on and henchmen, the 50-odd stable of cheque-signers whom he has made into his dependents. Then he introduced showbiz into boxing and now he needs to consume a fresh audience a day just to stay alive. Mortality gets to him.

"The world is changing," he says, "and the man who's the same at 50 as he was at 20 has lost 30 years of his life." Meanwhile his wife Belinda's taking up polo and at four in the morning he talks

> "Ali moves through a subservient world that echoes his every word and, friendless, lives in a luxurious 25th-floor cave to which all come seeking to be his friend."

about death, cotton wadding, embalming fluid and real worms. He's passing a shadow-line: "One day you're happy and the next day you don't want to get out of bed." Age is alongside: "You're still looking at girls, but you ain't feeling the same way any more."

Meanwhile, the show must go on. King Ali endorses beer and breakfast food, the Muslim faith, Colonel Gadaffi, Malaysian gentleness and invitations to Manila and Cairo with equal conviction. He moves through a subservient world that echoes his every word and, friendless, lives in a luxurious 25th-floor cave to which all come seeking to be his friend. How, one asks, would Bugner survive success?

Soon enough, we'll know. Kuala Lumpur, with its skyscraper hotels packed with Aussie package-tours alongside kampong shacks perched on stilts from whose balconies white-skirted and topless men shout "are you for Ali?", probably deserves better than what it is likely to get: a dour, slightly distasteful, not very good and possibly controversial fight.

Both men will survive, I would think, to a humid and sour finish, and when the final bell has rung, but for a miracle, neither man will have moved an inch. *June 29 1975*

PS: And that was how it turned out: 15 rounds of playtime, a duet in meditation. Time stood still, Ali remained champion, and Bugner was still just an ordinary Joe.

Enter the gladiators to a world not big enough for both

In the first few years of Muhammad Ali's dazzling carousel which he created with the world heavyweight championship, he took to deprecating Joe Louis, the formidable former Number One, as "the biggest Uncle Tom of all." Politics aside, his reason was probably motivated by fear that the continuing presence of the Brown Bomber, even outside the ring, undermined Ali's claim to be The Greatest of all time. Arguments raged—maybe they still do—amongst the fight fraternity over which of the two was superior. Was it Louis, whose left jabs felt "like busted light bulbs in your face," or Ali, whose trainer Angelo Dundee considered, "the strongest son of a bitch you've ever seen in your life?" A real life match being impossible, a notional one brought them together, based on film and photographic records, reports and the complete ring histories of both men.

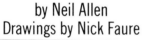

by Neil Allen
Drawings by Nick Faure

THE fight of the century

JOE LOUIS v MUHAMMAD ALI

71	FIGHTS	47
1934-51	BOXING	1960-74
68	WINS	45
34	K.O.'s	10
6ft. 1½ in.	HEIGHT	6ft. 3 in.
14st. 6lb.	WEIGHT	15st. 4lb.
76 in.	REACH	80 in.

ROUND ONE: ALI STRAIGHT INTO THE DANCE..

ROUND FOUR: .. BUT SUDDENLY ATTACKS WITH BITING LEFT JABS.

ROUND SIX: LOUIS FINDS HIS RANGE AT LAST AND...

ROUND ONE. The 50,000 crowd in the Houston Astrodome quieten down at last, except for some exuberant Ali supporters, at the sound of the bell. Joe Louis, face impassive, comes out faster than usual, like he did in his one-round destruction of Max Schmeling. Ali moves immediately in a wide semicircle, gloves dangling, chin well back, mouth half-open. Louis tries to cut his man off in retreat, lands one jab to Ali's shoulders, is short with half a dozen more as Ali pulls back his head. We've watched three rounds of Ali retreating, sometimes putting on the style as he shuffles his white, high-sided boots. He leans back into the ropes, trying to tempt Louis to punch himself out, but with little luck. **ROUND FOUR.** At last Ali begins to use his four-inch advantage in reach, sinking the left jab into Louis's face so that a spray of sweat and water shoots away from the Brown Bomber's head. But Louis moves inside some of these lefts—not at all slow-footed, as Ali used to claim—and whips a left hook into the body, and then a right under the heart. **ROUND SIX.** Ali kept up the tattoo of left hands in the fifth. By now, though, Louis is becoming more adept at cutting him off at the pass. Surprisingly, Ali finds himself beaten to the jab not once but three times. Louis at last hooks off the jab too, scores to the ribs with a right and then crosses the right to the jaw though Ali half-smothers this last, dangerous blow with his left glove. He spits "ghetto talk" at Louis in contempt, but his opponent has won the round.

ROUND EIGHT: ..CATCHES ALI WITH A CRUSHING LEFT HOOK...

...WHICH FLOORS HIM FOR A SHORT COUNT.

ROUND TEN: ALI, BACK TO LONG RANGE AGAIN, CLOSES THE EYE OF THE BROWN BOMBER...

ROUND EIGHT. Ali is taking too many risks. He reaches forward a shade too far with his left lead, not balanced behind the blow, and then swings awkwardly and tries to throw a lazy, unconvincing right to Louis's head. Before the blow is even half-completed, Louis steps inside the arc of Ali's right arm with the classic left-hook counter and we can clearly hear Louis grunt as he lands, wrist turning downward at the moment of impact . . .
THE KNOCKDOWN . . . Ali's head arches back,

and then his body is falling towards the floor . . . Television's action replay later proves that Ali's eyes are still closed as the referee bawls "Two." But at "Five" Ali is miraculously rolling over, almost instinctively, on to all fours and he's up, shaking his head to clear his cobwebbed brain, at "Seven." Before this unforgettable round is over, however, we at the ringside can see that the right side of Ali's jaw is swelling up just as it did in the final round of the first fight with Frazier. **ROUND TEN.** After a ninth

round of running, blocking and clinching, nursing his bruised ego as well as his swollen face, Ali comes out with much of his old zest. His lefts peck, snap and finally pound away at the face of his opponent until even those farther back from the $300 ringside seats can see that Louis's left eye is almost closed, and there's a trickle of blood down the cheek. Ali gets bolder, opening out with brief but vicious double-handed attacks which surely only someone as strong as Louis can withstand for long.

ROUND TWELVE: .. WHO, AT LAST, SINKS TO THE CANVAS FOR 'EIGHT'.

ROUND FIFTEEN: THE PACE SLACKENS AS THE REFEREE STRUGGLES TO KEEP THEM APART, BUT...

THE WINNER, AND STILL CHAMPION, IS MUHAMMAD ALI ON A SPLIT POINTS DECISION

ROUND TWELVE. The 11th had been unrelenting for both fighters. But now, late in the 12th, Louis's left hand begins to droop, his vision is almost restricted to the right eye and so he never glimpses the right cross which Ali explodes to the side of his head. Ali's follow-through is so complete that for a second the two bronzed figures seem frozen in the smoke-ridden air under the arc lights. Then Louis slowly sinks to his knees. "The bull is dead," howls Bundini, "it's all over, champ." But not for Louis.

Somehow he is up at "Eight" (or was it "Nine"? the cheering is too loud), and then comes the respite of the bell. **ROUND FIFTEEN.** The crippling pace has to tell at last as two weary bruised bodies locked together prove that the supreme heavyweights are only human after all. For the past two rounds Ali and Louis have been able to fight only in half-hearted, inconclusive bursts, leaning their heads on each other's shoulders. **THE DECISION.** The winner is what we and all the world wait for now. The three

judges' verdicts come from the MC with agonising slowness: Ali nine rounds, Louis five and one even; Louis seven. Ali five and three even. The boos and cheers subside until the vital vote. "Ali eight rounds, Louis six . . ." and there is Bundini Brown pulling down Ali's swollen face to plant a kiss, Angelo Dundee leaping high in the air and Louis, as dignified as ever in defeat, gently pushing aside the trainer who dabs with an ice-bag at his tight-closed eye. The dream fight of the century is over.

It still hurts to say, but if both men were at their best then Ali would (just) beat Louis. With 78 per cent of his victories gained inside the distance, Louis is obviously the more explosive puncher. In 25 championship defences he scored clean knockouts over 17 opponents.

Louis was knocked down eight times in 17 years, and beaten three times—outpointed by Ezzard Charles, stopped by Rocky Marciano at the fag-end of his

THE VERDICT

career, and knocked out by Max Schmeling when near his prime.

In 47 pro fights, a record truncated by a three-year lay-off, Ali has never been knocked out or stopped. He was put down by Sonny Banks, Henry Cooper and Joe Frazier.

Ali is taller, longer-armed and slightly

heavier then Louis. And the fight in Kinshasa against Foreman proved that when Ali settles himself he can really hit.

Louis had an invincible aura which often froze his opponents and might unnerve Ali. But he was outboxed for 12 rounds by the 12st 6lb Billy Conn, and floored by Tony Galento. For me Ali, with his greater tactical range, is the greatest, with Louis followed by Rocky Marciano, Gene Tunney and Jack Dempsey.   *December 8 1974*

The craft of Cruyff, a Dutch grand master trading in dummies

Football of the 1970s demanded not only talent but also temperament and ability to apply it in an over-functional era. That combination made Johan Cruyff the outstanding forward of his time; moreover, he could describe his craft better than most.

by Brian Glanville

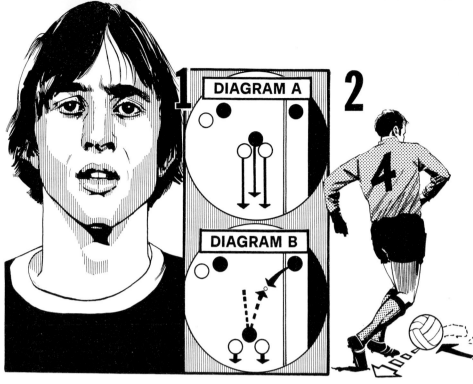

One sure mark of the outstanding footballer is his ability to play well when things are going against his team. By this criterion, Johan Cruyff, whose Ajax side were beaten 3–0 by Arsenal in the Fairs Cup last week, is a very fine player indeed.

With Ajax, foolishly cautious, reduced for most of the game to a token attack of two or three men, Cruyff nevertheless played with steady commitment, fire and enterprise, on a muddy pitch which was anything but ideal for a player of his flimsy build.

Twenty-two years old, long-haired, thin as a lath, direct and outspoken, he confirmed the impression he made when he played for Holland against England at Wembley this season: that he is one of the world's most exciting players. Certainly he has his critics. "He plays for himself," murmured one Dutch journalist at Highbury, darkly.

But with Keizer, normally his chief lieutenant, showing so little appetite for the game that his manager pulled him off at half-time, what else was there to do?

When the ball comes to him or near him, he reacts with electric speed, sublime assurance, his long, thin legs fairly pumping him along, even from a

Step by step, the movement of genius

by Rob Hughes

Johan Cruyff brings to football what Dick Fosbury did to the high jump: an original mind combined with a rare athletic talent. Improvisation guides him through this triangle of Belgians.

Before moving a muscle, he looks to see if a simple pass will put a colleague in a better position . . . and if not? "I go. Sometimes it is necessary to take responsibility to beat more than one guy."

Rinus Michels, his club and national manager, sums up: "Cruyff's variations are so many, his skills so bewildering, you only know afterwards— when he has gone—what he will do." Cruyff, however, knows exactly.

June 2 1974

A World Cup qualifier v. Belgium. Cruyff maxim: body between challenger and ball. Weight firmly on the left, the ball shielded outside the right boot, Dewalque (at Cruyff's shoulder) cannot win possession without fouling.

A

B

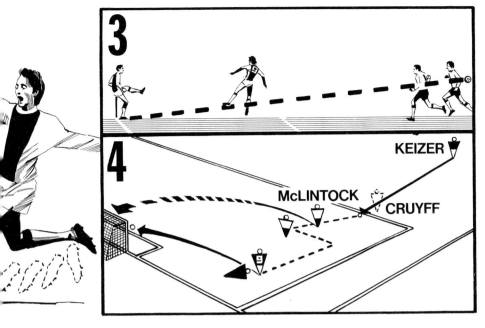

1. In diagram A, Cruyff policed by two defenders bluffs an upfield dash and leaves the throw-in for a teammate. The dummy sold, Cruyff doubles back—diagram B—to collect the ball in free space.

2. At top speed and full stride, Cruyff tricks defenders by tapping the ball one way, committing the defender, then, with a full leg sweep, redirecting its path.

3. Cruyff has feinted to collect a short pass. Two defenders run to prevent him turning. Cruyff's answer—a simple jump over the ball, which cuts both out of the game.

4. Collecting a pass from Keizer, in Wednesday's game, Cruyff taps the ball with his left foot inside McLintock and then outside another defender with his right. Goalkeeper Wilson leaves his line, dives at the feet of Cruyff, who chips the ball at an acute angle towards goal.

standing start. He's a great chaser, too, of lost causes. Once, in the second half, Storey had to slide desperately to kick for a corner, while Wilson had to plunge into the mud to snatch the ball, as Cruyff's hot pursuit made danger where there would normally be none.

His combativity can overstep the mark, but perhaps we should accept that as the obverse of his courage, without which so slight a player in so defensive an era could not prevail. His name was taken at Arsenal after a foul on McLintock provoked what is known these days as a scuffle with two opponents.

Asked whether he subscribes to Pele's philosophy of retaliation, he replied: "My way to hit him back is to pass him, and not to pass him once but twice, three times. If somebody hit me, not accidentally, but just to attack me, I put him for a fool before 60,000 people." His pantheon includes Corso, of Italy, Eusebio, Best "of course," while "in another style I like Charlton." *April 12 1970*

B. Shifting his weight, Cruyff squirms clear. Dewalque is unbalanced, Van Binst (No. 2) committted to closing the gap to his right. No attempt to trap the ball: "Kill it, and you have no momentum; it's better to hit the ball one metre and move."

C. The charge. Off on the right foot, Cruyff puts Delwalque and Semmeling (No. 7) to the sprint test. "I'm not a fast runner," insists Cruyff. "But in football, speed over two metres is more important than 20." Speed of thought, too: Cruyff's instincts are so heightened, he senses when an opponent or two are wrong-footed . . . the moment to move. While they strive to respond, he has a yard start.

D. The explosive nature of that acceleration is best judged by Van Binst's position (furthest from camera). While Van Binst stops and turns, Cruyff is away. Note Cruyff's weight again thrown guardedly over the left leg. By now, his momentum has burned off the threat of all three men.

E. The Belgians, however, are familiar and stubborn opponents. Two new challengers—Verheyen (furthest away) and Van Himst (No. 10) are drawn. With a sharp body swerve, Cruyff switches inside to find time and room (ultimately to hit a penetrating right-foot pass for his left-winger). By now, half the opposition has been taken out of the play. Genius? It helps, of course, if you've practised turning and kicking with both feet from the age of 12.

C

D

E

WHAT A SHOT! BUT HOW LUCKY SHE GUESSED WHERE TO JUMP

IT WAS NOT LUCK BUT BILLIE JEAN KING'S REGULAR AND EXPERT USE OF MENTAL REHEARSAL ...

LONG BEFORE ANY BIG CHAMPIONSHIP SHE REHEARSES EVERY DETAIL OF HER GAME IN HER MIND ...

The mental moving picture show which helps Billie Jean to reign supreme

Billie Jean King dominated women's tennis from the mid-sixties, arguably till the present day, firstly by her physical and mental strength, latterly by her equally determined campaigning for women's rights within all sports, but especially tennis. She is one of the most successful exponents, on the court, of a little-known technique of match preparation.

by Clarence Jones
Drawings by Nick Faure

Billie Jean King, by far the most successful woman tennis player, this week bids for a world record $32,000 in the Virginia Slims Championships in Los Angeles. An essential part of her training will be done, literally, in an armchair. For Billie Jean firmly believes in a scientific process of mental rehearsal: she is convinced that if she can sit and think of herself hitting perfect strokes and deploying perfect tactics over and over again, she will repeat this perfection on the court.

The process has helped make her the richest competitor in the history of women's tennis. Yet, while "mental rehearsal" is an acknowledged technique, many specialists dispute its validity and attribute the benefits to "mind over matter" or "psychology."

So, even if Mrs King keeps "laughing all the way to the bank," few of her contemporaries follow her example. One of her American rivals, Julie Heldman, is an exception. She began learning the process from a British coach 18 months ago. Her decline was halted. She has subsequently risen from 27th to 9th in the world. Few British players even know that such a technique exists.

Despite the sceptics, the practical worth of "mental rehearsal" in many activities was known at the turn of the century and recent research is establishing some fundamental backing for believing in its value.

Carrying out any physical or mental task sends minute electrical impulses up and down the relevant nerve paths. Each repetition helps to "burn a groove" along the nerve path somewhat in the manner of an automobile wheel rubbing a path in a road. However, unless concentration is complete, and the movement technically correct, the chance of "grooving" unsoundly is immense.

Actually performing a task sets up specific brain patterns which can be recorded by an electroencephalograph.

Making the movement without racket or ball produces identical brain patterns. And if the arm is strapped down immovably and the movement is made in the mind, the patterns are *still* identical. Thus imagining—mental rehearsal—"grooves" in the same way as on-court practice.

But there are pitfalls. Intense concentration, be it when physically practising or mentally rehearsing, sets up a reaction known as "reactive inhibition": the brain sinks into a "waking" sleep state and the chances of wrongly "grooving" the nerve paths increase a hundredfold. So, as a rough guide, 10 minutes is about the longest time that should be spent without variation on any one exercise.

Indeed, carried to excess, such practice can completely inhibit a natural movement. Professor Hans Eysenck used this fact to cure certain nervous ailments, e.g. eye ticks. The patient is put before a mirror and instructed to wink continuously for 20 minutes or so. He does this twice daily and after about a fortnight the eye tick usually disappears.

The techniques of effective mental rehearsal are far harder to master than it may seem. Complete quiet and absolute concentration are essential. Only then can vivid pictures be imagined and techniques or tactics evolved and mastered. The effort is far more demanding than on-court work-outs ... but far more rewarding.

PERFECTING HER STROKES...

AND HER VOLLEYS. IT WAS MENTAL REHEARSAL THAT GROOVED HER REACTIONS AS SURELY AS ON-COURT PRACTICE

ANYONE CAN IMPROVE, EVEN IN AN ARMCHAIR IF THEIR WILLPOWER IS STRONG ENOUGH

BILLIE JEAN KING EVEN REHEARSES THE MOMENTS OF HER CRUSHING VICTORIES

● If you want to use "mental rehearsal" to improve your own golf, cricket, cooking, car driving, and so on, how long should you spend on each session? A rough guide can be gained by considering the following two chestnuts. You may not think either particularly funny, but share 10 points between them according to their relative appeal to you.

Story A: "I've been a bachelor all my life and I intend to bring up my children the same way."

Story B: "Why don't you use both hands," said the pretty blonde as her amorous boyfriend's arm stole round her shoulder. "I can't," he replied, "someone has to steer the car."

Whether you preferred story A or B, according to Professor Eysenck, gives an approximate indication of your place along the extroversion-introversion scale. Extroverts tend to prefer story A, and are less capable of maintaining full concentration than introverts. You should thus adjust your "mental rehearsal" periods, regardless of your objective: if you rate A higher, mentally practise for one minute for each mark you give it; if you prefer B allow one-and-a-half minutes per mark; and if you rate the stories equally, practise for six-and-a-half minutes per session.

October 13 1974

PS. On this occasion, Mrs King's method let her down. She was beaten in the semi-final by Evonne Goolagong.

Inside track

Press On?

"A bunch of old women," snorts Oscar State, secretary of the International Weightlifting Federation. "They haven't got proof." Thus he dismisses a worrisome question: How dangerous is the press in weightlifting?

The press has long been lumbered by an imprecise rule forbidding "exaggerated" leanbacks. Yet in a recent European championship, a Polish heavyweight pressed 250lb. in the manner diagrammed here. Dr Duncan Troup of the Royal Free Hospital's Biomechanics Laboratory comments:

The barbell and the upper body, totalling some 310lb., create a "shearing" force of 200lb. (S) and, at right angles, one of 225lb. (F). To maintain equilibrium the abdominal muscles produce a force of 475lb. (A). Therefore, the total spinal compression is 700lb. (C).

"This alone isn't dangerous," says Dr Troup, "but the extreme posture is. The spine and the muscles are strained to their limits. It could result in injury to the spinal ligaments and/or the vertebral cartilage, leading to early degeneration.

"A trained weightlifter may get away with this, but the undeveloped adolescent, after only a brief experience, may suffer irreparable damage. And, after all, every budding athlete who practises weight-training has a go at the press."

The Sports Council agrees. Hounded by an ex-weightlifting official, Tom Mason, it recently despatched queries seeking world-wide attitudes on weightlifting: "Our or-thopaedic specialists indicate that the possible age when the epiphyses (lining) of the vertebrae are fused is not until around 18... weightlifting of maximum loads can be harmful to boys." *June 29 1969*

PS. Weightlifting's press was discontinued after the 1972 Munich Olympics.

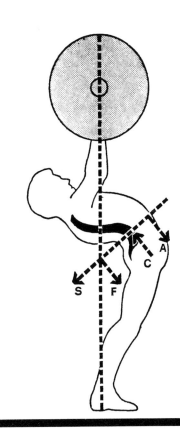

Augusta '75, and the tournament which made Jack Nicklaus a master among masters

The 1975 Masters produced some of the best golf and the highest drama in the history of the sport. By the end, all attention was focused on three of the game's finest players, Jack Nicklaus, Johnny Miller and Tom Weiskopf. The chart logs their hole-by-hole fortunes.

by Dudley Doust

Jack Nicklaus was standing on the final green of the Masters in Augusta last Sunday when he heard an explosion of applause from the 17th green. He backed off his putt, waited, looked at the scoreboard. "Before I hit my own putt," he said later, "I had to know who had got the birdie down there, Weiskopf or Miller. And if the score hadn't gone up on the board, I would have walked over to the score tent and asked."

The scores went up: it was Miller who had birdied and now, with one hole to play, he and Weiskopf were both a single stroke behind Nicklaus. Nicklaus was relieved. There was no need to go for the birdie putt aggressively, so he gently lagged his putt short of the cup and tapped it in for a par. Nicklaus then went to the scorer's tent to watch the finish. Miller's pitch came first: it settled 15 feet from the pin. Weiskopf, off an enormous drive, flipped up to about eight feet. Both putts were downhill.

"What do you think?" young Tom Watson asked Nicklaus. Nicklaus said either one man or the other, not both, would hole out, and he was in for a play-off. He later explained the conflict of his emotions: "Obviously I didn't want them to make their putts, but I didn't want them to *miss*, either. I couldn't root *against* anybody."

Miller, the boldest putter, stroked his ball firmly. It curled low and past the cup, and Miller clamped his elbows round his head in disappointment.

Weiskopf settled his shoes over his putt. His caddie, who is both Weiskopf's tour caddie and a regular Augusta caddie, told him: "Go for the right lip of the hole." Weiskopf did. The ball didn't. It wandered right. Weiskopf, baffled, felt he had struck the correct putt when he saw the replay on television.

So Nicklaus had won it with 276. Sharing second place were Miller and, for the fourth time in his career, Weiskopf on 277. Thus ended one of the most memorable tournaments in the history of golf. Lee Elder had become the first black man to play in a Masters. Hale Irwin on that last day had equalled the course record of 64, but, mainly, Nicklaus had won his fifth Masters.

The three players Nicklaus himself considered the strongest in the field arrived at the final round in the top three positions: Weiskopf 207 strokes, Nicklaus 208 and Miller 211. They were joined in a battle which Nicklaus was later to call: "The most exciting tournament I've ever played in."

Miller, not surprisingly, caught fire and shot the lights out, as they say, over the outward nine holes, scoring a 32 against Weiskopf's solid 34 and Nicklaus's remarkable 35 achieved after he dropped a shot at his shaky first hole.

The scoreboard at the turn showed: Weiskopf and Nicklaus, 11 strokes under par, Miller nine under. Weiskopf was confident: "I never doubted I would win."

By the long 15th hole Weiskopf, who had shed his sweater in the warm sun, had just regained the lead. He strode up to the tee very relaxed. "For some reason I felt very, very relaxed all day," he later recalled. "I wish I had been a little more nervous."

Nicklaus was far down the fairway. He was made aware by the sounds at his back that his lead might be gone. He frowned and muttered: "You've got to play this shot well."

Some 245 yards away, over a deep-sided pond, the flag fluttered and drooped in the breeze. The Golden Bear moves slowly under pressure. He twice took out his 3-wood and, undecided, twice put it back into the bag. He pondered: "I don't want to hit a 3-wood. I want to hit an iron. But I can't get an iron through this breeze. I'll wait. I'll fiddle around for awhile." He waited. He fiddled. The breeze died down. Nicklaus addressed the ball, cocked back his jaw and let loose with his hair-flying power.

Nicklaus usually stands watching the flight of his ball. This time he marched

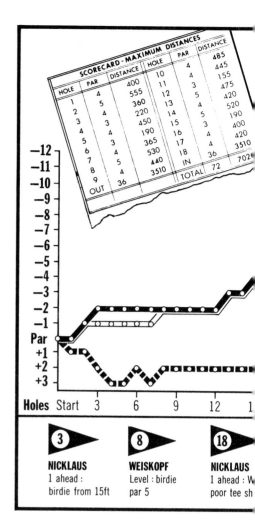

SCORECARD - MAXIMUM DISTANCES					
HOLE	PAR	DISTANCE	HOLE	PAR	DISTANCE
1	4	400	10	4	485
2	5	555	11	4	445
3	4	360	12	3	155
4	3	220	13	5	475
5	4	450	14	4	420
6	4	190	15	5	520
7	3	365	16	3	190
8	4	530	17	4	400
9	5	440	18	4	420
OUT	36	3510	IN	36	3510
			TOTAL	72	7020

NICKLAUS
1 ahead :
birdie from 15ft

WEISKOPF
Level : birdie
par 5

NICKLAUS
1 ahead : W
poor tee sh

right along after it. A thin smile crossed his lips. "That's going to be good." The ball flew string-straight, dropped daintily on to the green and nearly ran into the cup. Nicklaus had struck, he later decided, the finest 1-iron shot of his life.

That great golfers avert their heads from a scoreboard is a myth. Walking on to the green Nicklaus searched the board for news of his rivals. Nothing. The officials had not put up Weiskopf's new birdie for fear of distracting Nicklaus.

"That was courteous of them," he later recalled. "But by straining my eyes I could see the scoreboard by the sixth green." Weiskopf had him by one. Nicklaus narrowly missed his eagle putt and, with a birdie, drew level.

The 16th hole lasted an eternity. Nicklaus took too much turf from the tee and left himself a twisting 40-foot putt uphill to the hole. He watched Miller nearly hole an eagle putt to draw level back on the previous green. He

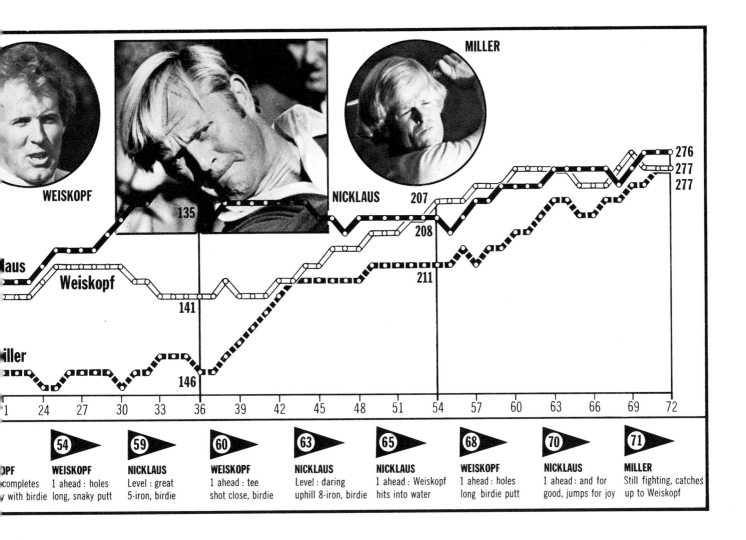

WEISKOPF

MILLER

NICKLAUS 207

135

aus

Weiskopf

141

208

211

iller

146

276
277
277

1   24   27   30   33   36   39   42   45   48   51   54   57   60   63   66   69   72

▶54	▶59	▶60	▶63	▶65	▶68	▶70	▶71
)PF completes / with birdie	**WEISKOPF** 1 ahead : holes long, snaky putt	**NICKLAUS** Level : great 5-iron, birdie	**WEISKOPF** 1 ahead : tee shot close, birdie	**NICKLAUS** Level : daring uphill 8-iron, birdie	**NICKLAUS** 1 ahead : Weiskopf hits into water	**WEISKOPF** 1 ahead : holes long birdie putt	**NICKLAUS** 1 ahead : and for good, jumps for joy	**MILLER** Still fighting, catches up to Weiskopf

watched Weiskopf tap in his own birdie putt to draw level. He watched his playing companion, Watson, hit twice into the lake by the green. He watched Watson putt, finally, and he magically saw the line for himself. "Sometimes you get the feeling—it's silly I know—but sometimes you get the feeling you're going to make a putt. On the 16th I had that feeling."

The feeling came true. The Masters could be his for the holding. In a rare burst of emotion, Nicklaus leapt into the air and did a war dance round the green.

"I knew that Tom was going to have a tough time playing that hole after watching somebody make two." Weiskopf did indeed have a hard time on the 16th hole. He lost the lead by three-putting, no doubt shaken, as Miller was, by such a burst of exuberance from the world's greatest golfer.

As Miller later observed: "I never have seen Jack jump around like that. I was happy to walk through the Bear prints."   *April 20 1975*

The one he left stone dead.

Big-game relaxation

About 1,000 people gathered around Jack Nicklaus last weekend as he weighed in with his 1,358lb. marlin, the biggest caught this year in Australia. Nicklaus made the catch while on a trip with his friend Kerry Packer off the Great Barrier Reef. Stuffed and mounted at a cost of $A5,000, the marlin is soon to be shipped back home to Florida.

Nicklaus is a tireless big-game fisherman and, according to reports, he was still fresh after his six-hour battle with the marlin. In fact, speculation that the encounter left him stiff and sore for the opening rounds of the Australian Open championship proved to be exaggerated. Despite a tennis injury on Packer's tennis court, Nicklaus had a second-round 66 and led by four strokes going into the final day.

"Fishing," he has written, "is an excellent way to rest the mind from golf before an important tournament."   *November 19 1978*

4

THE BODY

Hefty or thin, tall or short, disabled, elderly or young, physical recreation provides proof of the astonishing versatility of the human body. Nurture it, and the benefits can be enormous; abuse or neglect it, and the penalties may be extreme. Athletes on anabolic steroids may be taking risks the full magnitude of which are yet only hinted at. Boxers who take too many head punches, and footballers who head too many heavy balls, may be putting a healthy future in jeopardy. The whole gamut of sport's training routines, dietary variations, sexual myths, is fascinating and compelling to scientists and laymen alike. For the majority, though, exploring the various benefits derived from physical fitness is something which has been the particular concern of The Sunday Times.

It was Christmas of 1975 when *The Sunday Times* featured Waltraut Midgeley (previous page) and five other individuals who attributed the vitality of their middle-age years to exercise. Many readers were attracted to the accompanying "aerobic" exercise schedules, and the suggestion was made to follow up the middle-age "good examples" by testing and monitoring exercise in comparatively unfit people.

An initiative which started with one reader was continued by others. When the highly successful, year-long Middle-Age Fitness series ended, readers pressed the paper further. New ways of looking at exercise emerged. Altogether it amounted to a great deal of writing on the fitness theme. Here the year-long experiment is summarised mainly through the experience of one man.

The guinea pigs who put life into middle age

by Norman Harris

James Donovan, an airline pilot, was one of 12 human guinea pigs tested at the Cavendish Medical Centre, London, in January of 1976. The 12 comprised eight men and four women from all over Britain, who were at various stages of "middle age". They believed themselves to be in average health, though comparatively unfit.

The first test (to be repeated later) involved walking on a powered treadmill to a maximum of seven stages. Heart rate and blood pressure were recorded during and after this stress test, on an electrocardiogram (ECG).

As well as giving a first barometer-reading of fitness, this test was also in effect, a screening: and in four of the 12 subjects there was some degree of irregularity in the ECG pattern, suggesting the possibility of a "condition" which could manifest itself in time. For the general population, this statistic seemed to have sobering implications.

While the eight were given the green light to take progressively vigorous exercise, the other four were given the amber light and encouraged to proceed with caution.

One of the four was the airline pilot. In fact, 43-year-old James Donovan was already concerned. The yearly ECG test required by aviation regulations had also noted a slight pattern change, and as a result his health status was qualified so that he had to be tested *twice* a year. The first Cavendish test also indicated a slow recovery from stress: heart-beat should have dropped to 100 much sooner than it did (as the "Before" section of our table shows.)

James Donovan said the implications of the test "were catastrophic for me". His initial exercise plan was novel. On his inter-continental flights he took a fold-up bicycle—at 18 pounds, lighter than many typewriters. He rode forth from his hotel in the land of the mounties (see photo).

Checked again at the Cavendish after two months, he went without difficulty to his previous limit, stage five, and the ECG was now entirely normal. Now he was cleared to take up any of the aerobic exercises in which the Flat-Out-Eight were engaged, like jogging, swimming, squash, cycling. James Donovan soon became a regular runner, timing himself every day.

All of the other Proceed-With-Caution guinea-pigs were similarly given approval to increase their training effort. Two chose swimming. Another, a 57-year-old housewife, found stair-climbing attractive. The Flat-Out-Eight were mostly embarked on running programmes; they followed schedules in Dr Kenneth Cooper's book, *Aerobics*, and tried to reach a goal of 30 aerobic "points" a week.

At the end of the year all the guinea pigs were tested again at the Cavendish and they met for a party—including a run—at the Crystal Palace sports centre. The all-important final tests

HEART RATE		Before	After
At Rest		92	85
EXERCISE Stage	1	115	105
	2	130	120
	3	154	133
	4	158	145
	5	168	145
RECOVERY Mins	1	150	110
	3	122	95
	5	112	84
	10	105	82
	15	104	82
Cholesterol (mg%)		305	260
Triglyceride (mg%)		140	77
Weight (kilos)		72.2	73.0
Waist (cm)		87.5	86.0

● James Donovan's test figures at the start and end of 1976, the year of the Middle-Age Fitness experiment.

showed that everybody was able to do the same amount of "work" as in January at less effort. At the highest workload there was a drop in the heart-rate figures from an average for the group of 160 to an average of 142; and after one minute's recovery, an even more dramatic decrease, from an average of 123 to an average of 94.

"Imagine," we said, "that you are climbing five flights of stairs; or hurrying towards a bus stop; or digging the garden. And your heart is pumping furiously, your pulse racing at about 160. You might even be provoking a heart attack. Now imagine that you have a twin beside you engaging in exactly the same activity, but instead of being 160, your twin's pulse rate is only 140. And that the difference between the two of you has been brought about by a period of regular exercise . . . This is, in effect, what happened to our guinea pigs."

The tests also showed improved blood pressure and triglyceride levels, and, particularly, lower cholesterol levels which the Cavendish described as "significant". Overall, the opinion of the Cavendish's Dr Robin Hedworth-Whitty was that "these results mean that taking regular, graded exercise, definitely makes living safer for the average middle-aged person."

One of the subjects who, said the Cavendish, "owes a lot to the programme", was James Donovan. A year after the end of the experiment, we surprised the guinea pigs by asking for a further test, and the airline pilot was one who had kept going and showed the benefit. He said there was no doubt that he felt fitter, and indeed, he had rid himself of the widespread occupational complaint, among pilots, of backache. But the very best of his news was that he now needed to take the aviation ECG test only once a year: following further checks, his medical status was no longer qualified.

Pilot James Donovan at the controls.

Aerobic exercise time for pilot Donovan in Toronto.

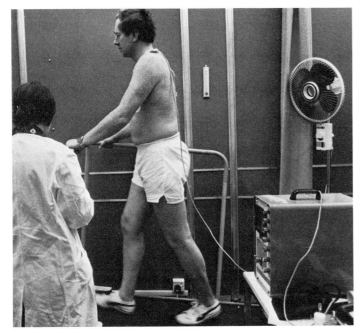

Another guinea pig at work on the ECG treadmill.

The guinea pigs' picnic: James Donovan, second from right, and other celebrants at Crystal Palace.

Festival of running jumping and throwing for the reborn

by John Lovesey

The competitors above are part of a total of 2,600 veteran athletes who came from 46 countries to participate in the World Veterans Athletics Championships in Gothenburg, the world's biggest track and field event. In a festival celebrating the joy and fitness to be derived from running, jumping and throwing for a lifetime, most competitors—like the 211 from the British Isles who won 64 medals bet-

ween them—paid their own way.

Since 1975 and the first world championships in Toronto, where 1,400 veterans competed, interest has soared. The biggest groups came from Sweden, Germany and the USA. In veteran athletics, men compete from the age of 40 and every five years move up a class until they reach the over-eighties. Women currently start at 35. Ultimately the system of age classification ensures, as one athlete said, that "every five years you are reborn."

Though records fell like ninepins in Sweden, it is a feeling of friendly striving, the victory over age, and occasionally disability, that epitomises these championships. It is mirrored in Fritz Assmy (photograph, upper left), a totally blind 62-year-old from West Germany who won the 100m sprint in his class, running alongside his son-in-

law; a cigar-smoking professor from California; Britain's first gold medal winner Charlie Williams, 46; a long-jumping Swedish mother and housewife; 72-year-old Winfield McFadden, a former American college athlete, high jumping nearly 4ft; and Britain's Bill Stoddart, 46, the winner of his class in the men's cross-country and then the marathon.

But if their spirit was mirrored in a single competitor, it was America's famous discus thrower Al Oerter, 40, who won four successive Olympic gold medals from 1956 to 1968, and who won the discus in his class in Gothenburg with 198ft 0½in against Czechoslovakia's 1972 Olympic champion Ludvik Danek's 189ft 6½in. "I came," Oerter said, "as a free soul." It was a sentiment echoed by everyone present. *August 14 1977*

Rushing feet in the Bois de Boulogne — the biggest running show on earth

by Robin Marlar

They ran through the Bois de Boulogne in their thousands yesterday, the French, and more will be running through the trees and over the acorns today. The Cross du Figaro has become the greatest sporting show on earth. It began modestly enough in 1961 with 1,800 runners; this year the entry for the 32 races was an astonishing 23,000. The ages range from 10 to 85, men and women, soldiers and civilians, athletes and shufflers, all puffing away.

From all corners of France they have come to Paris following the pattern of history. They are joined in the woods by tens of thousands of other Parisians and all the more this year because the weather was perfect. Experts from the clubs affiliated to the French Athletic Federation take part to lend a touch of class, whether from Bordeaux or Aix les Bains, Rheims or Poitiers.

But the open entries, those who just turn up for a run, are even more numerous and they, too, travel for miles. Three printers from Figaro's presses in Marseilles regularly drive 1,600 miles for a 25-minute run over six kilometres between putting Saturday's paper to bed and starting work on Monday's edition.

Some come to win. Michel Jazy took the athletes' prize for the first four years. For all that the most treasured achievement by an international athlete in the race is that for Alain Mimoun, who came 20th in the top race at the ripe old age of 45. Then there are other winners. The family Dupois-Quinet won the Cross's version of the generation game— grandparents and children, for four consecutive years.

Sun gone, nip in the air. Two laps of the 3,000 metre course ahead. Think it quickly—altogether, just over 4½ miles. There are the company teams, 15 strong. And there's Oxford and Cambridge, for whom the first 20 past the post will count in their own private contest. In all, 1,300 of us milling about under the four tricolours which mark the start.

I'll be trampled to death—the gun, a rush of humanity. How *does* anyone get to the front, one or two elbows used like gendarmes' truncheons, the track narrows, watch your feet, ouch, right eye whipped by low branch, what in hell's name are you doing here?

It must be a mile before we pass as opposed to being passed. Where is the end of the first lap? And all this *encore une fois*. Round again, whiff of belched garlic, voices from the woods "300 metres to go". Resist the temptation to a sprint finish whatever happens, but the sound of flat padding feet behind stirs the blood.

The exhausted foreigner asks himself Why? Just for taking part? For masochism, experience, fun? Yes. Oh, by the way, Oxford beat Cambridge.

But essentially it is a *jour de fête* during which *le picnic* takes over and 10,000 private bets are struck. The yell of encouragement from a 10-year-old soon after the start of the women's race "*allez maman*" was one to move anyone concerned with fitness, health and happiness. In fact, maman was allezing for all she was worth trying to keep up with the leaders over the 3km course.

The French called this race *seniors feminines*—though how anyone persuades a French woman to reveal whether she is over or under 35 is a secret only Frenchmen know. In that particular race something had gone wrong, for there was a Frenchman not a day under 60 in it; perhaps his blue rinse was a qualification.

For France the weekend has taken on the status of a sociological event, one for which members of the Academie Francaise will not only take part but also philosophise. How agreeable to take part in a competition without violence or tantrums or protest, merely an exercise in physical fulfilment with which entire families can identify, not to mention industrial companies and comedians.

There was no mention of steroids or dope, and the only major structure demanded by the event was a specially built restaurant. This is indeed Sport for All in the French way.

December 19 1976

"Allez maman!" Senior women revealing their age, and the spirit of competition.

JOGGERS RUN IN MY FAMILY · I JOG, U JANE · JOG, JOG, QUICK, QUICK, JOG · BE THE JOGGER IN THE PACK · U ORTA JOG · JOGONAUTS HAVE LIGHT YEARS AHEAD · JOGGING IS SOLE MUSIC · CHE JOGGERA LIVES · YOU' NEVER ALO

The day that Hyde Park was pounded alive by an invasion of 12,000 Fun Runners

by Norman Harris

A jogging-slogan contest, in November of 1977, re-emphasised the interests of our readers in this subject. Twenty thousand slogans were submitted, some of which appear above. And our readers insistently asked: What is *next*? It was to be *The Sunday Times* National Fun Run, announced early in 1978 and held in Hyde Park on October 1.

Twelve thousand entrants were attracted, in age classes ranging from the under-15s to the over-60s. In the latter group, underneath a T-shirt which proclaimed "Look After Yourself", the owner sported a long scar from coronary surgery: Ben Bennellick finished well up and received terrific applause. So did the first over-60 home, Chris Mason, who a year before joined a jogging group in Boston, Lincs. So did the first lady, Jennie Hawthorne, who won a delighted audience by saying she was "only from Surrey" and had run just five times in preparation.

Every one of the thousands who ran was a hero unto himself or herself. Or unto his or her wife, husband or family. Throughout the day roles were swiftly reversed, and one of the course marshals later recalled "seeing one boy of about 11 urging his mother on, and a few minutes later she was standing at the same place encouraging him."

One woman came during the morning to have a look. "And straightaway I went home to make a picnic and get hold of my family and bring them back to the park." For a Sports Council leader, it all amounted to "The most attractive group of people *en masse* I've ever seen."

In fact, Hyde Park had just played host to the biggest participatory sporting event ever held in Britain.

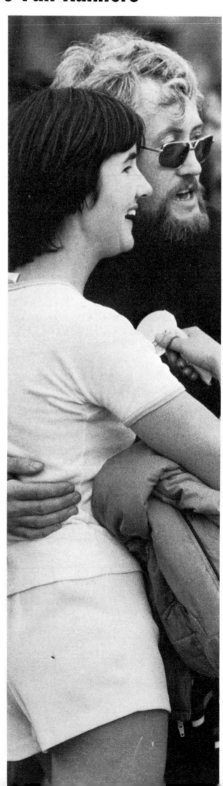

THE SUNDAY TIMES — KEEP ULATING, WITH RIEND

THE SUNDAY TIMES — JOG INTO THE GARDEN MAUD

THE SUNDAY TIMES — IF DODOS HAD JOGGED!

THE SUNDAY TIMES — MORE RUNS IN A LONG INNINGS

THE SUNDAY TIMES — JOG TODAY, HERE TOMORROW

THE SUNDAY TIMES — I'M ONLY DOING MY JOG

THE SUNDAY TIMES — JOG B4URA MEMORY

THE SUNDAY TIMES — JOGGING MAKES YOUR LEGS GO UP AND DOWN

THE SUNDAY TIMES — I JOG, THEREFORE I AM

The years of growth and the teenage sports drop-out

Beer bellies or a fit life? One PE teacher's battle for the hearts and minds of schoolchildren at the critical stage of their development.

by Chris Lightbown
Drawings by Nick Faure

"Kids do not want to play sport", says Barclay Edwards, 31, head of the Boys PE Department, at Sedgehill Comprehensive School in South London. "That is not what it is about, it never has been. If I told our kids 'There's a football fixture on Saturday. Be there at 11 o'clock;' you would get about three kids turning up. The only way you can be sure that they are all going to turn up is if they know that you are aware of all the pressures on them to not turn up. In other words, that you respect them."

Sedgehill sport only works because respect is mutual. Children have a confidence in Edwards and his staff that is, at best, rare on the academic side.

Edwards is the first to agree that in gaining children's respect, PE has built-in advantages, but points out that with children's increasing sophistication, "You cannot say that everything follows on from that. You have to sell it to kids; it has to be presented properly, to be organised, exciting, demanding—otherwise they reject it."

Sedgehill's "selling" of PE is obviously successful, as children in difficulties frequently turn first to members of Edwards's department. The huge out-of-hours commitment of the PE staff, and the closeness which comes from travelling with teams to outside events, undoubtedly helps, but Edwards argues that there is a deeper side as well. "Everything is down to basics on this side; it seems that out of the physical comes something much closer."

However, closeness is often interrupted at 14 by forces which are anything but close. If, as Edwards argues, PE is based on personal relationships, then not surprisingly children drop out at the age where personal relationships are most difficult. With the rapid advancement of children's maturity, staff speak of the

"Dropping Out" syndrome, traditionally encountered in the Fifth Year, starting to reach down into the Third.

Generally, children do not find fulfilment in personal relationships to replace the closeness Edwards talks of—one suspects teachers like Edwards

---

Up against the clichés about achievement through suffering: no one ever presents sport as fun.

---

would be quite happy if they did. But they turn instead to a whole series of material objects whose selling appeal is that they bring such relationships closer; but this is rarely the case.

For what both Edwards and the children are up against is a multi-million-pound beer industry, the highly calculating music business, the fashion world with its commercial and media allies, and all the entrepreneurs whose life is spent convincing children of 14 and 15 that they are somehow missing out on The Good Life.

For however new some of the pressures are that PE staff have to face, their basis is the oldest pressure of all—fear. What good PE teachers are up against is children's fear of being the odd one out if they do not go to the pub, of appearing unmanly if they do not go with girls and do not show disrespect to teachers. And an ample proportion of the commercial pressures on children play shamelessly on such fears.

However distasteful one might find the use of such pressures on young children, the fact remains that what they are working on is the simple idea of having a good time. Nobody with the children's interests at heart would want to deny them that. The question remains; what is the correct path?

Edwards feels there is room for both. "I tell our kids they can remain good at their sport, and still go out and have a good time; that it is a matter of determination and organisation." But this approach is rarely successful, it comes up against sport's blood, sweat and forbearance image, and children

assume it is a straight choice between that and The Good Life.

Here, much of the blame belongs to 100-miles-a-week athletes and the authority figures from headmasters to politicians who mouth clichés about achievement through suffering. No one ever presents sport as fun; and when Edwards does, he has precious little support from the players, officials and image-makers of the sports he is feeding from the grass roots.

Nor do Edwards and fellow thinkers have resources equal to the commercial pressures that descend on children at 14. "Half an hour is not much time to change a kid's whole life, is it?" says Edwards, referring to the time he gets with children in a single period.

On the girls' side, it is worse. With girls maturing earlier than boys, women PE teachers do not have even the breathing space until 14, which of course is no constraint on the commercial pressures that persuade young girls to assert their femininity before they have properly finished the ex-perience of childhood.

Women PE staff have considerable sympathy: "At the back of your mind you understand, and you feel for them and what they are facing. But you still push them because, surely, it is right that they be offered something different?"

Outside school, little is "offered", and almost everything is forced; it is almost impossible to exaggerate the severity of the outside pressures PE

The idea of co-operation and enjoyment of sport—constantly betrayed by media obsessed with winners.

---

staff face. While teachers like Edwards are trying to enthuse children with the germ of ideas like co-operation and enjoyment of sport, they are constantly betrayed by media that have an obsession with winners.

It seems grossly unfair to expect schools to produce reasonably fit adults who will later do some sport for fun, within a sporting culture besotted with superstars.

At Sedgehill, the superstar ethic means First Year parents disappointed at sons not making the school football team, and parents throughout the school providing no encouragement when their children are not doing well.

The result? Edwards reckons children with little ability, success or parental backing, are the first to drop out. The children who drop out early are usually the first to make money and start exploring the adult world. In trying to give such children a ground-work of confidence for this step teachers like Edwards have scant chance against forces that constantly work on children's inevitable lack of confidence and stability.

Society does not often see it that way, as Edwards observes. "Kids have a veneer of sophistication and confidence, particularly in London. But," he adds, with the insight of someone actually involved with children, "they are really crying out for something to hang on to." *February 16 1975*

The unacceptable face of the noble art unveiled one Tuesday night in Shoreditch

Boxers still die as a result of injuries which are an integral part of their sport, a fact cited by the abolitionists as conclusive evidence that boxing should be outlawed. Ulric Regis died after surgery for a blood clot on the brain the day following a bout, although he had been examined before and after fighting by a doctor.

by Peter Pringle

There will be no one to blame for the death yesterday, at 27, of Ulric Regis, Trinidad's professional heavyweight boxing champion, who had been knocked out only twice in his life. But must the death of this father of a two-year-old girl be written down as "just one of those unfortunate, unavoidable accidents"? Must it happen to another boxer in another year in another bout in another ring? Or will the British Boxing Board of Control be forced to look again at its provisions for post-fight medical checks and supervisions?

Events which led to the removal of a blood clot from Regis's brain at the National Hospital for Nervous Diseases in London where he died at 1 a.m. yesterday began on Tuesday morning. A blue BMC 1800 collected him and his Dutch second, John Batist, from the Winton Hotel, Inverness Terrace, Bayswater, and took them to the Royal Oak, Canning Town, for the weigh-in.

The same car was to deliver Regis, unconscious, to the hotel at 2 a.m. the next morning—*four hours* after the bout. Two of those hours which Regis may have spent with the taxi driver could provide a clue to his death. But the origin of the car and its driver—described as a stocky man, aged about 35, with receding fair hair—is a mystery. Batist says the taxi was booked for him by the hotel and the hotel says it was booked by Mr Batist. Neither can remember the name of the company.

After the weigh-in for his fight with Joe Bugner, the same driver took Regis and Batist to the Paramount restaurant in Irving Street for lunch and then back to the hotel. At 7 p.m. the driver picked up the two men again and took them to Shoreditch Town Hall and stayed there during the fight.

Dr A. L. Whiteson, chief medical officer of the BBBC, who examined Regis before and after the fight and found him to be as "fit to go into the ring as any boxer ever was," saw the whole contest. He says: "Regis took a fair amount of punishment during the eight rounds. He went down for a count of seven and again later but the second time it was more of a stumble.

"After he had been knocked down he didn't take too many punches on target and Bugner (aged 19, who has k.o'd 13 of his 14 opponents) just couldn't knock him out. Towards the end of the fight Regis was fast and alert and boxed much better." (So much so that the crowd booed Bugner because he could not put him down.)

"After the contest Regis went to Bugner's corner to congratulate him. He was in good spirits. I examined him in his dressing room and he had no complaints—no headaches, no double vision, perfect co-ordination and no amnesia. If there was anyone who shouldn't have had a head injury it was Regis."

Instantaneous brain injuries can be of three kinds: straightforward concussion which sends a shock wave through the brain and renders the victim unconscious for a certain length of time; the blow that tears a blood vessel and produces unconsciousness quickly; and, third, the knock that produces slow bleeding with delayed onset of unconsciousness.

The symptoms of any of these types may be dilation of the pupils, partial paralysis of the limbs, amnesia or loss of co-ordination. The BBBC rule book lays down a post-fight medical check for every boxer who has been counted out. Although he had not been k.o'd it was thought advisable by medical officers at the contest to give Regis his check, after which further treatment was not considered necessary. Whether he could have been saved if put under immediate observation in hospital will never be known.

At about 11 o'clock Regis, in jovial mood, and Batist left the town hall with their driver and returned to the hotel where they drank coffee.

Batist paid Regis his prize money—about £300, some of which was in Spanish pesetas because the boxer was living in San Sebastian—advised him

to give it to the hotel manager for safekeeping and to go to bed. "But he wanted to go off on the town," Batist told me, "and laughing, he left the hotel with the taxi driver." Shortly before 2 a.m. the driver returned to the hotel with Regis, now unconscious. The boxer had vomited in the car.

The hotel's manager, Mr P. Gnaegi, and a night porter carried Regis from the car. Mr Gnaegi says. "Regis was unconscious, his breathing was heavy and he smelt of drink. We assumed he had had too many and put him to bed. A quarter of an hour later I went to his room again and found him lying face down on the pillow so I turned him over.

"We booked a call for him at 9 a.m.,

Regis, who went down twice during the fight, in the ring with 19-year-old Joe Bugner.

but when the receptionist rang him at that time there was no reply. I came down at 9.30 and tried to wake him by slapping his face. When there was no response I rang a doctor who said we should call an ambulance.

Regis was taken to St. Mary's Hospital and later to the National Hospital for Nervous Diseases where he was operated on for a sub-dural haematoma, the late complication of a head injury, the condition of which may easily have been aggravated during the boxer's two last hours and before his admission to hospital. The vomiting may have been the result of drink or concussion.

Doctors at the National Hospital say that had Regis not been in "such a fit condition and very strong he would have been dead before he was admitted to hospital."

Only six professional boxers have died after contests in Britain since the war—the last was Lyn James, a featherweight, who collapsed in the sixth round against Colin Lake, also at Shoreditch. He died the next day of a brain injury.

The Regis story enforces the long-standing lobby by doctors outside boxing for more elaborate post-fight checks. This week there is a meeting of the BBBC's Southern Area medical panel. An item on the agenda is medical examinations before and after contests. The sponsor is Dr Whiteson.

March 16 1969

Inside track

Fancy Them

British racing pigeon fanciers gathered last week in London to select a team of birds to send over to Belgium next February for the Racing Pigeon Olympiad. If ever there was a strange competition it's got to be the Racing Pigeon Olympiad. The birds don't even fly, let alone race; they just sit there and get handled by judges.

"The winners are picked entirely on physical appearance," says Colin Osman, editor of The Racing Pigeon, organisers of the show. "Because there is no way to organise an international race."

The problem is simple: if the best birds are gathered from the four corners of the earth, they will fly off in four directions. That wouldn't do. Osman adds that even if birds were brought together for training they would not equally acclimatise.

Therefore, prizes are given for the look in a bird's eye and its body configurations. "I go first for the back," says a top judge, Charles Miller. "Nicely firm and arched slightly upwards. A flat back, you see, won't stand the stress. Then I like pectoral muscles to stand out like pencils. The flights of the wings should be in a straight line with the end flights a bit on the narrow side, to nip through the air. Finally, I want some depth and quality in the eye."

Three cocks and three hens were chosen for Belgium but, the Best of Show was a cock bird from Wales. He has seldom raced in his life. He merely *looks* a winner.

December 6 1970

● What a nave! A leading Soviet official, alleging that Western churches are attempting to identify with sport, says: "The alliance between religion and sport is a forced type of ideological diversion directed against the progressive education of youth against the growing unity of workers in the capitalist world in their struggle for freedom, democracy and socialism." Amen.

January 29 1978

The psychological, physical and moral inextricably muddled in a writhing heap

In September 1970 the World Congress of Sports Medicine was held in Oxford. The lectures covered doping, death and even the influence of wind resistance. But there was no opportunity to air one of sports medicine's most enduring controversies—the effects of sexual exercise on sporting performance.

by Robert Lacey

Is sexual intercourse *really* more tiring than a five mile walk? Most sportsmen think so. "Keep off the nest, lad" is the trainer's traditional warning to his champion in the days before the big event.

It is standard practice for Italian football clubs to take their players into *ritiro* from Thursday to Monday because they believe that sex would harm performance in weekend matches, and Pele considers the months he spent away from his wife to be one of the crucial factors in his World Cup success. Many doctors agree. "I would say that sexual abstinence is almost essential for sporting success," says Dr J. L. Blonstein, President of the Medical Commission of the International Boxing Association. "Even out of training the ambitious athlete should not have intercourse more than three times a week."

But other doctors are questioning the basis of sport's most enduring taboo. "There's absolutely no evidence to indicate that sexual exercise has any deleterious effect on sporting performance," says Dr John Williams, who has delivered a paper on the subject at an International Federation of Sports Medicine study course. "Obviously an athlete can't roll straight out of bed on to the starting blocks and hope to set a world record, but there's no *physiological* reason why he shouldn't make love the night before or even on the morning before an afternoon event."

Then why has abstinence become a fetish? "You have to make a crucial distinction between the mind and the body," says Dr Williams. "A top class international sportsman may feel strongly that he wants no distractions of any sort before a big competition, and that he can only excel if he concentrates on the event and nothing else. Now if he feels like this, then sexual intercourse can be a disaster—but for psychological, not physiological reasons."

Most racing drivers insist that their jet-set social life neutralises the strain of Grand Prix rivalries. But Stirling Moss can think of no real champions who have taken chances before competition. "At the beginning of my career I wouldn't go near a woman for five days before a race. Then I decided that was crazy and cut the limit down to 48 hours. But I'd never make love any closer to the event than that, no more than I'd jump over the moon. It was a matter of discipline."

What about after the race? Was he exhausted? "You must be joking. After two days without it?"

Henry Cooper, still Britain's best heavyweight boxer, agrees that when the training is over there are few things he enjoys more—and nothing he is better prepared for. "It stands to reason. If you feel healthy and fit you obviously feel more like it." But getting in shape for a fight is a different matter. He goes away for six weeks to a training camp. "It's not just sex. If you want to

win a fight you've got to go into the ring *mean*, and for that you've got to go without home comforts."

It is normal for managers to take their boys "into the woods" for seclusion lasting weeks on end—and Dr Blonstein, who is also honorary medical officer to the Amateur Boxing Association, thinks there are sound medical reasons for this.

"I strongly advise my boxers to abstain from sexual intercourse for two weeks prior to training and then for the three or four weeks that training occupies. You see, my argument is that in the course of training the blood develops extra adrenaline. Then during competition the blood also develops noradrenaline to assist the effort—and it's the noradrenaline you particularly need for physical effort. Sexual intercourse uses up the noradrenaline."

There is little scientific justification for this theory. It is a medical commonplace that adrenaline in the bloodstream tunes up the heart of the sportsman before competition: noradrenaline may well help to keep him going once the competition has begun. But specialist research provides no evidence that these chemicals can ever be exhausted as Dr Blonstein suggests.

"Look at what happens to rowers," says Dr Williams. "They may be exhausted after a race—at least as tired as anyone who has just made love. But they recover and they can row as many as three races like that in an afternoon. Athletes have been known to set up records only hours after the most strenuous qualifying heats. Of course one is weakened after intercourse—*omnia animalia post coitum tristia sunt** is an old and true saying—but the weakness is transient and largely subjective. The truth is that physical passion and top class sporting competition make both physical and emotional demands on the individual, and it is how he balances these in his *mind* that determines the sportsman's success in either or both activities."

As Casey Stengel, the American baseball manager, used to say: "It ain't the girls that bother the players. It's the booze they drink and the time they waste chasing them."

What about the suggestion that people who are super fit have an increased sexual appetite? "I'm afraid there is little physiological evidence for this either," says Dr Williams. "Sportsmen can perhaps manage more athletic sexual postures and can call on reserves of endurance at crucial moments—but apart from that it's a matter of psychology."

To non-sportsmen, of course, the entire debate is largely academic. Our sporting activities tend to peter out as our sexual ones develop. And sportsmen themselves aren't really too keen on getting the facts of the matter sorted out beyond contradiction. "Terribly sorry, but I was on the job all night," remains the least challengeable of excuses for the champion's defeat.

September 6 1970

*All animals are sad after intercourse.

"Watch The Ropes of Time and ask, could a footballer survive?"

Rudolf Nureyev, after the first 2½ hour session of the day, compares the "fantastic responsibility" of his training and workload to what is demanded of other athletes.

by Dudley Doust

In Hammersmith, overlooking the playing fields of St. Paul's School, Rudolf Nureyev trains daily at the Royal Ballet School. His classes, accompanied by a piano and about 20 other male dancers, begin with long and cautious sessions of limbering up at the barre and end an hour and a half later with more vigorous leaps and pirouettes in the centre of the studio.

"Training is a fantastic responsibility for a dancer," said Nureyev, wet with sweat after a session last week. "If you miss it, you regret it very soon. After three days off, my back, my legs, even my spine begin to deteriorate. And after a week"—he grinned—"ah, my legs would shake at the barre. I'd faint."

After years of dancing—he's now rising 32—Nureyev mentions only one hampering injury. "At school in Russia my teacher said 'sit down after you jump' and I did. I hurt my ankle,"—he designated the ankle, then hurriedly scrubbed it out of the air, "don't say the left or right"—"and since then it tires more easy. It doesn't stretch, the foot doesn't point like the other." That suggested that dancers, like footballers, worked with a favourite foot. "It's done by the choreographer. He'll take that into account."

Nureyev is fed up with manipulators who have worked on the foot. "I don't believe in them," he said with a brief flash of his celebrated temper. "They're crap. They've just weakened my foot."

Up close, what strikes one most about Nureyev, apart from his disarming grin, is his physique: at 5ft. 8in. he is hardly tall for a contemporary male dancer; at 11 stone, braided with muscle, he was the sturdiest man in the class "Now I am seven pounds overweight," he estimated. "In the winter I like to be a little fat, to keep warm."

Nureyev, a keen admirer of Muhammad Ali.

Lately, he has added more vegetables to the customary soup and entrecote steak, blood rare, which he eats some five hours before a performance and then again after one. He asked about footballers and disapprovingly pursed his lips to learn they usually eat nearer than that to match time. He sleeps 10 to 11 hours a day.

Did he use weights in training? Not any longer, although the Russians did. "I was once slim and very weak and I couldn't lift anybody. It was a terrible struggle, learning how to use your thighs and buttocks to lift a girl. The girl must jump correctly, too. In Russia, if she jumps badly, you are told to let her drop." The recollection amused him. "She soon learns."

His day's work was hardly over. He might rehearse in the afternoon. If he went on at Covent Garden that evening he would work at a barre for 45 minutes, "sort of grinding the floor until my legs are supple," or if the role was classical perhaps dance the entire assignment before curtain time.

"I have to be tired before I perform," he said. "If I am on my second wind, I know it will work. Otherwise I might jump and not know where I am going." On the morning after a performance, Nureyev takes two hot baths; he despairs that masseurs are not more readily available in London. "This is not a body-conscious country."

As for sport itself, Nureyev showed a passing interest in rope-climbing and, not surprisingly, gymnastics, and was "terribly slow runner" as a youth in Russia. He is a keen admirer of Muhammad Ali ("It's the skill of the man, and his footwork") and from time to time watches wrestling on television, yet to be truthful the thought of sport brings a blank and infectious grin to his face. "Watch me in a modern ballet like The Ropes of Time," he said, "and then tell me, could a footballer survive it?" *March 8 1970*

The long and the short and the tall —
a living framework for excellence

The tough, competitive needs of sport make increasingly specialist demands on the body. During the summer of 1974, we looked at the stresses of individual sports, at diets which fuelled the hugely diverse needs of Geoff Capes's 21 stones to the strained frame of Lester Piggott, who wouldn't know a calorie if he saw one.

We looked at other contrasts: the highly tuned boxer with his "exaggerated thighs", against the long-distance runner with his stubby legs, "short levers" to stand the pounding. The long-distance swimmer, blubbery as a whale, against the adolescent bodies of young girls held at puberty to enhance their sprint swimming. And the goalkeeper's trade—hardly one renowned for remarkable physique—which found in Peter Shilton a fanatic for fitness training: "I want the opposing forwards to think 'By golly, he looks big and fit'."

Yet, above and beyond the impact of any of those, were the repercussions caused by the photographs on these two pages. In Peter Gabbett and Monica Rutherford we found two modern athletes who paid homage to the Grecian ideal of the perfect body—the classic poses of the early Olympics, with their unashamed, unselfconscious pride in personal beauty.

From the sports pages one week, Monica's photograph—or rather Victorian attitudes towards it—achieved the rare status of front page news the next two. First Monica's nude pose lost her a job as a physical education teacher at a Dorset comprehensive school but, five days after their decision was aired on page one of *The Sunday Times*, the school reinstated her.

"The one thing which worried me about the photograph," said Monica, "was attending an interview at the school the day after it appeared. But I decided that not even a local authority could take exception to a serious and tasteful silhouette photograph in a sports context. In the end, I'm glad they removed the hidden stigma."

by Michael Bateman
Photographs by Tony Duffy

potatoes. I'd get the lot, shovel it down. At 9.30 I'd eat a couple of sandwiches, and bed at 10.30. I'd crash out, a pretty good kip till 7.30.

"Sex? Why not? It's better when you're fit, not doubt about that. Within reason it aids performance, because it relaxes you.

"But before a top competition I put everything out of my mind, for two or three days. I'm not on the same wavelength as the family thing, I'm divorced from everything around me. I run the competition through my mind, create a mental picture of me doing it. Then, when you're competing, all you've got to do is reproduce that picture in your mind, and not have to search for it, provide it from your bowels." *May 19 1974*

● *Monica Rutherford is 30. She was British gymnastics champion when she was 16, 17, 18 and 19. Represented Britain at the 1964 Tokyo Olympics. Married to diving champion Brian Phelps, two daughters. Height 5ft 4in. Weight 8st 8lb.*

"I still look at myself as a gymnast and keeping fit is the prime object of my life. My idea of an outing is an outing to the gym. In everyday life if I'm going for a bus, I run for it. I leap around the house. It almost seems crazy to imagine. Most people bend their knees to pick something up, but a gymnast bends with the legs straight. Bending all day keeps the body supple.

"I used to do the splits position in bed, one foot under the pillow. You get a greater degree of suppleness. I could go to sleep like that, it didn't bother me.

"I avoid a high protein diet, because I don't want too much muscle. I eat almost everything, but lots of nuts, meat and cheese. I eat potatoes once a week, roast on Sundays. And a lot of fresh fruit. Only one main meal a day. If it's the evening then I just have a soup, apple and cheese for lunch. Most people in this country eat far too much.

"I have to have at least seven hours' sleep because I burn up a lot of energy. I go to bed at 12. *Die.* Then up at seven.

"Speaking objectively I don't think sport affects sex life. You can equally exhaust yourself mentally reading a book all day. It's better when you're fit, the body's more highly tuned.

"My husband Brian looks at Miss World and knows she's nothing. But he looks at Ludmila, the Russian gymnastic champion, and he thinks she's fantastic." *May 19 1974*

● *Peter Gabbett is 32. He holds the British and Commonwealth decathlon records. He has also competed for Britain at 400 metres and long jump. Height 6ft. Weight 13st.*

"I think the decathlon is *the* athletic event. It takes about four years to build up to a decathlon. It's the full achievement, throwing, jumping, running. For the hurdles you've got to be supple and floppy. The event immediately afterwards is the discus, and for this you've got to be rigid and your back has got to be strong; the opposite.

"I was in the Navy, so training was no problem. I'd train from 9 till 11 after a light breakfast, toast and coffee, and then take an early lunch of energy and protein foods, Casalan and Complan. I mix it with Ribena. Then I'd train from 2 to 5 p.m., when I'd sit down to a pretty big meal of meat, gravy, bread,

A game of calories: beating the scales or stoking the furnace

● *Lester Piggott is 5ft 7½in., tall indeed among the world's smallest athletes. He's 38 now and he should weigh around 10 to 11 stone, but for 20 years he's never been many ounces above 8st 4lb at any time in the racing season.*

Champion jockey seven times maybe, but such is the toll of wasting to keep his weight down, and the nervous tension of racing seven days a week (flying to France many weekends), Piggott decided two years ago to take it rather more easily and not to go for the championship.

Piggott was always a good sportsman (not a bad bat at school, and a 200-yards sprinter) and has ridden from age four. He explains that in racing you need the concentrated strength of the circus acrobat. It's important not to upset the balance of the horse. Most jockeys come into the final straight moving about as they use the reins and whip, but Piggott minimises his movements while still exerting powerful force with his legs. He has very strong legs.

His riding style is unique. You can pick him from the bunch because he rises up above the others, rather like a water skier.

What a jockey doesn't want is weight, of course. Piggott's view is what you don't put on, you don't have to sweat off. Earlier in his career he used to travel to races with a sweat suit under his ordinary clothes, and the car heater turned on full. Nowadays he depends on consistency "I never let myself get heavy, even in winter, because I'm afraid I'd never get it off."

A jockey's breakfast is hardly a gourmet treat. A thin slice of toast plus coffee, without milk. Lunch, a sandwich. The evening meal something like tongue and salad, finishing off with ice cream. "I don't eat potatoes, rice, bread. I only take one pint of fluid a day." Piggott smokes three or four cigars a day to keep his appetite at bay.

Stripped down, Piggott doesn't look as if years of wasting have taken a toll on him as it has on some jockeys. "You can take dehydration pills and lose two or three pounds in a few hours. But they are bound to affect the kidney and liver." *September 1 1974*

Piggott: never heavy.

Shilton: deep sleeper.

● *Peter Shilton, at 24 one of the world's best goalkeepers, stands 6ft and weighs 13st 8lb. His footballing colleagues call him Tarzan.*

Sweating off the summer flab is a pre-season torture footballers dread. But, long before the clubs start, Shilton is in touch with Sergeant-Major Jock Scott, a Royal Signals PTI, who sets him 15 strenuous exercises of 30 seconds each, every one followed by a sprint to the end of the gym and back.

Mentally and physically whacked, Peter then goes on to the trampoline. "You're forced to think when you're tired," he explains. "It calls for split-second responses, or else you come down with a crash.

"I also do gymnastic and Bullworker exercises and I'm forever working out new technical exercises." Actually, when he was a boy he used to hang by his arms from the banisters to stretch himself. He claims it worked, too.

All this for what? Ninety minutes spent mostly standing around creates a huge static tension. He plays the whole match at the limit, flexing his body, making 1,000 imaginary moves, assessing build-ups, watching for individual skill, readying himself. "You've got to dominate things. I want the opposing forwards to think 'By golly, he looks big and fit.' But if you have a peak, you have to get a valley to ease it off; I try to look on relaxation and meals and drinking as part of training."

After a summer's holiday, he may put on seven pounds. "But I don't have a weight problem. I feel as if I'm stoking up a furnace. If I haven't got a full belly, I don't feel energetic." He eats what he wants, when he wants . . . "a lot of fruit, especially apples and oranges. I'm trying to like honey, I know its good for me. I don't eat fish or fatty bacon. My favourite meal is steak and salad, followed by rice pudding. Sometimes twice a day."

Each night he sinks into a sleep of

fearsome depth. Every morning, his wife Sue wakes him with breakfast in bed, newspapers, and enough cups of tea to revive him. Usually four or five. "I go to bed at nine, never later than half-past ten. I can't do without 10 or 11 hours' sleep." *July 28 1974*

● *Geoff Capes, 24-year-old village policeman whose shot-put record stands at a huge 68ft 3¼in, eats the equivalent of two heifers a year. He's a Goliath of 6ft 5in, a twenty-one stoner.*

Capes eats £15 worth of meat a week, along with 35 pints of milk, six dozen eggs, seven loaves. He eats three cooked meals a day, which his wife Jill prepares, and countless snacks like fried cheese which he does himself.

He burns this up at 12,000 calories a day, twice the rate of Peter Gabbett, the decathlete, and four times the rate of an average person.

"I've actually lost two stone in the last three years, while improving my distance by 10 feet. I've lost almost all my fatty tissue. I eat no fat, practically none at all. Just protein, the meat, eggs, cheese, milk, plus some greens and spuds. "I also take Pollen B, Pollitabs and Stark protein."

Capes's father was a mere 5ft 7in high, but Geoff had chosen him well, because he was a regular Lincolnshire poacher who made sure his four huge sons got all the protein they needed, downing deer for venison, bringing home pheasants and rabbits.

His mother provided greens and spuds, vital minerals and Vitamin C. She was 6ft and 18 stone in her prime. "There was a teacher at school who tore my ear lobe. My mother found him in the tea-break and thumped him.

"As a boy I remember picking up two four-stone weights the coalman uses, just to show off. At 16 I had an eight-stone bar I used to do press-ups with in bed until I went to sleep. But around these parts that's nothing.

"There's a man of 67, Joe, who can still lift two eight-stone sacks of wheat, one in each hand. When he was younger he ran from Market Hill to Mint Farm for a bet, with an 18-stone sack on his back and beat a man who ran without."

Geoff has always been the all-round athlete, weightlifting, playing football, boxing. He considered a boxing career until he decided it was too dangerous. *Chickening out?* "No, I was scared I might hurt somebody."

May 26 1974

Capes: meat eater.

Blocking the urges of growth, pain, hunger and... yes, sex too

● *Jenny Turrall broke the world 1,500 metres freestyle record when she was 13½, a slip of a girl at 5ft 2in and 6st 12lb. Six months later, she weighs nearly a stone more and she's two inches taller.*

World championship swimming is dynamics and dedication. Jenny can sustain the dedication, but how long can she control the dynamics? Just as long as her coach can make her play Peter Pan and never grow up, it seems.

Her coach is Forbes Carlile who, with his wife, runs probably the world's biggest swimming school near Sydney. The secret, he says, is keeping puberty at bay. "The proportion of body muscle to weight begins to fall off at puberty. We try to hold them back. This is an area of sacrifice: We allow no empty calories, no cakes, no biscuits, no sweets."

Carlile's swimmers are on no freak diets, though, no vitamin or mineral supplements. They don't even count calories. They are simply encouraged to eat plenty of beef, fish, eggs, fruit and vegetables.

Every day they put Jenny on the scales. "We begrudge her every pound. It is essential she remains lean. We like to see their ribs, we say. The most successful swimmers have been like greyhounds, even Mark Spitz."

But you can't resist nature for ever. Jenny, like all swimming nymphets, *will* eventually grow up. *June 16 1974*

Turrall: playing Peter Pan.

Murphy: training on fish and chips.

● *Kevin Murphy, 25, swims further than anyone in the world. He tries to stay a fat, 12st 7lb, 5ft 8½in to combat the cold.*

He has swum the Channel two-ways non-stop, twice swum the Irish Channel (the Graveyard swim), rounded the Isle of Wight, and spent a staggering 43 hours covering the 50 miles of Lake Balaton in Hungary.

Murphy was seven when he discovered this "aptitude". In Kingsbury baths, North London, all the kids beat him over one length, but he beat them over two. At 14 he won a three-miles race. At 17 he swam the Channel.

"Three-quarters of distance swimming is willpower," he says. "The body tells you to stop, you feel you are going to die. Then you tell your body,

'Get the hell away with you'. I know I can come out the other side of pain."

Six hours later, Kevin showed no signs of tiredness as he continued to list minute details of his anatomy—the colours of hairs on his wrist, his contact lenses, the shape of his nose, the little gristly nodules in his shoulders.

This is how some of it goes:

My stomach: I have a 35-inch waist. I drink Guinness and eat fish and chips to build up calories. Before a swim I have a double helping of cereal and scrambled eggs. During it, I'll eat biscuits, chocolate and rice pudding.

My chest: It's 44 inches expanded and abnormally strong. I crashed my Austin Healey at 80 mph in Ireland. My chest bent the steering wheel.

My armpits: I cover my body with lanoline to conserve heat, and put vaseline under my arms to stop chafing.

My legs: My thigh bone, the femur, is twice as thick as normal. I use my legs more than necessary which makes me bouyant in rough water.

My pelvic girdle: A doctor discovered I appear to have grown extra buttress-bones to support my pelvis . . . it might just be gristle though.
August 4 1974

● *Ian Thompson, 24, the Commonwealth marathon champion, is 5ft 6½in and 9st 6lb.*

"For a marathon runner, I've got rather stubby legs, short levers which stand the pounding. My knees get sore,

Thompson: ignoring the pain.

Conteh: breaking the ice and forgetting the dollies.

but Derek Clayton, the only man who's ever run a faster marathon than me, had five knee operations.

"But you'd be wrong to emphasise the pain. Pain is anaesthetised by the euphoria of running. You're going to get blisters, but you stop paying attention so they stop handing out signals. There's a part in every marathon where you lose a sense of identity in yourself. You become *running* itself.

"I've always trained hard. At 17 I was running 70 miles a week; now its 100 and by the European championship in Rome it will be 140 miles. I'm a trainee teacher, which gives me time.

"I have a light breakfast, two boiled eggs, bread and butter, tea without sugar. After a mid-morning coffee with sugar I go for a five-mile run in open countryside.

"Then I have stodgy school lunch, like cheese-and-egg flan, salad, potatoes, semolina. In the evening, I run 10 miles, then eat almost anything. Today it was a chop, potatoes, oh, and semolina again.

"The marathon is 26 miles 385 yards, and the important factor is to store energy sugars—glycogen. You can only store 1,500 calories worth, which is the amount you'd burn in 1½ hours of running. My best time is 2 hours 9 minutes, so you not only use up physical reserves but burn into actual muscle.

"I race on the high-carbohydrate diet. It's still controversial. You can make yourself liable to infections. Six days before the race you cut out car-bohydrates, eat only protein, and continue to train at high intensity. You exhaust the body's reserves of glycogen, expecially in the leg muscles.

"Three days before the race, you switch to carbohydrates and light training. You feel good, sleep well. The glycogen increases to a much higher level than normal and enables you to go on running when everyone else is dying.

"Before my Christchurch marathon I felt so calm, I *knew* I was going to win. I'd been running 10 years, I felt Master of Myself. Afterwards my legs were leaden for four or five weeks."

June 30 1974

● *John Conteh, 23, world light-heavyweight contender, is 6ft and 12½st. of lethal fight-muscle. His manager, George Francis, puts it down to a Marine-tough training programme.*

Conteh has one of the finest physiques for his weight ever seen. "So many have highly-muscled trunks, hunched frames," says George. "I've tried to keep John supple. I don't build him up on the pectorals (across the chest). For every exercise there is a counter-exercise which prevents exaggerated muscle development. If there's any exaggeration, it's in the thighs which are long and strong."

They are strengthened every day by kicking at a loaded medicine ball. Conteh runs, wearing heavy-duty boots, over a seven-miles hill course, ending up every morning with a swim in Highgate pond "even if we have to break the ice." George goes too.

John's ability to take one on the chin is because of a routine of exercises designed to toughen his chin, jaw and neck. He bites through an imaginary piece of wood 200 times a day, chewing till his face flushes and the radiating muscles to his neck show white.

Then he rolls his head from side to side, and up and down, forcing it against the pressure of hands and forearm. Next, on the ground, he puts his hands behind his back and rolls on his head from side to side. (One way of breaking your neck if you're not in training.)

After that, he lies down on an inclined board of 30 degrees: a stump of tree weighing 1½ stones is placed on his neck, and he lifts it repeatedly by arching his back.

"The hardest thing is the birds," says George. "Success brings all the dollies round. One climbed up a ladder to his dressing room . . . we had to pour a bucket of water over her. Sex is a nasty business. I say no sex a month before a fight. You've only so much energy to burn; you can't have that stuff between the sheets and box at full capacity. Muhammad Ali will tell you that."

John eats fairly conventionally for a top athlete: hungrily. On the day of a fight? "Plenty of glucose, lashings of honey. Consommé, Dover sole, grilled chicken or steak, green salad, ice cream, tinned fruit, glucose tablets. After five o'clock, nothing." *September 8 1974*

●

Head damage: paying a painful price and risking more than early baldness

An inquiry into football's unmentionable subject—that there could be danger in heading a ball.

by Rob Hughes

The roar of the crowd stirred in anticipation as the centre-forward, sleek black hair parted down the middle, galloped into position. The ball was met sternly by the broad forehead . . . goal!

"Scored, But He Did Not Know", echoed the headlines.

Indeed, it was three days before Tommy Lawton could recall heading that England goal in 1946. Then 27, he had played 70 minutes with concussion, and was seldom quite as devastating again. Today, Lawton makes no bones about it; constant migraine, leading to the dole and attempted suicide, is his legacy of legendary days as the nation's all-powerful head.

Two months ago, his life turned full circle. Convicted in Nottingham for petty fraud, he works out 200 hours' community service teaching boys to head. Doubtless his methods are less barbaric than his own education at Burnley where, under threat by cane, he lunged again and again at a ball suspended from rafters until skin peeled either side of his head.

Lawton was not the first to reel from head pain. Before him England and Arsenal full-back Eddie Hapgood used to faint after heading, and pre-war captain Stan Cullis retired prematurely with blackouts. Nor has time removed the dangers. The plastic-coated ball may carry less weight, but its speed is greater, and players come under greater pressure in twice as many games.

That represents a lot of headache. David Cross, Coventry's 23-year-old £150,000 target-man, has broken his nose five times (twice in contact with the ball). He too has scored whilst concussed, and regularly swallows aspirin, even after training "during which I may head more balls in 15 minutes than an entire League season."

Double vision—"it usually last 45 minutes"—hasn't blurred Cross's awareness of occupational hazards others refuse to treat seriously. Overriding all shades of opinion is the fact

that, of 55 players known to have died playing football, 26 had head injuries and eight were attributed solely to heading.

Medical research into heading is as thin as bone china, but consider the correlation between boxers hit by gloved fists and footballers struck by balls travelling at, say 45mph—half the measured kicking power of Leeds's Peter Lorimer. According to Polish studies, a boxer is likely to take 60 or 80 blows to the head during a three-round fight; a London doctor has recorded 40 to 50 headers a match by Mike England, Tottenham's Welsh defender. A boxer may fight eight times a year; a footballer plays twice a week.

Yet Mike England speaks for most specialist headers: "Look, I expected some doctor would eventually claim heading makes you punchy. I know I'll probably end up in 20 years with pain in my knees, but my head? No, I can't accept that."

Eloquent England may now be, but Dr Nicholas Corsellis, a neuropathologist with inside knowledge, fears too much wishful thinking. Dr Corsellis's survey amongst 200 British neurologists unearthed 290 brain-damaged boxers, 12 national hunt riders, two rugby players, two footballers and a parachutist.

"The figures may be minimal," concedes Corsellis, "but I wouldn't dream of suggesting there is no risk. Constant heading may have its repercussions not in classic punch-drunk symptoms, but in degeneration of nerve cells at the spinal column, a tendency to irritability, loss of memory and premature senility."

To be fair, England tells us: "There is no discomfort if you head correctly. I teach juniors to throw their eyes at the ball, watch it onto the forehead, and cushion the force by bracing the neck muscles.

Sound advice—in theory. In practice, it becomes a cardinal sin to allow a "clean" header; often three defenders jump against one forward, intent on forcing him off line and balance. That is why we see players—from Pele down—"going in where it hurts", eyes closed, heads vulnerably thrust amongst the boots and elbows.

Courage, we call it, don't we? Mike

Tetley, a physiotherapist who treats brain-damaged children, became alarmed when he treated a Red Star Belgrade player for headaches and arthritis of the neck. Some bone structures, he points out, may simply be the wrong shape or too thin to withstand the impact of heading.

Look at the drawing (centre illustration) of the skullcap. Whatever the merits of correct heading, as demonstrated by Gunther Netzer, slight misjudgement may transfer contact to the top of the head. In most of us, the *sagittal suture*, a serrated saw-like joint, knits the bones into a spherical shape which may withstand blows with a minimum of eye-watering. However, a minority of skulls never smoothly bed down; they leave a ridged roof-like joint which Tetley believes offers less resistance or protection.

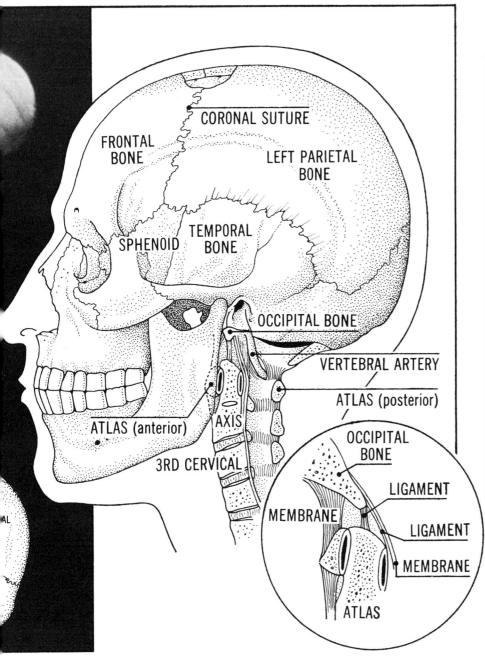

CORONAL SUTURE

FRONTAL BONE

LEFT PARIETAL BONE

SPHENOID

TEMPORAL BONE

OCCIPITAL BONE

VERTEBRAL ARTERY

ATLAS (posterior)

ATLAS (anterior)

AXIS

3RD CERVICAL

OCCIPITAL BONE

LIGAMENT

LIGAMENT

MEMBRANE

MEMBRANE

ATLAS

Now look at the larger drawing. If, says Tetley, the *frontal bone* is driven a mere 2,000th of an inch into the *coronal suture*, it could cause great pain behind the eyes. A displaced *sphenoid bone* might impair vision. More widely acknowledged is the accumulative wear on neck muscles. If they are over-strained, small ligaments and membranes could tear, causing arthritis which, like brain damage, may occur 15 years later.

What says the Football Association? Nothing. Our national sport has no medical adviser to direct the millions who play. Two international team physicians, however, believe there *is* cause for concern. Dr Alan Bass: "Being hit by a fast-moving soggy ball can't be all that different from the effect of a punch ..." Dr Neal Phillips: "Players should never resume after concussion."

Meanwhile, it remains an absurd paradox that, whereas the British play football in the air, they concentrate coaching below the belt. Mature players may believe if they choose that they risk nothing more than premature baldness, but doctors must respond more constructively than handing out aspirin for headaches. Would it cost too much to screen for structural weakness?

At least the FA could throw out the cold sponge and learn why boxing and racing strictly control any return after concussion. The Schools' FA, with no policy for coaching boys—as opposed to men—to head, could consider that skull bones are not fully formed until 18. The idea is not to stop people using their heads—but to use what is inside and at risk ... the brain.

November 10 1974

Inside track

Flicks

Remember London to Brighton in Four Minutes, the classic speeded-up film of a rail trip on the Brighton Belle? Well, much the same thing has been made of a cricket match at Lord's. The film, in 16mm colour, is made by Films of Today Ltd., and Darrel Catling, a 63-year-old television commercials director, who are seeking sponsorship for a more ambitious 35mm film.

"Some sports are too fast to follow," says Catling. "Cricket is too slow. At the normal pace, you miss the patterns, the organic shape of the game." So, in shooting a Middlesex-Nottinghamshire match last year, Catling "under-cranked" at two, four or six frames per second rather than the usual 24 frames per second. He then edited down from four hours to five minutes.

"You don't notice the mannerisms of a cricketer at normal speed. After he finishes what he's doing he lifts his arm over his head to get his sleeve uncaught. The bowler, if he bowls round the wicket, walks *back* round the wicket. But the most extraordinary thing of all is the pulse of play. The players move in-and-out, in-and-out, rather like a lung."

For an encore, Catling hopes to tackle soccer. "If one could only get a God's eye view of a football match with the whole field in," he says. "It would be staggering to see the way the game flows from one end to the other." *February 20 1972*

Running Tummy

Bruce Tulloh's attempt to run across America in 66 days will be as big a strain on his digestive system as his legs. "If he can't handle the enormous food, water and salt intake he'll need," says Dr Griffith Pugh, Britain's leading exercise physiologist, "he'll weaken and he won't make it."

Dr Pugh knows his subject. This winter, he measured Tulloh's energy expenditure at various running speeds. "Tulloh's a small man (5ft 7½in, 118lb)," says Pugh, "and the 4,500 calories he'll need to run some 45 miles a day is equivalent to about 6,200 calories for a 165lb man. I myself don't know any occupation where people use anything like as many calories. On the approach marches in the Himalayas, for example, the intake was 4,500 calories with bigger men than Tulloh."

Moreover, the doctor says that Tulloh, partly due to fatigue, won't have the appetite equal to his additional needs. "If he makes it there won't be another feat like it, physiologically, in history." *April 27 1969*

PS. Tulloh did make it: in a time of 64 days 21 hours 50 minutes. At the end he had lost 8lb, which he regained in ten days.

The mountain range of the woman athlete's achievement, complete with peaks and valleys

The three feminine champions on the right are famous not simply for their eminence but for the consistency with which they triumphed. But the regularity of their victories is rare among sportswomen. The reason for this is set out on the chart (far right) which shows the peaks and troughs that the performances of most sportswomen go through every month. The chart is based on observations made by Dr Katharina Dalton, who stresses that it is only a roughly sketched impression and covers all women, not simply athletes.

by Robert Lacey

Gymnast Vera Caslavska.

Skater Peggy Fleming.

Sportswriters are fond of patronising the inconsistent performances that women put up in competitive sport. One weekend's champion is next weekend's runner-up to a degree significantly more frequent than in male games and events. But through delicacy it is seldom pointed out that there is a simple explanation for this varying level of achievement—the female menstrual cycle. Or that the effects of the cycle make up a *continuous* and *regular* pattern affecting a woman's sporting potential.

The pattern set out in the chart accompanying this article is based on the work of Dr Katharina Dalton, author of *The Menstrual Cycle*, which drew together some fascinating examples of the way in which premenstrual tension acts. It is during the days immediately before their "period," for example, that women are most prone to road accidents. "In a sporting context," says Dr Dalton, "these tensions can make the difference between defeat and victory."

The pre-menstrual syndrome is the term coined for a collection of symptoms affecting at least half the women of reproductive age (15 to 45). It is the time when a woman's weight is temporarily at its maximum—which can obviously slow down her sporting performances; her pain threshold is lowered, her resistance to infection is weakened and she may suffer from migraine, giddiness and fainting. Her joints, muscles and back may ache, and excess fluid in the brain cells may make

for emotional disturbance. Few sportswomen suffer all these symptoms but rare is the female athlete who claims to be totally free of them.

"I have in the past had to withdraw from competitions," says Della Pascoe, the British Olympic sprinter. Ann Wilson who last year won a silver medal in the Commonwealth Games pentathlon, agrees with her. "For the first five hours I feel a lot of discomfort, and for two days the tops of my thighs are like lead."

Marea Hartman, secretary of the Women's Amateur Athletic Association, finds that many girls suffer with this particular problem—heaviness at the top of the thighs—in addition to tension and general pain. "We take this into account when selecting international teams. If we know that a girl was handicapped when she turned in a particularly poor performance, then we disregard that result. But if we know that her period will coincide with the competition that we're selecting her for, then we pick her just the same. We often find that faced with a real challenge, girls excel themselves."

This raises the as yet unresolved ladies' dressing room debate—how can mind be made to overcome matter? Della Pascoe remembers running one of her very best races on a day that made her physically sick. She was worrying so much she had no time for "race nerves."

But no matter how much a female athlete, golfer or tennis player concentrates on overcoming the problem, she does suffer a definite loss of co-ordination. "At such a time," explains Dr Dalton, "there may be a rise in intra-ocular pressure. Excess fluid presses on delicate structures within the eyeballs. This may have a physical effect on a woman's eyesight. She finds it harder to judge distances or quickly spot small moving objects like, say, tennis balls or shuttlecocks."

Golfer Vivien Saunders confirms this: "I find I just can't see well enough

Athlete Mary Rand.

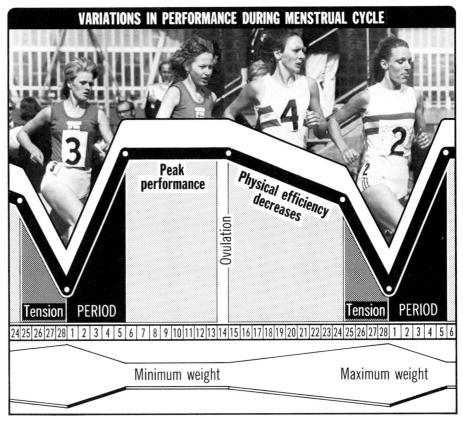

VARIATIONS IN PERFORMANCE DURING MENSTRUAL CYCLE

Peak performance

Physical efficiency decreases

Ovulation

Tension | PERIOD

Tension | PERIOD

| 24 | 25 | 26 | 27 | 28 | 1 | 2 | 3 | 4 | 5 | 6 | 7 | 8 | 9 | 10 | 11 | 12 | 13 | 14 | 15 | 16 | 17 | 18 | 19 | 20 | 21 | 22 | 23 | 24 | 25 | 26 | 27 | 28 | 1 | 2 | 3 | 4 | 5 | 6 |

Minimum weight

Maximum weight

to putt properly." A Wimbledon finalist also agrees: "The loss of sight and co-ordination are impossible to cope with."

Around Dr Dalton's apparently simple pattern of regularly varying performances sportswomen present a bewildering contradiction of personal experiences. Sheila Carey, the 800 metres runner, notices a 4–5lb weight variation every month but keeps up consistent training and competition results. Val Peat, who won two bronze medals at the 1969 European Athletics Championships, calculates that most of her best performances have occurred on the theoretically wrong day.

Some international athletes use the contraceptive pill—or similar compounds—to bring on or postpone the regularity of their cycle at the time of important competitions. But doctors like Raymond Owen of the British Olympic Association, believe this can harm performance. Eastern European and Russian competitors quite frequently employ testosterone, the male hormone, totally to suppress menstruation—and, incidentally, to build up male muscle formations. But the WAAA fiercely opposes this.

Perhaps the most helpful line of future enquiry could be Dr Dalton's own hypothesis that pre-menstrual tension—which is especially severe in adolescence—creates a huge barrier that cuts many girls off from sporting activity at school. Thus the minority of girls who get "creamed off" for special attention and training and go on to compete internationally are the ones whose exercise is not shattered for several days each month.

The implications of this are twofold. First, that though female athletes follow the normal pattern of varying physical efficiency, they experience a comparatively small degree of suffering. The reasons for this could perhaps help many women outside sport.

And the second, even more long-term, possibility is that there may be in our schools a vast reservoir of games-playing talent that requires medical rather than athletic assistance to fulfil its true potential. *February 7 1971*

Inside track

Mr President

Avery Brundage, who died on Thursday aged 87, was president of the International Olympic Committee for 20 years. His name has become a byword for simplistic virtues and undiluted amateurism. Brundage described himself as a "110 per cent American, and an old-fashioned Republican." People like him, he added, had not had anyone to vote for since Hoover and Coolidge.

Other typical Brundage-isms:

"You know, the ancient Greeks kept women out of their athletic games. They would not even let them on the sidelines. I'm not so sure but what they were right."

"I have never known or heard of a single athlete who was too poor to participate in the Olympic Games. If in certain countries there are people who are too poor to play, which is doubtful, let the government raise their standards of living until they have some leisure time instead of asking us to lower our amateur standards. After all, we of amateur sport cannot be expected to reconstruct society."

The Brundage quotes that will probably be remembered longer, though, than any others:

"The Olympic Movement is a 20th-century religion. Here there is no injustice of caste, of race, of family, of wealth . . ."

"The Olympic Movement appears as a ray of sunshine through clouds of racial animosity, religious bigotry and political chicanery . . ."

"The Olympic Movement today is perhaps the greatest social force in the world. It is a revolt against 20th-century materialism—a devotion to the cause and not to the reward . . ." *May 11 1975*

How a long distance runner can cover 14 miles with a temperature of 106.3

The hazards of altitude became a highly emotional preoccupation during the build-up to the Mexico Olympics; one British doctor saw the problem in a different light.

by Dudley Doust

The fear of a 1968 Olympic death seems finally to have vanished in the thin mountain air of Mexico City last week, but the estimable Dr Griffith Pugh lingered on. Long after the last horse had jumped the last fence in the Little Olympics, Pugh, the British physiologist, was testing his new sports theorem: body temperature can play the major role in the long-distance events at next year's Olympics.

With his two young subjects, British runners Mike Turner and Tim Johnston, Pugh drove late one morning to the practice stadium at the National University. The day, in the doctor's clinical view, was perfect: 22 degrees C. (71.6 degrees F.) temperature, with only a small breeze, bright sunlight and a flock of white clouds grazing on the hot horizon.

At the track they were joined by a Mexican professor and a team of technicians. Together they set up what looked like a meteorological outpost: a four-cup wind gauge, various solar radiation computers, a heart-rate telemeter, a hydrometer, a compact VHF radio receiver, some thermometers (both weather and rectal), assorted clipboards and a pair of bathroom scales.

Johnston, who had swallowed a radio temperature pill with his breakfast, weighed in and jogged off at what was planned as a 30-kilometre run. On an autumn afternoon in England, it might have been easy-going for him: Johnston once held the world's record for the distance.

Each lap time was recorded, and during each fourth lap Turner ran beside his fellow guinea-pig, holding the radio receiver beside the runner's gut. Gradually, in the blazing sun, Johnston's temperature climbed. Pugh browsed about, taking the temperature of the porous volcanic rock wall beside the track, and of the grass infield (both of which could pass heat to the runner), and of the track itself, which he found had risen from 30 C. to 42 C. in half an hour.

Just how hard is it to win an Olympic medal the hard way?

Disabled athletes rightly win our admiration but it is hard to assess their achievements. We rarely appreciate their difficulties fully and there is no proper yardstick. In an effort to find one we arranged an unusual match.

By Ulick O'Connor

Claude Stevens is 57 and paralysed from the chest down, but in the Disabled Olympics in Montreal he managed, while sitting in a wheelchair, to throw a discus 75ft. The throw won him, and Ireland, the silver medal.

But how startling an achievement was this? To find out we asked Phil Conway, 27, a former Irish discus record holder (167ft 7in) and current Irish shot-put record holder, to get into a wheelchair and throw against Stevens.

The stipulation was that Conway should not use his legs for leverage, since Stevens cannot. But it was not possible to eliminate one advantage: Conway could twist his hips, where much of the impetus in a discus throw comes from, whereas Stevens can achieve no movement at all below the chest.

First Stevens prepares to throw.

Conway: national champion, threw only 76ft.

In moments of waiting, he brooded. "Why didn't they take Gaston Roelants's temperature after his marathon? That's what matters—body temperature, not altitude. Why did they throw a blanket over the Japanese boy who collapsed? They should have thrown cold water."

By the 15th lap, Johnston's internal temperature had reached 38.4 C. By the 34th, sweat lay like saliva along his jowls, and by the 43rd he pleaded to stop. Turner coaxed him on, lap after lap.

"What we're looking for," said Turner, "is a threshold of heat endurance. Once we find it, perhaps we can plot a graph showing what speeds we can run at certain temperatures."

On the 58th lap—after only 14½ miles—Johnston was finished. He wobbled in, cold with exhaustion and on the verge of collapse. He was weighed and his rectal temperature

Tim Johnston: making medical history.

taken. The result made medical history.

Johnston's temperature was 41.3 C. (106.3 F.). This was the first time that such a high temperature had been observed in a healthy human being. Moments later, he would have collapsed. All this reinforced Pugh's idea—shared by nearly all but crowd-drawing promoters—that marathons should be run in the cool of the day. He

seemed satisfied for the first time all day. "Now," he mused, "if we can work out ways to keep body temperatures down. . . ."

If Johnston had been doped, he would have died in his tracks. "High altitudes and high temperatures are the worst conditions for the amphetamines," said Dr Albert Dirix, a Belgian member of the International Olympic Medical Committee, "and the amphetamines are a favourite drug with athletes. It is no good losing your fatigue at this altitude and with this heat."

It is fortunate that compulsory spot-checking for dope will be conducted at Mexico City next year for the first time in Olympic history. This year some 350 urine tests were taken at the mini-Games, and no traces of dope were found. Next year 50 random samples will be taken each day.

November 5 1967

Interestingly, his preliminary swing closely resembles the pose in the classical Greek sculpture, the Discobolus of Myron. His best throw (of three) is 74ft 2in, 10in short of his Olympic throw.

Now Conway settles into the wheelchair. On his third throw he manages to reach 76ft, just 22in in front of Stevens.

After the contest Conway acknowledged the muscular advantage he enjoyed even without his legs being on the ground. "I could feel the muscles in my lower back give me a base to throw against, something Claude simply hadn't got."

Ironically, Stevens had no interest in sport before he was paralysed. He had been in the Merchant Navy for 20 years where he fell into the hold of a ship and became crippled. He was in hospital for nine years. "I was swathed in rugs," he says. "I couldn't hold my head up without a steel collar. I had no interest in life until (looking with a grin at two other wheelchair athletes), this pair of blackguards got at me to take up sport. I'd never been near a sports field before that. I was literally an old man, almost dribbling. Then my whole life changed."

That was three years ago. Now he is fit and bronzed. His daily training schedules under his coach Jimmy Bryne are ferocious and Stevens maintains that the exercise affects his whole outlook. "It makes you mentally alert, aware of things in an almost psychedelic way—the cure for depression."

October 17 1976

Stevens: partly paralysed, threw 74ft 2in.

How they learned to love the Bomb and escape the fear of consequences

Anabolic steroids, the muscle bulk-building drug, has been used increasingly, surreptitiously, and illegally over the past two decades. Proven cases exist in athletics, but swimming has also had its suspects.

by John Hopkins

The world swimming championships ended last Sunday but the controversy surrounding the East German women's team continues. Were they taking body-building pills, such as anabolic steroids, which might account for the powerful shoulders and build displayed by the swimmers on the right? Or were they just very well-developed, the result of long, tedious hours of physical training?

Anabolic steroids were first used to build up concentration camp victims after the war; it is basically a male hormone which helps the body to absorb huge doses of protein which build up muscle when linked to a strict training regimen. The weight gain can be stupendous—the Swedish shot-putter Rudi Bruch claimed he had put on four stone in five months.

The reasoning behind the use of anabolic steroids—"the Bomb" as athletes call it—and the like is that they rapidly increase body weight and, with hard training, this can be turned into muscle which will help swimmers pull themselves through the water faster. But the use of such pills as steroids in this way in sport is strictly illegal. And the allegation against the East Germans that was made at Belgrade, and has been reiterated since, is that they have been taking steroids.

One man who knows more than most is John Hogg, Scotland's national swimming coach. In Belgrade he talked for three hours to an East German team doctor about their training methods which include daily blood and physiological tests and regular checks on performance by computers.

In addition East German swimmers train for five hours every day. In winter, three hours of land work (in the gym, doing weightlifting and circuit training) and two hours in the water. In summer, three hours in the water and 2 hours in the gym.

"If what they told me is true," says Hogg, "then it would account for this increase in size and weight. Their type of work would build up this type of musculature."

One question remains unanswered, however. Why were the East German men so unsuccessful in Belgrade when they have been doing the same training as their stunningly successful women colleagues? "The doctor told me they were disappointed with their men swimmers," says Hogg.

So the East German training methods could in theory, says Hogg, show the results we saw in Belgrade—but so could regular doses of anabolic steroids, allied to heavy training. The allegation against the East Germans remains unproven, but so too does the East Germans' defence against the allegation.

"I can't say they are taking steroids," says Hogg, "and I can't say they aren't. What I can say is that if the East Germans are giving steroids to their swimmers they will be doing them, and swimming, the biggest disservice ever."

In the world of athletics, this has already happened, both in the East and West, and earlier this year a meeting of the Medical Commission of the International Olympic Committee in Moscow confessed they don't know how to stamp out the use of steroids.

They were used freely at Munich by competitors in a wide range of sports: discus, shot, hammer, weightlifting, the decathlon and pole vaulting. Professor Arnold Beckett, Britain's representative on the commission says there's no hope that they will find a test to spot the use of these hormone wonder drugs before the 1976 Montreal Olympics. "If we can't find a suitable test, then we can't enforce a ban," he says.

The debit side of building up extra athletic oomph can be heavy. There are documented cases of heart trouble, liver and kidney damage and cases of an abrupt cessation of sex life. In *The Lancet* last year there was a suggestion that it was a possible cause of cancer of the liver.

For women, anabolic steroids are the answer to Rex Harrison's prayer in My Fair Lady: "Oh, why can't a woman Be

Roswitha Beier, 15-year-old East German swimmer.

more like a man." Using anabolic steroids she can. She can lose unwanted curves, her voice will become lower and gruffer, and she will sprout hair where she shouldn't.   *September 16 1973*

by Cliff Temple

The athletes' attitude is simple. Most world leaders are using steroids, and when our boys go abroad they get beaten by whopping margins. They come back from throwing the hammer or discus beaten by 10 to 20 feet and their friends say: "Hey, you're not much good, are you." So they get fed up. They've done all that work and they've apparently got nowhere.

Much of the motivation for athletics is the chance to go on foreign trips. But because Steroidal Man has pushed up the qualifying standards, British ath-

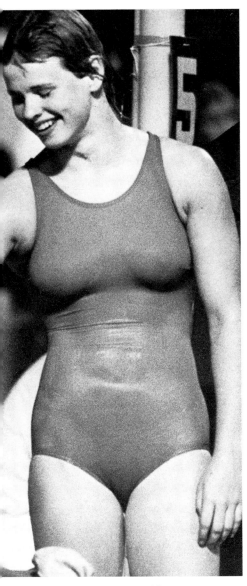

Compatriot Ulrike Richter, 14.

letes cannot get abroad unless they go on to steroids too. There's no glamour in training hard and being a loser.

Athletes think that controlled use of anabolic steroids may be safe. But there is always the temptation when one competitor sees the progress of a rival, and he starts shovelling the pills in like sweets. They reckon they know it's time to stop when they find themselves getting a bit short-tempered.

The spread of the use of anabolic steroids may be bigger than the Olympic officials realise. It is not only in throwing events, but in the explosive events, like long jump, high jump and sprints. The whole outlook for the Olympics is rather sad. I get very depressed looking back over the 80 years of the Olympics, seeing how it grew up in an amateurish way. It's falling apart medically, financially, politically.   *June 10 1973*

Andrea Huebner, 16: five hours daily of blood tests, sweat and tears.

The resilience of a champion — battening down the hatches of the mind against pain

by Brough Scott
Photographs by Chris Smith

It happened at Hexham just six months ago. For Tommy Stack, it has been like half a lifetime. The accident was quick and brutal. As he landed in the saddle for his last ride of the day, his horse reared straight over backwards, pinning him to the paddock tarmac. More than one observer turned away muttering: "That's a dead 'un for sure."

Stack was not dead, unconscious, or even paralysed. "I could wiggle my toes." But his situation was still desperate by any normal standard. His pelvis was badly crushed and displaced, his bladder damaged and the ambulance drive back to town was torture.

In the 14 years since he had come over from his native Ireland, he had grafted his way up the tree, finally to take the jump jockeys' championship in 1975. Last year he had become a household name with his record breaking Grand National win on Red Rum. But now visitors to Hexham's magnificent hospital echoed the first medical opinion that Stack would be lucky to ride again this season, if ever again.

When he came out of hospital he had a very limited movement, says one doctor: "Something like 30 degrees in the right leg and only about 10 degrees in the left. I told him we would get him fit to ride Red Rum in the National on April 1, but at that stage it was more to give him hope than being realistic."

That he has already ridden, and had two other rides besides Red Rum yesterday, could be called a miracle—even though there is a further bladder operation this week. But the word miracle seeks to avoid an explanation which is not hard to find. For Stack is a champion in one of the most demanding sports of all. He has had to do his share of battening down the hatches of the mind when the going gets rough, and those are just the qualities that were needed in his ordeal.

He summed it up one night last October: "I've had six weeks so far. Another six to go. It's like riding a bad jumper in a three-mile chase at Wetherby. We've done one circuit, and we've got to go out into the country again."   *March 5 1978*

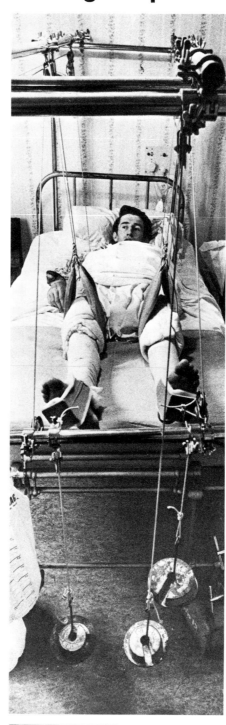

SEPTEMBER The Rack. Stack's pelvis was severely crushed, and his bladder damaged. On the first evening he had over two stones on the left leg, and was X-rayed every half-hour as they tried to pull the pelvis into line. After that it was a mere stone-and-a-half on the left leg, a stone on the right and the intermittent torture of a tube in the bladder. He stayed like this from September 5 to November 28.

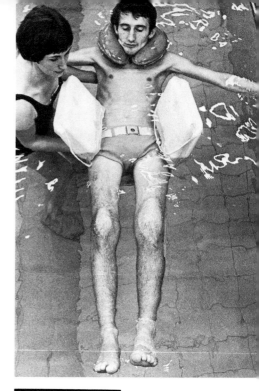

NOVEMBER The 10st jockey was reduced to a painful eight stones by the time he was cut down. "I had no appetite. It was like trying to push your food uphill." His hips and legs were lowered on successive days. The moment they tried to stand him up he passed out. "It was like someone pouring a huge bucket of hot blood down my legs." The swimming pool gave him supported movement.

DECEMBER Leaving hospital. Despite the smile, this was the worst period of all: "Somehow I felt after all that time everything would be all right once I got home. But I could only just walk, couldn't even dress myself and could do nothing else at all. I've never felt so helpless." At their brightly decorated farmhouse near Tadcaster, his wife Liz remembers: "He seemed desperately tired. He would just keep falling to sleep for no reason."

He didn't plan to ride a racehorse until the following

FEBRUARY

Thursday, but he got legged up on Scatter, his neighbour's pony, four days early. Since then, he has been riding out four hours a day with local trainer Peter Asquith, riding progressively short to develop his thigh muscles. He rode Red Rum in a gallop on February 23, had his first practice jump the next day and his first race ride at Doncaster on the 27th.

Tommy Stack and Red Rum were re-united at Haydock

MARCH

yesterday. They finished sixth—27 lengths behind Rambling Artist, winner of the Greenall Whitley Chase—after nearly parting company at the 12th fence. Tommy, obviously relieved to have survived Red Rum's uncharacteristic blunder, said: "He ran as well as I expected and was staying on at the finish." Referring to his own battered frame, Tommy added: "I feel fine."

JANUARY

The long grind to fitness. Stack checked in to the Sports Medicine Unit at Leeds Hospital when he got home, but was so weak that he could not start the exercises until the New Year. Soon he was doing an hour-and-a-half circuit training a day, and besides the bicycle and rowing machine there was a progression of weights and exercises that gradually restored his vitality and weight to a muscular 10st 3lb.

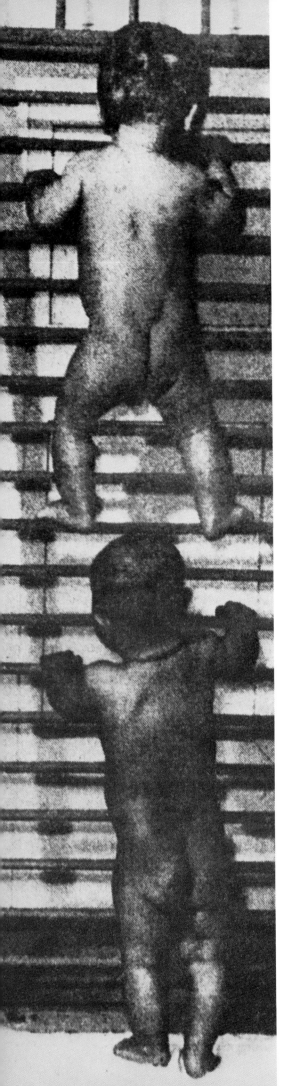

The 'curiously environmental dwarfs' who are being pushed into a sporting unknown

As sport became ever more kindergarten, so concern began to grow over the possible harm that rigorous training might impose on growing bodies. *The Sunday Times* consulted 20 specialists in sport and child growth in 15 countries, and screened the "careers" of 17 fledglings for this report.

by Rob Hughes

Two babies climb wallbars in a Prague institute (left). Each is seven months old, and doing his bit for the furtherance of scientific knowledge. The photo, taken during a study in "motor precociousness," nevertheless serves equally well as a chilling vision of what we are heading for in sport . . . the ultimate in catching 'em young.

Prodigies have always been catered for; in sport, however, we are on the threshold of casting moulds and bending infants into them. The selection and processing that produces flawless 14-year-old Olympic champions and 12-year-old European ice-skating medallists begins at four, when other little girls fondle dolls.

Child health experts look at Korbut and Comaneci, and marvel at the suppleness and creativity of the human frame; they look again, and they see "curiously environmental dwarfs—whose puberty and growth is delayed"; and finally they look once more and think that, for every champion, some 5,000 children are put through the hoop.

After the child health experts, the bone specialists, psychologists and biologists come into the picture. No need for heart specialists since it is now established that activity cannot damage a healthy heart or lungs.

The rest are groping around the outer fringes of knowledge, and alarming patterns are beginning to emerge. Spinal defects in the young, particularly girls, are being unveiled. These defects, commonly stress fractures in the lower back, are being coupled openly in some medical circles, guardedly in others, with the gymnastic explosion in the wake of Olga Korbut's televised performances in the Munich Olympic Games.

One American study of 100 gymnasts documented damage to the ring around the vertebral canal four times more prevalent than that found in the general female population. The gymnasts were girls of 14 who practised 20 to 40 hours a week. And even in Britain, where sports medicine is a lame duck, doctors acknowledge back pain in "girls trying to do a Korbut when they are not built for it."

Gymnastics must not be pilloried disproportionately: if skilfully and correctly coached within the scope of the children, doctors agree it is a beautiful and healthy pursuit. But parents push beyond safety limits; like the sister-in-law of a Midlands doctor (who spends hours treating children with bad backs) who recently boasted to him that her eight-year-old daughter does six gymnastic sessions a week over and above the norm.

"If I had my way," says Dr John Williams, secretary of the International Federation of Sports Medicine, "I'd make it illegal for parents to get involved in sports training. They do untold harm. I'm horrified by the children wheeled into my clinic, the parents gabbling on about growing pains, when what I see are genuine overuse conditions which, sometimes, will be there for life."

Progression towards training from the cradle accelerates apace, not merely through the parental push in the West or the state drive in the East, but also at the hands of obsessional coaching. In America a year ago two coaches admitted feeding pills to kids to help beat weight limits.

Meanwhile, Dr Vincent Grantham, medical officer to Oundle School, Northants, published a study of 224 boys with back trouble. This demonstrates that at 13 to 14, when the adolescent spurt is at its maximum, strain causes severe damage in a host of sports, particularly rugby.

Dr Grantham for seven years refused to allow boys to perform "this wretched Fosbury Flop" because of the danger of them competing at schools with landing areas "so unsafe they could cause total paralysis for life."

The world over, doctors are warning against dismissing aches as "growing pains". The earlier maturity of boys and girls, the growth of organised leagues (which in America embrace nine million children) and the excess training loads are without doubt vastly increasing the incidence of stress injury.

The area of most concern and least knowledge remains long-term repercussion. Can excessive wear and tear in childhood lead to crippling middle-age?

Dr Trevor Hoskins, secretary of the Medical Officers of Schools Association, puts into words what others darkly hint at: "I fear that within two decades we shall see arthritic backs as common in women who trained fiercely at gymnastics as we now see footballers with arthritic knees." He adds, as he must. "I have no scientific base for that, but there is no proof it won't happen."

Nobody can say categorically that the growing body can cope with stresses applied in the name of sport today. A visit to the Physical Fitness Laboratory in Prague, however, is at once heartening and frightening.

Milos Macek, a professor in paediatrics, is chairman of an international medical committee which attempts to collate information on the subject. "Studies here prove," he says, "that an infant's capacity to exercise heart and lungs is greater than we think. But a child works far harder in unsupervised conditions—and anyway spontaneous play is more varied and balanced than the maladaptation of the anatomy which can result from specialised repetitive training."

Macek's deepest fears are of minute, almost undetectable, stress fractures building into irreversible injury. He is convinced we must redirect children towards recreational play, away from strict coaching. "The criterion has to be prevention. If we have to say stop, it is too late."

This fear echoes that felt by Dr Ronald O. Murray, an eminent orthopaedic radiologist in Britain, who believes osteoarthritis of the hip may be a direct result of prolonged road running before the bones mature.

"To prove the origins of wear and tear is a 40-year follow-up," he observes. "My ideas remain hypothetical, but I'm convinced constant jogging along hard roads, and the jarring of bones not finally formed, *must* be detrimental."

Factors which led to Dr Murray's hypothesis include that in 79 of 200 sufferers studied there was a common deformity at the hip joint and evidence of previous *epiphysiolysis* (displacement of the growth centres). This stress condition occurs between the ages of 10 and 15 and a symptom is surprisingly mild pain in the hip or knee.

Dr Murray's long-term thinking has backing from independent studies in America and Bulgaria where damage to other load-bearing joints is linked to sports and where arthritic deformities are predicted.

The message is clear: we have taken sport away from nature, why should we be surprised that the body breaks under the strain? We learned long ago to steer clear of a car which has been thrashed too soon in its life, yet we haven't begun to think out the legacy of doing the same to children.

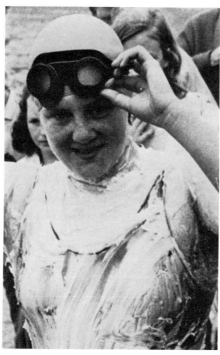

Tina Spry: a 13-year-old at sea.

The purpose of this report is not to discourage active participation. Far from it; but there is a duty to try to ascertain the risks of subjecting children to laborious training rituals. The medical studies now emerging are the first sprinklings of hard evidence supporting what some of us felt in our bones to be wrong.

We must, as Professor Macek says, use this evidence to return to a balance between sport and play which again promotes games as a dimension to growth rather than a harmful obsession. And, perhaps, to call for an entry age of 15 to be imposed on international competition. *July 3 1977*

CASE HISTORIES

Once it was the piano or ballet; now sport is the instrument of parental ambition. How proud would you be to rear a prodigy like these?

● Charlie Clover was Commonwealth javelin champion and world junior record holder at 18; months later, disillusioned and physically unsound, he quit.

"Insufficient motivation," they said. Truth was, Charlie saw nothing at the end of it; a dislocated bone in his foot wasn't mending; gristly lumps in his shoulder wouldn't go away, and his collar bone was bent like an arthritic finger. "Stress fractures, they call 'em," says Charlie. "But the pain was mine."

He believes his injuries " were from my being such a hard thrower so young. I was javelin mad since I was eight, I had no time for anything but throwing and lifting weights." One other thing broke the javelin's hold on Charlie: "To improve, I'd have had to start on anabolics. I didn't fancy it." In Olympic year, persuaded to chance his arm again, he found the snap wasn't there but the injuries still were. He's in the army now and throwing again.

● Tina Spry's chubby, beaten face still haunts one exactly three years after they fished her out of the English Channel after 14 hours and 45 minutes in the water. She'd failed, by two miles, to become the youngest swimmer to cross the Channel. She was 13 years and two months old. Clutching a teddy bear, Tina had been allowed to enter the sea at Dover against coastguard advice that sea mist hampered navigation.

Within a month she failed again, this time because of a storm. Then, with time and tide running out, she heard that Abla Khairi, a 13-year-old Egyptian girl, had swum the Channel. Anyone who has witnessed the mental straitjacket the swim imposes must wonder that the law allows minors to try.

● The most precocious champion? In Britain, Beverley Williams became an international high-board diver at 10 but, despite "disciplined" coaching from Dad and medals at all levels, she had had enough and quit last year, aged 19.

In America, Kevin Strain (yes, Strain) claims more than 50 world records for an eight-year-old, including a full 26¼-mile marathon in 3hr 15m 42sec. That, however, is child's play to Mary Etta Boitano. She's been marathoning around the States since she was six . . . this over a distance that causes stress fractures and loss of control over bladder or bowels, vomiting and hallucinating in mature men. Mary, of course, doesn't run as fast, but she's working up to it.

PICTURE FILE

The much-loved Manchester United have won the Cup, and tonight
there will be celebration for their supporters not only in Manchester but
also in cities as remote as Belfast and Bridgwater. But although the
modern football fan may share the outward emotion of his team's
success, he can never experience the reality of high-level sport in
which—as the following pictures show—essentially private emotions
are laid bare by stress and conflict.

Ilie Nastase's main opponent is himself, but this time—progressing to the Wimbledon final of 1972—he is on terms in the Inner Game.

For Olga Korbut, an injured ankle in the gymnastics World Cup, and a silver medal, are almost equally painful.

In 1968, in their fourth attempt at the European Cup, Manchester United seemed to have fallen again at the semi-final hurdle. Away to Real Madrid, they trailed 3—1 before a stunning recovery elevated them to the final: for Bobby Charlton the end of the rainbow was in sight.

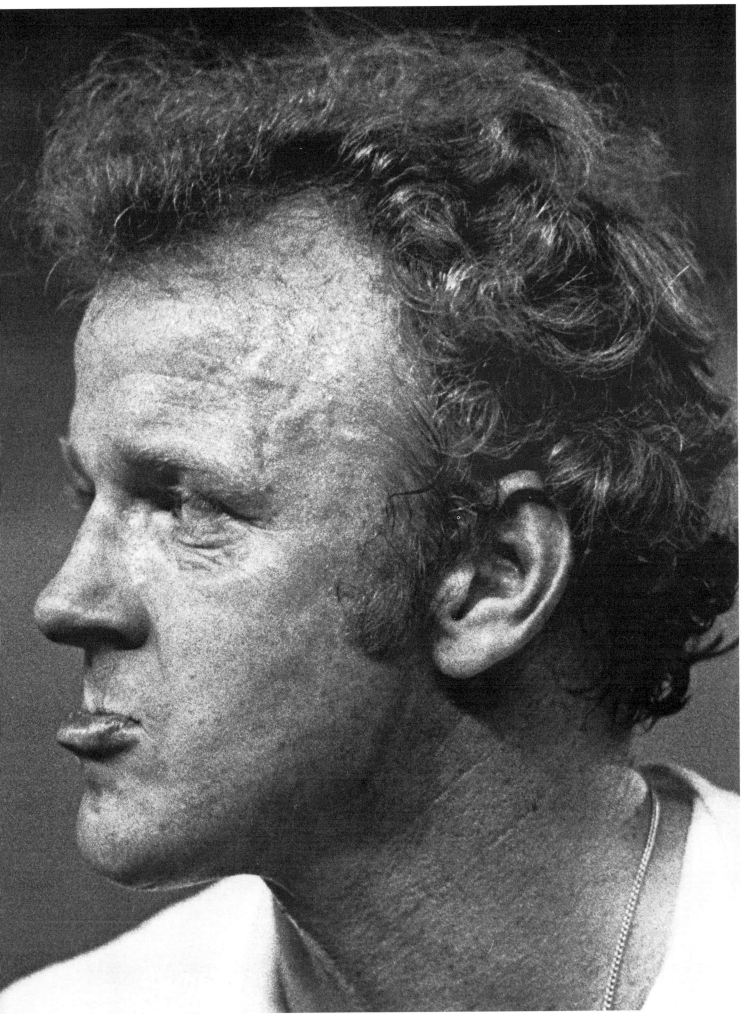

Billy Bremner, an aggressive footballer who, even more than most, hated to be beaten or bettered. But professional sports also demand professional discipline, and Bremner became an even better player when he learned—sometimes with difficulty—to control his temper.

Tattenham Corner at Epsom has been a graveyard for the hopes of several great horses, as they suffer in pressing for position on the long, downhill bend. Some in this large field at the Spring meeting will also, in effect, be practising for the Derby.

In the winner's enclosure, Gerry Gracey has reason to smile through the mud. Rain at Cheltenham has made the going terribly heavy, and for the Irish jumpers that's always grand.

In theory, lacrosse is played in the air, with no bodily contact, but it may still create the impression of running combat as opponents try to check, block and intercept. Here, United States defenders are stationed against their equally determined prey, Judy O'Connor of the English Midlands.

For Jim Dietz, an American sculler training for the Olympics, the ergometer machine offers hard training, and a chance to re-measure fitness. He hates the device that he uses willingly. "It's all the pain of rowing but none of the pleasure."

Swimming offers training hours that are as long as in any other sport, and more monotonous; and British swimmer Brian Brinkley chose to specialise in swimming's toughest events—the 200m butterfly, the 400m medley, the 1,500m freestyle.

On one side, Ian Gillard of Queen's Park Rangers; on the other, Dennis Mortimer of Aston Villa. It is not possible to say which footballer is challenging the other. Football, the hard, combative game, is perpetually offering conflict with "the 50–50 ball".

In training at the Noble Art Gymnasium in
1971, Henry Cooper has young Joe Bugner on
his mind, and the doubts of any athlete who
knows he is also fighting against age. He is 36,
his challenger 21. Our 'Enery, the favourite of
the British public, stands to lose much more
than just his British, European and
Commonwealth heavyweight titles. In fact,
this will be Henry's last fight.

First came Kip Keino, then Ben Jipcho, then
Henry Rono. At this moment, in 1972, it is the
turn of Jipcho. He has just run away with a
5,000m, race at London's Crystal Palace. The
steeplechase event is already his oyster, and
various world records are within his reach. The
photographer captures the face of a young
Kenyan for whom life is exciting.

5

HEROES

Sport's heroes do not necessarily have to fit the classic mould, though we begin this section overleaf with a story about a woman who surely does. One person's hero is, after all, another's anathema; some heroes are scoundrels, others play out lonely roles on the sea or in the mountains, some never fulfill their promise. Television too has created modern heroes whose appeal knows no national boundaries, like the remarkable Soviet lifter Vasily Alexeyev, who is also included in these pages. But what is certain, and has always been so, is that sport provides enough heroes to satisfy anyone.

England's Brendan Foster and Mick McLeod – first and third in the 1978 Commonwealth Games 10,000 metres

In the demanding and tough world of three-day eventing women compete on strictly equal terms with men, a tradition that dates from 1949 when women first took part at Badminton in Britain's premier event, and a period when a former military activity was switching to being a civilian sport. In 1954, in the European championships, women competed for the first time internationally, and today female riders rank among the greatest in the world. The most formidable of these is Lucinda Prior-Palmer, who is the only person to have won Badminton three times on three different horses. She is also the only rider to have successfully defended the European individual championship. She first won this in 1975 and shortly before she triumphed again, in 1977, she spoke about the hazards of her sport and her doubts about herself.

Lucinda Prior-Palmer: the dangerous challenge

by Dudley Doust

In defence of her European horse trials championship, the dressage phase over and done, Lucinda Prior-Palmer will walk the 4¾-mile cross-country course at Burghley next week: down the Leaf Pit, through the dreaded Trout Hatchery, over the new Jubilee Table. She'll walk alone, planning her attack, aware of the dangers.

"I don't enjoy fear, but I need the challenge of it," she says. "I wouldn't be any good without it. I'm always worried if a course doesn't frighten me. I know I shan't ride as well." She smiles. "Often when I'm using a whip on a horse, I'm really using it on myself.

"It's sport's old adrenaline story, only, this time, with an added dimension: What about the horse? You can't shield fear from a horse. How do you transmit such useful power to a 1,200lb animal? This is the problem, of course, and I'm adamant that I should control my fear, turn it into determination which comes out by pushing forward, rather than melting into a jelly."

She's a striking girl, perhaps beautiful. Blonde hair, blue eyes, fine bones, long neck, thin legs, 5ft 8in tall, as she pads barefoot round her family's Georgian home near Andover. *Of all the riding gifts which I would like most to be blessed with?* She ponders the question. "I'd like to be six times more elegant. I'd like to be lighter on my feet, less clumsy, because I'm sure it would help me in my dressage."

She begins to fiddle with her jewellery—a striped enamel ring, an evil eye set in a silver bracelet—and suddenly you notice the oak under that elegance. Her hands, wrists, and forearms, well shaped, are big and strong. She's fit. She skips every morning, 200 slow, 100 fast. She schools her horses daily. In less hectic times she plays squash and rides gallops with Toby Balding's string of racehorses.

At 23 Lucinda is one of Britain's great intuitive sportswomen. Her record: three times winner (on three different horses) at Badminton, Britain's premier horse trials, reigning European champion, and almost certainly, but for a literal slip (bad luck isn't in her vocabulary), a Montreal medal.

Her cross-country is bold, wise, her show jumping good, yet Lucinda accepted the fact that her (indeed all British) dressage is falling farther and farther behind the Americans, and, more pressingly, the West Germans. She took a decision. Lucinda scrapped her basic position for dressage last winter, and went back to square one. She studied dressage for a month near Hamburg, a courageous, perhaps dangerous decision.

Lucinda holds fast. "It made an enormous impression on my mind. It gave me a bit of an idea of what I'm trying to do. But it will take me at least three years to put into practice what I think I now know." She frowns with absolute humility. "I've really *got* to try to give and sink into my seat. Yet, if you think too hard about body control, you're as rigid as a rod. It never ceases to amaze me." She laughs. *Eureka!*

Eureka, too, because Lucinda has been lent a replacement for her beloved family horse, Be Fair, the Montreal casualty, now 13, now pretty much out to grass. Her new man is George, 11 years old, a 16.2 hands bay gelding, bred, owned, trained and hunted by Mrs Hugh Straker in Yorkshire.

"George has got big ears, big lungs, a big heart, and, as a four-year-old, he

Lucinda and George: "It's sport's old adrenaline story."

"A lot of horses keep something for themselves, but George doesn't keep anything. No kinks."

could get out of trouble like a 12-year-old," says young Nick Straker, who madly dashed him round Yorkshire, over castle walls, gates, and the A68. "The only thing he's scared of is pigs."

Lucinda is grateful. "I first saw George four years ago. Apart from Be Fair, he was the only horse I ever loved on sight. He's so genuine, so generous. A lot of horses keep something for themselves, but George doesn't keep anything. No kinks. If he sees a geranium, he doesn't have a fit."

Lucinda gobbles up the challenge, probably expects things to go her way. Born on November 7, 1953, daughter of Lady Doreen Prior-Palmer, and Major-General George Erroll Prior-Palmer, who died last month. The General led the amphibian forces up the beaches at Normandy on D-Day, earned the Croix de Guerre *avec palme* and later served as British military attaché in crucial post-war years in Washington. Lucinda's determination and courage, they say, descend from her father, her insight and sympathy from her mother.

An indifferent, rebellious pupil, Lucinda left St Mary's, Wantage, an Anglican boarding school, before sitting her O levels. Luckily she came under two fine instructresses: as a child, the local Mrs Betty Skelton, and later, the remarkable Mrs Pat Burgess. At 15, with Be Fair as a birthday present, her talents crept out of the bang-bang Pony Club clamour.

She worked. In 1973, in her second appearance at Badminton, she sat in the stable and, deeply concentrating, talked Be Fair through the forthcoming course. They won. "I was convinced it was sheer fluke." In 1976, she won again, on the ill-fated Wide Awake. She won again this year, on George, came third on Killaire, and, between the two rides stretched out and switched off in the horse box.

Mrs Straker's breeding and training of the horse, Mrs Burgess's almost mystical insight, and Lucinda's downright riding skills, combined in George's astonishing triumph. Hunted by the Strakers in the winter, Lucinda and Mrs Burgess had only two weeks to

work with him before Badminton. It worked. Lucinda grins, genuinely modest: "Nobody was more surprised than I was when he won." Mrs Burgess says: "Lucinda has this great peace, harmony with her horse."

Mrs Burgess and a friend, the instructor, William Micklem, have made Lucinda more aware of the possible depths of perception between man and horse: *Tune in*, Mrs Burgess implores her pupil, *reach a harmony not only with your horse, but with the trees and the stars.* Lucinda, believing, makes haste slowly. "I'm in the baby stages with this idea. Basically, you can't feel at ease with the trees until you've done a really good job. But I know we're on a threshold. The whole of riding is so much more in the mind than I ever realised, and once you're successful, it really becomes a battle of the mind."

She laughs, recognising the dilemma facing all thinking sports people. "On the other side, of course, one has to stop thinking and say, 'Shut up,' and get out there and relax and let it all happen."

September 4 1977

A trio of survivors: Niki Lauda, who came through fire and the most appalling injuries to return to the top flight of Grand Prix motor racing; Emil Zatopek, perhaps the greatest of post-war distance runners, who has come through the trauma of political disfavour in Czechoslovakia; and Mary Peters, surmounting the agonies of a divided Belfast to win an Olympic gold medal.

Niki Lauda: the private man reborn in public

by Keith Botsford

Niki Lauda: not just remade physically, but a man who has conquered himself.

If you look back at Niki Lauda over the years since he walked into the March camp in 1971 with £8,000 to buy himself a Formula Two car, you'll see a clear picture of the grandeur and misery of the life of a Formula One driver. The period since his near disaster at the Nurburgring last August has been the great trial in his life, an ordeal by fire and a trial by single combat between Niki and the Press, Niki and Ferrari, Niki and Carlos Reutemann, Niki and politics and most of all between Niki and himself.

Niki's beginnings in the sport were not that obviously successful, and whatever he did achieve, he had to achieve by himself. If it hadn't been for a personal friendship with Count Luca Montesemolo, he might never have driven for Ferrari: the Old Man wanted Jarier, and made his reluctance obvious.

Ferrari was wrong. That year Lauda finished second and by 1975 he was world champion. Which is when his real troubles began. As champion, he became King Rat: because he wouldn't play the game, because he stayed Niki, a private man not a glad hand, because he was arrogant, lofty, disdainful.

I know people (not, however, his rivals) who literally prayed for something to happen to Niki. And something did. Another Niki was born out of the seared flesh and scarred lungs of the Nurburgring. For two weeks his life hung in the balance, and when he said he would race again few believed him. In September he drove back to fourth place at Monza, and became a hero to the world. In October, on a rain-drenched track at Mount Fuji, he dropped out and Hunt took his championship. The hero had become, to a virulent Italian Press, a coward, unworthy of Ferrari, a failure.

None of which took into account the journey Niki had to make from death-bed to cockpit. Last year's battle with Hunt was joined on unequal terms. Niki was not then, and could not be then, the same man he was before the Nurburgring. And even if he were spiritually the same man, and did what he could, physically, to become the same man, he no longer had the car. Without Niki testing it, adjusting it, sensing it, it became a very ordinary car indeed.   *January 23 1977*

Emil Zatopek: the unsung hero

by Rob Hughes

The picture is agony, a flailing run, torso heaving inside red vest, head rolling, tongue out and face a crimson, contorted mask that suggests his next gasp will be the last. But the lungs and the legs were magnificent: 25 years ago this week they drove him to an achieve-

Mary Peters: back home in Belfast with her pentathlon gold medal.

Mary Peters: too much time to think

by Cliff Temple

Mary Peters spent all one night last week long jumping and running 200 metres around her bed. For when you're leading the Olympic pentathlon competition, and when it is spread over two days, which she hates, you have a lot of time to think. Too much.

"Buster McShane, my coach, had worked out after the first day's events what I would have to do on the second, in the long jump and 200 metres, to win. I didn't sleep at all for thinking about it. "Everyone was saying, don't worry, you'll get a medal. And I was saying, with tears running down my face, 'I know, but I want the gold'."

The magical moment of which every athlete dreams had come in the high jump: Fosbury-flopping her way almost to a British record to the accompaniment of the crowd's chant, "Mary Peters (clap-clap, clap-clap clap)".

"Sheila Sherwood said that I waved so much and blew so many kisses to the crowd that I could get a job appearing at the end of the Morecambe and Wise Show." *September 10 1972*

ment at the Helsinki Olympics that to this day remains unique.

In the space of eight days, Emil Zatopek won the 10,000 metres, the 5,000 metres and then the marathon, the last an event he had never run before. Time can neither diminish nor embellish that. But in Czechoslovakia Zatopek has not only been systematically stripped of the hero worship which was his right, but also of his pride as a human being.

The extraordinary willpower which ran him beyond known limits had, in the summer of 1968, openly defied Russian tanks as they rolled across the Prague cobblestones to quash Dubcek's liberal socialism. Afterwards Zatopek was deprived of his Colonel's rank, his position at the ministry of defence, his job as a coach, his membership of the Communist party and his passport. And today the marks on his hands testify to the menial work of the past nine years—sweeping streets, collecting garbage and drilling holes.

Sports officials in Prague still remain nervous about helping anyone to contact their country's best-known Olympian. In the end, we spotted him in the great hall of the Cerninsky Palace at a reception by the Czech head of state honouring the International Olympic Committee.

In the lapel of this man who once won four Olympic gold medals, who set 18 world records, who was undefeated in 38 consecutive 10,000-metre races, and who won his country's highest decoration, was a cheap mock-silver button, bearing the insignia of St. George; it was pinned there by his wife to help him feel dressed. There was a melancholy request to sit with him out of the limelight of the great hall, a trancelike recollection of British runners, Chataway, Pirie, Ibbotson; and then reluctant acknowledgement that he must circulate amongst honoured guests.

Nowadays, of course, the 55-year-old Zatopek goes nowhere outside

Czechoslovakia, And one is aware of the eyes watching his every move. Not (noticeably) the eyes of the state, but the deep, disturbed, grey eyes of his wife Dana, the Helsinki javelin champion. Years ago, before it happened, Dana had said: "Emil is always talking too much, too often, too long. He rebels too much, he always has to do things his way."

He's unaware of the nervousness of Dana. "You know, the athlete today is *not* an athlete," he says severely. "He's the centre of a team—doctors, scientists, coaches and so on. My running was very simple; it was out of myself. Perhaps sometimes I was like a mad dog; when I run today it is for my pleasure, but before I did what I felt.

"Two months before Helsinki, the doctors say I must not compete. I had a gland infection in the neck. Well, I don't listen . . . and what happen? Three gold medals. The sportsman, the *real* sportsman, he knows what is inside him." *July 17 1977*

Henry Longhurst: good wishes from the Sunday Times golf correspondent

The late Henry Longhurst of *The Sunday Times* was that rare writer who, in his own time, became as beloved as many of the golf heroes he wrote about. It took a special visit to his home by the sports editor and the help of Mrs Longhurst to persuade him to write this comforting account about himself, about his cancer, his contemplation of suicide, and the nectar that saved him.

Well, well, now, where were we when so abruptly interrupted? Ah yes—at Troon, watching the tall soldierly figure of Tom Weiskopf, smiling all over his handsome countenance as he strode up the last fairway to win the Open Championship and be duly embraced by his ex-beauty queen wife.

If I offer a personal account of why I have been AWL, i.e. "absent with leave," for so long, it is only because I have been specifically requested to do so.

Life on the whole had been kind to me and enviable. I had achieved a certain notoriety both in writing and broadcasting about golf, and most people who remembered the frightful things I had done and said in the course of the past 40 years or so were no longer with us to recall them to a later generation.

During the course of the Open I was presented with the Walter Hagen Award, "for furtherance of golfing ties between Britain and the United States," which , if the truth be told, gave me infinite satisfaction, for I had been going to and from America since captaining a Cambridge University team there in 1930 and had in recent years been found acceptable on American television.

I had also during the Open taken part in a BBC chat show (another which may interest golfers is due, by the way, on BBC2 at 6.45 pm on Boxing Day) and had conducted various interviews, including one with one of the very great men of golf, Gene Sarazen. As US Open Champion, he had failed by one stroke to qualify on this same course 40 years ago and now had done the short "Postage Stamp" hole in one in the first round and in two in the second. I had met innumerable friends and drinking companions, about a hundred of whom must have told me how well I was looking.

I had even had the temerity to provoke providence by entitling an autobiography *My Life and Soft Times*.

Fate, however, had decreed that they had been soft for long enough. I tried to keep a bold face on it but the fact was that only two or three days before the Open I had visited the doctor with a complaint which, though a trifle coarse, proved to be so ludicrous that I venture to set it down. I had found emerging from my person what I could only take to be the end of a tapeworm, or some such unwelcome lodger, and on, pulling it, about eight inches came to the light of day.

"No," said the doctor, "tapeworms only shed half an inch at a time." I thought at once of Sherlock Holmes and the worm "hitherto unknown to science," but the doctor identified it as a piece of cellophane wrapping from a cigarette packet. "I have not smoked for 12 years," I said, with what dignity I could command in the circumstance, "and furthermore am not in the habit of eating and swallowing eight inches of cellophane wrapping without being aware of the fact"—but so it proved to be.

I then revealed that I had been conscious not of any pain but of a sort of "awareness" in the lower abdomen, as a result of which a day or two later a neighbouring surgeon, who turned out to be a plus-4 at this sort of thing, and whom it still infuriates me to be unable to name, inserted his telescope and, at one of those moments when life stands momentarily still and you know it will

Inside track

Our nomination for the best unseen TV golf footage of the year must go, we think, to the American company which didn't use its take from the last US Masters of two owls sitting in a tree, along with the voice of Henry Longhurst murmuring: "There, looking solemnly down on the proceedings at the 16th green, are two spectators who don't give a hoot for the Masters."

Evidently, in the USA, this was not considered good sports television.

June 13 1976

never be the same again, said quietly: "Ha! A tumour."

This would mean a "colostomy," i.e. removal of part of the colon, and furthermore, if you will forgive me, an artificial orifice in the side of the body.

It was the thought of the latter which really decided me—though, to give comfort to others who face this, let me say that the modern apparatus designed to cope with it is really wonderful.

Lying soberly in bed during the Open Championship, I decided that I had done all I had set out to do and that all good things come to an end. In the words of the late Errol Flynn, I felt "I've seen everything twice and am ready to go."

I enquired of three doctors (not, of course, including my own) as to whether I had obtained sufficient pills to exercise man's inalienable right, as Hamlet put it, to "shuffle off this mortal coil," and all said yes—one recommending rather splendidly "half a bottle of whisky and make sure they don't find you for 12 hours."

My life was prolonged, though he will be astonished and, I hope, gratified to learn so, by last year's captain of the Turnberry Club who, in an example that cannot be too widely followed by golf captains, had presented me during the John Player Classic with a bottle of Highland malt whisky called Glenmorangie, which proved to be of such superlative excellence that I have never been without it since.

The fatal night, with my mind still made up, called clearly for a bottle of this powerful nectar with which to slide peacefully away and I attacked it with maudlin vigour, but alas, or rather hooray, I must have exceeded the stated dose and the Glenmorangie got the better of me before I got round to taking the pills.

Thus the condition in which I was presented next morning to the Howard Ward of the Royal Sussex County Hospital and its devoted staff makes it all the more miraculous that I should be still here, restored physically to the "normal channels" and with, I am assured, a three in four chance of further survival, to offer our readers my good wishes for a Christmas which in July I never expected, nor indeed intended, to see. *December 23 1973*

PS. Henry Longhurst continued to write for *The Sunday Times*, and to broadcast regularly for the BBC, until his death in 1978.

Henry Longhurst: "Life on the whole had been kind to me and enviable."

John H Stracey: ninety minutes of hard sweat

John H. Stracey lost his world welter-weight title to Carlos Palomino in June 1976, but before qualifying for a return fight he was required to beat the up-and-coming Dave 'Boy' Green. (In the event, he failed). Stracey went into training at the Royal Oak in Canning Town, London.   (*March 20 1977*)

by Chris Oram
Photographs by Chris Smith

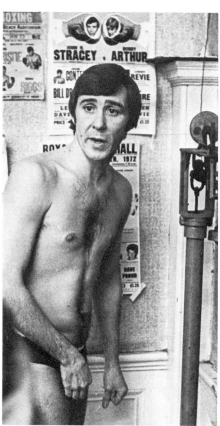

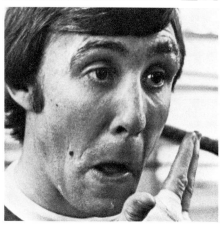

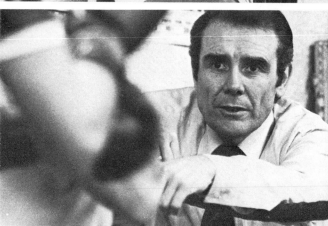

4·17 pm In nine days time, John H. Stracey will step into the ring for the first time since last June, when he lost the title. With the fight so near, there is no such thing as a day off, only days of lighter training. Every day John H runs for an hour in the morning and goes to the gym in the afternoon. Weighing is a daily ritual. Stracey is 10st 6½lb: half a pound under the maximum for his class. On the walls are fight posters whose design hasn't altered for a quarter of a century. On another wall hang grisly bunches of black leather headguards, protectors and gloves; on another is a large mirror with an ornate frame that would look more at home in a suburban dancing class. After a spit he climbs into the ring and shadowboxes to loosen up. This exercise, like nearly all the others, is carried out in bouts of three minutes to knock into the boxer's head an awareness of the time a round will last on the night. Stracey greases his face. Not allowed before a fight, this deflects punches. For sparring, everything must be done to prevent a cut, which could be opened again by an opponent during the course of a real fight. He also bandages his own hands for protection, with an arthritic-looking result.

● Frank Black, trainer, holds a glove and grimaces with the effort as Stracey forces his hand inside. The heater in the gym is turned off now, and "Blackie" makes sure the temperature stays constant by dealing in strong language with anyone, whatever their status, who leaves the door open. He also walks round the gym, avoiding flying punchbags with the uncanny accuracy of a bat. When the gloves are on, Stracey stands helpless while Blackie and manager Terry Lawless lace one glove each: then Blackie puts in the gumshield, as solemn and gentle as a priest with a communion wafer.

● Terry Lawless watches closely as Stracey spars. A dapper man, who moves with the confidence of a fit body under his well-cut suit, Lawless has a reputation for being a caring manager, for not matching young fighters against a boxer out of their class, for crying with Stracey when he lost the title last June. Stracey has an insatiable appetite for training: "You think it's beyond you (regaining the title) and you put more into it." He spars seven rounds: four with Jimmy Batten, British light middleweight champion, and three with Sid Wright, chosen to spar today for the first time ("Who's 'e?" mutter the onlookers) and subsequently proudly nursing a bloody nose.

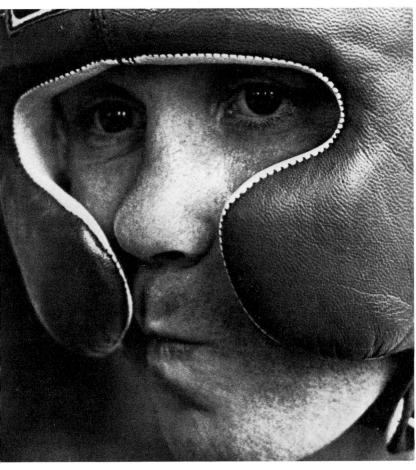

● The headguard converts Stracey's face from Norman Wisdom's kid brother to a gladiator. However close he is to his manager the ring is a lonely place. What goes on here seems strangely irrelevant to what will happen there. This knowledge is shared by the older members of the fraternity, watching and wisely assessing. "The punches are there, but the viciousness ain't", says Sid Wright. "Don't want any cuts." The tattoo of punches landing on leather combines with the characteristic sound of feet on canvas, like linen tearing. John Stracey's father (extreme left in picture) doesn't say a lot. Later one of these men will be vested with the temporary authority of putting the watch on Stracey as he skips. What's their opinion of Dave Green? "'E's ugly. Good at picking carrots." Mr Stracey senior turns and beams suddenly "'E's well fit, inne—my baby?"

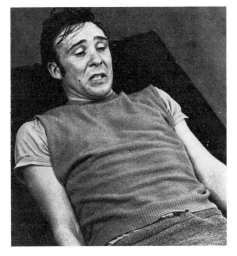

● Still working in three-minute rounds, Stracey attacks the punchbag. He says to a boy watching: "Good fight Saturday—heard you should have won." The boy blushes deeply and tries to look offhand. Floor exercises for 15 minutes, and instead of doing sit-ups from lying flat to sitting up, he repeats the most difficult part, rocking to and fro at 45 degrees to the floor. Ten minutes' skipping, and 90 minutes after entering the gym Stracey is in the shower. However John H. Stracey chooses to relax tonight ("I never think about the fight till a few days ahead") he'll be back on the roads again in 12 hours time.

5·47pm

John Lever: keeping the spirits up at Number 12

Life among the spare bats, the drinks, the sweaters and the aspirations of a Test match 12th man.

by Dudley Doust

John Lever, England's 12th man, sat on the balcony outside the England changing room at Lord's and watched his teammates slowly grind away at the batting New Zealanders. A Union Jack, flying above the pavilion roof, cast a fluttering shadow across the outfield. "They'll want their sweaters pretty soon," Lever said of the toiling bowlers. "Look how wet Willis's shirt is getting." Lever then explained how signals for sweaters are passed from the field to the balcony: a pluck of the shirt-front means a man wants his sweater, a chop at the wrist signifies a long-sleeved sweater, a chop at the shoulder calls for a sleeveless one.

How Lever finds these sweaters, or indeed anything, in the England changing room, is a mystery. The place is cluttered with cricket cases, clothing, letters, telegrams, autograph books and dozens of bats, full-sized and miniature, a battered and ill-focused television set, old and bursting over-stuffed furniture and, curiously, an Edwardian dressing table with a swinging mirror.

"It gets lonely round here when the lads are in the field," said Lever. "When we're batting, you see, I only have to look after the two men on the field. Also, it's the best time to get these things autographed." Among the 12th man's chores is looking after the autographs: bats for future benefit matches, autograph books and fan letters. "It's the worst thing ever, losing an autograph book. But the lads are pretty good—they don't throw them around." Oh yes, and he just might get into the game to field substitute for an injured or ailing player.

The 12th man is an unsung cricketer and, with Essex in desperate need of his left arm over-the-wicket bowling against Kent, Lever's feelings were ambiguous. "If you're not playing, it's never easy watching cricket," he said, back on the balcony "but, on the other

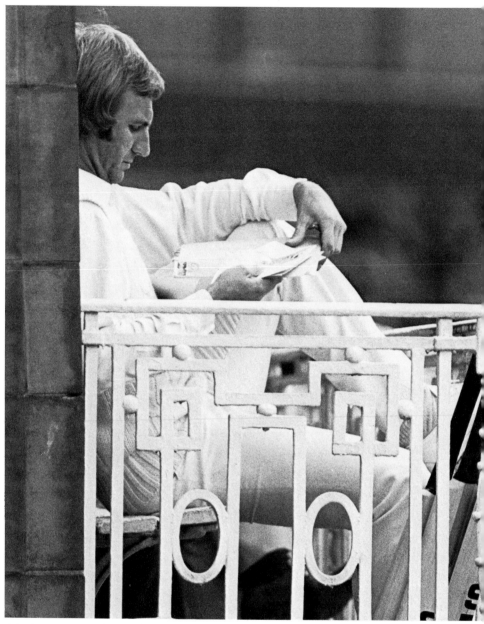

John Lever sorts out the team's letters—just one of the day's chores.

hand, it's a great honour being picked in the 12."

Lever had also been 12th man in the Nottingham Test a fortnight before and with the new cap, John Emburey, to be blooded, and a winning side otherwise unlikely to be changed, he long ago smelled the assignment in the offing. That morning, at nets, captain Mike Brearley had said: "You guessed it, J.K." Lever's chores had begun, there in nets: "Since Collinge, who is left-arm over, was to play for New Zealand, I was ideal for giving the lads a little left-arm swing."

On the field now, Radley looked up and tapped the top of his head. A cap? Lever signalled back by tugging at an imaginary peak. No, Radley indicated, and yanked both fists down past his

ears. Lever nodded. Radley clearly meant to move to silly mid-off for Botham, and he wanted a crash helmet. The dumb dialogue later reached Marx Brothers dimensions when Radley alternately tapped his head and jabbed a finger towards Emburey. Lever finally got the message: Radley wanted a cap, not for himself, but for his Middlesex mate Emburey.

In all, Lever fetched and carried to the field about eight times that day, rabbiting dutifully down the 36 stairs, returning puffed, more than once stopping on the way to check the fortunes of Essex on the tickertape outside the Long Room. He took water for Hendrick and Botham, the cap, and again the crash helmet.

At lunch, Lever became batman and

waiter. He helped the bowlers out of their sweat-soaked shirts, carried the clothing into the drying room: "It's a good thing for them to sit down and get the weight off their feet and have a lad carry away their wet things. It makes for a happy side. It's good for team spirit." Lever spoke without irony or guile. His selfless concern for his mates was genuine and suddenly touching.

Lever's chief chore in the afternoon, apart from visits to the field, was to help the attendants lay out the tea and arrange for drinks to be available at the close of play. The order: mostly orange squash, a double tonic water for Boycott, and for the bowlers Lever himself went to get pints of bitter.

Being 12th man was a boring and frustrating two days for Lever, but he carried out the job in good spirit. "It's a job that's got to be done," he said, before setting out on Friday night, released to join his Essex team against Surrey at Southend. "And, in the circumstances, I'm glad that I got it."

Lever was replaced at Lord's yesterday, and for the rest of the match, by Ian Payne, of Surrey. If he didn't already know it, he would soon learn the form. Bill Bowes, a Test player half a century ago, was at Lord's last week, and he put the 12th man's job into historical perspective. In Bowes's day, and particularly during the notorious bodyline tour of Australia, the 12th man's role under the captaincy of Douglas Jardine was splendidly varied. Jardine, for example, would give his 12th man strict orders to draw and guard the baths after close of play, so that Hammond, Sutcliffe and Larwood would be first into the water.

"Jardine also was the only captain I ever knew who made *tactical* use of his 12th man." Bowes said. "He actually would build his bowling strategy round the drinks interval. The 12th man would, for instance, be left instructions to bring on the drinks at, say, 3.10. Not 3.05 or 3.15, but 3.10. Then he would rotate his bowlers so that Larwood, the key man, would get his drink at the pre-arranged time. I remember he once told the 12th man: 'Bring Larwood a glass of champagne, he'll never know the difference.' The poor fellow had to run around Australia looking for champagne, which wasn't an easy chore in 1932."

The champagne may be easier to find at Lord's, but the job is just as demanding as it ever was, and no more exciting.

August 27 1978

The Alphabet Test — or how to send yourself to zzzZulch

by Benny Green

It is a universally accepted fact, to me at least if to nobody else, that one of the occupational diseases of cricket lovers is close-season insomnia, an affliction caused by the spectacular discrepancy between our own climate and Australia's.

To the dedicated follower there is nothing less conducive to sleep than the maddening knowledge that while he lies there shivering in the dark of a winter night, somewhere on the far side of the world fresh statistics are being fed into the annals of the game. For years I was a martyr to this condition before discovering what I took to be its cure. (That in time this cure became itself the source of a more acute phase of the original condition is beside the point, which is that for a while I thought I had the answer.)

The story began about 10 years ago when I stumbled, quite by intent, on an essay by Compton Mackenzie in which there appears the following:

The H's of cricketers past and present give much the most powerful side on paper ... Hayward, Hobbs, Hutton, Hammond, Hearne, J. W., Hendren, Hutchings, Hirst, Huish, Haigh, Hearne, J. T. ... No other letter can supply a full team.

At first I was too preoccupied with the validity of the first claim to bother with the second. Why had he left out George Headley and Clem Hill! I was also about to start canvassing for Wes Hall when I noticed that the essay had been written in 1945, when Hall was only eight years old and therefore only just starting his Test career. I felt also that Hassett and the Hardstaff family might have a grievance, that Percy Holmes could consider himself unlucky, as usual, and that Humphries of Derbyshire, who kept wicket three times for England, might wonder about the inclusion of Huish of Kent, who never did.

I then saw that by adding to my list of rejects Harvey, Hunte and Hollies, I had virtually an H reserve side, and that the second of Mackenzie's claims must be questioned. If there were two H sides, was it really possible that no other letter could raise even one?

That night in bed, my mind anguished at the thought that at this very moment Dexter was engaged in mortal combat with Benaud at Brisbane without my help. I remembered the Mackenzie theory, and began to attack it. Within minutes both it and I lay in ruins. What I arrived at was: Shrewsbury, Sutcliffe, H., Spooner, Stoddart, Sutcliffe, B., Sobers, A. G. Steel, Strudwick, Statham, Spofforth and, in case the side should be faced with a request for charades, Sir C. Aubrey Smith.

From now on falling asleep was never a problem, as I learned to find my way around the cricketing alphabet. I used to wonder sometimes what it would be like captaining the L's, wondering who to give the new ball to out of Larwood, Lockwood, Lohmann and Lindwall.

The connoisseur's side was T. with Trumper, Herbie Taylor, and the Tyldesleys. (Always a pleasure picking T, because by including Tate, Tyson, Trumble, Turner, C. L. Townsend and Albert Trott you could omit Trueman with a clear conscience.)

The law of diminishing returns began to operate on the night I started toying with the odd letters, and wondering if there had ever been a Test player beginning with Z. The desire to know was irresistible, so soundlessly I slipped out of bed, waking my wife in the process.

She went back to sleep, whether or not after quickly picking a cricket team I wouldn't know. After breaking the golden rule by looking up Wisden I went back to bed, as soundlessly as before, waking my wife again. "What's happening?" she said. "Zulch," I replied. "J. W. Zulch. Sixteen caps for South Africa. Everything's all right."

February 20 1972

To Topaz: on March 24 a bouncing daughter for Charlottown

A first-hand report of the birth of a racehorse, daughter of the Derby-winner Charlottown and a 19-year-old brood mare Topaz.

by Caroline Silver

Topaz belongs to Mr H. J. Joel. She is a big old mare with only one eye—the right eye was lost through an infection—and a stomach distended by ten foalings. She was once (now hard to imagine) a winner on the racecourse.

In the second week of March, Topaz's udder "bagged up" full of milk. On March 21 she "waxed"—a thickish secretion oozed from each milk canal and hardened into wax-like blobs on her teats. Drops of milk fell from her udder. Her 11-month gestation period was almost over.

On the morning of March 24, the muscles around Topaz's tail looked hollow and slack. Slackening, caused by the hormone *relaxin* which softens the tension of the strong pelvic ligaments to ease the passage of the foetus, occurs 12 to 18 hours before the foal is born. The stud groom, Michael McFarling, moved the mare into a foaling box, and Ali Kroon, a Dutch girl, sat in with the mare.

At 7.45 pm Topaz broke out in a light sweat on the neck, soon spreading to a heavy sweat on the neck and girth which steamed in the cool air of the box. She seemed calm.

At 8 o'clock Topaz got down in her straw and rolled, breathing in short snorts of discomfort because her stomach was so large. Then she got up quickly. Colostrum—the important first milk containing antibodies to immunise the foal against disease— spurted from both teats.

At 8.10 the mare went down again, rolling. McFarling reckoned she knew the foal was not quite in the correct position and was rolling to get it right. He washed his arms up over the elbow in warm, disinfected water and reached into her vagina to check. Topaz knuckered to him softly.

Her birth canal was blocked by the partly-ejected water bag. McFarling burst it with his hand so that he could

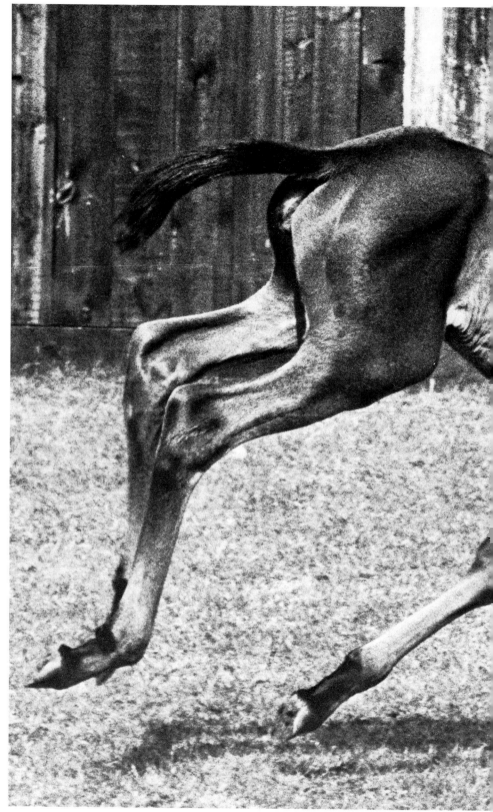

In the foaling paddock and (inset) with her mother: "The old mare's like a kid with a Christmas present."

reach through and feel that the foal was in the proper position (if not, this would be the moment to straighten it). Water poured out of Topaz, and one of the foal's forelegs stuck out from under her tail, encased in thick white membrane.

McFarling felt the other foreleg lying a little behind the first; touched the head, lying neatly along both legs like a diver's. Satisfied that the foal's shoulders would pass on a slant through the narrow pelvic area and that its nose would not get stuck against the

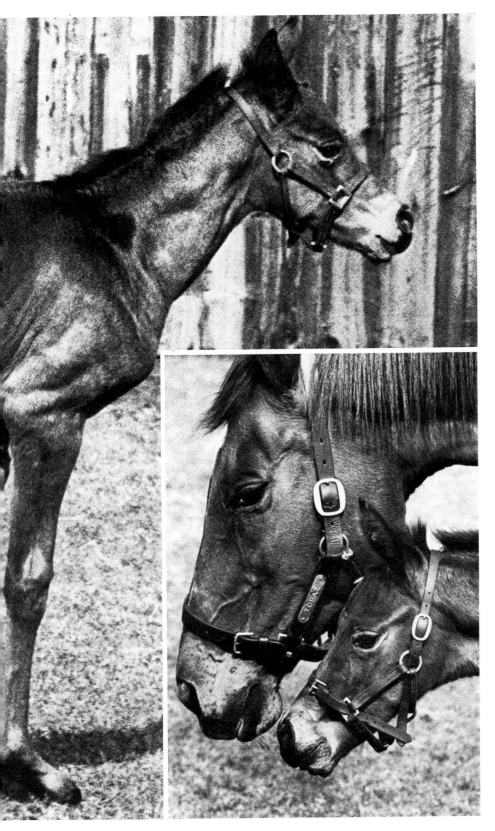

foreleg, which was dragging back into the mare.

The foal's nose stuck out clear of the amniotic sac, nostrils closed and tongue hanging out. It wasn't breathing yet. Lying in the straw, Topaz turned her head and hummered (McFarling's word for the intimate voice a mare uses to her foal). "Not there yet, old girl," he told her.

Topaz bore down hard. She stuck her legs out stiff, and curled her lips back over her gums in effort. At 8.29 the foal slipped easily out. As its ribcage slid clear, it gave a little gasp and started to breathe.

As the foal's hind feet slipped away from Topaz, she got up fast and turned, eager to see her foal. The umbilical cord snapped, and bled in spurts. McFarling held the end of it tight until the bleeding stopped.

Topaz bent over the foal, hummering to it and licking it dry. It was a bay filly, daughter of a Derby winner. A wisp of beard hung from its lower lip, and it was soaking wet with fluid. It lay in the straw limply buffeted from side to side by Topaz's tongue.

Eight minutes from birth the foal tried to get up, rocking backwards in the straw with its forelegs splayed out in front. Topaz continued to dry it, talking to it all the time.

"Funny old girl," McFarling said. "You'd think an old mare like that would be used to it, but she's like a kid with a Christmas present." Topaz began to frisk a little, raising her elderly body in tiny rears of delight.

At 8.58 the afterbirth came away. McFarling removed it, checking that it was complete as a partly retained placenta can cause infection. The foal, walking now, stuck its nose out questingly towards him. "I'm not your mother," he said to it.

It lurched away to Topaz, feeling along her side for the teat. It had no notion where to look. It poked its mother in the armpit hard; she swung her head around and pushed it away, kicking out fussily. Saliva ran down the foal's lips in a fine white foam. It licked its mother's udder, didn't drink. Topaz blew air down her nose impatiently.

At 9.44 it found the teat and began to suck. *April 1 1973*

PS. Topaz's foal, later named Brilliant Gem, broke a blood vessel at Epsom soon after the start of a promising racing career. She subsequently stood as a brood mare in Ireland.

roof of the vagina, he withdrew his arm.

At 8.15 the other foreleg showed, just behind the first. Topaz began to work, a contraction every few seconds drawing her stomach up from underneath.

One of the foal's hooves burst through the amniotic sac. The end of its foot was white and soft, and looked like flabby gristle at the tip.

At 8.24 the foal's head appeared, covered in membrane. When the contraction passed and Topaz had relaxed, McFarling pulled gently on the second

Tommy Docherty: symbol of a game in moral disarray

After a playing career with Celtic, Preston, Arsenal and Scotland, Tommy Docherty went on to manage Chelsea, Rotherham, Aston Villa, Queen's Park Rangers, FC Porto, Scotland, Manchester United, Derby County and QPR again. In his 30 years in top level professional football, he has been a perennially controversial figure, displaying at least one outstanding ability—a talent for survival. He needed it in 1978, when he lost a disastrous libel action which he had brought against a former Manchester United player.

by Rob Hughes

The fresher face of Docherty in December 1967 while manager of Rotherham United.

Tommy Docherty's hara-kiri in the High Court last week was justice of a kind. His lying during a libel action he brought to trial was shockingly comical, brutally sad.

The "pack of lies" has cost him the earth: a libel suit he might nominally have won, court fees of £30,000, possibly his £25,000-a-year managership at Derby County, and perhaps his right to work in British football.

It is hard to separate the emotions of compassion and contempt, and it was harder still as the case unfurled. Should the man stand condemned alone? Or are there others, at Manchester United and throughout football, who ought to share his humiliation? He, after all, was there because he wanted to be, wanted to make Willie Morgan, his former admirer, friend and club captain at Manchester United, pay for his refusal to withdraw remarks transmitted by Granada TV into 930,000 homes.

What a silly, trivial case it started out to be. How could Morgan legally justify his claim that Docherty was "about the worst manager there's ever been" or that it "will be a good club again when he goes?" Docherty's United reached two Cup finals, won one, came third in the League and enthralled spectators with their impetuous attack.

Equally, what pecuniary damages could Docherty hope to draw? He was in full employment among the highest paid men in the game, and fond of bracketing himself with Brian Clough

as the only men to whom the biggest clubs need apply. How could he truly believe that the comment of one player he used to manage had injured the reputation he enjoyed?

His barrister, Peter Bowsher, QC, spent virtually the entire opening day last week describing the counter-allegations which would be made in "a dishonourable campaign to denigrate Mr Docherty."

Out of this address came the headline stories which we have all read this week and which the FA will now have to investigate. Docherty denied a series of allegations his counsel claimed would be put, but agreed, however, that he was sacked after leaving his wife and children to live with Mrs Mary Brown, who had been the wife of the club's physiotherapist.

"This case," commented Docherty's counsel, "is all about the reputation of Mr Docherty."

But a jury which might ordinarily have sought the autographs of both plaintiff and defendant—and indeed of Denis Law, Lou Macari, Paddy Crerand, Alex Stepney, Ted MacDougall and others called to give evidence for Morgan—were there to decide who, as the judge Mr Justice O'Connor put it, "was telling a pack of lies."

The Docherty we know—the compulsive, brash wisecracker whose out of court preview included "I've been in court more often than Perry Mason"—did not appear in the witness box. Instead of the love-me-hate-me wheeler dealer who had transferred 130 players for more than £6 million we saw a nervous man out of his depth.

The first thing one noticed was the tie: black, red, white—the colours of Manchester United. Next the demeanour, not merely subdued, but reverent, bowing stiffly to the judge, the nervous tic of his left eye working overtime, the answers short and staccato.

Morgan sat, eyes fixed on Docherty's face, head shaking occasionally, giving a nod when Docherty told how he reversed a £500,000 deficit to a £850,000 profit in his five years at Old Trafford; figures denied yesterday by chairman Louis Edwards, who said that the club's bank balance was £5,000 when Docherty arrived and £147,000 when he left. But Morgan sat upright when Docherty described Crerand as a "disaster" in management, yet a man Sir Matt Busby has recommended to Northampton Town as manager.

The name Busby appeared frequently, on and off "stage." Both men,

PB

Docherty cross-examined: "I don't mean to be disrespectful sir . . . not being clever, sir . . . but what does pro*berty* actually mean?"

it seems, had asked him to appear; Morgan was "still hopeful" he would appear for the defence, but Docherty was prefacing the majority of answers to his counsel with "Sir Matt and I felt . . ."

Day two brought the cross-examination and Docherty reminded one of a small child, locked behind the school gates for the first time, as defence counsel John Wilmers hitched and pulled on his gown and Docherty's own QC sat down. In the legal skirmishes which preceded cross-examination Wilmers had looked a particularly unforgiving and sharp legal mind; and so it proved.

Docherty barely survived the first, loaded opening question: "Mr Docherty, would you agree that a football manager must first of all have complete and utter probity?"

Docherty swallowed, as any manager would. "It would be very nice to have such a complete . . ." He tailed off.

"That is not what I asked," persisted the QC. "Answer the question please Mr Docherty."

Docherty looked across at Mary Brown, attempted a second answer, was again rebutted and said: "I'm not trying to be disrespectful sir . . . not being clever, sir . . . but what does pro*berty* actually mean?"

Wilmers swung on him: why had he attempted to answer the question, what had he thought the word probity meant? Docherty guessed once, twice. . . . "No, Mr Docherty, nothing like either of those. Let me help you . . . honesty, integrity, are those words you have come across . . .?"

Docherty replied they were "essential qualities."

"And a manager's word must be his bond?" Yes.

Wilmers gave him a torrid, 30-minute cross-examination, floating words like dignity, trust, just and fair and Docherty jousted feintly: "No football manager today is a saint," but Wilmers persistently questioned him on gentlemanliness, asking him to read his own contract with Manchester United and the FA rule book on ungentlemanly conduct.

As the world knows, Wilmers's perseverance eventually trapped Docherty into admitting he had told a pack of lies in court relating to the transfer of Denis Law. Hypocrisy outside was swift; newspapers which had paid handsomely for The Doc's columns of revelation were now damning him in the largest typeface. Doubtless one is already negotiating to buy up his court losses with the exclusive Docherty

version, perhaps before he gets absorbed into some Arabian oil fortune.

Manchester United is an important institution in our game, one which most of us have loved at one time or another, but through it the entire fabric of the game has begun to come apart in open court. When the FA has sat in judgment on Tommy Docherty, on the allegations against him in court, will they also probe deeper to discover who knew what, and condoned what, about things which so many from inside the club were prepared to allege on oath?

And who, anyway, is to sit in judgment? Sir Harold Thompson, the FA chairman, at present involved with an attempt to impeach him on the grounds of maligning a certain FA councillor? Or another gentleman I cannot name, whose club is being pursued by solicitors for possible malpractice?

The honest men in authority have a job to do, and should start with the statement given us by League secretary Alan Hardaker last year:

"Football people are funny people. They can be good at their business, good to the wife and kids, and yet still try to break every rule in the book and claim that it's right for their club."

November 19 1978

Virginia Wade: a view from an opponent facing her on the other side of the net

For years an enigma and, until her Wimbledon triumph of 1977, something of a disappointment to her British fans, Virginia Wade has always made a strong impression on her fellow players. This light-hearted profile was by one of them—a high-ranking American player of the time.

by Julie Heldman

If you should ever find yourself one set up on Virginia Wade be prepared for anything; the roof could cave in, the umpire come down with bubonic plague, or the beer could run out in the cocktail bar. In case you miss the incident, Virginia is sure to bring it to your attention and also to that of the umpire, the crowd and the passing motorists.

She is one of those nearly-great players who seldom actually lose a match. Defeat for Virginia could be the result of an unfair conspiracy by the world against her. Dependent upon her fine serve and power game, screwed up with thoughts of her superiority, she can crumble before the humblest of opponents into uncontrolled tantrums. It's all very unBritish.

Now there's nothing wrong with being a loser. I ought to know for Virginia usually beats me. In fact it is an essential qualification for popularity in British tennis. Remember the admiration of Christine Truman, when, as a large schoolgirl, she would hit streams of winners off the wood on the Centre Court. She was far more popular than the cool professional Ann Jones who counterpunched her way to the most consistent record in women's tennis.

Beside the strawberries and cream image of the British tennis player, Virginia appears almost Latin in her temperament. She has all the equipment of a great player, yet she falls short of the mark. Most of her tournament wins have been of smaller titles. In the last two Wightman Cups she has let Britain down disastrously; even her US Open victory in 1968 has to be set against her first round loss at Wimbledon three months before.

Virginia has been the British No 1 since 1969, and it is usually her temperament which makes the headlines. But first let's examine her game.

Most good judges agree that she has the physical equipment of a champion. She is tall, thin, strong and quick. Her first serve is consistently the fastest in tennis, even counting Rosie Casals and Margaret Court.

Attack that serve and you have Viginia's measure. She depends upon it for her confidence and she cannot bear to be broken. Her second serve, hit with too much topspin, tends to sit up on a slow court.

Her main technical weakness is her tendency to slap at her forehand volley under pressure. It's a fault which, with correct advice, could have been eradicated years ago. Therein lies the cause of her failures.

She is a dominant lady, with a superior air on and off the court. Seek her out at any British tournament and you will find a small band of acolytes sitting at her feet and telling how truly great she is. Although she has refused to join the women's "Lib" group in the US, Virginia's lifestyle is that of a modern liberated woman.

The trouble, of course, with too much adoration is that you tend to start believing it, and in Virginia's case it is one factor which may have helped her lose her chance of greatness.

Take the contrast with Billie Jean King. After a losing match the reaction of both will be pretty much the same;

Master stroke: Virginia's forehand volley

As part of a photo-sequence analysis of some of the greatest strokes of the world's leading players, we show the dynamic forehand volley of Virginia Wade, our leading woman. It is a stroke that she has improved dramatically in recent years. The importance is seen of moving *to* the ball rather than waiting for it to come to you. A quick shuffle of the feet *towards* the ball, to connect with it as near to the net as possible, makes all the difference between hitting it dead centre, as Virginia has done here, mishitting it altogether or catching it on the wood. Such volleying allied to her wonderful service, could serve Miss Wade well at Wimbledon. She has never fulfilled her great potential on grass at The Championships, as she did at Forest Hills in 1968 when she beat Billie Jean King to win the US Open title. *June 24 1973*

by John Ballantine

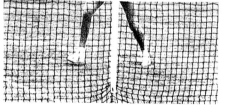

● Keeping the racket head well up, forward and "cocked" is a crucial part of good volleying. Having dashed towards the net, Virginia has braked to a temporary halt near the service-court line, and has prepared to dive either way for the volley. The ball is going to be on the forehand, so she pivots slightly that way.

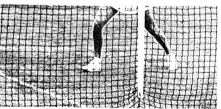

● Moving still more to the right, with her weight on the right foot, Virginia keeps her racket straight up, like a Belisha beacon, to await a high ball. Her left arm and hand stretch out as a balance. Note how intently she watches the ball's flight trying to see it right on to the strings of her racket.

defeat, they will tell you, may have been caused by the strength of the wind, the seating arrangements, in the grandstand, or the colour of the umpire's trousers. Billie Jean however, usually admits the truth to herself, if to no one else. Look for her at 7 am the morning after and you will find her on the practice court with her own bunch of disciples, hitting tennis balls. Virginia seems to lack that insight into her weaknesses, and her career has not really been helped by the lurid portrayal of her dramatic ups and downs in the Press.

Every professional player has her favourite story about Virginia's temperament, but I will always remember Perth, Scotland, in 1969 when I was serving against her at 9–10 in the second set. At 15-love, Virginia announced that a light had gone out on court. By the time the referee had been brought from the bar my concentration and cool were gone. So needless to say was the match.

I don't believe that Virginia plans her tantrums; they are the product of her life and her strong belief in her superiority, a belief which unfortunately has insulated her from true self knowledge. Virginia should have been Britain's greatest player, but at 26 she risks leaving her brilliant future behind her. It would be a pity.   *November 14 1971*

The Wade image: beside the strawberries and cream of British tennis, almost a Latin temperament.

● She stretches right up to get on top of the ball to deliver the downward chopping action that is the essence of the crisp volley. The racket arm is stiff, as is the wrist, and there is virtually no back-swing. The best volley is short, sharp and heavy, like a jab in boxing. Most mistakes spring from too long a backswing.

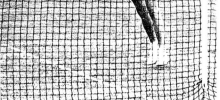

● The perfect hit as Virginia brings her whole body weight down on to the ball. Arm, wrist and racket are locked together. She has, as the players say, simply "leant" on the ball. A great difficulty with novices is to stop them flailing at a volley as at a ground stroke. Little movement is needed if the racket is held solidly.

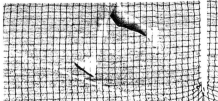

● A typically flamboyant Wade finish, with rather more follow through than is necessary. She makes the stroke now resemble the end of a drive-volley, used by most players only when they have the easiest of kills. "My object," says Virginia, "is to get myself behind the ball very fast to screw it with control for a winner."

Ingemar Stenmark: the silent gymnast gliding through the snow to a fortune

A trip above the snowline for an interview with a less than talkative skiing champion.

by Dudley Doust

The photographers (15 Swedes and our own Chris Smith) were summoned to a snowy slope at Lermoos, just over the Austrian border from Garmisch Partenkirchen, and there they were given the rare privilege of shooting the greatest skier in the world, Ingemar Stenmark of Sweden, in practice. Soon a VW Scirocco slewed to a stop, and out stepped Stenmark, a tall, freckly youth of 21. He fixed a small, glacial smile on the photographers, and said not a word. "That's funny," someone murmured, "he usually says 'No comment,' or 'Go talk to my coach.'"

His coach, Torgny Swensson, was embarrassed by his prima donna. He shrugged and kicked his boots together: "The Swedish Ski Federation would like him to give interviews, and so would his ski manufacturer, Elan. But we live off Ingemar, and we must do what he says."

Sweden and Elan, the unlikely Yugoslavian ski firm which was founded by partisan mountain fighters after the Second World War, have the hottest property in skiing. On the World Cup circuit this season, Stenmark already has captured the title for the third successive year. At the World Championships on Thursday he won the giant slalom by a colossal 2.04sec, the most conclusive triumph in world skiing since Jean-Claude Killy took three gold medals at the Grenoble Olympics in 1968.

At the photo session, Stenmark unloaded his skis from the car roof and, in the blatant manner of skiers, turned the trademark towards the cameras. In a sport that treats the ethics of amateurism with outright contempt, it is impossible to get honest answers about the earnings of its superstars. For example, Elan claims to pay its silent Swede a paltry £6,000 a year, yet a rival maker, Fischer of Austria, says it unsuccessfully offered £120,000 a year for Stenmark's services. A victory in the slalom today is said to be worth £60,000 to Stenmark.

The Swedish team went up the chair-lift, and as coincidence would have it Stig Strand, the first one down the practice course, comes from Stenmark's home town, Tarnaby, a fishing, hiking and skiing resort in the Lax Mountains, some 60 miles south of the Arctic Circle.

At school, Strand went on, they would nip out between classes and take quick runs down the adjacent slalom course. Ingemar's father, a former ski-racer, would drive a wavy line down the mountain in a snow-buggy, and the boys would follow it before being buggied again to the top. Ingemar is now so famous—he twice has beaten Bjorn Borg to the title of Scandinavian Sportsman of the Year—that tourists steal stones from his garden.

Another skier, Torsten Jakobsson, came down. He had tried Stenmark's skis in practice the previous day, he said, and found them unusable: "I can't turn with them, and when I sit back they shoot out from under me." In fact, the centre of gravity in Stenmark's skis is marginally farther forward than in normal skis. A Yugoslavian professor of physical culture from the University of Ljubljana often travels with Stenmark, studying his skiing positions, and he feeds the data back to the ski manufacturers in an attempt to find even better ways of distributing Stenmark's weight.

Jakobsson said: "Look, here comes Ingemar!" Stenmark came down the mountain, rising and falling in an ecstasy of rhythm, altogether effortless, the gates flicking away from his shoulders. Indeed, he was leaning well forward over his skis, pointing them downhill upon leaving the gates. Stenmark checked and stopped with an insouciant swish and clatter of bindings. He hung forward, relaxing in his pole-straps, giving the photographers a view of the graceful sweep of his thighs.

Stenmark's legs are the mainspring of his awesome power: from a standstill, he can high jump 1.60 metres or long jump 3.20 metres or, better still, link six non-stop long jumps and cover 18.50 metres. Swedish physiologists, great probers of sportsmen, have found that only Borg has an oxygen-intake capacity equal to Stenmark's.

The greatest skier in the world gazed silently up the mountains. There was still one Alpine discipline to conquer, the downhill, but he had neither the time nor the inclination to do it. Another coach, Tyrolean Hermann Nogler said: "In three weeks, Ingemar could master the downhill"—he grunted disdainfully—"but the downhill is for weightlifters. The slalom is for gymnasts." *February 5 1978*

Champion at speed: a Stenmark victory in the giant slalom.

Champion aloft: an uncharacteristic Stenmark grin framed by a pair of characteristically well-displayed skis.

Jackie Robinson: the social pioneer

by Stephen Fay

In 1947 Jackie Robinson crossed one of the most potent social barriers in America: he became the first Negro to break through the colour bar and play major league baseball with whites, so becoming the most famous black man in the country.

Robinson was specially chosen by the owner of the Brooklyn Dodgers, a man named Branch Rickey, because Rickey thought he was not only good enough, but tough enough to play a symbolic role. He proved everything that Rickey had hoped for.

In his last public appearance, two weeks ago during the World Series, which is baseball's extended Cup Final, he made a speech which deliberately avoided the bromides which accompany such occasions. He said it was a rotten thing that the major baseball teams had happily accepted black players since he first played for Brooklyn, but that no team had appointed a black manager.

Robinson died last week, a sad figure, at the age of 53. He was almost blind and had a weak heart. He was a wealthy man. His son had been a drug addict and died a year ago in a car crash. He was almost cured then and Robinson had devoted much of his time lately to the drug problem.

He was a short-tempered man, but he had a good deal to be short tempered about. When he started to play with the Brooklyn Dodgers some players said they would not play with him because he was black. They did, of course, but it left a scar that would never easily heal. Robinson was always conscious of colour prejudice in sport and never hesitated to expose it. But his experience opened up American sport to succeeding generations of blacks. When he died he was already a legend, but unlike many legendary sportsmen, he actually had some claim to be.

October 29 1972

Inside track

All Black

The off-field conduct of some of the All Blacks has been so foul-mouthed and menacing during their visit that many former friends will be glad when they go home. "For some reason," the New Zealand News, a British-based newspaper wrote last week, "the All Blacks seemed to have failed as ambassadors."

The reasons are obvious. The New Zealanders have shunned traditional postgame receptions, broken a share of hotel furniture, and frightened away autograph hunters with a churlish "F— off!" Sir William Ramsey, past Rugby Football Union president, was given a toe-curling critique of pommie rugby by an All Black. "I told him," replied Sir William, unamused, "I could beat him at swearing."

"THEY SEEM TO BE PAINTING US ALL BLACK"

Complaints centre round Keith Murdoch, the All Blacks' 18-stone prop, the Otago bouncer with a *bandido* moustache. Murdoch last weekend manhandled our writer Norman Harris who, ironically, is a New Zealander himself. The assault took place near midnight, after the Scottish Districts match, in the Peebles Hydro Hotel. Harris approached the night clerk's desk where he overheard Murdoch request another guest's key. Harris innocently commented that this man was K. Murdoch. The big prop wheeled blindly round, picked up the six-foot newsman by the hair, and hurled him to the floor. "You had better," bellowed Murdoch, "f——ing watch out!"

The manager of the Hydro wasn't sure whether he would invite the New Zealanders back to his hotel. A spokesman for Cambridge University Arms was more forthright. "You could say some of the All Blacks were not as diplomatic as they might have been," he said. "When they were hungry, they used four-letters words to our staff." *December 3 1972*

John Curry: a champion defying tradition

An assessment of the genius—and the struggle for recognition—of a future world skating champion, by the former Sunday Times ballet critic.

by Richard Buckle

Nine a.m. at the Richmond Sports Drome seemed quite an early date for me, but John Curry, the British figure skating champion, said he had been on the ice since 6.30. Curry, 23, born in Birmingham, was leaving the next day for Czechoslovakia to have his third shot at the world championship being held this week.

"I won't get it," he told me. Well, I hope he's wrong, but the reason he *thinks* he won't get it is the crux of the matter and why I am writing this piece.

Curry is a revolutionary. Skating has always been an athletic activity, a skill which can be measured and judged like pole-jumping. But Curry is only interested in it as a means of artistic expression. He wanted to be a dancer, but his Dad said No, and skating was the next best thing. The reason he thinks he won't be world champion is that most judges are interested exclusively in technique. Curry can do all the difficult tricks as well as the next man, but in free skating (as opposed to figure skating) he is against displays of virtuosity for its own sake. "You wouldn't believe it, but judges have told me I make it look too easy." I laughed. So it's a question of *Ars est celare artem* versus Look-Ma-I'm-Dancing.

John Curry, who is 5ft 11in, slight and dark, has a reticent quality, which may come from shyness or good manners and reminds me of Anthony Dowell. He goes to ballet class three times a week. What are the chief differences between ballet and skating, apart from the skates? The turn-out of the legs is important in both, but a skater cannot point his toe, so that in the extended position we call *arabesque*, instead of holding the raised leg stiff, Curry bends it very slightly: this improves the line. Spins are easier for a skater than pirouettes for a dancer, but jumps are harder. Skaters can move backwards with far more freedom than dancers.

I asked Curry if he could skate to the music of a typical male classical solo, usually short with a pounding rhythm, *allegro risoluto*. He said Yes, but it

probably wouldn't give him the chance to cover the space and to introduce all the technical feats which are obligatory even in a display of free skating.

I noticed the various arm movements borrowed from ballet, which make the act so much richer and more satisfying. In traditional skating the arms were nearly always held in an extended position, palms downward. In his "sit-spin into cross-toe" Curry had his arms curved together above his head. He can spin about 30 times, and does everything in both directions except jumps, which he does to the left. Ballet dancers can usually only pirouette well one way.

I learned the names of several marvellous jumps—Triple loop, Double Axel and Triple Salchow. I was told that Salchow, who invented this jump, could only do one at a go: now three are

obligatory. Which brings me back to the point about technique and artistry. In skating, people learn to do more and more difficult stunts as the years go by, just as in ballet. There is no end to it. It becomes boring without the addition of grace and style. In the 1880s a number of Italian ballet dancers showed Russia some dazzling acrobatic steps.

To the strength the Italians taught them, the Russians added their own style and feeling. The wonderful artists who were the result of this process, Pavlova, Karsavina, Nijinksy and Co., conquered the West in 1909. I am convinced that a similar process is inevitable in the skating world. It will be interesting to see whether the judges at the championship recognise that Curry is making history. The new wave may take another year or two, but it is bound to come. *February 25 1973*

① TRIPLE TOE LOOP ② TRIPLE SALCHOW ③ DOUBLE LUTZ ④ DOUBLE AXEL

Leaping to the crown

The jumps, blended into a programme of consummate artistry, which brought John Curry the men's world figure skating championship last week:

1. The Triple Toe Loop. This jump carries the maximum difficulty rating of 8 from the International Skating Union. Skating backwards, Curry flings himself

into the jump, digging the toe of his free skate into the ice just before take-off. He revolves three times, and lands backwards on the same foot from which he took off.

2. The Triple Salchow (ISU rating: 7). He takes off backwards, does three complete revolutions and steps back on to the ice—this time with the other foot.

(In Curry's now classic opening sequence, he adds to these two a triple loop (ISU rating: 8). This is identical to the first jump

but without the toe-assisted take-off.

3. The Double Lutz (ISU rating: 6). The toe-assisted take-off is vital in this jump in order to get the body turning against the natural rotation set up by the skating edge.

4. The Double Axel (ISU rating: 6). A spectacular but not difficult jump which with its 2½ rotations looks as impressive as a triple. In a forward take-off, Curry swings his free leg round and up, lands backwards, and signs off kneeling. *March 7 1976*

Tessa Sanderson: young, gifted, and black... and liberated

Back in the days even before she became a world-class javelin thrower, Tessa Sanderson struck us as the epitome of a gracefully sporting young lady.

by John Hopkins

Searching for a liberated sportswoman in International Women's Year, we came across friendly, sexy, bubbly and pretty Tessa Sanderson, an outstanding athlete, a natural games player and a liberated young lady. Swimming begins her week and dancing in Birmingham, Wolverhampton or Stafford ends it. In between she squeezes in athletics training, swimming, dancing —and work.

Tessa was born in Jamaica 19½ years ago and now lives in Wednesfield, Wolverhampton. For most of her life she has enjoyed sport. "At school I hardly bothered with lessons, specially maths," she says. "But I always looked forward to games."

Malcolm Allison: May I present Miss Richmond

A steaming game of consequences which rocked the Palace to its foundations.

by Helen Muir

A vicar's daughter
met
a football manager
at
Selhurst Park
on
a fresh morning in March
She said to him:
Mr Allison, I can put you in pictures. I write for a men's magazine. I would like to make a documentary study of yourself and the Crystal Palace players in training. Of course, my father played for Rotherham United before he took the cloth.

He said to her:
Very well, Miss Richmond, we will treat you as one of the team. I am a young 48 and I cannot recall your father.

What they did:
The vicar's daughter parked car FU2 and dressed in football clothes, raced about the pitch kicking the ball and boisterously tackling the other players and the manager. When the game was over, they all threw off their football clothes and had a bath, splashing and frolicking in the water, as players do when they are tired and dirty. A photographer took many pictures because the vicar's daughter was really very famous and renowned for her writing and sexual intercourse and the football manager was also a playboy, well known for his cigars and champagne and chicks.

The world said:
Oooh . . . ooh, have you seen those pictures? How disgraceful. What a terrible shock for the decent people of football and the decent wives. This is why the club is in the Third Division. Disgusting. Are there any more?

The consequence was:
The football manager is parting company with Crystal Palace.

After three years of battering personal publicity and sliding defeat for Crystal Palace, the nude bath episode seems to have been one of the final straws in Malcolm Allison's career as manager. But Fiona Richmond, the girl who at 29 has made such a lucrative existence from using men as sex objects, takes no responsibility for her part in his departure to America and dismisses the uproar as ridiculous.

Dressed in a black PVC collar, a black PVC hip belt with a fringe and black thigh boots, she discusses it between acts of Come Into My Bed at the Whitehall Theatre, a play in which nearly everybody takes off their clothes. There are whips and black romps with King Kong and joyful audience participation, the dialogue of which the Editor would not allow to be repeated in *The Sunday Times.*

She was one of those enviable girls who could do anything athletic—sprint, do the high and long jump and throw the javelin. Her hockey was good enough for her to represent her school; at netball she was even better.

At 13½ and, typically, larking about in a schools' athletics competition, she was spotted by John Moogan, who is now her coach. "There's a multi-talented girl" he thought to himself as he watched her traipse from the high jump to the long jump and then pick up her javelin. Now she is Britain's No. 1 javelin thrower and has enough talent left over to be among the country's top ten in the pentathlon, a five-event competition that does not include the javelin. Last month she ran her first 400 metres hurdles. Her time: 65 seconds, which ranks her in the top 20 in Britain.

"Javelin throwing requires a combination of strength, speed and technique" says Tessa. "You need sprinting speed to get down the runway, strength in the upper arms and upper body, notably the shoulders, and flexibility in the hips."

Exercises to increase the suppleness of her back have helped her to arch her back when throwing the javelin while also enabling her to Fosbury Flop to a height of 5ft 6in.

"She is potentially world class at the javelin," points out Moogan. "Yet I also have to bear in mind that she might be world class at the pentathlon and the 400 metres hurdles as well."

October 26 1975

"I think Malcolm's done a great deal for football. At least, he's colourful. He shoots his mouth off but he's very open and honest about what he does. And he gets other people interested. As a woman I would never have normally taken an interest. I don't find footballers particularly attractive but I went to the semi-final at Chelsea when Crystal Palace lost to Southampton.

"The other managers are a draggy lot. Most other men are bitchy towards me because I'm doing what they've been doing for years."

Fiona is an extraordinary mixture of middle-class manners and tough flamboyance. She makes the new Ms woman seem like a knitter from the Outer Hebrides. Her father actually was a vicar and her mother taught French in a convent but the uproar she causes slides off her. Her reaction to disapproval is to award the Limp Dick of the Month to her critic. Malcolm Allison certainly won't be receiving that award. They became firm friends, she says, after their bath. *May 23 1976*

CONSEQUENCES

When the vicar's daughter got it together with the football manager.

Enzo Ferrari: life in a world where the only positive element is fear

A rare and privileged conversation with the hidden giant of motor racing, for 60 years at the heart of the sport and for 25 years, since the death of his son Dino, a virtual recluse.

by Keith Botsford

There is simply more to Enzo Ferrari than any other figure in the world of motor racing. But little of the inner man is ever revealed to the public. The man who is God to most in the sport has private sorrow to match public triumph, and for 25 years since the tragic death of his only son Dino, who at the time of his death suffered from terminal muscular dystrophy, he has consistently refused to become public property.

There have been just two passions in his life: cars and his son Dino. The cars have been his joy; his son, his private grief. The shadow of that death, and his own, obviously hangs over him.

I went to see him at Maranello, near Modena, the home of his world-famous marque. A simple office. A near empty desk, a sculptured glass version of the famous Ferrari prancing horse—the emblem taken from the plane of an Italian war ace—a portrait of his son Dino and little else. His talk, from the start, was about "the hallucinating fragility of life." And his daily visits to his son's grave.

"Suicide," he said, "is an act of courage. No man who takes a journey into the unknown is cowardly or vile. A man is nothing until he is dead; it is death which puts a stamp on his personality. Death has led me to constant self-examination, but I know life is an illusion, mainly the illusion that we are something. So that when people talk about my fame, I know better than to be taken in by it. I am a man who has pursued an adventure. But it is probably an error to say who I am; if I am unable to see the defects in the machines I build, how can someone else judge me?"

Ferrari is a big man. Next February he will be 80. His almost colourless eyes, usually concealed behind tinted glasses, are withdrawn; his nose and mouth are fleshy and prominent; his speech is formal and eloquent, his bulky body in repose. Latterly he has been intermittently ill, a lung infection due to a lifelong inhalation of noxious engine emissions frequently leaving him weak and spent, but his mind is as alert and categorical as ever.

His talk is of almost brutal frankness, as though all the pretences of the younger Ferrari had been stripped away and left only the heart of the matter. Which is egotism. "No one loses anything or does anything for someone else," he said. "We live in a vast prison, like Kafka's. The world is a penitentiary and we are the inmates: caught in an instinctive egotism, we have to depend on our own force and nothing else. Whatever we pretend, we value others not for the good they can do us, but for the evil they might. The man who might kill us receives our full attention. He requires it, for we live in a cruel world where violence has taken

Ferrari: "an endless corridor."

the place of reason, a world where the only positive element is fear, the chief instrument of power."

Constructors come in all shapes and sizes: shrewd, cunning, autocratic, affable, some in it for money, some for the glory, a few for the sport. But Ferrari has been in that world since it started, born when it was born, and ever since a force in every aspect of it: as driver, engineer, promoter and elemental force. Yet the world he inhabits—for the last quarter century with its stripped down routine of house to grave to office, to the Ferrari circuit at Fiorano and back home—remains perplexing. Creating cars is another Kafka labyrinth.

"You are in an endless corridor, along which every door is closed. You want to get out but you can't. You have to find a solution. I find it sometimes in the night, sometimes as if in a dream. When I see a possibility, it is like a blinding light, like lightning. In my head, I say, 'Why not a machine like this, or like that?' I become a thinking instrument, I guess at a concept, I formulate a theme.

"But the constructor is not free. Not as the poet is free. To realise a dream is the work of a team, like the birth of a superior mind. A new motor comes into the world with the cry of a newborn child; raw material is transformed into a living being with a voice of its own. Machines bear the marks of their makers' minds, but also of conviction, otherwise how to convince others that your dream is possible?

"I think of myself as a promoter of ideas. My task? To explain an idea to those who must realise it; to argue until they find the right thread; to persist, keeping the thread in mind, until a solution comes; to test those solutions. But I am a constructor. I remember all my errors. I think there is no such thing as luck. Nor is there misfortune. Ill luck is what we didn't know or failed to foresee. In such collaborations there is an ascendant curve: its peak is a moment when this common effort all works, its base when it breaks down. It's elite work, not made for most. Two of my oldest collaborators are ill, I put in young men. But as soon as young men acquire cultivation, they acquire personality. Will they then work together? It is my job to choose people. And then give them total confidence."

Ferrari's own background is, like the man, modest and simple. The beginnings were humble. Modena was a simple, sleepy provincial town, his father the proprietor of a small engineering works with some 20 workers, his education scant: "I myself didn't study when I was a boy," he said, "so I have very little formal education and my cultural patrimony is small. I have acquired a modest erudition, that's all, which is not to be confused with culture. But I am surrounded by people who have more than I: that is my secret.

"I don't believe a constructor need be an engineer or technician, but someone with a passion for cars, a man who knows enough about human beings to harmonise the ambitions of his colleagues. Aren't all conquests ultimately the consequence of superior human and technical capacities? Had I had a voice, I might have become a singer. I liked operettas and pretty singers and dancers. Or a journalist: fortunate men who can do again tomorrow what they did today and forget their errors. Economic facts determined my profession. In 1918 I was poor. My father had died two years earlier. I was in Turin, an ex-soldier, hungry. Today I can dine around the world, but then, no one invited me home for a meal. But I had then, and have now, my pride. Yet is there a worse profession than that of a constructor, whose judges are infinite, whose critics are numberless?"

We lunched, across the main road, in the private room of a restaurant: a plate

views: they are responsible for the wholesale inflation of the sport.

"Some people say that without sponsors there'd be no Grands Prix. Nonsense. The car was invented, races followed. The sponsor is a source of destruction. I can allow those who contribute to the sport, but cigarettes and prophylactics, no! That's prostitution. They depersonalise cars; by allowing it, we depersonalise ourselves. They call it spectacle. It was a spectacle in my day, too, but a spectacle of technique, honour, humanity and sport."

Ferrari's drivers are an honour-roll. Nearly all, but the one driver he most admired, for his all-round ability, under all conditions and in any car,

lives for nothing, but the sport came before the cash.

"But I can describe the parabola of today's driver. You take him on and his first task is to prove to you that he's better than his teammate, his next that he's better than any other driver. To prove that, he has to extract economic and technical advantage from the constructor and, having obtained that, he reaches the top.

"He risks his life, yes, but it is a glamorous death he faces and all racing drivers are volunteers. There is no justification for death, even in war, and we constructors have a responsibility, which is to determine the causes. These are seldom single.

"But man is presumptuous. No

Monza 1923: young Ferrari (right) with Nicola Romeo (centre, founder of Alfa-Romeo) and Giorgio Rimini, who sold Ferrari his first racing car.

of pasta for the Ingegnere, local, fresh, rosy wine with a faint bubble, roast veal, much fruit. On the table, a small portable radio for Ferrari, playing music. He being both together with us and apart.

In his lifetime, the sport has changed beyond recognition. "There is no sport today which lives outside the hard laws of cash. I go back to the days when cars bore their national colours, blue for France, orange for Spain and so on. Today, it's a hunt for profit. We used to be honoured to be invited to a prizegiving; now drivers get cash for signing photographs. Money is the boss. Sponsors have the dominant role; circuits are rearranged for their convenience: their hoardings block the spectators'

Stirling Moss, have flown the emblem of the rampant horse: Nuvolari, the unforgettable Ascari, Mike Hawthorn, Phil Hill, Fangio, the ill-fated von Trips, Bandini, John Surtees, Chris Amon, one of his favourites, Jackie Stewart, Andretti, Ickx, Regazzoni, Peterson and now Lauda and Reutemann. He has loved them, fostered them and always, ultimately, remained aloof.

"I understand drivers' problems," he said. "I was one myself until my son was born and I knew I should no longer race. But they are no longer of the race I knew. Today they are athletes who hire out their capacities for profit; they have been assimilated into their surroundings. The old drivers didn't risk their

driver thinks he will be next. Not only that, each thinks he's too good to make the mistake his dead colleague made. They don't reflect: if they did, would they take unacceptable risks?

"I've had dead drivers. They were psychologically in an anomalous state, or ambiguous about death. Drivers need quiet private lives: how to reconcile that with burning the candle at both ends? Egoism tells them, make a living, get rich, go out again, do not become a creature of regrets. That is the world today; one is first or one is nothing. The modern world creates idols, which is cruel, when the intent is then to destroy them. Because today the great hunger is for emotion. It is ego which rules us all." *June 26 1977*

Max Faulkner: after 49 years of golf, a man with roots deep in Sussex soil

The author, who died in 1973, was a traveller with a gift for the humorous phrase, who presented reality through his own particular prism. Among several pieces for *The Sunday Times* sports pages, this visit to Max Faulkner is especially remembered.

by Anthony Carson

I drove down into Sussex on a lovely day with spring dancing on the Downs. I had come to see Max Faulkner, the champion golfer, at Hill Barn Golf Club near Worthing.

When I arrived at the clubhouse, there was no sign of him. The rooms were full of pullovered players relaxing before the next day's tournament. None of them had seen him. I asked officials wearing white discs and important frowns, but they could tell me nothing. I hung about, sank a few draught Guinnesses, lunched on veal and ham, and got on to the telephone.

I was told that Mr Faulkner was very sorry, but his wife's father had just died in the house, and he couldn't come to the clubhouse. Would I find details about the next day's tournament—with whom he was playing, and when—and bring certain necessary documents to him as soon as possible?

I did this and drove deep into unknown Sussex. The countryside, as we swayed along Gay Lane, had the stillness of the ages. Finally we arrived at Moon Farm, and there was Max Faulkner, a tall, slightish, young-old figure, standing beside his front door.

"I'm sorry about all this," said Max Faulkner, "but I was trapped in the house. I just couldn't have gone anywhere. The body is upstairs. We've put him in his best pyjamas, and he looks clean and neat. He was 91. He had to go."

We went inside his beautiful rambling house. "Mentioned in the Domesday Book." he said. He introduced us to his son, Guy, a farming journalist, his daughter Hilary. He also has another son, John, 17 years old, whom he intends to turn into a golf champion.

We all sat around drinking tea and I felt that Max Faulkner didn't want to say anything very much. He's too close to the Sussex soil, and doesn't want to show his roots. I asked him to join me alone in another room, and then there was a wavelength and he began to talk.

"I don't really care for golf at all," he said. "I don't like thinking earnestly about it, and I'm glad when I've other things to do."

"When did you begin being a golfer?" I asked him.

"When I was four years old," he said without any hesitation, "I had untidy black hair like the yobs wear now, and was starting on the same swing as I have now. When I was twelve and a half, the schoolmaster at Bramley let me compete in a boys' tournament and I won by sixteen strokes. My father said: 'It's golf for you.' I went to school till I was 15, but spent six months studying in the mornings. The rest of

"I daren't look my caddie in the eye."

the time was golf. I used to practise till after dark. You could see the holes by moonlight. I remember the glowworms.

"Now I'm 53," said Max Faulkner, "and all that's a long way back. In 1934 my father sent me to Sonning Golf Club, under the pro Arthur Young, who'd been with James Braid. Those were terrific names. Braid, Vardon and Taylor. My father was seventh assistant to James Braid up to 1914."

"I thought you didn't like golf, Mr Faulkner," I said.

"You get tied up," he said, "but I'm damn good at untying myself.

"How else can I blow the old trumpet? In 1951 I won the Open Championship at Royal Portrush, Northern Ireland. I've played golf twice round the world, and followed the sun round

the States. That's where the money is. I'm too old for it now. Brian Barnes will be a millionaire before he's 35."

Max Faulkner paused and looked out of the window. "I'm not a millionaire, but I live like one."

He looked back from the window and flexed his muscles. "I'm a fisherman," he said. "I'm a professional bass fisherman. I bought a Selsey fishing boat and a tarred hut for lobster pots. There were plenty of gaps in the tournament season. I caught prawns, cooked them and sent them to London. I caught bass on spinners. Bass are jet black with silver sides and white flesh: beautiful fish.

"D'you know, whenever I'm in a tournament by the sea, I take off my shoes and paddle. I wash my face in the salt water. I love looking brown on the golf course. Think of all the walking a golfer does. I never get sores on my feet. I tell you I hate freshwater and freshwater fish."

We stood up and shook hands.

"I'm off to feed the hogs now," he said. "I'm glad you met me where I belong. Let's finish our tea."

In the kitchen before he went to feed the hogs, Max Faulkner suddenly gave an inspired talk about caddies. In his Domesday home, the spotlight shone on him and the entertainer took the stage.

"They're mostly old soldiers. They only live for golf. They know much more than me. Sometimes I daren't look my caddie in the eye. He knows every blade of grass between me and the 14th hole."

He sat down, sipped his tea, and stared at my car driver. "I remember I was driving off in a tournament and I saw my caddie swaying a bit. Not too much but a bit. Mind you, I know my caddies. I know every tremble.

"'Are you all right?' I asked him.

"'Trim as a daisy,' he said. 'I've just finished a bottle of brandy, and I'll have another one when you've won the tournament.'

"As a matter of fact I did the hole in two. There was no sign of a flag. I looked around and there was the caddie flat out, clasping the flag in his arms. I put the flag in the hole, and carried the caddie behind a gorse bush."

The last news I heard about Max Faulkner was at the tournament at Worthing on April 30. He was wearing lilac trousers, lilac socks and lilac shoes. At last it really was spring.

May 3 1970

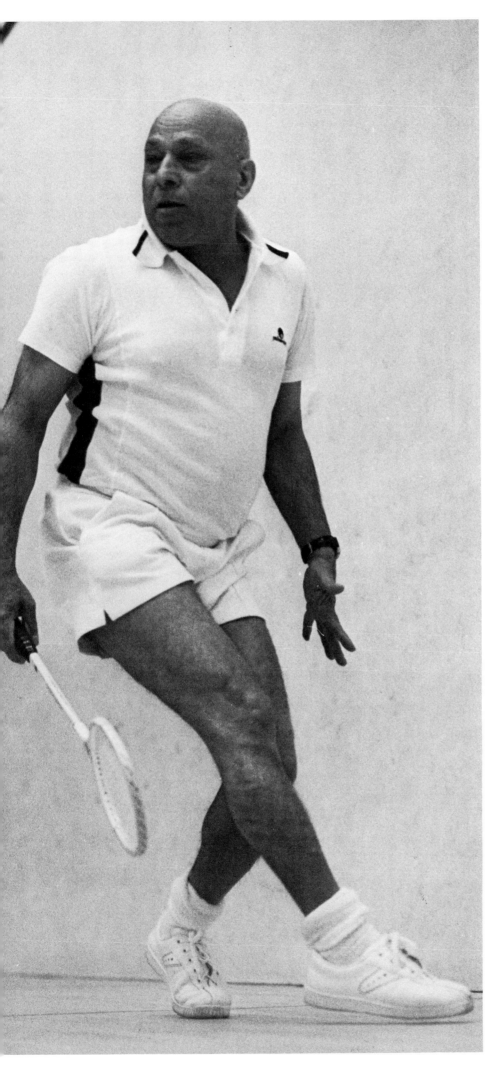

Hashim Khan: ungainly but still inspiring

A legend returns to claim his court.

by John Hopkins

He is over 60 now, weighs 50lb more than he did in his prime, and fathered his 12th child, a girl, 10 years ago. His ear-to-ear grin remains, his giggle is still as high as a nervous debutante's and his bald head gleams as brightly as the most polished town-hall doorknob. Hashim Khan, the world's greatest squash player, was in London for the first time for 20 years.

At Wembley last week, a generation of squash enthusiasts for whom Hashim is the most famous, the most revered of all, gave the maestro a welcome that made him feel more nervous than when he met Prince Philip after his record seventh win in the British Open, was feted by a million fans in Pakistan, had a railway station named after him, and a public holiday called in his honour. Last week they interrupted his tea, chased him into the showers and made moving from place to place a test of patience.

Hashim does not know his precise age ("For reason we never born in hospital"), but he settles for 63. Thus in 1950 he was in his mid-thirties when he won his first British Open, and rising 50 when he won his last. His return to Britain from the United States, where he has lived for 20 years, to play in the Open, was a clarion call.

At first, one's heart sank. His barrel chest and chicken's legs remained. He held his racket halfway up the grip, as always, but he hit shots off the wood of his racket, he hit them into the tin. He looked ungainly. But then he always did. Speed, not style, was his asset. After playing, he used to leave behind on court the smell of burning rubber, not the impression of grace. "Even now, I pretty fast for my age."

He watched the world champion, Geoff Hunt, play his semi-final last Thursday. "He very fast," Hashim conceded, "but my brother (Azam) and I, we play better for reason we play more shots. Zaman play like we used to, but he not got speed we had." He paused, and then added: "Put that nicely. I not mean it bad."

April 9 1978

Vasily Alexeyev: the anatomy of a supreme Soviet lifter

Weightlifting has attracted a prodigious television audience to the last three Olympic Games, perhaps because of the swagger and ritual reminiscent of the strong man at a country fair. Alexeyev, as the world's strongest man at the 1972 and 1976 Games, maintained Soviet domination of the sport, and amply filled the world's TV screens.

by John Goodbody

Russia's Olympic super-heavyweight weightlifting champion Vasily Alexeyev is demonstrably farther ahead of an ordinary human being than any world champion in sports that can be measured and do not require special equipment. And his feat in lifting $534\frac{1}{2}$ pounds overhead at Crystal Palace last Wednesday is the ultimate demonstration that man's capacity to increase his strength is greater than any other purely physical attribute for sport.

Alexeyev's effort is over four times what a man in the street could probably manage. Weightlifting experts agree that few untrained humans can raise more than 130 pounds. They simply do not possess the muscular strength, largely because they have not de-

veloped their inherent ability. Even those who have now appear unremarkable compared with Alexeyev.

The heaviest weight lifted in the 19th century was 355 pounds by William Turk, but even with the advent of widespread international competition, poundages did not increase rapidly until after the Second World War, when America's John Davis became the first man to raise 400 pounds with a standard barbell. It was not until the USSR first took the honour of possessing the world's strongest man at the 1957 world championships that man's strength feats became extraordinary. Successive Olympic champions Vlasov, Zhabotinsky and now Alexeyev have largely maintained their domination.

John Lear, Britain's national coach,

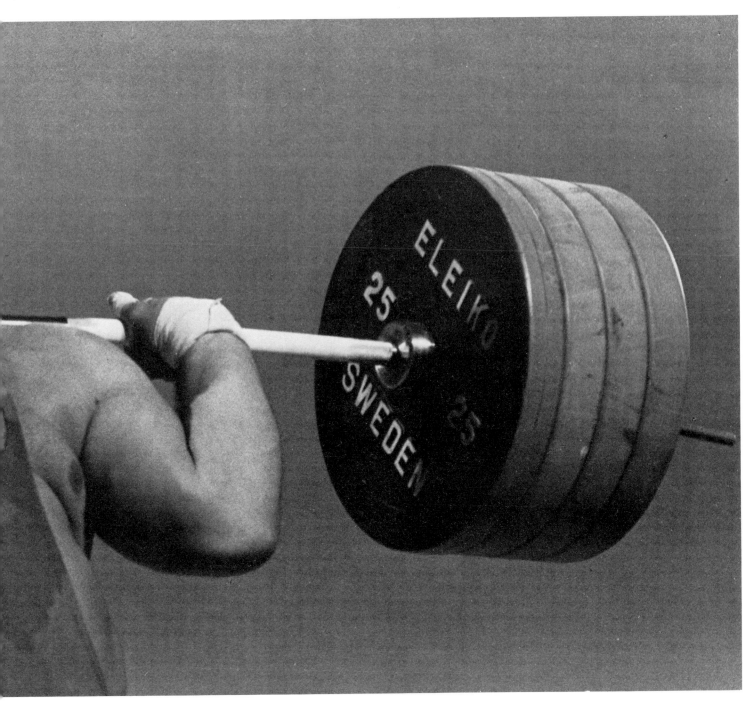

provides five reasons for Alexeyev's present supremacy:

Technique: Weightlifting consists of gymnastic movements against increasing resistance. A man-in-the-street would not use his strength to the most advantageous mechanical principle. However, Alexeyev rarely uses the jerk in which the bar is driven overhead in training, concentrating on the clean, in which he pulls the weight into his shoulders by squatting underneath it.

Physique. Super-heavyweight weightlifters are extreme mesomorphs-endomorphs (combination of muscle and fat). Only a few men have the physique to be champion weightlifters, and still fewer to be super-heavyweights. Long arms and legs are not useful. A top basketball player would not become a top weightlifter because his levers are wrong. Alexeyev, apart from his stomach, is in proportion to himself. It's just that his size is on such a gargantuan scale. He has a 58-inch chest, 48-inch waist, 21-inch biceps and 34-inch thighs (bigger than most men's waists).

Bodyweight. Alexeyev last week weighed 23st 12lb, his bulkiest ever. The heavier a man is, the more weight he can lift; this is why there are nine categories in the sport, with a super-heavyweight class starting at 17st 4lb. Fat gives the stability about the waist necessary for pushing heavy poundages overhead.

Diet. Although most weightlifters, like other competitors in sports with weight categories, have to guard against an increase in bodyweight, super-heavyweights are an exception. Food consumption is gross. Competitors last week were eating 12 eggs whipped in milk for breakfast, and a whole leg of lamb for lunch.

Motivation. The extreme example of this was when Mrs Maxwell Rogers, an 8st 11lb American housewife, in 1960 lifted one end of a 3,600lb stationwagon which had fallen on her son. She cracked some vertebrae. Alexeyev attempts to get as close to this hysteria as possible.

There remains the question of anabolic steroid drugs. But whether or not Alexeyev takes them, they would only be a slight aid to his raising 534½ pounds. He remains sport's supreme superman. *December 1 1974*

Sir Alf Ramsey: an end of term report on a professor's part in his downfall

The fate of Sir Alf Ramsey as manager of England's football team and his eventual replacement by Don Revie was sealed, in part, by his own intransigence. It foundered finally on the equal determination of one unlikely figure, Sir Harold Thompson.

by Brian James

As England team manager, Sir Alf Ramsey's great gift was an ability to assess the calibre of the opposition. Yet his dismissal last week was the consequence of a total failure to appreciate the power and determination of the opposition movement that finally overthrew him.

And, in particular, to detect the strength of one man. Professor Sir Harold Thompson, around whom antagonism towards Ramsey polarised and grew. To understand Thompson's cataclysmic influence, it is first necessary to know the attitude Ramsey adopted when offered the post of team manager in 1963.

"I'll do the job, but *my* way," he told the late Joe Mears, then chairman of the Football Association. By that Ramsey meant an end to the power of the amateur selectors who had chosen and re-chosen England teams since the beginning in 1872.

A clue to his attitude came on the last day of his first summer tour with England. At a party in Basle, given by pressmen, Sir Alf made a speech. He thanked the trainers, he thanked the reporters for their hospitality.

And, finally, he thanked the FA councillors present for "their sense in keeping out of our way." The remark was greeted with thin smiles, a ripple of laughter cold as hail on a tin roof. That remark has never been forgotten or, by some, forgiven.

Faintly contemptuous

Ramsey had begun as he meant to carry on. It became noticeable that when boarding aeroplanes he would sit next to the trainer or doctor. If not, one of his senior players. In desperate circumstances, he'd sit next to one of the Press. But only if there was one single seat left would he perch next to any of the official party.

He seldom attended banquets or receptions, even being prepared to give offence to remain with his team. "Dinners . . . speeches," he used to say. "That's *their* job . . . that's why those people are here."

"Those people" was his collective, and faintly contemptuous, phrase for anyone in the party not a playing or working member of the FA squads.

Once the Selection Committee was re-named the Senior Committee, Ramsey also took great care to ensure that the members had no say in his teams. As a polite gesture, he let the committee know the team before he told the Press. As a formality he allowed the custom of committeemen to go on "scouting" expeditions around League matches to continue.

But it was only a gesture. A First Division manager said last week: "One of these committeemen came to one of our games, and told me he was watch-

Ramsey: the arch professional.

ing so-and-so for Sir Alf. Next time I saw Ramsey I asked him: 'Do you really take notice of what *they* say?' Alf laughed . . . 'You must be bloody joking' . . . and he made a gesture as though screwing up a report-sheet and slinging it away.

"I remember thinking then he'd got the committee where he wanted it . . . in the background, without influence, just a figurehead, really. But I remember thinking, too, that they'd only stand for that as long as he kept

winning. If he ever had a bad run, they'd rise up and eat him alive."

So long as Ramsey was successful, so long as the committee had no leader of real presence to stand up to him, he was allowed free rein.

That leader appeared last summer with the coming of Professor Sir Harold Thompson, CBE, MA, DSC, FRS—chummily known as "Doc" or "Tommy" to the senior citizens who control English football, but a very considerable man indeed.

It takes 59 lines in Who's Who to capture his brilliant career as an academic, scientist, committee-room politician and adviser to governments. An expert in molecular spectroscopy, he had sat at the head of international commissions, and been much honoured by foreign governments.

Massive intellect

At the end of this litany of achievement is listed his one recreation: "Association Football." An Oxford Blue in 1929, the 66-year-old Thompson also founded the Pegasus inter-varsity club which won the Amateur Cup in 1951 and 1953. He joined the FA as Oxford's representative in 1941, and became vice-chairman in 1967.

Thompson's massive intellect overwhelmed many of the long-serving butchers and bakers who make up the numbers on FA committees. A close friend admitted this week: "Tommy? Brilliant, but a touch autocratic."

When, therefore, Thompson last summer decided to take a closer interest in the full international team, he would have been appalled to discover how Ramsey ruled the councillors as he travelled for the first time with an England team to Prague on May 24, 1973. He and Sir Alf were at odds from the start.

The second day of our stay in Prague, Ramsey strode up and demanded in the hotel lobby. "Who is this bloody man Thompson?" Then he proceeded to recount an incident over breakfast in the team's private dining room—in which FA councillors did not normally intrude—when he had had to ask Thompson *not* to smoke a cigar.

There seemed to be some dispute, also about Thompson's immediate assumption that he was welcome on the team coach, while the players were equally unhappy about Thompson's habit of addressing them by their surnames. That "I say, Chivers," rankled.

Ramsey probably dismissed

Thompson from his thoughts between this match and the next important game in the World Cup in Poland, which resulted in a disastrous defeat.

Next day the Press, with whom Ramsey had once again blundered into conflict, were in full cry.

After previous upsets the FA had closed ranks around Sir Alf. Not this time. On the plane taking the party to the next match, in Moscow, the then secretary, Denis Follows, sat with the FA councillors passing out newspaper cuttings. Criticism of England and Sir Alf was circled in blue . . . and much pointed at and nodded over.

But it was the next match with Poland, at Wembley in October, that gave Ramsey's personal crisis new impetus. He had asked for a rise just before the game, but his application got a very cool reception. England were eliminated after a match now famous for the injustice of its score, and Ramsey was under fire from without and from within.

Immediately the FA announced the setting up of an executive committee to consider "all aspects of England's international football." Members say now that the future of the team manager was "clearly understood" to be within the committee's terms of reference from the start. The facts suggest that such an understanding was not at all clear.

At a meeting of the full International Committee, reported to the FA on November 5, a minute recorded that on behalf of members of the committee, Dick Wragg, chairman, had expressed: "Sincere regrets to Sir Alfred Ramsey that the England team had been eliminated" . . . but added that Sir Alf had the unanimous support and confidence of the committee.

Similar expressions of confidence were later expressed by Sir Andrew Stephen and Wragg in the official FA News.

Wider discussion

Prof. Thompson seemed not to share this view. At a subsequent committee meeting, and then at a full council meeting, he challenged the minute, claiming that "it did not represent the feelings of all members of the council . . . it should not preclude a wider discussion by the council, *or some other select group*, at a later date.

On February 14 the Executive Committee agreed to the setting up of a sub-committee. Few present doubted that it

was to be a commission of inquiry into Sir Alf's future.

The composition of this six-man team is interesting. Sir Andrew Stephen, now a clear doubter of Ramsey, was its head. Prof. Thompson, naturally, was included, and another important figure was Len Shipman,

Thompson: the old Corinthian.

president of the League and a man open to persuasion.

In retrospect, it can be seen that if Thompson and Stephen had swung Shipman to their side, their authority might sway the two "new boys," Brian Mears (ironically, the son of the man who appointed Ramsey) and Bert Millichip, and thus leave Ramsey's main defender, Wragg, isolated.

That sub-committee met twice. That its task was to decide on Sir Alf can be hardly doubted, for Alf Ramsey was never invited to meet its members. Indeed, he did not even know it had met, until one day by chance he noticed a draft minute recording a meeting on a desk in another FA office.

I approached him around this period, to ask: "How could a committee discuss England's future without talking to England's manager?".

"Maybe that's the point," he replied. He clearly had seen the warning.

Two more curious incidents came in the next few weeks. Ramsey was about to pick teams for the Inter-League match with Scotland on March 20, and the international with Portugal on April 3. Talking to him just before, I wondered about the shape of those teams. "Perhaps this time I'll have to give them the players they want," he said. Them? The Press? The public? Or the men in the background now openly criticising?

Certainly the squads announced contained many surprising names, including Bowles of Queen's Park Rangers, McKenzie of Nottingham Forest, Tueart of Manchester City . . . all players of the type Sir Alf had seemed not to admire. I had the strong feeling then that these were tongue-in-cheek selections. If they played and succeeded, he'd be delighted; if they played and failed, he'd covered himself against criticism.

Then there was Ramsey's attitude to the Press in Portugal. Suddenly, a man who had been so unwilling to discuss his plans and his problems, was smilingly ready to tell all. In Lisbon he came out with an astonishing broadside against the "cheating clubs and managers" who had denied him use of players.

Some reporters dismissed the incident as a lucky fluke, "catching Alf on a good day." Others, more perceptive, discussed the theory that this was a deliberate attempt on his part to emphasise the difficulties of the job; the need to give the team manager more power, not less.

In Lisbon, too, Prof. Thompson was heard again, significantly. The story is that he complained to another FA councilman that he couldn't "communicate" with Ramsey. "Tell me," he was asked. "What do you call him when you try to speak to him?"

"Why, Ramsey of course," said Thompson. "Perhaps that's precisely the trouble between you," was the reply.

This is a perceptive point. Ramsey, no matter what he might privately feel about FA councillors, was by nature scrupulously polite in addressing them . . . "Mr This . . . Dr That" . . . every man to his title. Prof. Thompson would naturally fall into the public-school habit of calling all men by their surnames, totally unconscious that among those from other backgrounds, the usage would be regarded as patronising at best, deliberately insulting at worst.

If Ramsey had hoped to save himself by the outburst in Lisbon, he was too late. Although he came back to compose and announce a 40-strong squad for the coming seven internationals, his fate had already been decided.

On April 22 the executive committee met and accepted "unanimously" the sub-committee's recommendation that he be replaced. Privately, this last week, council members have stressed again and again the unanimity of their decision. *Over*-stressed perhaps. The offguard comment of Len Shipman: "What can you do when your hand is forced?" suggests some degree of embarrassment at least.

In the final analysis, those not concerned with the deep clash of personalities in all this were persuaded by other arguments to go along with Ramsey's sacking. It was pointed out that although his teams had lost only 17 of the 113 games played under his direction, those defeats included the vital matches with West Germany and Poland, which eliminated England from the European Nations Cup and the World Cup finals. Such defeats, it has been estimated, cost the FA £500,000 in revenue.

Polarised opinion

Ramsey was told of the decision on Tuesday, April 23. The FA still will not say who had the task of breaking the news, but it would be unthinkable that anyone other than the chairman, Sir Andrew Stephen, was charged with the duty. Ramsey asked for eight days' grace to make plans to drop out of sight, went in and cleared his desk last Monday and by noon on Tuesday the statement was made.

Nothing that has happened in football for years has so polarised opinion within the game. A First Division manager summed up for the players: "This is bloody awful. I played for England before Alf. It was a shambles. The way teams were picked was a joke."

"The greatest thing Alf did for England? Not winning the World Cup, but putting the amateurs in their place, turning England into a team as professional as any club. That's his real achievement . . . that's why they've got together and slung him out. The clock's gone back 10 years this week . . . the amateurs are back in the saddle."

That would hardly be Prof. Thompson's view. In interviews since Tuesday he has barely bothered to deny his position on Ramsey, yet it is extremely unlikely that he would have been motivated by personal feelings.

Rather it is that in his amateur, Old Corinthian way, he has felt that football ought to be a game of instinct and adventure, uncluttered by theory. As do we all. But again, in his amateur, Old Corinthian way, he would be totally unaware of the pressures and realities of international football as they are seen by Alf Ramsey, the arch-professional. *May 5 1974*

Irina Rodnina and friends: a modern romance on the Olympic ice

The popular Soviet couple, the Protopopovs, boosted pairs skating by winning the 1964 and 1968 winter Olympic titles. Their mantle was taken over by compatriots Alexei Ulanov and Irina Rodnina, and all went well for them until the 1972 Games at Sapporo, Japan, when uncharacteristic passions flared to disrupt the delicate equilibrium required on ice. The Sports Editor of *The Times* filed this report to his sister paper.

by John Hennessy

A crunching handshake tended to give an immediate answer to one of the questions fed into thousands of miles of wire by *The Sunday Times*. As I nursed my battered fingers back to life I had time to reflect that there was no question about the virility of Douglas Berndt, of the United States. As my inquiries broadened and my hand became a palsied palm, so I came to accept that these young men of the pair-skating fraternity, who throw women about with such careful abandon, are as well adjusted as any.

Small wonder therefore that the Russian camp is riven with a romance that had the *Daily Mirror* man hopping about at 3 a.m., inconvenient for him and his three flatmates, of course, but the eyeshade hour of 6 pm in distant Fleet Street.

Has Alexei Ulanov, the World and Olympic champion, developed an unquenchable passion for Ludmila Smirnova, a runner-up in both events? This was the burning topic that set us all by the ears. In due time rumour crystallised into fact as the two skaters were seen, if not in blackmailable situations, at any rate in poses that only lovers find other than acutely uncomfortable.

There was a contrary flurry of rumour on Thursday when it was discovered that the seductive Ludmila, for whom I would willingly risk divorce, had left for home. It seemed at first glance another lip-smacking source of gossip, but there was a disappointingly tactical explanation: Miss Smirnova and her partner, Andrei Suraikin, do not relish the razzmatazz of exhibitions and they are now spared the slight embarrassment of revealing their lack of versatility. Their place on the final day goes, instead, to the American pair, Kenny Shelley and Jo-Jo Starbuck (spelt *$ in Japanese), crowd-pleasers all the way, however much the judges may frown on their performance.

Nobody I know has dared to question Irina Rodnina on the behaviour of her partner. But then nobody has had to. Her whole attitude on the ice has been eloquent enough. Only when she is ready do they come together in a warm-up and only when she is satisfied do they leave the ice for the surrounding area.

Both Rodnina and Ulanov speak reasonable English, and the young English pair, Linda Connolly and Colin Taylforth, are full of admiration for their friendliness towards a raw pair in need of encouragement.

On the other hand, bitchy as it may sound, they have little to say to pairs whom they regard as possible rivals, though Ulanov and Smirnova have found a time-honoured means of bridging the gap. Whether they can also bridge the gap of 300 miles that separate Moscow and Leningrad when Ulanov returns home is another matter. It's a situation that has all the making of another Zhivago.

Successful pair skating usually requires a delicate balance of personalities, involving not only the two skaters and the coach, but even the two families. It is common for the three central characters to hit it off, only for something of a feud to develop between the two mums and, zing, you've got two solo skaters again.

A married couple, on the other hand, neatly sidesteps this kind of acrimony, but domestic harmony is at risk and, since the downfall of the Protopopovs, who were classically supreme in 1964 and 1968, it is rare to find a husband and wife skating together. The West German pair, Herbert Wiesinger and Almut Lehmann, though, may be regarded as something more than "just friends," which may explain the occasional outburst by Miss Lehmann.

The Germans apart, the relationships among the leading couples is mainly platonic. If it may seem odd, even unhealthy, for a young man to paw a little dolly tricked out in a

Andrei and Ludmila: lip-smacking gossip.

Alexei and Irina: flurries of rumour.

fetchingly brief costume without developing some sort of carnal passion, it has to be recognised that this sort of thing begins at an early age and the transformation into full-blooded adults is so gradual as to approach by stealth. "Then suddenly, boom-boom, they have grown into brother and sister," said John Nicks, British trainer of Starbuck and Shelley.

No brother and sister could be so platonically in tune than Shelley and Starbuck, in spite of the fact that he is a serious Mormon and she a devout Roman Catholic. "We date in four-somes sometimes," Miss Starbuck, a blonde beauty, told me, "but if some creep comes creeping at other times I nudge Kenny and pretty soon he'll throw an arm round me and say it's time to be moving on honey."

Apparently no creep has yet survived the brush-off. Shelley says that holding Jo-Jo's hand is like holding his own. I asked the delectable Jo-Jo if she was offended. "Not at all with Kenny," she said in her Californian high school drawl, "but if some other guy said it, why I'd spit right in his eye."

The girl in pair skating has to have complete trust in her partner, or else she tenses up and the lifts become impossible. Spectacular as the overhead lifts are, they require not so much strength as split-second timing.

I felt a few biceps during my tour of

Sunday Times duty and none made me ashamed of my own. It is much more important that the male should be a strong skater than rippling with muscles in unexpected places. Shelley is a strong enough skater to be American champion and he has never given Miss Starbuck any cause for anxiety.

Despite everything, pair skating is no exercise for cissies. I remember the second American pair, brother and sister Militano, lying on the ice, with Melissa unconscious at Ljubljana two years ago, but they skated their free programme the same evening to tumultuous applause, with the girl's head swathed in bandages.

The same night a Canadian pair collapsed in a concussed heap and it must have been fully ten seconds before they gathered their senses sufficiently to pick up the threads of their performance. Miss Connolly has twice had her leg ripped open and still bears the scar where six stitches were recently sewn into her.

The choice of music, too, is important, not merely because it can produce a mood that suits the skaters' temperaments or even because it can have a lulling effect on the judges, but because of its influence in establishing a rapport between the skaters and the audience. It can set the andrenaline coursing and raise the whole performance.

I asked Nicks for his impressions of

Mark Militano's strikingly casual wear in the pairs free (from where I sat it looked like second-class gardening gear). "Very unwise," he said, "because in any panel of nine judges at least six or seven will be conservative. It may give the man more freedom of movement than the conventional straight-jacket, but it ruins the line between the two skaters, which is important."

And skating judges can be hard task masters to those struggling to win recognition. Once you have reached the top you can take a tumble as Janet Lynn did in the women's free and still get the full six marks from one judge; or present a single Salchow instead of the statutory double, as Ulanov did in the compulsory programme; or have your marks unaffected after fluffing a double Axel, as Rodnina did—undoubtedly disturbed by Smirnova's conquest of her partner. *February 13 1972*

PS. Two weeks after publishing John Hennessy's story, *The Sunday Times* reported the sudden wedding in the USSR of Ulanov and Smirnova, who also paired up on ice. They were promptly beaten by Rodnina and her new partner Alexander Zaitsev (whom she subsequently married) in the 1973 European Championships for the pairs skating title which Rodnina has won, with her two partners, an unprecedented ten times.

Howard Winstone: how fame exiled the friendly Freeman of Merthyr

Contemporary professional boxing seldom bears any resemblance to the original definition "the noble art of self-defence." But occasionally Britain has produced a boxer whose skills can be appreciated in terms of aesthetics. Such a one was Howard Winstone. However, his life since he quit boxing has lacked the grace and dignity he displayed in the ring.

by Rob Hughes

Howard Winstone is Walter Mitty in reverse.

Exactly 10 years ago, he was up there; the little wizard whose name echoed through the valleys, whose fists made him featherweight champion of the world. Today, never having mastered the art of cashing in, Winstone dreams of reverting to being one of the boys.

But others prevented him going all the way—kindly, well-meaning folk, who think he ought to have *ambition*. "I reckoned I'd done that," recalls Howard, "so for 18 months I went around for a job. Nothing special, like. Hod-carrying, maybe. The bosses looked me in the eye and said: 'This isn't for you, Howard, boy; you're a Freeman of Merthyr, you've the MBE, you can do better'."

Eventually, having bought and sold a snack bar and a haberdashery he rented a secluded pub in bleak Robertstown. Revisiting him there, a man you knew well in his prime, an artist of the ring whose sheer friendliness embraced you, is a compulsion. It may also be a mistake: heroes should perhaps be preserved in their time, and certainly shielded from harrowing rumours of what became of them.

His first joke peels back the years. Winstone, now 38, has two grandsons and, prankster still, delights in presenting them as his "boys." Tomorrow is the anniversary of so much in his life, the decade of his crowning, a night in which he took the night sleeper from London to Cardiff to divorce the mother of his four children on the grounds of adultery. And January 23 also represents the seven steady years of his second marriage, to Bronwen.

However, the anniversaries find him drawing national assistance because the £40,000 won in his final year in the ring has gone (much of it in surtax) and a trapped sciatic nerve forbids him even pulling pints. Robertstown is a ten-minute drive from Merthyr Tydfil, his birthplace; yet he reacts like man exiled: "Things'll get better when we go back," he says. "I'm going to have my own pub."

Rumours around the Rhondda are cruel. "Hitting the bottle, he is, on double brandies for breakfast . . . the hangers-on have blown his cash, took them all on holidays, he did . . . they had him in hospital New Year's Day, drunk I shouldn't wonder. . . ."

Winstone listens, mild as a pussycat. The pale blue eyes smile: "Some of it's true man. The comical part of New Year's Day is I wasn't even drunk. I had a blackout, man, woke up in the ward seeing all these old boys drinking. I thought it was a party and I wasn't invited; kicked up a terrible fuss, I did. Thought they'd put me away, I did."

What he hasn't done is adjust to life outside; retirement, which most people barely cope with in their sixties, hit him below the belt, and the coincidence with his divorce "shattered" him.

He had married at 17, and in Eddie Thomas had a caring, even loving, manager who absorbed his every responsibility. Released from the constrictions, Winstone admits to having been free and easy with money, to "boozing like a madman" for the first three years, and to "going *massive* on pints."

And now the dream. "I'm hoping to have this pub—I'll call it Rhydian after my youngest son. It'll be a freehouse and the brewery is putting up £100,000." But won't that be a lifelong millstone? "Would be, aye; but the site I've chosen is a good 'un. It's next to the hospital. Now there's 1,000 beds there, that's 2,000 visitors a day . . . gotta be 5,000 comin' into my pub every week, y'see?"

"Oh aye?" asks a friend. "The way things go for Howie, you'll probably find that over half the visitors have signed the pledge. He's such an optimist, he's like a little boy."

January 22 1978

Record of a champion

● The Winstone of the ring was a craftsman extraordinary. He never lost a fight for British or European titles, yet won the world title at his fourth attempt only when he was beyond his prime. Reasons for that were three missing fingers which deprived him of a right-hand punch—"a one-armed bandit, I was"—and a Mexican called Vicente Saldivar who outrivalled him in three exhausting battles. On January 23 1968 he stopped Mitsunori Seki (above) in nine rounds to take the title. His full record was: won 61, lost six. He was never knocked out and today his face scarcely betrays the raw courage that accompanied his skill. "I still love boxing," he says.

Howard Winstone in the bar of his Robertstown pub, framed by his past, uncertain of his future.

Inside track

The Shadow

On the subject of shadows, those grim defenders whose sole job it is to stop the top rival scorers, one's mind turns sooner or later, usually sooner, to Chelsea's Ron (Chopper) Harris. "I've marked Geoff Hurst five times and he's scored once," Harris told us. "Jimmy Greaves has got five in about thirteen matches—and Georgie Best? He's never scored against me."

Harris, 24, is slope-shouldered, mild-spoken and remarkably small; he stands 5ft 8in. and weighs 11st. 10lb. "For 90 minutes my job is to get close to a forward—keeping in mind that the ball's not kicked over my head—and put him under pressure. If Georgie's got time to pull down the ball and look where he's going, it's one thing, but it's a different kettle of fish if I'm up his backside. Before he turns round, I get a tackle in. I've got a ruthless reputation, but maybe next time, he'll turn round to see where I am."

Fouling, Harris said frankly, is in the eyes of the beholder.

Going forward, Hurst likes the ball played to the near post and runs on for flicks: "I play him near enough shoulder to shoulder." Scorers skilled in the air, Harris said, tend to take crosses near the far post: "A little nudge in the air." And on Greaves: "When I first started marking him, Jimmy played into my hands by not moving. Now I try to keep him from turning around and away from the penalty area."

Clearly, there are skills to shadowing for Harris said he has scored only about four goals in seven seasons. "Some fellows get paid to score goals," he said, "others get paid to stop them." With that he unravelled his week's pay slip: with bonuses, after deductions, it totalled £152 14s. 2d.

September 14 1969

Olga Korbut and Ludmila Tourischeva: rivals in an emotional arena

Three gymnasts have dominated the field of women's gymnastics over the past decade—two contrasting Russians and a remarkable young Romanian.

by Edmund Stevens

Deceptively fragile-looking, more like an elf than a full-blown Olympic champion, Olga Korbut hardly seems measured to her 18 years. By contrast, her fellow champion gymnast and bosom friend, Ludmila Tourischeva,

at 21, is a shapely pin-up brunette.

Olga was born and brought up in Grodno, which at various times in history has been under Lithuanian, Russian and Polish rule. Ludmila was born in Rostov-on-Don, historic gateway to the Caucasus. Their birthplaces, many miles apart, shared the trials of wartime occupation by the Nazis, but Olga and Ludmila belong to a generation that knows of such things only by hearsay.

Both of Olga's parents have jobs, her father as a civil engineer, her mother in the local Adminstration of Internal

Affairs. Olga explained: "I've always been the family baby." There are no brothers, but three elder sisters, two of whom are out at work. The third is one class ahead of Olga at the Grodno equivalent of a teachers' training college. "When I retire from gymnastics," Olga said, "I shall be a history teacher."

The two girls agree that 30 is the outside age limit for their style of gymnastics, and they predict that as the programmes become more complex, and physically more demanding, the limit may be as low as 25.

Ludmila lives with her parents when she is at home in Rostov, which is seldom nowadays. Her father is a chauffeur, her mother keeps house and there is an older married sister.

She never goes out dancing on dates, she explained—she gets enough dancing as part of her gymnastics. "All one's emotions go into practising the exercises, many of which are set to music. Somehow the dance floor doesn't attract me. One thinks about gymnastics the whole time; one analyses one's performances."

These answers in a clear voice carried the strength of conviction. But when asked whether she had marriage plans, she almost blushed and her answer, "Not yet," was barely audible. To the further question, did she have a boyfriend, her reply was more decisive: "Frankly speaking, no."

Olga also denied any marriage plans. She said she had gone on holiday to the Black Sea with friends, but preferred visiting her maternal grandmother in a village near Smolensk. As for the future, Olga declared her great ambition is to become absolute world champion. Her opportunity for this will come at the Montreal Olympics, when she will be 21. *October 21 1973*

Nadia Comaneci: how to grow old gracefully

by Cliff Temple

Nadia Comaneci, the unrivalled Romanian star of the Montreal Olympic gymnastics tournament as a 14-year-old, was last week in danger of being swallowed into a group of the most agile young ladies in the World Gymnastics championships at Strasbourg. Just the vivid memories of Montreal set her aside from the others, who look now as she did then: flat-chested, wispy-light, with pipe-cleaner limbs.

Nadia, who will be 17 next month, is definitely a young lady now, with an almost regal presence on the beam. She has grown four inches since Montreal, and put on a stone and a half.

Not unnatural, of course, but ever since that week in July 1976, when she won three gold medals, she has been the subject of rumour and speculation. Had she, and other gymnasts, been given special pills to delay the onset of puberty and thus retain her boyish body, so reducing the chance that years of patient and precise technical preparation could be disrupted by nature?

In Strasbourg last week she looked restricted, less bouncy and flamboyant, and appeared to have reverted to her sullen pre-Montreal expression. Instead, it was the winning Soviet team who seemed to play more to the crowd, with big grins and vigorous waving.

October 29 1978

Red Rum: a brief assignation with an undoubted star

A dream ride on a unique horse—who in 1977 became the first ever triple winner of the Aintree Grand National—was former steeplechase jockey Brough Scott's first assignment on appointment as *The Sunday Times* racing correspondent.

by Brough Scott

It was like suddenly finding yourself in bed with a film star. Would she be as fantastic as you had imagined, and would you match up to her the way you had in your dreams? The salty rain-swept emptiness of Southport sands at 8.15 last Wednesday morning was a pretty odd place for an assignation with a star, but in racing terms the rest of the comparison was accurate. For I was riding Red Rum.

Red Rum? Yes, *the* Red Rum, winner of the 1973 and 1974 Grand Nationals, the star attraction in next Saturday's Hennessy Gold Cup, and all in all the most charismatic National Hunt horse since Arkle. Yet here he was cantering beneath me, and about 100 miles of sand ahead for us.

The first feel of Red Rum is a little disappointing. He seems a shade narrow and lightweight, much more ex-flat racehorse than big strong 'chaser. But then "ex-flat racehorse" is exactly what he is, having started out eight seasons ago with a dead heat at that same Liverpool track he has since taken by storm.

It was old pro's weather on Wednesday morning. Solid Lancashire rain only eased to a threatening drizzle as we left the little yard at the back of McCains' Car Sales, out on to the Aughton Road and through the streets of the Birkdale part of Southport until we finally came to the beach with its warning notice: "Drivers beware of soft sand."

You can't imagine a style of exercising racehorses further removed from the traditional Indian-file-up-the-lane-to-the-downs style of tradition. Horses walking in a cluster, Red Rum in front, with his lad Billy Ellison beside us on the big, white-faced Glenkiln, past the pet centre and the Chin-

Above: Red Rum with Brough Scott (below) aboard, burning up the Lancashire sands.

ese fish-and-chip shop, over the level-crossing and the main road. It certainly works for Red Rum. I don't think it at all fanciful to say that this equine hero enjoys the bustle of the town.

So we were safely on to the beach, and after the briefest of instructions were cantering in pairs southwards along "the gallop," a newly-harrowed stretch of sand between seaweed and waves. At first the impression of "ex-flat horse" remained. "I'm not sure that I would feel that confident going to

Becher's on this," was the way I put it to myself.

But then, as the sands swept by, there came a feeling of relentless power about the stride. We seemed to have been cantering for about five miles, and although I hadn't ridden for a few months I thought I was showing plenty of the old magic ("What magic?" asked an unkind friend with all too clear a memory of my brief career in the saddle). "Do we pull up now?" I called across to Billy Ellison. "Oh no," came the reply. "We've got a *long* way to go yet."

Suddenly there was a threat of disaster. Alone with a film star, I was going to ruin everything by being sick. Then of all things, on this beach 100 miles from nowhere, there was a hoot on a car horn, and right beside us was Ginger McCain. "He means us to go a bit quicker," shouted Billy.

This wasn't going to be funny, for you know that as you release the brake a little the load becomes greater. The sands stretched to 1975 and, far from a beaten-up ex-flat horse the length and power of Red Rum's stride made me

Richards or Piggott: an argument without an answer

Who is the greatest British jockey of the century? The two leading contenders assessed by _The Sunday Times_'s former racing correspondent.

by Roger Mortimer

Yesterday the flat-racing season drew peacefully to its close. For the seventh year running, and for the eighth time in all, Lester Piggott achieved the distinction of being champion jockey. Piggott will be 35 on November 5 and has spoken of retiring in five years' time, so he will never equal the record of Sir Gordon Richards who was champion 26 times and only once, and then because of an injury, failed to hold that position between 1931 and 1953. Steve Donoghue was champion 10 times, Fred Archer 13 times and George Fordham 14 times.

Piggott stands out today among jockeys as Richards did in his prime. There is one essential difference, though. Richards was riding in the golden age of English jockeyship with rivals such as Donoghue, Elliot, Carslake, Childs, Bullock, Weston, Wragg, Fox, Perryman and Beary. By comparison, this is the ice age.

Richards possessed a style that lesser men were unwise to attempt to copy. The same can be said of Piggott, and whereas he can get away with riding exceptionally, some think unnecessarily, short, others who try to do so are liable to look merely absurd. Richards was perhaps more consistently good and rarely lost a race he ought to have won. On the other hand one experienced rider told me he considered Piggott the more effective in a classic because he is cool and imperturbable. Richards was far more highly-strung on the big occasion and because of that was occasionally lacking in restraint. Richards won one Derby and 13 other classics; Piggott has so far won five Derbys and 12 other classics.

No-one in his right mind could judge Richards inferior to Piggott in courage, dash or sheer determination to win, but the cool, unflappable Piggott has a turbulent record with the authorities which formed no part whatsoever of the career of the tenser and more sensitive Richards.

Unquestionably Piggott is the outstanding personality in English racing today and not even a drab evening meeting at a minor track can be wholly dull when he is riding. I doubt if he will ever be regarded with quite the same warmth of affection that Richards was. He is a very much cooler character with an engaging disrespect for the plaudits of the crowd. "You might at least have smiled, Lester," remarked an owner after Piggott had entered the winner's enclosure amid cheers. "Why should I?" replied Old Stoneface. "If I'd lost they'd be chucking muck at me"—or a four letter word to that effect.

Easily recognisable through his arse-in-the-air style, Piggott has won admiration not just for his professional skill, but for his dedication to his work and his astonishing toughness. A man less robust and more imaginative could hardly survive the long season of ascetic dieting, of riding day after day, frequently during the summer at both afternoon and evening meetings, and of travelling to the Continent on Sundays.

Piggott   Richards

Only a man with an iron constitution and a phlegmatic temperament could endure it.

Most small punters have always been loyal Piggott fans for they feel that fundamentally he is on their side and that most of his offences have been committed through exuberant dash unfettered by discretion and by sheer determination to win at all costs. Their dislike is reserved for jockeys who all too often are permitted to get away with a noticeable economy in effort. Some racing people used to resent the fact that on occasions Piggott seemed to be cold-bloodedly severe on the horses he rode, but with age and experience he places far less reliance on the whip, using it more as Richards did, to encourage rather than chastise.

November 1 1970

feel that he might win next year's National pulling a cart, let alone an unfit and panicky journalist.

One more notch and we would have gone. But then an angel in the unlikely form of Billy Ellison saved us. "Whoa up! That's it," he called. Red Rum eased up knowing where he was all the time, and in a couple of minutes we were across the sand and into the sea.

Yes, into the sea! All McCain's horses go into the sea, and Red Rum, who previously suffered from the usually incurable foot disease of pedalostitis, owes much of his dramatic improvement to his regular exercise in sea and on sand. "He hates trotting on the road, you know," says Billy.

"You know, when he works he likes to get another horse ahead of him so that he can sort of get it in his sights and then come and do it at the finish," says Billy. "Watch him going home. He always likes to buck opposite the convent." He did, and plenty more, and having spent one and a half fantasy-come-true hours on Red Rum's back, it is my privilege to report that his spirit is burning strong. _November 17 1974_

Shilton or Clemence? The happiest dilemma for English football

For ten years Gordon Banks was un-disputed No. 1 goalkeeper in England, and latterly in the world, until an eye injury finished his international career. England were fortunate to have not one, but two understudies for Banks's position at the beginning of 1973. It was a difficult choice for Sir Alf Ramsey, the England manager, and remained so under Don Revie and Ron Greenwood.

by Rob Hughes

Ray Clemence considers goalkeeping an art, which can only be improved, not created, by endeavour. He is contented by nature, happy with his flexible 12st 7lb six foot frame, though not blind to his faults. And at 24, he believes that he is learning and improving with almost every match.

Clemence never wanted to be a goalkeeper. He preferred playing at left half, and was thrust into goal at 16 by Skegness schoolmaster Frank Moft. Scunthorpe happened to have a scout at that match and Clemence gave up studying to become an accountant—"I was a fool, football is such a short life"—and found himself on the wrong end of six and seven goal defeats in Scunthorpe's A team. He was on the verge of quitting when the club's coaches dissuaded him.

Within a year he had played "badly" for Sir Alf Ramsey in the Under-23 side and at 19 joined Liverpool for £15,000. There he eventually succeeded Tommy Lawrence after playing only three first team games before his 21st birthday. It was Geoff Sidebottom at Scunthorpe and Lawrence, plus Liverpool training, that got to grips with his "glaring" weaknesses: poor kicking and hesitancy going down at forwards' feet.

Quite recently Banks told him, during an England training session, to *look* more confident. "But I don't feel," says Clemence, "as though lack of confidence shows in my work out on the park. That's where it counts. It's not me to shout my mouth off, even though it has made doors open for Cassius Clay and Malcolm Macdonald."

He speaks quietly with a hint of naivety. He hasn't an agent: Liverpool's consistent involvement in two matches each week, he says, doesn't allow him room for outside business.

Then he remembers something as he leaves the ground to drive home to his semi-detached in Formby: "I do do a bit of business," he says. "Endorsing football boots and making appearances at shops. That is, when I've time."

Peter Shilton was nine when he decided he wanted to become the best goalkeeper there's ever been. Most of us will have had similar designs: the difference is Shilton is still working at it. He has become, at 23, the slight favourite to take on the Gordon Banks mantle. Indeed he wants more than that: to be known initially as a different goalkeeper from Banks, and ultimately even a better one.

Already, on and off the field, Shilton tries calculatingly to dominate everything he touches. He is a solidly manufactured product, a tribute to his obsessive dedication. By the age of 10 his talent had been spotted by his home club, Leicester City. And from then until he joined the club at 15 he was schooled twice a week by George Dewis, a former centre forward. At 17, unhappy with his position as the reserve team goalkeeper, he helped to determine the course which led to Leicester selling Gordon Banks to Stoke City for £52,000.

In his early teens the budding goalkeeper recruited his mother for "stretching" exercises, she hanging on to his legs while he suspended himself from the banisters. Now 6ft and 13st 8lb—"all muscle"—he still earnestly lifts heavy weights. "I want to *look* invincible," he says. "When Alan Hinton took a penalty against me, he said he could hardly see the goal. I was chuffed. I've tried to build myself to look and feel this way."

His clothes are those of a man who thinks of himself as important, and also of a player who has become intensely aware of the lucrative potential in the business world an image can fire. One of his financial advisers says: "Peter is going to be the biggest name ever in goalkeeping—as well as the best goalkeeper." Shilton, quick to sense the pitfalls of overstatement, adds: "Only time will tell. Even if I'd won 100 caps by the time I was 33, I like to think I'd still be looking to improve."

January 21 1973

CLEME

On the field as well as off it, Shilton and Clemence use almost opposite techniques. Shilton controls Leicester's entire penalty area, at times using legitimate physical intimidation. He spends almost his every thought assessing angles and situations, programming his mind, and building his body to enable him to force issues. In contrast Clemence relies heavily on reflexes and concentration, guarding his line while the big Liverpool defenders meet the challenge in the air. In short, Shilton acts, Clemence reacts.

Thus, First Division attackers have found it increasingly pointless to attempt to bully or shoulder the powerful Shilton. They tend instead to hit even corners out to the edge of his area and attempt volleys from there. Yet Clemence, more than any other goalkeeper, is capable of pulling off a "miracle" save. Against Southampton in the FA Cup at Anfield two years ago

Clemence made his greatest save. Ron Davies had beaten Larry Lloyd 12 yards out and headed the ball over Clemence. The goalkeeper, well off his line, appeared lost as the ball dropped behind him when, suddenly he launched into a backward somersault, caught the ball a foot from the ground and held it despite being baulked by Gabriel. Gymnastic agility and reflexes honed up by badminton had compensated for Clemence's bad positioning.

Whether Sir Alf Ramsey selects Shilton's aggression or Clemence's natural flair for Wednesday, it is important to remember the lesson of Leon, when Peter Bonetti was called nervously into the England side at short notice and without a World Cup game under his belt. He and England lost to West Germany. Ramsey must ensure that at least two goalkeepers have the faith of themselves and the England defence in good time for Munich.

The differing styles that say 'they shall not pass'

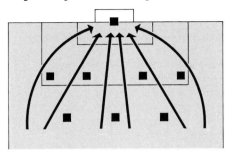

Clemence is aware that the England style obliges him to come off his line more readily than at Liverpool. There his game is fashioned (diagram above) by standing behind massed defensive lines, tied to his line by imaginary elastic, arched like a bow ready to spring to deflect shots or chips which appear late through a conglomeration of bodies.

Clemence feels that in the national side he should blend his style to work with established and experienced players like Bobby Moore and Roy McFarland.

Gordon Banks stresses that an England goalkeeper needs to be dominant in the air, which suits Shilton. "But above all," adds Banks. "you've got to concentrate because you rarely get put under prolonged pressure."

That suits Clemence, who has long spells of concentration in every League game. He maintains contact by assuming a role as an extra full back.

At Leicester Shilton frequently shouts to dismiss his own defensive cover. In a recent League match (diagram below), West Ham's Pat Holland, having beaten a defender near the byeline, ran the ball back to a square-on scoring position near the penalty spot. Shilton advanced a yard, narrowed the angle, stood his ground and forced Holland to either "run," him or shoot quickly. The goalkeeper easily engulfed Holland's shot to his right.

Significantly, Shilton's dominance, which could go too far and make him predictable, clashed with Liverpool's Larry Lloyd at England training.

"Larry liked to get things in the air," says Shilton. "But I had to make him see I didn't want him in the six-yard box. The goalkeeper should dictate to the men around him."

Shilton (left) and Clemence: two young lions battling for the succession to Gordon Banks.

SHILTON

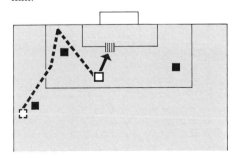

David Bryant: young master gives bowls welcome new image

The greatest bowls player of today, David Bryant, had achieved pre-eminence even by 1968. The English National Championships of that year, which attracted 70,000 competitors, provided a fitting opportunity to pay tribute to the young master.

by Clarence Jones

By all of the million players that the sport of bowls now embraces, David Bryant is reckoned to be the most outstanding performer who has ever lived. Happily for the sport, Bryant is not an old man with a cloth cap. He is in fact 36, wears spectacles and smokes a pipe, is a qualified teacher of handicapped children, and every Sunday morning can be found gardening at his home in Clevedon, Somerset.

In a sport which demands touch, finesse, force, stamina, judgment and an icy command of nerves, Bryant makes people catch their breath and jump out their seats. "I sometimes get a little nervous" he says, "at the crucial stage of a match when I'm needing a neck or nothing shot. But if I'm losing confidence, I tell myself to take my time, concentrate and get right down (when delivering). But if the conditions are good and I'm bowling well I don't get nervous."

His secret is concentration; it is rare for Bryant to finish less than 30 minutes after all the other matches on an average championship green.

Bryant's father, Reg, is a former indoor international. From him, David developed his revolutionary style. The style springs from a reversal of priorities. In the pre-Bryant era, accuracy of delivery and the emphasis behind any coaching was based on the arm's swing. Bryant reasoned that the arm could swing consistently, smoothly and accurately only if it was anchored to a steady base. He decided to experiment with the foundations of the human base—the legs.

He arrived eventually at a highly individualistic technique in which he exercises leg control as finely as a tightrope walker, relating the length of his backswing to the extent of his forward gliding step.

As a result he can mix the infinite range of bowls shots without the slightest loss of accuracy, a feat that no other bowler in Britain or the world can match.

His closing shot in the final round of the Sydney World Championship classically illustrated this. The South African champion, Snowy Walker, generally considered his only serious rival, had two bowls by the jack which Bryant needed to disturb to win the game (see illustration). Bryant's running through shot which took Walker's two bowls away leaving the bowl Bryant had first played nearest the jack, would have been astonishing even on a billiards table. On a 42-yards long bowling green it was miraculous.

May 19 1968

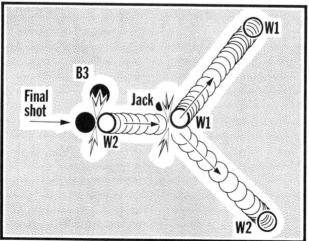

Bryant's already legendary last delivery in the world championship. The drawing shows the situation he faced, in which his opponent Snowy Walker seemed to have victory ensured with bowls W1 and W2. Bryant's reply was to cannon W2 on to W1, forcing both away to leave his first bowl, B3, closest to the jack.

Lillian Board: one in a lifetime — the athlete and the girl

Few athletes have won the affection of the British public as Lillian Board did. Few people understood her as well as the athletics correspondent of *The Sunday Times*. He wrote this appreciation of her after her death from cancer at the age of 22.

By Cliff Temple

Britain has lost a champion. Athletics has lost the greatest advertisement it ever had. And I have lost a friend.

I knew two Lillian Boards: the Athlete and the Girl. The Athlete frantically tugging her blonde hair into place at the finish of a race, before the photographers had a chance to take close-ups, was a girl too. But the Girl, dressed up for a party, was never, surely, an athlete?

Lillian the Athlete would chatter nineteen to the dozen after a race, a release from the tension. She'd confess her fears, her thoughts during competition, and her hopes. Then she'd ask how so-and-so was doing in the long jump, and sign autographs for the inevitable horde of kids that surrounded her, carefully thanking each one for asking, as she did the first time she was approached four years ago.

She had the memory of a public relations officer for names, faces and incidents. And she would like the colour of your tie before you had a chance to congratulate her on the race.

Then she would go home and become Lillian the Girl: rather isolated, despite her fame. A girl who had met a lot of people briefly.

Yet it was this isolation that made her a champion: no distractions. She would arrive at the training track, say hello to regulars, then get down to running. No more, no less. Her example, and her achievements, made her an obvious choice as captain of her London club, for whom she would turn out when she could. But she was never "one of the girls."

During an evening training session last summer she suddenly said: "I know it sounds big-headed, but don't you think it's a pity so many people come here to just stand around and talk

instead of training? I mean, all the time they spend, and they're just mediocre, aren't they?"

It was a disarming remark, and not meant to be as callous as it sounds; she left the back-scratching to others. But she just couldn't understand why anyone should aim at less than the top.

Lillian was never the loser making good; she was always a winner. When I first knew her, in 1965, we both used to make our way as aspiring teenage runners around Wembley's depressing Alperton track on Sunday mornings at, alas, distinctly separate speeds.

She trained alone even then, already a long jump and sprint champion whom people tended to think of superficially as aloof and stuck-up. In fact she was often too shy to initiate a conversation, and behind that shyness was a charming articulate girl seeking, through athletic success, to break down that barrier. It proved a successful, though roundabout method of doing so. Her intelligent observations and interviews became not only the journalist's dream, but also a worthy replacement for the giggles and mumbled half-hopes so often associated with the amateur sportswoman. And ironically, some of her own clubmates got to know her, for the first time, through Press and TV.

At home she was more relaxed, whether curled up on the sofa listening to the wistful music of Simon and Garfunkel, or thundering up and down the stairs, three at a time, looking for a lost shoe before training. To go to a meeting from home was invariably to wait 10 minutes outside with the engine

Lillian Board: she was never the loser making good; she was always a winner.

running while she dashed in and out fetching all the things she thought she had packed, one at a time. To stay as a house guest with the Board family was to be aware of Lillian constantly on the prowl for food, though she never put on an ounce. She viewed her mother's accusation that she was a "human dustbin" with vast amusement, and agreement.

Her constantly self-effacing manner showed her a funny side to everything. When she lost the Olympic 400 metres gold medal in Mexico by inches she was making jokes about having the silver medal sprayed gold, though it was a deep disappointment to have come so close.

I remember, poignantly, one particular moment shortly after her return to England from Mexico. She was kneeling on the floor at home, cutting out a dress, and saying about the Olympics: "At the closing ceremony, when the words 'Munich 72' went up on the giant electric results board, I felt very inspired and immediately thought of the 800 metres. A couple of days later, though, I decided not to think too hard about 1972, because to aim solely at that would be to throw part of my life away. So much can happen between now and then." *January 3 1971*

Mike Brearley: instinct against reason — the dilemma of the sportsman-scholar

During the England-Australia series of 1977, Dudley Doust, an American on the *Sunday Times* staff with only a basic understanding of cricket, began a series of long conversations with Brearley, newly appointed as England's Test captain. Their subsequent friendship resulted in their collaboration on two books.

by Dudley Doust

Mike Brearley felt pleased as he sat over his lunch steak, medium-rare, in the Headingley pavilion yesterday. The England captain had asked the Australians to follow on and now, with two wickets down, the visitors still needed 298 runs to make England bat again.

Brearley was amused by radio commentators criticising him for bringing Greig on to bowl. "Well, Mike Hendrick was a little bit tired and Greggie is a fine bowler and he gets a bit of bounce and this is an uneven bouncing pitch and, besides, he wanted to bowl," Brearley grinned.

"But the *most* significant thing in the morning was that the ball went out of shape and we changed it and the second ball swung much more than the first. Greggie got his second wicket with it.

"Cricket is a second-guessers' game. Worse even than baseball."

Brearley got up, popped the inevitable cud of chewing gum into his mouth and, thanking the waitress, said no, he wouldn't be having the chocolate gâteau for sweet.

That was one of the less significant decisions taken by Brearley, who is on the point of winning the Ashes on home ground for England for the first time since 1956. It was "just" one of a number of decisions, on and off the field, which lately have occupied Brearley's considerable mind: his own Middlesex team's struggle to retain the county championship; the Packer Affair and the future of Knott, Underwood, Amiss and Greig; his own fan mail ("My grandson broke his bat, could you send him a new one?"); his Middlesex benefit in 1978.

"At times, I find these things exhausting," Brearley said after a good snooze in the pavilion on Friday afternoon, "but when I get out on the field everything drops away, the world, the news, anything unpleasant in my life."

Brearley looks tired these days; his black hair is flecking grey, bruises of fatigue have appeared under his eyes and yet, at 35, he retains a handsome, boyish look. When speaking, he pauses for long, anguished moments, precisely marshalling his thoughts, then his words flow swift and clear.

Brearley's open-mindedness, sometimes seen as indecision, speaks of his intellectual unselfishness. The eminent philosopher John Wisdom, who profoundly influenced him at Cambridge, looks back at his famous pupil with respect and affection: "Brearley was a fair-minded, sympathetic man. He never set out to demolish another man's argument and, before making any objections, he would look for something valuable in what the man was saying. I should think he also applies this in cricket."

It seems natural that Brearley was headed for a life as a sportsman-scholar when he was born on April 28, 1942, in Harrow. His father, Yorkshire-born Horace Brearley, read maths at Leeds University, played in one first-class match for Yorkshire in 1937 and, coming south to Ealing to teach at the City of London School, twice for Middlesex. Brearley's mother, Midge Goldsmith, at London University, also read maths, and played netball.

Brearley batting: a question of trust.

Brearley's first memory is a curious and extremely vivid one: he recalls a large wooden table under which one would take shelter in the event of an air raid, which never came. "'If a bomb fell on the table,' I would ask my mother, 'would it save me?'" Brearley leans over a cage of his long fingers: "I came from a very secure, conventional, friendly, decent, pleasant and warm family, but there were constraints on extremes of emotion."

He became absorbed in cricket. An early cricket memory dates back to the age of seven, in 1949, the year Jack Robertson scored 331 not out for Middlesex against Worcestershire. Brearley manicured his own little pitch in his back garden and, throwing a tennis ball against the brick wall, gripped his bat and played all the shots; correct, precise, like Robertson.

"Great fantasy matches came out of this. I was always Middlesex, and I always arranged for Robertson, the opening bat, to get more runs even than Compton. Modelling myself on Robertson was interesting because, of course, he was not as spectacular as Compton." Oddly, he seldom saw Roberston play: "I rarely went to Lord's by myself. I wasn't very independent."

At 10, Brearley was at the City of London School playing the clarinet, studying classics and scoring runs like thunder. In his final two schoolboy seasons he scored 11 centuries in about two dozen matches, an imperishable record. "We took summer holidays at Bognor Regis. I opened the batting in a colts side once against John Snow, who also was about 14, and scored two fours in the first over, which pleased me very much." It also pleased a spectator, John Snow's father, who said within earshot of Brearley's mother that here was a boy who would one day play for England.

Brearley went up to St. John's College, Cambridge, on a scholarship, and earned a first. His cricket exploits there are well documented; captain two years, the most runs (4,068) ever scored for Cambridge, and bowling under-arm against Oxford and Sussex: "The real tragedy is that I had an under-arm stumping chance against Sussex. The man came down the wicket, missed it and the wicketkeeper missed the chance. Pity, it would have shut everybody up. There is no reason why under-arm bowling shouldn't come back. It's a good, freakish variation if you're stuck."

Brearley in repose: "At times I find these things exhausting, but on the field everything drops away."

according to his medical chief, "he has unusual empathy and very considerable vigour." It is a field Brearley plans to pursue when his cricketing days are done. He also is expanding his self-knowledge through psycho-analysis and psycho-drama, areas from which most sportsmen would flee in terror.

"Some of this, of course, connects with cricket," says Brearley. "Instinct versus reason, for example. There are very few batsmen who don't set themselves in certain ways, look for certain things from the bowler, and unless you're a genius like Compton, you don't go out and bat without thinking what you are going to do next. The number of times a player like me gets to that moment is very rare indeed. If I could trust my body, and let my body go, I would do better."

He cites examples: during last winter's tour of India, when Fletcher was hurt, Brearley went into the slips. He had been reading Far Eastern Philosophy: "The idea that one should not try to control the outcome—let it take care of itself—that helped me." About five years ago an old coach, Tiger Smith, now 91, pointed out to Brearley an error in his batting: "Look, you're frowning, and you won't see the ball any better for frowning at it." Brearley took it to heart. "That was when I adopted my new stance," he recalls. "It was mainly to relax, and to trust my body more."

Brearley will talk about sessions of group psycho-drama: "I took the role of a four-year-old, which was great fun except that I was left out of the decision-making and ruled out as the leader." And about art therapy. There is a spontaneous drawing by Brearley of an anonymous city gent in pinstripes and furled umbrella, with his face obscured by *The Times*: "I meant to label him Mr Normal, but it came out Mr Nobody, which suggests a neurotic fear that you *are* a nobody if you're normal. There may be a little streak of that fear in me."

An enormously interesting man, a proven county and Test captain, the former philosophy lecturer Mike Brearley is by no means a nobody. He also has come to terms, at least for a few more years, with playing games for a living. "I have this particular ability," he says, "and when I get up in the morning I never feel like I'm going to work." Or, with apologies to Descartes: I stink, therefore I am.

August 14 1977

This unorthodoxy coincided, perhaps significantly, with a realignment of Brearley's intellectual interests. He grew less fond of classics. "My objection to classics was that at the end of it I couldn't, or at least *didn't*, read Virgil fluently. Also, I began to doubt the shibboleths about discipline and classics. I think there is discipline involved in learning anything. I switched to philosophy. I realised now that what was beginning to interest me, apart from playing cricket, were things to do with people's minds."

This interest took seed during Wisdom's tea parties at Cambridge. It grew, following one-and-a-half seasons at Middlesex, when Brearley was a research assistant in philosophy in California and finally came to flower in 1968 when he turned his back on full-time first-class cricket to become a lecturer in philosophy at the University of Newcastle. He cut a colourful, paradoxical image there; lecturing by day, travelling in the evenings and at weekends to the former mining community of Percy Main, where he taught and played, often with a north-countryman's red flannel round his waist to fend off aches in the back.

Brearley also began his Ph.D thesis: Emotion and Reason. It is a concept with which Brearley has since been grappling. He is interested in psycho-analysis and psychotherapy. Once a Samaritan, he has been for two winters an assistant at London's Northgate Clinic for disturbed adolescents where,

Paul Elvstrom: a man sailing to immortality

The master yachtsman calmly—and correctly—predicting an end to his own record-breaking run of Olympic medals.

by Dudley Doust

From the wall of a Copenhagen sitting room, four Olympic gold medals look out over the sea where, at weekends, a sailing boat is blown about by the wind. The medals and the boat, a Finn, belong to Paul Elvstrom who sails, bare-handed, through the winter. "I love to go out, " he says, "when the coast is full of snow."

In Mexico this autumn, when the coast is full of sunshine, Elvstrom, if chosen to represent his country, will be unique among Olympians. He is the only person in modern history to win first place medals in four successive Games: in a Firefly class yacht at Torquay (1948); in Finns at Helsinki (1952), Melbourne (1956) and Naples (1960). These single-handed craft are the best test of Olympic sailing skill; identical ones are issued to each competitor.

What's more, having won world championships in five other yachting classes, Elvstrom is indisputably the greatest small-boat helmsman of all time. "In any other sport," says British yachtsman David Hunt, "Paul would be a world hero. In yachting, he's a god."

He looks more like a rugger player. He stands, bow-legged, 6ft. 2in., weighs 13 stone and wears steel-rimmed glasses. A natural and determined athlete, he might be useful in any sport—but his instincts are those of a helmsman: a fine sense of ocean currents and winds and, best, a feeling for boats.

"While waiting just off the starting line," says Charles Currey, second behind Elvstrom at Helsinki, "Paul can stop nearly dead in a 10-knot wind. For a *minute*. Somehow, he'll wriggle up, head to the wind, and feather his sails, just waiting—it's an inexplicable technique—then *bang*, he's away, past the line at 60 per cent. of his maximum speed."

His earliest boating recollection is a mini-saga: "When I was six or seven I decided to row my boat one nautical mile to a harbour. There were heavy winds against me and a fast-running current. It took me eight hours to get there — and fifteen minutes to get back."

Although his mother soon dissuaded him from the lonely sea captain's life, although a five-year-old brother drowned, Elvstrom spent much of his youth on the water. "It was something I did, like walking." At 12, in a local dinghy regatta, Elvstrom for the first time beat the grown-ups. "The water was nearly dead-calm that day," he recalls—totally, "so I set out to sea to find the wind. We did the course in two hours—

"In any other sport Paul would be a world hero. In yachting, he's a god."

and won by 28 minutes." He was crewed by his 22-year-old brother.

At 20, now a building contractor, Elvstrom won the Danish Olympic Trials in a National 12. He came unknown and unnoticed, except for his bright red jersey, to Torquay, the youngest yachting Olympian. "They gave me a Firefly, which was fine," he recalls, "but I'd never seen one before. I was shy and I sailed too carefully." Peter Scott, in charge of those Games, says: "What I remember most about Paul was the way he soaked his jersey so he'd have the weight to sit far out in his boat." Elvstrom, winning his first gold medal, advanced the legend.

Preparing for Helsinki he ran 10 kilometres a day for the next four years, lifted weights and strengthened his already oaken thighs by leaning back, toes hooked under a bench, while doing the business books.

Then came Melbourne. "I went there expecting to win and when I came fifteenth in a race I couldn't believe it. My nerves collapsed. I gave up—and suddenly the air was cleared." He went on to sail brilliantly through the last two races and won his third gold.

Then, again, at Naples: "I was doing very well indeed, but I couldn't keep my mind off the damn sailing. After the fifth race, I was getting ready to go out to dinner with my wife and I passed out in the bathroom. The next day I seemed well again and I won. I hated sailing and I had to stop it. I went into hospital and they said I was healthy enough, just forget about winning." Elvstrom laughs.

He did not sail for Denmark in the 1964 Tokyo Games. "I thought I'd relax," he says, "and see what I could learn by watching." In fact, the Danish Olympic Committee feared a storm of protest if he sailed. Under Olympic rules he could be considered professional.

Though hardly more openly than other yachtsmen, from California to Brazil to Austria, Elvstrom violates Olympic Rule 26 which bars a sportsman who capitalises financially "in any way on (his) athletic ability or success. . . ." Elvstrom, long out of the building trade, owns sail lofts in Copenhagen, Bermuda, the South of France, Australia and South Africa.

But Elvstrom has spoken hopefully of sailing a Star in Mexico. "This time, I'm going to have fun. For the first time in my life I'm prepared to lose."

January 14 1968

Ada Kok: 12st. 8lb. 6ft.1in. butterfly with a 41-inch bust

The cheerful Dutch girl during her successful campaign for an Olympic title in Mexico.

by Dudley Doust

Ada Kok is Holland's great swimming champion. She holds four world butterfly records, and in Mexico this autumn she is likely to become the first Dutch woman to win an Olympic gold medal since Mrs Blankers-Koen and the breast-stroker, Nel Van Vliet, did it twenty years ago. "If I lose," says Ada, "I'm sorry. But sport is just a game."

Ada is a big, laughing girl, 20 years old, with green eyes and corn-coloured hair. She stands 6ft. 1in., weighs 12st. 8lb. and is thick-set, from her massive shoulders to her 41in. bust to her thighs.

Oddly, she eats like a bird. "When I'm training hard, I'm not very hungry and I must force myself to eat," she confides. "The only things I *really* enjoy are apples and oranges."

Rising at 5.45, she hurries through breakfast and fills her shopping bag. She puts in half a dozen apples and oranges, and sandwiches. She then rides a bus and a train to Amsterdam where she slips into a public swimming bath by seven o'clock.

Then to work. As an Amsterdam coal company receptionist, she is allowed unlimited (unpaid) time off. But Ada *does* get fed up. "When I got back from the Little Olympics last autumn in Mexico," she says, "the smell of chlorine in a pool made me sick. I quit training for two months and slept late and went to parties and stayed out late at night."

At 15, Ada set a European 100 metres butterfly mark. She was on her way. In Tokyo, she came second in the 100 metres event, and this autumn she gets her last chance for an Olympic gold. Thereafter . . . ? From her shopping basket she takes out a treasured Press cutting. It shows a picture of Ada walking hand-in-hand with a young student through the streets of Valkenburg. The headline reads: Ada Kok engaged to an economics student.

"It's not true," she protests, but she blushes just the same. *April 21 1968*

Willie Carson: an exhausting but routine day in the life of a champion jockey

Mobility for a successful jockey means more than riding like the clappers round a racecourse, and if you're champion, much, much more. For one thing, you'd better not have a fear of flying, or of fast cars, because in one week you can be called to ride in six afternoon and four evening meetings. Here is an example of Willie Carson's regime. *(July 14 1974)*

by Brough Scott
Photographs by Gerry Cranham

07·25 The big gold Mercedes comes whirling up the drive. Willie Carson's face, still crumpled with sleep, lights into an irrepressible schoolboy grin as he meets trainer Barry Hills. It is the start of the busiest week yet in Carson's relentless battle to retain his crown. By the end of the week Carson will have had 50 rides. Monday brings simple delights of racing at Pontefract and Wolverhampton.

07·57 Whispering hoof-beats, straining horses and trainer Hills's intent eyes as Carson leads the morning work-outs over specially prepared sawdust gallops on Lambourn Downs. After one gallop, Carson returns for the next, his face transformed into the high cheek-boned determination of a professional gunman. We are now halfway through the season: Carson has had one solitary day off in three months.

15·15 Carson's first ride at Pontefract. The course is all hot Yorkshire shirt-sleeved sense of humour, and racing has actually been cancelled on occasion because of subsidence into the disused pit-shafts beneath. Hula Hula, Carson's ride here (No. 2), starts second favourite at evens. First out of the stalls, they lead for three furlongs in a mile race. But, for all his pushing, for all that the champion never lets up, Hula Hula can only finish third. "I tried to slow the field down early on," he explains. "But she just didn't seem to get the trip at all." Always the animals are talked of like people; not softly, but as if they were business clients. His second mount, Knockers, ran second in the 3.45. For the first time in the day there is an annoyed edge in his voice: "I should have won there. Jock Skilling's horse (Uncle Vanya—unplaced) rolled all over me three furlongs out."

16·30 Airborne again, heading for Wolverhampton, garden suburb one minute, straggling slum the next. Coffee, but no food, and Carson sleeps during the 45-minute flight. His success is founded on appetite for work; last year he rode 883 times for 163 winners; this year, racing seven days a week in Britain and the Continent, he may top the 1,000. At the end of each season Carson sleeps solidly for three days.

09.30 While others feast on the Hills' boundless breakfast hospitality, Carson bounces in after phoning his secretary to arrange travel and scheduling. "Marvellous!" he says. "Lightest ride is eight stone one—let's have some breakfast," Bacon and eggs compares with the less substantial—and rather more usual—morning ration of coffee and toast to which he reverts next day to meet the scales at 7st 8lb.

12.15 Newbury airstrip, ready to fly to Pontefract. Carson, spruce in blue shirt and blazer, is asleep within five minutes. Over South Yorkshire chimneys and pitheaps, land Doncaster at 1.20 pm. Taxi called "Dog" to complete 15 miles to Ponty. Dog does the dirty. Flat tyre. Half-hour wait. Second taxi. Worse than Cresta Run: driver last of Hell Drivers. Still arrive late: Carson misses 2.45 race.

14.55 On the scales. He will go there 100 times during the week. Time always desperately short. Saddles, leg cloths and pads have to be changed and adjusted for the right weight. Different horses need special equipment such as blinkers or breastplates. All have to be checked by the valets. All equipment has to be gathered and carried on to the scales within minutes of the previous ride, win or lose.

18.15 Wolverhampton. First ride is Willow Song, first daughter of the famous Park Top. Equally famous straw-coloured silks of Duke of Devonshire. Carson gets another good start, but finishes "in the middle." The race-winner, Pat Eddery, goes five winners ahead in the jockeys' championship. Does Carson worry about his rival? "Oh yes, I want to be champion. But Pat's going really well at the moment."

20.20 Carson's turn to go well. Wins the 8.10 on Redesdale, and then talks with trainer Bernard van Cutsem, who helped establish him. After Wolverhampton, driven home by Ted Eley, his race secretary. Eley booked for motorway speeding. Carson grudgingly eats steak and drinks a motorway shandy, gloomily predicting: "I'll have to sweat tomorrow". He manages to get some sleep in the car.

01.15 Back at Falmouth Cottage, Victorian house in Newmarket which goes with the job of Lord Derby's jockey. Sipping whisky Carson begins to study the runners, the weights and his chances on the next day's card. Ted Eley had said earlier in the day: "My little fella breaks the others' hearts. Pat Eddery will be dead by the end of August." Writer and photographer decide we don't want to be champion jockeys at all.

The two most successfully competitive British runners of the Seventies as seen by the *Sunday Times* athletics correspondent: Steve Ovett, who won the European 1,500m in 1978, introverted and suspicious; Brendan Foster, who won the European 5,000m in 1974 and an Olympic bronze medal in the 10,000m in 1976, outgoing, full of grit and good humour, the people's runner.

Steve Ovett: on the way up a sandhill to a dedicated search for self-perfection

by Cliff Temple

The first occasion that Steve Ovett can recall having to run fast was when, at the age of five, "I smashed some kid over the head with a milk bottle, and had to run like hell to get away from his mother."

He hasn't crowned anyone with a pint of gold top recently, but he can still shift. Last month he became, at 18, Britain's youngest ever four minute miler with 3min 59.4sec—exactly the same time as Roger Bannister's barrier-breaking race in 1954, but "just a training run really" for Ovett. Such is the revision of standards in 20 years.

Ovett is also the AAA's senior 800 metres champion, though it is his range of competence, from 100 metres to cross country, which sets him aside. Britain has never been short of runners who could sprint after a gentle early pace, or run at a strong, monotonous speed without being able to raise the necessary crescendo. Ovett has no obvious weaknesses, which is why more than 30 American colleges want him on a track scholarship.

But his heart belongs to the Regency air of Brighton, and he has no plans for leaving. "In the winter, when I was just getting over glandular fever, I started back training with some mates from the Brighton Surfers Club. We'd run along a really flat part of the promenade to the West Pier, up and down, about 9 o'clock at night. Marvellous."

Not so marvellous to train there in summer, of course. So then he runs in the woodland at Stanmer Park, or on the grass cycling track close to his home at Preston Park. "I'm a bit of a loner really, in all respects," he says. "Ninety per cent of my training is done alone. But I find that makes me more competitive in a race, because it seems so unusual to be actually running with someone else."

He left school after his A levels in June, and his academic future on the other side of next month's European championships is hazy. Right now he is enjoying his state as a full-time athlete. That state could continue, as his parents are so keen for him to develop his sporting talent to the full. "I mean, what better way of life is there? They back me all the way, cooking meals at odd times, or driving me to different places to train when I'm fed up, or holding the stopwatch. But they don't push me. Push is the wrong word. They spur me."

Art and design are his big career interests. He pulls out a folder of work: pencil sketches of Brighton station, pastel portraits of an athlete girlfriend, and a string of Chaplin silhouettes. But previous thoughts of study at a college outside Brighton have been dismissed.

"If I went to a college in a strange environment, I'd have to start worrying about getting meals, and shopping and laundry and all that. I'm not saying I couldn't do it. But at the moment things couldn't be better. My coach takes care of my training schedules and race invitations, and my parents smooth the way in everything else. All I do is the running."

According to your evaluation of sporting achievement, he is therefore either in a situation perfectly contrived to build confidence in facing the state-aided athlete, or just terribly spoiled. But his father, Mick, who runs a farm-produce stall founded by Steve's grandfather in Brighton's open market, doesn't view his son's races through rose-coloured spectacles. "I remember," says Steve, "last year when I ran four minutes for the mile. I was feeling quite pleased with myself, but he said 'What a bloody awful race that was.' In fact, I'd run the last lap in about 55 seconds, much faster than anybody else, but still lost the race. I'd misjudged it, so he was quite right."

The background has produced its success. He went to the European junior championships in Duisburg, last year, as 800 metres favourite and won the gold medal. This year his unbeaten racing record lasted right up until last week, when Andy Carter got the better of him in a 1,000 metres race at Gateshead.

Before that, he had been the despair of the experienced Carter, who first lost his AAA's title and then an in-

ternational match race against Czechoslovakia to Ovett. "Not only that," said Carter at the time, "he even won the sweepstake." Ovett's guess of 5min 14sec was the nearest of the entire British team to the length of time British Board chairman Harold Abrahams was to speak at the post-match dinner.

One of the free wheeling joys about the running of the 6ft 1in Ovett this season may have been that it is achieved on a kind of borrowed time. Earlier this year, a bout of glandular fever seemed to have torn the summer pages from his racing diary.

"When I had just started training again, about April, I went over to visit a distance running course at Merthyr Mawr in Wales, where they have the gigantic sandhill called the Big Dipper. I didn't think Harry Wilson, my coach, would ask me to run up it, but he did. Somehow I got to the top, but I just lay there, feeling like death and being sick all over the place. I couldn't do anything for the rest of the day. But next morning I felt better, and after that everything started to click into place. Looking back now, I think that one big effort up the sandhill was the difference between me going to Rome and not doing anything all summer."

August 11 1974

Brendan Foster: true to himself

Brendan Foster is astonished that you should want to go to Gateshead to see him. "It's not just north," he warns. "It's right up near Newcastle." But once you have established that there is life beyond Watford, he'll tell you about the foot racing tradition of the North-East; a tradition he's continuing. Olympic 1,500 metres finalist, bronze medallist in European and Commonwealth Games, and 3 minutes 55.9 seconds for the mile.

His best days may lie ahead at 5,000 metres, for his proven track speed and cross-country strength should make him a world class 5,000 metres man. But he's having two races first, to see.

And despite his doubts, half serious, half joking, Gateshead is a very fashionable place for distance running now. Gateshead Harriers won the National Cross-Country team title last month, and on a mid-week training session might have around 120 runners going out.

Earlier this year Foster actually held in his hand a professional contract with his name printed on it. One more autograph and he would have been assured of a minimum £5,000 a year doing what he loves; running. But he handed the contract back, unsigned. No, not even tempted, he says.

"There are enough pressures in athletics without having to run to make your living. What you earn would depend on your results. I'd hate that. Imagine what it must be like to go out training, thinking, 'Am I a £5,000-a-year athlete or a ten-bob-a-week one'."

So he puts in his 100 miles training each week for a Commonwealth Games title in New Zealand next January, instead of for the thousands of dollars the American professional circus hands out for winning races and breaking records.

There was also his teaching career to consider, and anyway he didn't want to leave the amateur ranks. "If you run 10 miles in training and you think it was hard, it doesn't really matter. If you race badly, your standard of living doesn't suffer. But in simple professional terms, if you don't run well, you don't eat."

At 25 now, he's pleased that he was never a teenage prodigy. The younger-faster syndrome passed him by. "Call it

slow development if you like, but I was never in a hurry. If you're totally dedicated to one sport too early in your life, there must come a point when you reach out for the forbidden fruit.

"If you're always running in your teenage years, when do you go to all-night parties and get drunk? When do you go away camping and walking by the sea? And when do you spend time reading and studying? I couldn't see life without running now, but when I was younger I'm glad I didn't have to worry about getting up on a Sunday morning to run 20 miles.

"I think some kids are missing out by being totally dedicated to sport too soon. Let them run, play football, or whatever. Let them find out what suits them, and then at 19 or 20 they can decide for themselves, and say: 'I'm doing athletics because it's my best sport,' not 'I'm doing it because it's the only sport I've ever been allowed to try.'

"For instance, I think maybe I missed out because I never played table tennis. For all anyone knows, I might be the world's greatest table tennis player. I've just never had a chance to find out."

April 22 1973

Dave 'Boy' Green: out of the Fens comes a Tiger with a snarl on his kind country face

The fight fraternity in London felt as if it had been shaken by the scruff of its neck when Dave "Boy" Green came down from Cambridgeshire early in 1975 with his wild uninhibited style. He passed his first big

Ian Botham: a study of a man grappling with his aggression

When Tony Greig departed the England cricket team in 1977, Ian Botham, a rumbustious 21-year-old, eagerly snapped up the vacancy for an all-rounder. He took five wickets on his Test debut against Australia at Nottingham that summer, and there seems no limit to his potential.

by Dudley Doust

The topic was the will to win, and Ian Botham, relaxed in his sitting room, suddenly looked up and fell silent. The door had opened, and his infant son crawled in and sped naked across the carpet. Botham smiled. "Now, there's a good example of what I'm talking about," he went on. "If we're playing some silly little game, Liam and I, I can't let him win. It's pathetic—I've even got to beat my one-year-old child."

The sources of his competitiveness are hard to root out; perhaps they come from his parents, both Yorkshire-born and former cricketers themselves. At his rented house in Weston-super-

test two years later by stopping former world welterweight champion John H. Stracey in the tenth round of a world title eliminator at Wembley. Nicknamed "The Fen Tiger", he said during his final pre-parations for the fight: "I put all my efforts into winning. I can punch a bit and that's what people pay to see. You've got to be keyed up in this game, and I get a bit nasty sometimes. Manager Andy Smith gets his share of the credit: "Mr Smith has learned me to box and control myself in my punching and brought me on a bomb. I don't think I'd have got where I am if it weren't for Mr Smith." *March 27 1977*

Mare, Botham stroked his spikey moustache and came up with an interesting and possibly valid view of his own aggression. "Maybe one of the reasons is that I'm an all-rounder. I can have a go. If I fail with the bat I know, subconsciously, that I can always redeem myself with the ball."

The difference between this year and last, in Botham's regard, is that he has learned to harness this sometimes wasteful aggression. "He's much less *macho*", says the England captain, Mike Brearley. "That's the basic reason, I think, for his vast improvement. Ian no longer has to bowl a bouncer at Richard Hadlee." If one running incident has elevated Botham from one of Wisden's Five Cricketers of 1977 to England's most secure all-rounder, a 22-year-old player with an almost infinite Test future, it lies in his maturing feud with the New Zealand fast bowler, Hadlee. The battle, glare for glare, bouncer for bouncer, was joined during England's tour last winter.

"The first time I ever saw the guy was at Canterbury, before the first Test," said Botham. "He bounced me a few times, and I hooked him a few times. Straight afterwards, in the Wellington Test, he got a bit keen. He glared at me, put a bloke back at square leg and bounced me again. I took the bait—hook, line, sinker and half the rod—stupidly tried to hook him and got caught."

Botham warmed to the story: "Well, the second Test came along, at Christchurch. Hadlee was fresh, and came racing in and started bouncing. He had a man at square leg, but there's no way I was going to hook him this time. I just smiled down the wicket. That geed him up, and he lost his line and length. So, second round to Botham. When he came in to bat I got a little bit carried away, and I bounced him, very first ball. He went a few different colours. Pretty soon, though, he played this characteristic shot of his, flat-batting a bouncer over the slips for four. I was very annoyed. I lost my rag. I bowled badly, and he smashed me all over the ground. Third round to Hadlee."

At 6ft 2in and 14½st, an agile man with a bull neck and legs like tree trunks, Botham might look more at home at Twickenham or Wembley, rather than at Lord's or the Somerset County Ground at Taunton. True, he played soccer and dutiful rugby while a schoolboy at Yeovil. He even won the Somerset under-15 badminton doubles championships. Otherwise, he has been a committed cricketer since about the age of four, when he used to go across the street to fetch balls for the boys at Yeovil Grammar School.

Botham's deepest regret this season is that his batting contribution to his county's success has been only modest. "I'd like to have got more runs for Somerset," he said, pointing to his county first-class average of 19.54, with a highest score of 86, as compared with his Test average (five matches so far) of 48.40, including two centuries: "What could be happening is that I am bowling too much in Somerset games. I have been getting tired, and when I am batting my thinking hasn't been switched on."

Botham now faces the most important fortnight of his crowded season. Somerset, joint leaders down the home stretch of the John Player League, play Middlesex today at Taunton; England begin the final Test against New Zealand at Lord's on Thursday and, a week Saturday, Somerset meet Sussex in the final of the Gillette Cup. After a short family holiday in a log cabin beside a loch in Scotland, Botham can confidently expect a winter in Australia with England.

Also, this remarkable youngster now faces the ironic challenge that once confronted Tony Greig, his predecessor as England's finest all-rounder. An established Test player, he must guard against a slackening off of his county performances. He's loyal, and much liked by his teammates, and he'll never fail for lack of effort. "What I now want most," he said, "is to help Somerset finally to win something in cricket." *August 20 1978*

Inside track

Sex Powered

You would think that swimming flat out for 800 metres at Olympic level would leave you fairly shattered—certainly in no condition to be thinking about sex. Not so, apparently. According to a team of Australian doctors, whose findings have been published in the British Medical Journal, this killing effort almost doubles the sex hormone level in the bloodstream.

The suggestion is that the rise is linked with the aggressiveness and drive needed to get to the top, and the feeling of well-being associated with peak physical fitness. A rise in the sex hormone level is directly associated with increased sexual desire and activity.

Swimmers do seem to be a special case. Medical students experimented with 20 minutes vigorous cycling in the laboratory, and oarsmen of Olympic standard knocked themselves out for the cause with a brisk spell of rowing. The sex hormone level did go up, but not half as much as with the swimmers.   *March 11 1973*

Fagged Out

So you think "smokesploitation" in sport is something new. The Sunday Graphic football album for 1905–6 contains an ad: "Why The All Blacks Triumphed. The New Zealand team think BDV cigarettes are a very excellent smoke, and they have been greatly appreciated by the members,

signed G. H. Dixon, team manager. The above testimonial was sent to Godfrey Phillips & Sons, by the manager of the New Zealand team." It was also accompanied by a stanza:

The All Blacks from over the seas,
Won most of their matches with ease,
Yet it's pleasant to learn,
They've been conquered in turn,
By the famed cigarette BDVs.
                    October 24 1976

Barry Sheene: life in the fast lane

by Dudley Doust

Lounging in a red chair at his home in Putney, London, is Barry Stephen Sheene, MBE, the world motorcycling champion. He is a vivid young man, engaging grin, blue eyes, long, fluffy brown hair and a strong jaw. He wore a cashmere sweater, clean jeans and cowboy boots.

After providing a live commentary to a videotape of his horrific crash at Daytona, Florida, in 1975, Sheene was back in his red chair, jewellery flashing, eating a big beef sandwich and drinking a glass of wine, stopping to send his girlfriend, former model Stephanie McLean, back for salt for his sandwich. You wondered, "Where does the legend leave off and Barry begin? Does nature follow art?"

Oddly, there is no legend. It's all true. Sheene is a palpable guy, courteous and intelligent, not at all bumptious, and he bubbles along, talking *with* you, rather than for you. "*Fantastic*, that MBE," he was saying about the New Year Honours List. "I like royalty and the Queen, and I don't give a damn what anybody says—I was brought up to look up to the Queen."

Born in Holborn, son of a motorbike

fanatic, nephew of a speedway driver, Barry sat on his first bike at the age of two and owned his first one—a slapped-up 50cc Ducati four-stroke—at five. At 27, Sheene has grown into one of the coolest men in leathers. His tip on what not to do when skidding on your backside at 180 mph down the tarmac, for instance, is a model of composure: "Just don't move your foot—it might snap off."

Although Sheene's income is nothing like the rumoured £200,000 a year, he is one of the highest-paid sportsmen in Britain, with his appearance and prize money and arrangements with Heron-Suzuki, Fabergé, Ingersoll Watches, and British Caledonian Airways.

Sheene, meanwhile, begins his physical preparation tomorrow for the defence of his title, which opens in Venezuela in March. It's a daunting daily programme: twenty furious minutes on a rowing machine, half an hour on the Bullworker stretcher, 75 press-ups, a dozen excruciatingly-held sit-ups, and—best for the wrists—six lifts of a 10-pound motor cycle flywheel with a stick and rope device. "Motorcycling is not all beer and skittles," said Sheene. "It's a lot of hard work."
                    January 15 1978

Conrad Dobler: acclaimed as the "dirtiest player" in gridiron football.

Conrad Dobler: being utterly offensive

by Dudley Doust

Conrad Dobler plays offensive guard for the New Orleans Saints in the United States National Football League. Dobler (that's him charging at the camera) stands 6ft 3in, weighs 18 stone and is universally acclaimed the "dirtiest player" in gridiron football. "The legal way of doing my job," he says, "is to get it done any way I can—without getting caught."

Dobler's job is two-fold: "I clear the way for my backs when they run with the ball and, more important, I protect my passer from the guys on the other team trying to knock him down." When he is forced to play dirty, Dobler contends, it really is the other man's fault. Dobler's short glossary of fouls, sometimes committed for the pure purpose of intimidation:

● SPEARING. "It's like throwing a spear into the ground. When a guy is down, or somewhat down, you dive on his back, face, neck or stomach with your helmet, which is a hard shell."

● CLOTHESLINING. "You hold out your arm stiff, and let a guy's neck run into it. It's like running along and catching your throat on a clothes line."

● LEG-WHIPPING. "Yeah, it's like a karate blow. If a guy charges past you and swings you aside, you use his momentum, keep swinging and kick him in the back of the leg."

● BITING. "What's the other guy's finger doing in my mouth anyway?"

Dobler's repertoire also includes grabbing and wrenching the face-mask of a player running past ("It tends to separate his head from his shoulders" he says) and most commonly, slugging a man in the face.

What are we to make of Dobler? Violent as he is, he never has permanently crippled a man. Clearly, though, he glamorises (and is allowed to glamorise) brutality in his game. Clearly, too, he is emulated by thousands of young Americans. Dobler doesn't see it that way. Transferred this season from St Louis Cardinals to New Orleans Saints, he views the charge with amusement. "How could I be evil?" he asks, feigning innocence. "I've been elevated from a cardinal to a saint."

October 15 1978

Joe Bugner: when Mr Smith lets go of the reins

Shortly before he left England for Las Vegas to meet Muhammad Ali in the first of two losing fights he had with him, Joe Bugner was interviewed without his apparently dominating mentor Andy Smith and emerged as a man with a stature of his own.

by Llew Gardner

Joe Bugner has been criticised as being a man of even fewer words than he has given exciting performances. So much so that there have been unkind souls prepared to suggest that apart from being a dab hand at pulling the wires when his creation was in the ring, manager Andy Smith was also a budding ventriloquist.

But last week, on the eve of his departure for America to prepare for his fight with Muhammad Ali, Bugner opened up and talked movingly of the relationship he shares with the perpetual-motion Scot: "If something happened to Mister Smith so that he couldn't go on being my manager, I'd pack up boxing. I *could* fight without him in my corner, but I *wouldn't.*"

Why? "Because it's a . . ."

"Partnership," I suggested.

"No, that's not the word. It's trust. Should anything happen in the ring, like I was going to be maimed or something, then I know he would stop the fight. More than that. He'd get in there and fight the other guy for me."

The fight manager of fiction chews 10-cent cigars and can look his fighter straight in his scar-tissued eyes while robbing him rotten. The reality, this side of the Atlantic at least, tends to be rather different. Most of the managers I know are more like Kensington nannies that hustlers.

Andy Smith is the Big Nanny of them all. For six years he has nursed Joe Bugner, hand-picking his opponents, cosseting him in the face of more public scorn than was heaped on Chesterton's donkey, speaking for him and, apparently, thinking for him.

But now it seems as if Smith is preparing to let go of the toddler reins and let his 15½-stone charge take a few steps on his own.

Manager and fighter live in St Ives, Huntingdonshire, on the banks of the River Ouse. I went there to talk to Smith about his subtle relationship with Bugner. But it didn't turn out like that at all. Mister Smith, as the whole Bugner household calls him, had gone to Peterborough to renew his passport, and there was Joe ready and happy to talk about *his* relationship with "the Guv'nor."

Away from Smith the fighter takes on stature of his own. No one would call him brash, but he has a nice humour. Such as when I asked if he had been affected by the critical obloquy heaped on him by the boxing writers: "I used to worry, but not any longer. Now I know most of them know as much about boxing as I do about writing."

On the fight with Ali? "It will be the *second* boxing surprise this year. After all, all I've got to do is win. If I do that they'll make me a knight . . . Sir Joseph."

On Mr Smith's love of boxing: "He's like a man with an old car or a dog. You can't say to him 'give that filthy thing away.'"

"It's like father and son," explains Bugner. "I know that everything he does is for my own good. I've been with him since I was 16, and more or less grew up in his household. He's got two boys, Andrew and Alan, who are near my age, and we were like brothers.

"As a fighter you've got to have faith in your manager. You've got to trust him. Know he won't let you down. The times I've lost, that hasn't been his fault. It's because I've let me down.

"As you get older you have to grow

out of childish attitudes. There comes a time when you realise that it's not a fantasy any more, but it's become a business.

"The thing is that when we have a business discussion he puts all the facts in front of me, and then gives me time to go away and think about it. Not all managers are like that."

So they never row? "Sure we do. We often blow our tops. Have a real fury." But he was vague about the kind of thing that caused rows. Positive only that they usually took place in the morning. "I've got a terrible temper in the morning. I'm best just left alone while I get on with training."

He claims Smith is the only person to whom he can listen in the gym. "He lets me do my thing. He has never tried to mould me in any way. He sees me as Joe Bugner the fighter, and that's what he wants me to be.

"I've been in gyms and heard trainers say: 'Throw a left like Ken Buchanan' or 'Do it like Tom, Dick or Harry.' It's all nonsense. Some fighters try and copy the Joe Louis shuffle, and end up with thick ears. And how many fighters have tried to copy Ali and ended up with a busted face?"

And the manager's influence in the ring? "Mister Smith's job ends the night of the fight. Up to then he puts as much mental effort into the fight as I do physical preparation."

Bugner has sometimes looked more in danger of boring his audience to death than suffering serious injury himself. In his last fight against Rudi Lubbers he was back to his old bad habit of letting his opponent off the hook, punching and then standing off to admire the view.

"Mister Smith gave me a right rollocking for that. But I just put it down to lack of experience. People say that I've had 50 fights, but they forget it's 50 fights over only five years. You know, I will most probably bring the world title back to Britain one day, but people already think of me as if I were a 29-year-old fighter. I've just been around a long time."

Why, after all these years together, does he insist on calling his manager *Mister* Smith? "People often raise that with me, say: 'Cor, Joe, you're big enough to call him Andy now!' Well, of course I am. I'm big enough to call anyone anything I like. But it's a matter of respect.

"You've got to have respect."

February 4 1973

Judy Hashman: blazing the badminton trail

By 1971 Judy Hashman had made a mark on badminton that probably will never be equalled and, the daughter of a famous Irish-American family, she was playing that year for England for the first time.

by Peter Dunn

Mrs Judy Hashman walked into the subterranean gloom of the Empire Pool at Wembley last week, to the opening of the All-England badminton championships, saw the rivals exerting themselves on court like young crickets, and felt weak at the knees.

It was a familiar sensation and one that she has never been able to master. Widely acclaimed as one of the world's greatest sportswomen, Mrs Hashman's self-doubt before each tournament has seemed an odd contradiction to the shelves of silver trophies at her house called Ricochet in Abingdon. A certain heartiness might have been expected in one who has taken the world's singles title in women's badminton 10 times: but that is not her style. Every important match has been prefaced by weeks of sleepless nights.

Even the uplifting influence of a special occasion has failed to ease her tension. She has always played and won her championships as an American. Last week, as a recently naturalised Briton, she was playing for England for the first time.

In morale terms it meant that she had the crowd behind her in what, for all the perfidious chauvinism of the "All-England" title, were the unofficial *world* championships in badminton. But Mrs Hashman, in striped blazer and with her sandy Irish hair clipped short, seemed not particularly consoled. "She's the world's most nervous person," said her husband, Dick. "Before a tournament, she's impossible to live with."

The post-war resurgence of badminton owes much to Mrs Hashman and her family, the famous Irish-American Devlins. Between them—Judy, her father and her sister Sue—they have collected an astonishing 40 championships. Judy's badminton was deeply etched into her life by her father, who even taught her to throw a ball like a

boy to improve her swing. Intense concentration, economy of style and an unnerving ability to dismantle her opponents by analysing their technique made her virtually indestructible.

But these days the threat comes from Asians, particularly the Japanese. "If it was only Europeans playing here," said Mrs Hashman at Wembley, "I wouldn't be half so bothered with training. Asians are quite content to let you do all the work and kill you off in slow degrees. They're utterly dedicated."

It is the kind of dedication that Mrs Hashman can admire even though she no longer needs to emulate it. At 35 she has made a mark on badminton that will probably never be equalled.

March 28 1971

Judy Hashman: the post-war resurgence in badminton owes much to her.

Rodney Marsh: acting the part of a man who is acting the part of a man who...

An attempt at self-analysis by a glamorous, extrovert, reformed clown.

by Hunter Davies

Rodney Marsh is so shyly arrogant, so humbly conceited, that it's not surprising he inspires so much love-hate. He turned up for training and took off his white Lotus Europa like an old glove, letting it lie where it fell. Typical of the bastard, said someone, leaving his car to block the way for everyone else. But they couldn't take their eyes off him, once he started turning it on. Rodney Marsh has star quality, even doing press-ups in the mist in the wilds of Ruislip.

He was knackered at the end, which is the point of training, so that the sweat stood out like melting cheese. There's one thing Mr Marsh prides himself on these days: he's a professional, working for the good of the team rather than the good of R. Marsh.

"I came into football to project myself. I wanted the limelight and the glory. At 18 when I was playing for Fulham I saw myself as brilliant as Denis Law, off the field as well as on. I worked on my extrovert image, playing the clown, being a joker.

"Then one day when I was 20 we beat Manchester United and I rushed home to watch it on Match of the Day. I saw myself for the first time as a very poor imitation of Denis Law. When I left Fulham six months later for Queen's Park Rangers, I became a different person. I decided to stop being a clown."

He was now sitting at home, half-serious, half-smiling. The phrases were coming out as if he'd rehearsed them in his head. I said I didn't believe them. He was looking back at himself, rationalising his actions.

"You're right. Nothing's true. Talking to you now I'm acting another part. It's all a façade. Perhaps acting the clown *was* me and I didn't realise it at the time. All the same, I regret it now, whether I was doing it deliberately or not. I know now what I didn't know then. Managers don't like clowns."

The resulting transformation has resulted in his being picked for England for the first time, at the great age of 27. He's not only the handsomest, the richest, the most glamorous player in the Second Division, he's now the most successful. He puts it down to Bobby Campbell, the Queen's Park Rangers coach.

"It happened about a year ago when Bobby came. I've always been a flash bloke. I thought I knew it all. But Bobby was the first person who got through to me about the need for discipline."

And now, do people no longer hate you?

"Hold on," he said, getting up to answer the phone. "Keep hold of that question, I've got a good answer for you."

His home is in the heart of stockbroker Epsom where he's realised the Footballer's Dream—blonde wife, a boy Jonathan, a girl Joanna, lovely house, lovely neighbours, lovely life.

"I've always been a flash bloke."

Not that he's taken in by it all, or by himself. "Stand back," he'd said earlier as he was putting his car in the garage. "I'll put on the suburban coach lamps and give you a treat."

He finished on the phone, then it rang again. It never stopped. All the world and his agent wants to talk to him. He took it off the hook in the end, by which time he'd forgotten what his smart answer was going to be.

Behind him was a book case, full of books. Boswell's Life of Johnson, Pears Cyclopaedia. He waved a hand and said there were more in the next room. A few months ago, so he says, he was thinking of going in for the Open University. "But what happens if you end up a teacher on £12 to £15 a week? Not much satisfaction there.

"I'll tell you what though, if I hadn't been a footballer I wouldn't have stayed in England. I don't like the English climate and the people are too reserved. I was invited to a party in Epsom the other day. The bloke was on the phone, telling me blah blah what a great party it was going to be, and then he said a couple of special friends were coming who wanted to see me. I never went, of course. That sort of thing happens in England. People want to see me . . . just because I play for Queen's Park Rangers."

Fractionally, just fractionally, he'd hesitated over the last three words. It looked as if he was going to say "just because I'm Rodney Marsh" or "just because I play for England." But the new Marsh, had corrected himself, just in time. Was he ashamed of playing for a Second Division side? Was that why he'd deliberately dragged it in? He refused to be drawn. He was being so well paid, he couldn't leave. He didn't know anything about First Division clubs offering £200,000 for him. Anyway, Rangers would be in the First Division next season.

When his playing days are over, he fancies staying in football, as a manager. Very few footballers say that: they couldn't stand the aggravation—directors, Press, fans, players, all on their backs. "A manager's aggravation is self-made. I wouldn't find directors or the Press a hardship. All a manager has to do is keep 11 players happy—the 11 in the reserves. The first team are happy, because they're the first team."

He doesn't intend to sit his FA preliminary coaching badge, the accepted beginning for any player wanting to be a manager. "No, sir. If I'm going to be a manager, I'm going to be a successful manager. I have most of the football knowledge I need, but I have to learn about management. All football managers are untrained in management. I'll do a business management course at a business college. I'm not bothering with any FA badges.

"Sometimes I think there is something in my life I'm lacking. I can't pin it down. It would take hours and, if I boiled it down I know I'd come to the same answer—football for me is the best way out of the crowd. Football has stopped me being ordinary.

"I don't worry that it's short-lived I've now got more cynical. I was taken for granted when I was younger. Now I try to get as much as I can, to do nothing for nothing.

"Managers don't like clowns."

"But what is it, being a footballer? In theory, if you take away Match of the Day and the Press and the fans and the hangers-on, it's all very empty and lonely. When you take it out of context, what is it?"

You mean you'd rather be doing something really creative, like discovering penicillin? "No, sir, Alexander Fleming knew that what he was doing was right and good, even if he'd never discovered penicillin. That must be a nice feeling."

But isn't it nice to think of the pleasure which football gives to millions of people? "I agree. Football's a great game. But it's being out there that matters most, not talking about it. That's what I like best. You can't cheat, not in football. You can cheat in life, cheat at home, cheat at work. You can talk yourself in and out of anything. I can talk about the great game I'm going to play on Saturday. But I can't out there. I'm out there to be shot at, simply for what I am."

December 19 1971

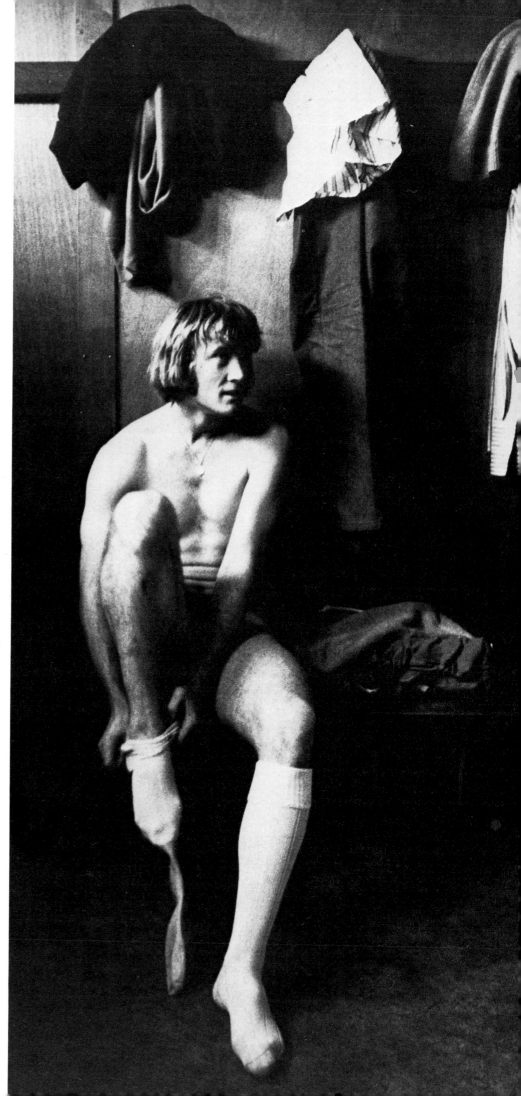

6

SKILL

For many people who watch sport at the highest level the drama, the heroes, the sheer spectacle are enough. But to others the sight of a true champion in full cry poses a whole new set of questions. How can a professional golfer place his iron shots with such consistency? How does a jockey remain in command of a high-speed classic colt? How is a Test batsman able to find time to consider his response to a 90 m.p.h. bouncer? And for anyone who has participated in sport, at whatever level, the cool analysis of technique, skill and the tricks of the trade provides an endless fascination.

Eyes on the ball : Jonah Barrington on the squash court

Attention to fine detail is important to most success in sport. In yachting, understanding the weather and deciphering the local pattern of currents can mean the crucial difference between winning and losing. Accordingly, in 1968, the British team took a professional meteorologist with them to Acapulco and solved a mystery. It helped produce the best postwar showing by our yachtsmen in an Olympics, and established a style of approach that produced even better results in 1972 and 1976.

Britannia rules Mexico's 'slippery sea'

by John Lovesey

If there is one part of Britain's Olympic effort that gives cause for justifiable optimism, it is our yachting team in the steamy heat of Acapulco with their own motor launches, their own meteorological forecaster and a thirst for victory.

For once British organisation is envied and admired and much of this is due to Vernon Stratton, 40, a fine yachtsman himself, who is managing our Olympic team for the first time.

He walks along the oven-hot concrete quay at the Club de Yates in a straw hat and with an intensity of expression that other sailors from all over the world are learning rapidly to respect.

In no other sport is such a high premium placed on gamesmanship and by the end of this week, with the excitement reaching a pitch that you could almost reach out and touch, Britain was already ahead.

The team has, for instance, caused the Dutch to cable home for a new Flying Dutchman centreboard like one that Rodney Pattisson has been using in Superdocious, and goaded the Spanish to having one made in Mexico. "What they don't know," says Stratton, "is it's no good."

What may be crucial to British success, however, is an exhaustive study that has been made of the weather and currents at Acapulco. This has been supervised by David Houghton, who is one of six senior forecasters at the Central Forecasting Office at Bracknell in Berkshire, and the editor of Weather magazine. His major triumph has been to unravel the mystery of what the team calls "Acapulco's slippery sea."

Stratton shrewdly realised that somebody like Houghton would be necessary to help the British team after visiting Acapulco at this time last year for the yachting contests of the mini-Olympics.

"A race would start," explains Stratton, "and there would be no current, but by the time you got to the first mark there would be one. We could never work out why. The wind, which averages 5 to 10 knots, instead of the 10 to 15 knots in England, was another mystery. I decided that if we were to master all these problems, we'd have to have a Met man."

With the aid of hydrographers, David Houghton worked out that the cause of Acapulco's slippery sea lies in its huge depths, plunging in places 125 fathoms. This, in the extreme heat of the place, creates two layers of water, a warm one above a cold one. The warm one, being less dense, is moved easily by the wind and slips across the cold one to create a current that can take as much as two days to abate.

"Most of the people here," says Stratton, "don't understand why this happens. And it's a hell of an advantage to know. If you go out and there's no current and very little wind, when the wind gets up you realise the surface is going to change and you can start taking avoiding action."

The currents just outside the Acapulco Bay also change direction in such a bewildering fashion they form a pattern on any chart that looks like a mass of snakes in a frenzy. Anybody who tries to unravel them at the last moment, comments David Houghton, "is going to be up a gum-tree, because they won't have the complete picture."

Houghton and the rest of the party have cloaked their investigation of the currents under the guise of fishing. Their fishing line has, however, been connected to a lead weight on the ocean bed and then attached to a plastic bottle on the surface to form a temporary buoy. After that it has been a simple matter to float a small stake from the bottle to calculate the direction and speed of current in any particular spot.

But this is not all. The British team have been rising early in the morning for physical training.

Everybody has then worked on the boats before breakfast and the first team meeting of the day. At this Houghton, who has already sent up a balloon, makes his weather forecast (he is having satellite pictures of the Pacific area sent to him regularly from Bracknell).

And at the day's second team meeting, at 8 p.m., everybody has then discussed what happened to the weather and sailing problems.

The Hotel Caleta, where all the Olympic yachtsmen are staying, has been nicknamed "the Monastery", since no women are allowed in after 10 p.m. It has produced, as a result, the British pin competition, which has to do with exchanging national badges, and has prompted a question on the notice board in the British HQ: "What does a girl have to do to get a Virgin Island pin?"

Rodney Pattisson, a blond, muscular young man of 25, and the leading favourite in the team for a gold medal, has been working on Superdocious every day. He never wears a shirt, a hat or sunglasses, and for the first few days he was very bad-tempered and impatient until a sun canopy was fixed up over his boat on land. He worries incessantly about every little screw and has a phobia about weight.

Pattisson threw out a stopwatch provided for each British Olympic yacht because it was "too heavy," had his sail fixed at the top of the mast so he could get rid of the halyard, and has a specially made electrical, lightweight wind indicator on board which he has kept hidden from all the foreign opposition.

The British team have also had the benefit of the accumulated knowledge of John Oakeley, here as a reserve helmsman and the man who won the

British hopes at Acapulco: left, Flying Dutchman Superdocious (Rodney Pattisson and Iain MacDonald-Smith), the eventual gold medal winner.

Flying Dutchman world championship with David Hunt in Montreal last year.

He has apparently passed on a secret starting technique, and the information that for the past two years he has been gaining energy on the water from a special food pack prepared by Horlicks.

The food packs will be important because, as Vernon Stratton says: "The game is going to won here in terms of sheer endurance. In this heat and glare the deciding factor will be how well you make yourself concentrate over every little wave."

As for Rodney Pattisson, on Wednesday he was planning to do some work at midnight on his boat. "I'm certain," he says, "one or two think there's a bit of magic in Superdocious, and I'm not about to disillusion them."

October 13 1968

Pots of confidence: the inimitable style of a world champion

The distinctive panache of snooker's uninhibited master, John Spencer.

by Clive Everton

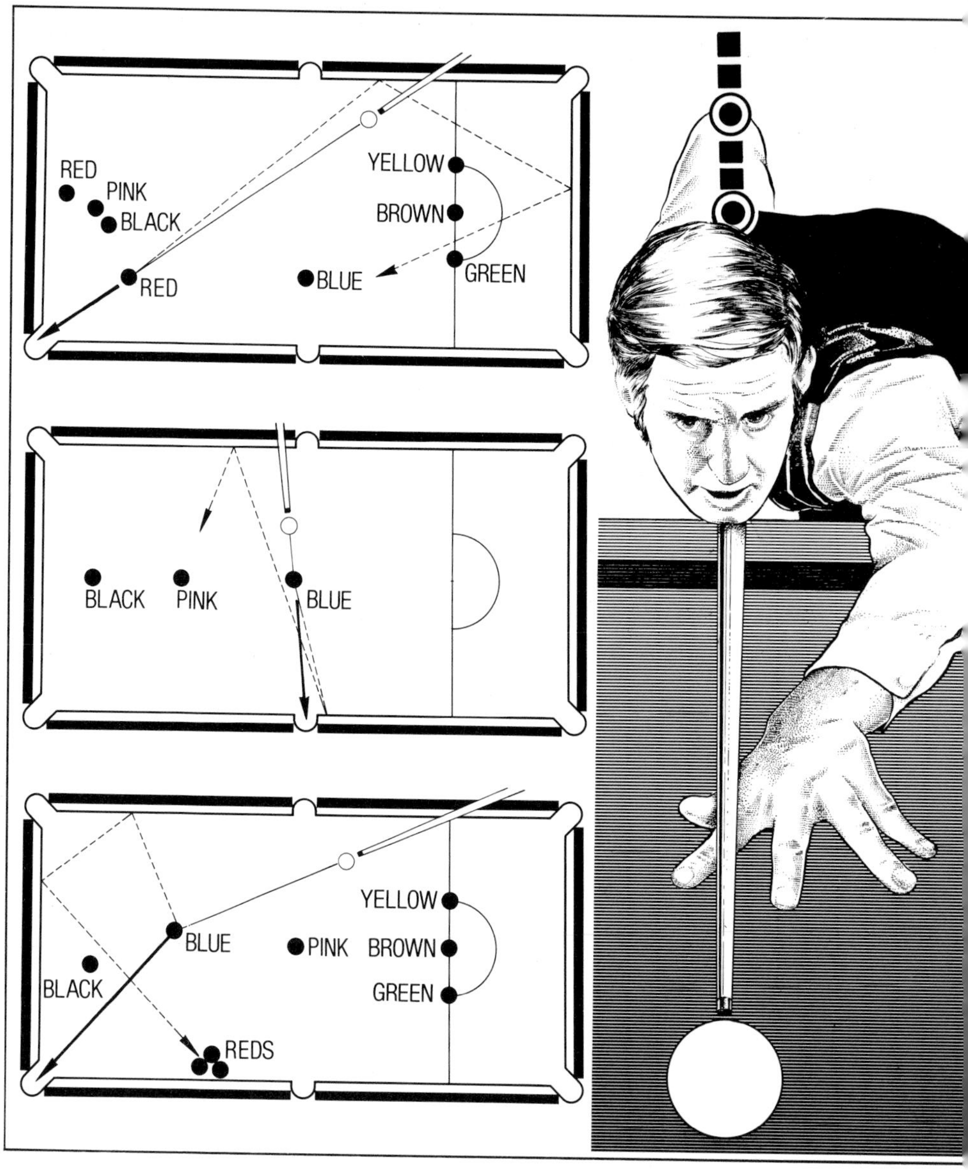

John Spencer, Britain's world professional snooker champion, currently starring in BBC2's Pot Black series, is an extraordinary champion with a very distinctive style.

When Spencer next appears on Pot Black, a week on Wednesday, look for his perfect stance and unique bridge which have remained unchanged from his childhood games of bagatelle, through a break of 115 (15 red, 14 blacks, one yellow) at the age of 16, to his present status, at 35, as undisputed world champion.

The stance forms a perfectly straight line, from the point of his right elbow, through his upper arm to his shoulder, and continues between his eyes and along the cue. As he shapes up Spencer's lower arm is perpendicular from elbow to cue.

His bridge is something different. His thumb is cocked, but, very unusually, the first finger is pushed almost underneath the thumb, so that the cue runs across it, rather than alongside it. He claims no particular advantage from this idiosyncracy.

But it is Spencer's long potting, his ability to play at speed with maximum backspin (screw) or sidespin (side), which make him champion. Added to that his great panache, in attempting shots in matchplay that others would only contemplate on the exhibition table, fills the halls.

The top diagram here depicts a fantastic shot he played last November while defeating Australia's Warren Simpson in the final of that championship.

The only pottable red was a straight one into the top left-hand pocket, but there was no obvious colour to follow it. Spencer struck the cue-ball as low as possible (to apply maximum backspin) and with tremendous power. The cue-ball hit the red, pocketed it, and then screwed back some 12 feet, via the side and bottom cushions into position for the blue. (The path of the cue-ball after impact is traced by the broken line.)

First to speak after an ovation lasting fully three minutes, Simpson, his opponent gasped: "That was impossible."

"I thought," said Spencer, "the best I could hope for was to get back two or three feet." The nap of the table helped the screw, and the fact that Spencer struck the cue-ball minutely to the left of centre meant that the ball was still carrying some side spin which caused it to gather speed off the side cushion.

The centre diagram shows another position Spencer faced in Australia, as he cleared the colours in rotation (yellow, green, brown, blue, pink and black). The problem arose on the blue, in itself a simple pot. However, playing it in orthodox fashion would have led to a missable position for the pink.

Spencer's cue struck the cue-ball at about 10 o'clock, high and to the left, with such side spin that the cue-ball returned at an acute angle, off the two side cushions, and finally into perfect position for the pink. It is a feat akin to a tennis player making a drop shot return to his own side of the net.

In the bottom diagram, Spencer again ignored the percentage game and elected instead to play the blue. He applied a combination of screw and left-hand side spin.

The screw caused the cue-ball to leave the blue almost at a right angle, with the blue being pocketed. And as the cue-ball hit the cushion, the side spin pulled it off the top cushion to splash into the cluster of reds. Thus, all three reds were pottable.

If he does not match the precise calculating positional play of the old maestro, Joe Davis, Spencer's naturally aggressive and uninhibited style make him without doubt the most exciting player ever. His confidence in playing the outrageous shot successfully in tight situations is unparalleled.

March 14 1971

Six days beneath the monstrous overhang on Britain's 'impossible climb'

Conquering the Scoop with new ideas, new technology and sheer old-fashioned courage.

by Peter Gillman

Strone Ulladale, an 800-foot high cliff on the remote Hebridean island of Harris, has long been known to many climbers as the most intimidating challenge in Britain. Its most prominent feature, at its northern end, is a monstrous scoop, 400 feet high, whose upper lip overhangs its base by 150 feet; for years the Scoop was considered impossible to climb.

But recently, with the development, first in the USA and then in Britain of new and highly-specialised artificial climbing equipment, the Scoop became a target for climbers—its ascent would extend Britain's climbing possibilities to new limits.

On May 21 two Scottish climbers found a route to the right of the Scoop; 700 feet long, it took them three days to climb. On May 23, Doug Scott, a 28-year-old Nottingham schoolteacher, veteran of four overseas expeditions and highly skilled in artificial climbing techniques, decided to attack the Scoop itself, choosing a line of grooves in its very centre. With him on the attempt were Jeff Upton, 20, electrician; Mick Terry, 27, toolmaker; Guy Lee, 24, climbing instructor. They had with them 120 pitons and many other items of specialised equipment. The climb unfolded.

● May 24. Scott and Upton climb 130 feet on almost continuously overhanging rock. The rock is fine-grained gneiss, containing narrow hairline cracks susceptible to only the thinnest pitons. Scott used a number of American rurps—their full name is "Realised Ultimate Reality Pitons"—whose blades are only $9\frac{3}{4}$ inches long. But the crucial pitons are the British HiTens, 80 / 1,000ths of an inch thick, tapering to 40 / 1,000ths, and immensely strong. "They saved the day time and time again," says Scott.

● May 25. After sorting rucksack loads, Scott and Upton jumar back up the rope they have left in place to the previous day's high-point; Scott climbs a further 30 feet. The day's

worst problems are caused by a vertical band of micaceous schist ("apt name," says Scott)—rock of treacherous, earthy looseness. Scott bivouacs that night on a three-foot-wide ledge, Upton in a hammock slung from the rock above. "Eight hours sleep," says Upton. "The best night of the holiday."

● May 26. Scott climbs a further 130 feet up a prominent groove, overcoming several large roofs. But he is halted by a large block of rock that is obviously loose—a dangerous problem. Scott has been in pain all day from acute diarrhoea, the result of eating five packets of dried fruit ("a mistake," he concedes). He decides to abseil back to the ground to spend the night there.

● May 27. Scott recovers, and worries about the loose block. But, on the ground, he is at least able to reconnoitre the route above. "Up there, with the rock overhanging all the time, it was very difficult to see where to go."

● May 28. Scott returns to the block and, as he pegs round it, tries to ignore the rising symptoms of fear—fast breathing, a dry throat. Upton, belayed below, is aware of the danger: if the block comes away he will almost certainly be dragged down by the rope too. But the block holds; Scott surmounts it, and assaults the crux of the route, a continuous 80-foot overhang. At the very lip of the overhang, he dislodges a rock: it hits the ground 150 feet out. Scott belays above the overhang, brings Upton up, and continues up the final 150 feet. The rock now is almost vertical: "Beautiful," says Scott. He reaches the top and Upton follows. Terry and Lee, who have been laboriously depegging the route, reach the loose block and bivouac.

● May 29. Lee and Terry reach the top; the Scoop has been conquered. "There was relief that it was all over," says Scott. "It was a good team effort and we were glad we'd done it—but thought, now let's get out. None of us were really comfortable on it at any time. But probably if we do a few more, this kind of climbing will come as naturally as climbing that's only vertical." *June 15 1969*

Pitch 1, the Scoop: the Hebridean wind tugs at Doug Scott's rope.

Driving round Brands at the limit of a champion's nerve ends

Graham Hill, who has since died in a plane crash, talked Brian James round a pre-Grand Prix ride at Brands Hatch. "In 100ths of a second," he reflected, "you make major decisions that some people don't face in a lifetime. It's not like choosing wallpaper."

BRANDS HATCH CIRCUIT

Westfield Bend
Portobello Straight
Dingle Dell
Hawthorn Bend
Dingle Dell Corner
Hawthorn Hill
Stirling's Bend
Pilgrim's Drop
Druids Bend
Pilgrim's Rise
Bottom Bend
Bottom Straight
Paddock Bend
Clearways
Start/Finish

The Grid. First time I'd seen a motor race I was driving in it! All they told me was: "Watch the flag, then give it all you've got." I snaked up the road like a rocket, and found I was in the lead. "Hell," I thought, "What do I do *now*?" The start is the most thrilling moment. Inside the car you are shut off . . . waiting. One eye on the flag, one eye on the rev counter and one eye looking for gaps in case the bloke in front stalls— three eyes, and you need them all. A bloke behind got off to a flier and whacked me up on to the bank on the left. I'd only gone 50 yards, and it was all over. It's worse in the wet. I missed my braking once, water was gushing up through the floor. The pedals got wet,

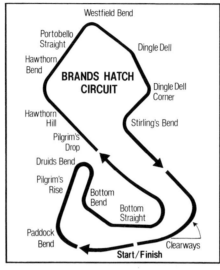

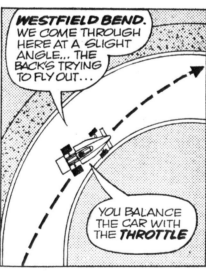

Hawthorn Hill. We're climbing, also braking for the next bend. The nose really gets onto the ground. With 40 gallons of fuel, about 300lb, the tyres squash out and the whole thing feels like a London bus. You have to be braced to resist the 1.4 G force, nearly one-and-a-half times the weight of your body wanting to fly out sideways on these curves. Your head, feels a bit of a lump and your neck muscles take a

hell of a hammering.
Westfield Bend. Out of Hawthorn Bend, along Portobello Straight, which we take very, very fast . . . and then brake very, very hard. At Westfield, it's a tight-rope act. You've got to be accelerating all the time and you've only so much grip through the tyres. It's all done by the canals in your ears . . . and you balance with the throttle.
Dingle Dell. Coming out of Westfield,

ripples on the track really jiggle the car up and down. It rattles your eyeballs. You blink and press on. After this you dive into Dingle Dell at 140 mph; cars tend to hit the ground, really skate down like a sledge.
Dingle Dell Corner. A funny old corner. You are so low you can't see the turn until you are on to it—all that undergrowth on the right. You take the bend from memory. A foot out com-

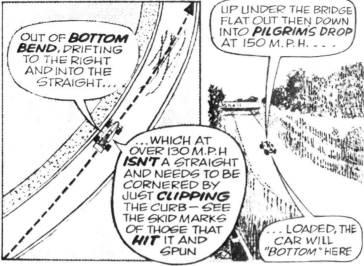

OUT OF **BOTTOM BEND**, DRIFTING TO THE RIGHT AND INTO THE STRAIGHT...

UP UNDER THE BRIDGE FLAT OUT THEN DOWN INTO **PILGRIM'S DROP** AT 150 M.P.H. ...

...WHICH AT OVER 130 M.P.H **ISN'T** A STRAIGHT AND NEEDS TO BE CORNERED BY JUST **CLIPPING** THE CURB—SEE THE SKID MARKS OF THOSE THAT **HIT** IT AND SPUN

...LOADED, THE CAR WILL "BOTTOM" HERE

and my foot slipped off the brake onto the throttle. Water flies off those big tyres and you scream off through a fog, taking the first corner by instinct. All very dodgy.

Paddock Bend. If you brake coming up the slight rise before the corner, you get the benefit of the slope. If you leave it until you hit the top, you don't actually become airborne but you feel yourself floating. It's fairly critical. You have to be accurate to within about five yards—at 150 mph! Lost a back wheel here once. Dumped on the track, bleeding like a pig—scared my mechanics spitless.

Druids Bend. This is very tight, a real bloody traffic jam. Inside or outside

there can suddenly be room for a spurt. Once driving a little A35, I slid through the inside when two blokes were so busy banging each other they didn't see me.

Bottom Bend. If you are not careful here you skin your rival going in, and if he's a bit clever he'll out-accelerate you coming out. The trick is to clip the inside curve, then drift to the right for the next left-hander. If you hit the curb too hard, you'll get pushed off line, put too much wheel over, you'll spin off.

Pilgrim's Drop. Stand on the throttle. We're flat-out, looking to pass under the bridge at 150. I once ended up with a bump on the head that made me look like a unicorn.

Red Baron

Big-time motor racing in the USSR is enjoyed by a minority—of one: none other than Leonid Brezhnev, all-powerful Soviet president, and general secretary of the Communist Party, who has a large private collection of foreign cars.

Apparently the 70-year-old supremo is beginning to view Moscow as his own Silverstone. Earlier this year he had one of the main streets, Prospekt Mira, closed off so that he could zoom down it in one of his Western models, with the rest of the Politburo hard at his bumpers in their chauffer-driven Russian-made official cars. No prizes for guessing who won.

Obviously Mr B does not read his own official sports paper, Sovietsky Sport. This year readers have written in inquiring why it does not report Western Grand Prix racing. Answer: "Don't let's forget that in the West car racing is controlled by businessmen. It's a circus rather than a sport. Victories are bought and sold, and a man's standing is assessed by how many dollars he has earned for himself and his bosses. True, racing drivers are brave men. But in a bourgeois society their courage is meaningless. They are only appreciated as long as they can make money."

See you at the circus, Leonid.

October 9 1977

CLEARWAYS TRICKY BECAUSE OF ADVERSE CAMBER WHICH CAN EASILY LEAD TO AN OFF-COURSE EXCURSION

BACK TO THE **START/FINISH** WHERE THE PIT SIGNALS WILL TELL ME IF I'M ON THE BALL...

...NOW ON TO THE NEXT LAP

pletely buggers the corner.

Clearways. Another dodgy old corner, it falls away to the left and you can't see it until you're there. The car gets very light and you wash right across the road. Concentration is crucial. When we had front-engined cars with the hot pipes I once had third degree burns and not known it until I got out.

Start-Finish. Get ready to read pit

signals. You take in three bits of information—position, lap time and how much ahead or behind you are—at 140 mph. If you're down, you may have to take a corner a foot shorter, brake a yard deeper. You can pick up a tenth of a second at every corner. That's a second a lap. Racing today is all about fractions. In one Grand Prix only 1¾sec. separated 25 cars. There's no way you hang about. *July 14 1974*

Jesse's Other Snub

One of the great sporting legends of history has finally been put into perspective in an interview that Jesse Owens, the winner of four gold medals at the 1936 Berlin Olympics, has given to America's Track and Field News.

Speaking about Hitler's famous refusal to shake hands with him, Owens, now 61, says: "That did not bother me. I did not go over there to shake hands with Hitler. I went to run, and I was not running against Hitler, but against the best that 54 other nations had to offer."

Later in the same interview, Owens talks about the way of life he had to return to in the United States, providing an uncanny foretaste of the treatment that Muhammad Ali received on his return from an Olympic triumph nearly 30 years later. "I came back to my native country and I could not ride in the front of the bus. I had to go to the back door. I could not do national advertising because the South would not buy it. I was not invited to shake hands with Hitler, but I was not invited to the White House to shake hands with the President, either. This was the social stigma we lived under."

October 6 1974

Reluctant star who shows them all the way home

Although he received less of the limelight than was accorded some other stars of the British Lions triumphant tour of New Zealand in 1971, winger Gerald Davies had joined rugby's immortals. A modest man, he was content simply to beat his man and win the game.

by John Hopkins

In the bleak midwinter long, long ago frosty winds weren't the only moans that were heard around rugby grounds. People often complained about the lack of use of wings. However, in this particular bleak midwinter, wings are something to look forward to, and none more so than Gerald Davies, the jinking, twinkling right wing for London Welsh and Wales, who will soon be in international action to cheer us all up.

More so than any other player on the contemporary rugby scene Davies can light up a whole game with one move, either a long run or a short, darting run that is over in the bat of an eye and usually ends in a try.

This latter is the quintessential Davies—a tight situation in which he can use both his sidesteps and his remarkably quick acceleration. Which one he chooses to get past an opponent depends on how much room he has and how many men he has to beat. In any case he chooses instinctively.

He comments on his technique shown in the pictures here.

Other players can tell what makes him the world's best right wing. "Of all the right wings I have played with," says John Taylor, a club and international teammate of Davies's, "Gerald is more conscious than any of what is going on around him. He can run flat out and when he does he will probably get there. But he can also make quite sure that if there is any chance of his being caught he will pass the ball in time."

Davies is a self-assured, though quiet person. He doesn't worry about opposing full-backs because he expects them to worry about him. That is a statement of fact not braggadocio.

December 23 1973

"I encourage the defender to think I am going to run straight past him by running to his left. At this point I just want to get him moving to cut down his options."

"Now he is moving to his left, I can move to his right, which is what I wanted to do all along. I come in off my right foot and sidestep past him. He is off-balance so he cannot recover in time."

"He makes an attempt to recover and he does get one hand back across in front of me. But because I have wrong-footed him it's only a half-tackle. I can brush it aside."

"Now I'm clear. With the defender left sprawling I can go hard for the line."

The 'cockney cool' of Jimmy Greaves the shooting star

Jimmy Greaves epitomised the London footballer, self-confident, ebullient, impertinent. His total of 357 First Division goals is a record. Adept at making something from nothing, he was an unmatched opportunist, aware of where chances would emerge, as shown in these drawings and analysis when he was playing for Tottenham Hotspur.

by Paul Trevillion

A Greaves likes to take the ball right up to a defender before beating him. By doing this he forces the defender to jockey back on his heels, so catching him flat-footed at the moment he accelerates past. This means Greaves is a yard ahead before the defender has had time to turn and pursue. A less-confident forward who pushes the ball wide of the defender too soon allows him time to turn and get in another tackle.

B Instead of challenging for the ball in a packed goalmouth, Greaves will leave it to a teammate and make for a spot where, if he receives the ball, he will be in a perfect position for a crack at goal. Greaves times his run—usually on the blind side—to arrive at the open space the same time as the ball. The less gifted striker will run into the space too soon causing defenders to follow and so plug the gap. Unfortunately in some matches Greaves will make as many as 30 such runs and never receive the ball. It is on these occasions that he is wrongly accused of contributing nothing to a match.

C The Greaves genius is seen at its best when he runs on to a fast-travelling through ball. Without checking his speed, Greaves will, simply by dipping his shoulders, either to the right or to the left, race past two or three bewildered defenders without once touching the ball. So unlike George Best, who likes to kill the pace of the ball as he feints, then dummies his way past the defenders with the ball, at all times, glued to his feet.

D When Greaves bursts through, he rarely has to make the vital decision of when to shoot. He takes the ball so close the goalkeeper is forced to commit himself and this is the signal for Greaves to jab it home. This jabbing action withdrawing the foot as soon as the ball is kicked, allows him to kick the ball without any check in his running stride, and denies the goalkeeper the chance of anticipating his shot.

November 30 1969

Holding steady, Holding fast: a hard time for English timber as the defences crumble

Photographs by Patrick Eagar

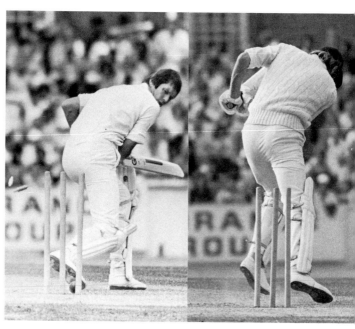

Balderstone 151–3. The first duck. On the front foot to a ball well up to him. He dropped his bat too late and the ball hit the off stump. Like most of the others, he was undone by sheer pace.

Greig 303–5. Twenty minutes before stumps. Greig had middled one drive. He i in no position to middle this. His flying bail were the signal for the worst pitch invasion so far. Drunks and kids. Not good.

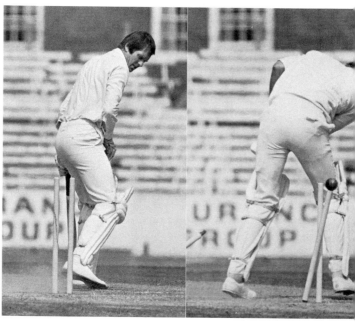

Balderstone 64–3 in second innings. A pair of spectacles . . . presented to Alec Bedser to help his search for new talent? Another near-yorker: this time the off-stump is flying. Holding had already removed the openers.

Greig 78–5. The picture for once does no tell the story. Greig takes guard with his ba off the ground. The target has to be the bottom of the leg stump—a tiny bullseye Holding hits it with his first super-fast ball

The England-West Indies Test series of 1976—which subsequently turned out to be the last major confrontation played out free from the shadow of Kerry Packer—resulted in a triumph for the West Indies, who beat Tony Greig's side by an almost humiliating three Tests to nil. The batting of Greenidge, Fredericks and Richards gave them an enviable foundation, but it was the fast bowling of Holder, Daniel, Roberts and Holding that destroyed England time and again. And it was Michael Holding (left), unknown to English batsmen before this tour, whose speed and hostility took the major honours. In the final Test at the Oval he took 14 wickets at the cost of a mere 10 runs each, and this despite a fine double century by Dennis Amiss for England. This remarkable sequence—a record of the nine occasions on which he hit the stumps—is a tribute to his stamina, his aggression and, above all, his sniper's accuracy. The commentary is by Robin Marlar.

August 22 1976

Underwood 323–6. Over goes the nightwatchman's brazier. Tail-enders are often beaten by pace, and pace is harder to play if the ball is pitched well up to the batsman. It was Holding's ace in this game.

Amiss 343–7. The double-century man bowled behind his legs. He went from 199 to 203 with a tickle. This was to be another. His new method—back foot to the off stump—makes room for the stroke, but the back door was open.

Knott 411–8. The lonely lion on the Prudential cap is, alas, no insurance against dragging one on to his leg peg. Knott is superstitious. See the protruding handkerchief. That was no protection, either.

Selvey 411–9. First ball. The batsman stands flat-footed. He, too, dragged this one on. And look at Selvey's so-called boots. Can any quick bowler make out a case for not supporting his ankles? These are just shoes.

Knott 196–8. Middle stump this time. Holding is entitled to be tired by now, but he is still bowling straight and hitting timber—nine bowled out in a bag of 14. And who could fail to respond to this enthusiasm?

"Her right-hand strength is equivalent to the average in 10 physical education men"

Margaret Court won the Wimbledon singles title for the third time in 1970. The week before the final she was sent by *The Sunday Times* to the Medical Research Council's National Institute for Medical Research in Hampstead, London. There she was measured on a grip dynamometer and other machines and the results compared to those from tests on men and women of varying ways of life. Dr Reginald James Whitney, who carried out the tests, and John Ballantine, our tennis correspondent, commented.

BODY SIZE

	Height	Weight
Average British Woman (2,884 were measured)	5ft 3¾in	9st 4lb
Women athletes (10 measured at Hampstead)	5ft 6½in	10st 6lb
Margaret Court	5ft 8¾in	11st 3lb

Dr Whitney: "Clearly, athletes are taller and heavier than average. Mrs Court is a big girl, with a good pair of legs, relatively long arms and longer and wider hands than average. But she's no Amazon."

Ballantine: "Many of Margaret's opponents are psychologically overwhelmed by her size and obvious strength, and are beaten before they start. This doesn't apply to Mrs King, although Billie Jean has said that, when you play Margaret, you get the impression that her arms nearly reach the ground.

"Mrs Court's magnificent physique means that she sees more of the court, and serves harder from higher up. Also, it enables her to cover the net and 'kill' most smashes. Adversely, her height means that she labours when running up and down court—going back for lobs, for instance."

BODY SHAPE

	Average woman (27 checked)	Athletes (10 checked)	Margaret Court
Leg length as a percentage of height	54%	56%	58%
Arm length	21¾ to 24⅝in	—	26¾in
Hip breadth	12¾ to 17in	—	15in
Shoulder breadth	15¼ to 21⅛in	—	18½in

Dr Whitney: "Although Margaret has very long arms, she has moderate breadth of hip and shoulder. But it's difficult to reach conclusions about ideal size and shape on the basis of just one player."

Ballantine: "Teddy Tinling, the Wimbledon dress designer, told me once that for Ann Jones and Christine Janes he had to make up dresses two sizes bigger on their racket side. The difference, normally, is far more noticeable in the over-developed racket arms of, say Rod Laver, Roger Taylor and Tony Roche."

HAND SIZE

	US Servicewomen and Nurses		Margaret Court		
	Mean	Range	R/Hand	L/Hand	Mean
Hand length	6⅞in	6 to 7¾in	8in	7⅝in	7⅞in
Palm breadth	3in	2⅝in to 3⅝in	3⅜in	3⅜in	3⅜in
Number of times breadth goes into length	2.3	2.2 to 2.3	2.4	2.3	2.35

Dr Whitney: "Margaret has relatively large and strong hands, the right longer and stronger than the left."

Ballantine: "Handsize is probably hereditary, since players vary enormously in this respect."

HAND-GRIP STRENGTH

	Grip strength	
	Right Hand	Left Hand
Average women of all ages (10 tested)	63¼lb	54¼lb
Average women under 30 yrs. (7)	76½lb	64½lb
Athletes (5)	92lb	85lb
Margaret Court	121¼lb	73¾lb

Dr Whitney: "The most amazing thing about Margaret is her right-hand (racket-hand) strength of grip, which is equivalent to the average we found in 10 physical-education men from St Mary's College, Twickenham. She's much stronger in her right hand than the left. The left is well above average for normal women, but comparable with that of other female athletes."

Ballantine: "All players know how important grip strength is in the racket hand. Fred Perry carried a squash ball in his pocket and squeezed it whenever possible to build up palm and finger power. Lew Hoad and Rod Laver have enormously strong racket hands, and pick up low volleys like ping-pong balls."

STANDING JUMP

	Average Jump	Range of several jumps
Normal women (6 tested)	15¼in	10½ to 19 inches
Skiers (8)	15½in	14 to 20½ inches
Athletes (2)	19¾in	15 to 22 inches
Margaret Court	21in	19 to 22¾inches

Dr Whitney: "Margaret was greatly above average compared with non-athletes, though some normal women leap astonishingly well. Women athletes are not always good jumpers, but Margaret Court made the highest jump of all the women we have tested. One man high jumper went up to 30in.

"Upwards propulsive force depends as much on co-ordination as on sheer strength. Margaret jumped very economically and her degree of motivation was interesting; after three

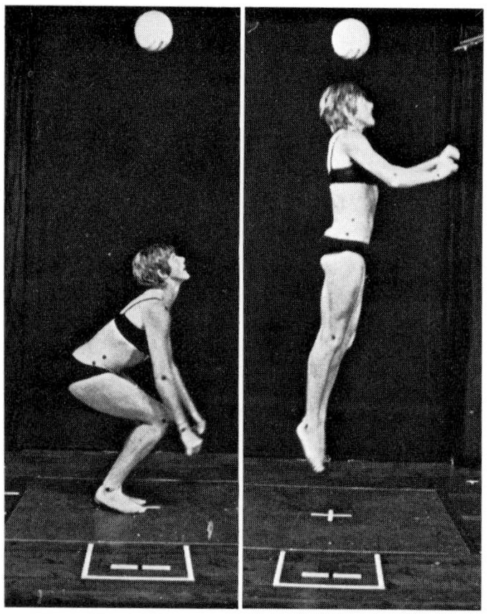

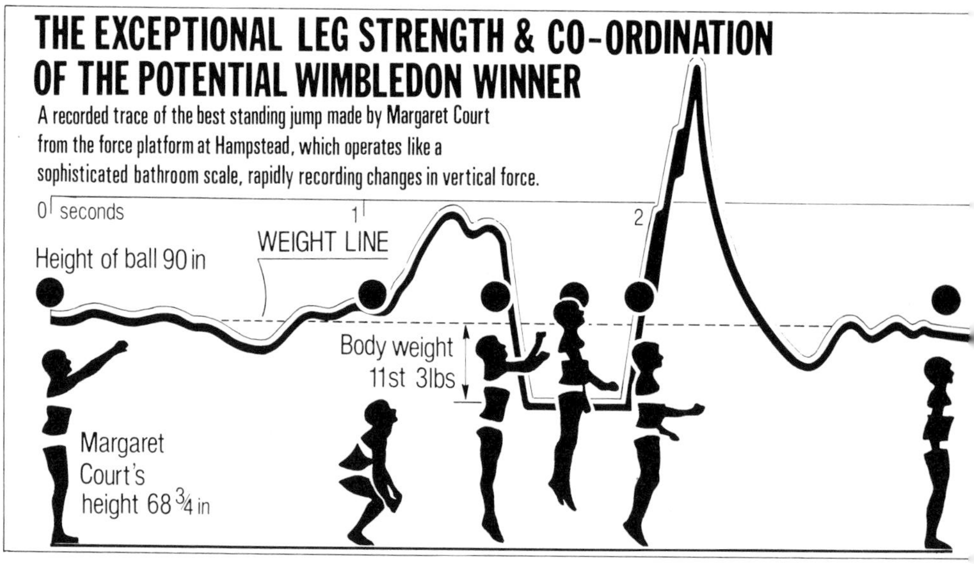
THE EXCEPTIONAL LEG STRENGTH & CO-ORDINATION OF THE POTENTIAL WIMBLEDON WINNER
A recorded trace of the best standing jump made by Margaret Court from the force platform at Hampstead, which operates like a sophisticated bathroom scale, rapidly recording changes in vertical force.
0 seconds
1
2
Height of ball 90 in
WEIGHT LINE
Body weight 11st 3lbs
Margaret Court's height 68 3/4 in

jumps she complained about not having time to jump again. She was certain she could do better. It showed how much ability she has to move and to change direction. Her three jumps were progressively better.

"How much is inherited and how much developed we don't know."

Ballantine: "Twelve years of training in places like Frank Sedgman's gymnasium in Melbourne, and leaping about courts for hours each day, have given Margaret her great jumping power."

Dr Whitney's conclusions: "In many characteristics other than her size, which is individual, Margaret resembles other women athletes, but she is far stronger in the right hand, and in the strength of her leg action, than other women we have tested.

"As a result of our tests on this one player, if I were asked to advise on the physique and strengths coaches should be looking for in aspiring tennis players, I would go for a tall woman like Margaret because she *starts* by being stronger. It's strange that most players I see today seem to be short."

Ballantine's conclusions: "The perfect physique for tennis would probably be one slightly shorter than Mrs Court's, but with the same magnificent muscle-power, co-ordination and movement. The era of "the good big 'uns"—Fred Perry, Don Budge, Bob Falkenburg, Dick Savitt, Jack Kramer, Tony Trabert—*does* seem to have passed in favour of little 'tennis tigers' like Chuck McKinley, Lew Hoad, Ken Rosewall and Rod Laver.

"If Billie Jean King, who is tiny, wins on Friday, it will be another triumph for the small player who has a lower centre of gravity, and so is nearer to the court and can get down to service returns more easily than the lanky one." *June 28 1970*

An early warning of anti-missile tactics to beat the Rocket

by John Ballantine

Tomorrow at Wimbledon Laver sets out to try to prove again that he is the greatest tennis player of all time. Even players who have beaten the Rocket find it hard to explain how they did it, for his weaknesses are only tiny chinks in his armour.

He has a tendency to start slowly while ranging his shots, to serve double faults with his unremarkable service when a wind blows the ball about; he has a dislike of slow high bouncing balls, and a forehand that is powerful but relatively more inconsistent than his backhand.

But the measure of a champion's greatness is his ability to overcome weaknesses and to understand Laver's is to appreciate his strength. Six players who have beaten him in the last two seasons describe below how they did so. Significantly, four are left-handers and another, Cliff Drysdale, has a double-handed backhand like a left-hander's forehand.

June 20 1971

PS. Laver did not reach the final in 1971. He was knocked out by Tom Gorman, who in the round before had defeated Cliff Drysdale.

  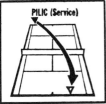   

Roger Taylor, of Sheffield, beat Laver last Wimbledon 4—6, 6—4, 6—2, 6—1: "You've got to believe you can beat him. I limited him to playing the shots he least likes by getting in my first serve and hitting my first volley very deep to pin him to the baseline, and forcing him to hit the ball awkwardly off his toes. "The wind stopped him serving well, whereas I served real good slices and kickers, and kept close to the net. If he came up, I lobbed him or hit acute angles.

"I tried to keep the pressure hard on all the time, and whenever I had a chance for a kill I hit the ball hard enough to stop him bringing off one of those fantastic passes. My beating him made other fellows believe they can do it."

Cliff Drysdale, of South Africa, beat Laver at Forest Hills and at Bristol two seasons ago: "I imposed my own pattern of play on him, using my double-handed backhand to take his serve early and hit cross-court under, or past him.

"His service is not the best among left-handers and I had confidence to hit it hard, return low balls into difficult postions, particularly to his backhand side.

"In rallies, I kept the ball on his forehand; it's powerful but more vulnerable. And I served mainly that side, too, because he's developed this dangerous early-ball topspin backhand, which he hits so quickly you can't see its direction. Occasionally he has a spasm of double faults, but it's rare for him to fail to rise to a crisis."

Nikki Pilic, of Yugoslavia, defeated Laver at Wills' Bristol Open last June 6—3, 1—6, 6—3. "I kept the ball very low and whenever I had a choice, hit to his forehand side which is weaker, if it's possible to use that word. He wanted to beat me very much—it was the final—and in the second set, he passed me as he pleased. I ran desperately for impossible balls.

"But in the final set, at 3—3 I hit two passing shots which were, on grass, just enough to get me the break. I gambled and hit a lot of hard backhands; he switched to my forehand late in the match, but then it was too late. I swung slice serves into his body to cramp him and stop him taking a full wide swing. He dislikes playing against left-handers."

Mark Cox, of Leicester, beat Laver on dew-wet grass under floodlights in the Australian championships in Sydney in March: "I didn't have any set plan; that can be fatal against his class. Rod began slowly, ranging his big drives and some went out and he lost confidence. He can't change to a steady game because he always attempts to hit and dominate.

"I served well and hit cross-court forehands to his forehand, and won most rallies on the wet court. I dictated the play and just managed to scrape out in tie breaks.

"Rod was using a new racket for commercial reasons and he was unsure on the slippery court; it's very rare for him to allow an opponent to make the running like that."

Dennis Ralston, of America, beat Laver in the last US Open quarter-finals 7—6, 7—5, 5—7, 4—6, 6—3: "I served and volleyed particularly well and hit many acute angles short that either passed him cleanly or stretched him so that he was set up for the next pass.

"Keeping the pressure on hard is crucial against him. I had to stick with him through his purple patches when there's nothing you can do. I happen to have a style that doesn't suit him; hitting the ball staccato and using extreme angles and it worked.

"Often, he plays fantastically for a set or two, and then slumps a bit; at those moments I screwed up the pressure. There are so many high-calibre players today he's bound to lose occasionally."

Tony Roche, of Australia, handed out Laver his heaviest defeat, 6—3 6—1, in the last Irish final in Dublin: "I caught Rocket on an off-day. He'd just lost to Taylor at Wimbledon and didn't feel happy. I played my own best game against him, not changing because it was him.

"Many players make the mistake of trying to hit harder, and beat themselves. I served the same way I do against other left-handers, slicing into his body from the right court and wide to his forehand from the left. He clipped his returns at the start, as he often does until he gets confidence to go over (topspin) his shots.

"It's not really possible to pinpoint any certain weaknesses, except in odd matches. I rely on my own strokes."

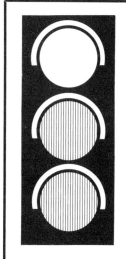

Red may
mean you
can only
get it
short
of the
green ...

... but
you've
got to
be aware
of an
amber
light ...

Stop... look... and listen... a fairway code devised by a human data process

At the beginning of 1975, America had discovered a new golfing hero in Johnny Miller. He brought the world of the computer to the game in order to sharpen his precision and banish chance and emotion from his game. Here he explains his mental techniques.

by Dudley Doust

Johnny Miller appears to have constructed a solid mental attitude towards golf which, should it survive the inevitable gales of defeat over the next several years, will allow him to follow Ben Hogan and Nicklaus as the finest active player in golf. "When I start losing," he said, with admirable caution, "I don't think I'll go into a mental slump and start throwing things at my wife."

At 27, Miller is remarkably mature. There can be few players of his age who strive for such a comprehensive view of their work. He, like so many lesser golfers, has read his Norman Vincent Peale. Miller has absorbed the positive-thinking commandments and made them his own.

"You have to come to a golf course saying 'I'll enjoy playing this golf course and this is a super tournament.' Then you set about trying to win it by playing your own game and, above all, percentage golf," he said. "It's not a matter of going out on the first tee and saying to yourself, 'I've got to birdie these opening holes,' because that's not the way to win a tournament. You don't win tournaments by playing flat out all the time. Most people, when they think about winning, they try to change their game. I try—and I don't always succeed—to play the same whether I'm eight under par or eight over par."

After playing a shot, Miller will discuss it with his caddy, Andy Martinez, as they walk down the fairway. If the shot was a poor one, Miller will be careful not to specify what he did wrong; he'll simply "talk it through" again, this time playing it correctly. He explains this mental device with a corny lyric from Johnny Mercer: "You've got to accentuate the positive, eliminate the negative."

Conversely, if the shot was brilliantly brought off, the two men will discuss it and re-live it for days, weeks, even months. "I never make a good shot and not comment on it to Andy," said Miller, allowing a brief smile, "You know, I'll say 'Oh boy, I did this or that and it really felt good.' You shouldn't toot your own horn. But I'm trying to ingrain what I did and how it felt into my muscle memory."

Martinez, aglow, spoke from across the room. "Tell him about that shot at Pinehurst, John. Tell him about the 3-wood you hit into the green."

To young Martinez that 3-wood shot summons the same heroic nostalgia as a bridge blown up by a World War resistance fighter. In truth, the Pinehurst shot was probably the finest Miller struck in 1973, possibly the finest he has struck in his life. Played from the fairway of the second playoff hole, it carried 250 yards into the heart of the green and earned Miller a sudden-death triumph over Jack Nicklaus and Frank Beard in the World Open, last September. It is worth examining through Miller's own microscopic re-collection:

"I had been having a little trouble with my wood. I had been hooking it.

... and when it's green, it's all go, go for the pin

So when I got the ball, I just thought the word 'fade.' I said to myself, 'I'll take a long lead into impact, like Lee Trevino does, and then I'll just go ahead and relax and release it and, with all the tension, it should end up a pretty straight shot.' What I've learned through past experience is that a guy gets pumped up in a sudden-death playoff and he's apt to release with his right hand and hook the ball. So I tried to think 'fade' and picture a fade swing in my mind and relax. I hit a perfect shot to the pin."

At the delicious recollection, Miller did not smile. He was totally serious. "That shot," he concluded, "was an example of using past experience under pressure, knowing the problems I was having with a given club and being able to picture the compensation for it. Then, of course, being able to stick to my decision."

Such a clear conception of a problem and, even more impressive, being able to bring it off under pressure, suggests a physical and mental harmony rarely reached in sport.

As Miller stands over a shot he "programmed," all the variables must quickly be fed ("bango, bango, bango") into his computer-like mind: wind, lie, limitations of the club, pin, etc. Then

Miller, quite clinically, slots the resulting print-out into red, amber or green light compartments and plays the shot accordingly.

"You've got to look at the game very objectively and not try to buck the odds," he said. "Most people can't recognise the statistical chances they have in bringing off a shot. For example, if my lie is perfect, there is no wind, and I can get a good level stance, and the pin is accessible according to the way I'm hitting the ball that day, the computer says go, go for the pin. Try to knock it close." With that, Miller is totally committed to the shot.

"*That's* easy," he said. "The difficult thing is to distinguish and make up your mind between the amber and red lights. If you've got a lie that's sitting down a bit, or if you are up near the face of a bunker or maybe you're not hitting it good at the moment, you've *really* got to play the percentage shot, which may be into an ideal spot short of the green and take it from there. As I say, some people can't recognise an amber from a red."

The red itself is a vivid, indisputable warning. "If you've got five trees in your way, fellah, that's red. Get the ball back in play. Don't get cute. You'd be surprised how many people can't re-

cognise a red situation in golf."

Any conversation with Miller gets round, sooner or later, to the afternoon of June 17, 1973, the afternoon he scored that spectacular 63 to win the US Open at Oakmont. The round included nine birdies; Miller's rounds often include bushels of birdies. "You know," he said, almost apologetically, "some of these birdies have to do with where your ball finishes on the fairway. I don't mean just the lies. I mean the yardages from the pins."

Miller expanded: "My prime range with a 6-iron is from 155 to 160 yards. My 7-iron at most, goes 150 yards. That means if my ball finishes, say, 152 yards from the pin I'll have to choke down on the 6-iron and play the half-shot. That's not precise enough. I prefer to hit the shot solid."

Miller finished an orange juice. He has a pleasant way of talking. "People ought to think, 'If I laid down 100 balls right here and played 100 shots, what would my success ratio be?'" he said. "You see, very few people can judge the results of the same shot played over periods of five years or even 20 years. No, people want to play golf for now. And now is no way to play golf."

February 2 1975

Tiger, lion, beaver, greyhound, trotting horse: the man is like a flying menagerie

In the summer of 1968 British athletes were in training for the Mexico Olympics. David Hemery, a young "greyhound", was perhaps the most talented of several hoping to compete in the 400 metres hurdles. Just before the AAA Championships he talked about his own individual strengths and problems; and in the event the victory was his in Mexico City.

by John Lovesey

Which event in athletics demands that a man moves like a tiger, has the courage of a lion, the balance of a tightrope walker and the sheer dogged stamina of a beaver?

The answer is the quarter hurdles, in which Britain is so brimming with talent that if there were a 400 metres hurdles relay in the Olympics, we would be near favourites.

This optimistic view will be thoroughly tested during the Amateur Athletic Association Championships at the White City Stadium, London, next weekend. After the quarter hurdles, a clash to gladden the heart of anyone who ever despaired of a primeval excitement returning to the sport, it might be possible to forecast that we will have more than one Briton in the final at Mexico.

Why this has happened will remain among the mysteries of British athletics, but recently David Hemery, 23, currently our best hurdler, leaned across a table in the Crystal Palace restaurant and said: "I sort of paw the air. My foot goes out and I pull over my leg and then drive. Like a trotting horse."

He is what John Cooper, one of his rivals and the Tokyo silver medallist, would probably call "a greyhound." Hemery is 6ft 1½in tall and weighs 11st 11lb.

Cooper, valiant and popular, is like a fighter trying for a comeback, and he calls himself "a carthorse." He is the same height but his racing weight is 13st 2lb. Building himself up again, nearly four years after he was welcomed back home with banners across the street, Cooper consoles himself that it was two carthorses that came first and second in Tokyo. "Hemery," John Cooper remarks, "could go back."

But Cooper and Hemery have not only each other to contend with. There are also John Sherwood and Andy Todd, who last week ran Olympic qualifying times in Switzerland, and Peter Warden, who makes up for his lack of height (5ft 7in) with strength and bravery.

Not without cause the event has been called a man-killer, demanding the clearing of 10 hurdles, each 3ft high, between the start and finish. Until recently, Hemery's best time of 49.8 seconds, run in the USA in June, put him alone behind the American Ron Whitney as the second best in the world this year. He is comparatively unusual

The view from the ground of hurdler David Hemery in action: "I sort of paw the air, like a trotting horse".

as a quarter hurdler in that he takes 13 strides between the first and fifth hurdles, and 15 after that, because he can only hurdle well off the right foot.

"I could continue 13 strides until after the seventh hurdle," he says, "but at that point my stride automatically becomes smaller and I have difficulty accelerating my tempo to get 15s—it's quite a problem."

After a hurdler has gone 330 yards, a fatigue factor enters the reckoning. If a competitor lands off balance, without his body landing so that the weight is exactly over the foot, he staggers around using up more energy trying to regain it.

Hemery learned the technique here and in America. His father is a financial consultant in the USA, and David went there at 11 but has retained his right to run for Britain.

He is so nearsighted that he sees at 20ft what people with normal vision see at 200ft and Hemery believes his bad eyesight has helped improve his hearing. On a cinder track he listens for the sound of other competitors landing in the grit, calculating then like a bat in the dark how far ahead or behind he is.

In the 120 yards high hurdles, the vigorous thrust of his lead leg across the 3ft 6in high hurdles imposes a tremendous strain on the back of his hamstring and rather than run the risk of injury Hemery has stopped going over them.

But in some ways he misses the attractions that are peculiar to the shorter event. "When you're down for the start, you can see a tunnel through the hurdles. If you look up with your hands on your knees, it almost looks like a road along the tops—I wish it was. When you start, it's almost like a sea you're going through, and it feels like being buffeted by a wave if you hit a hurdle.

"At the end the athletes look as if they've come through the surf, all wet with sweat and strained."

When Hemery was learning to high hurdle he had cinders continually in his knees from falling. "You could have grown potatoes in my left knee," he says. But in the harsh facts of athletics he sees a direct relation to life. "On the track you get almost everything that hits you in life."

About Hemery's own event, a noted American coach called Dean B. Cromwell put it more bluntly in a book. "The 400 yards and 400 metres hurdles," he wrote, "were clearly invented with homicidal intent." *July 7 1968*

Fosbury approaching.

Spinning 180°.

Clearing 7ft.

Flopping.

The man who invented his way of jumping

by John Lovesey

High jumping backwards may not seem the easiest way to do anything except damage yourself, but a 21-year-old American named Dick Fosbury may win an Olympic Gold Medal doing just that.

His technique has been named the Fosbury Flop for the way that, after his approach run, he plants his right foot, spins a full 180 degrees and then launches himself backwards into the air. His uninhibited, child-like take-off and lack of fear (landing on his shoulder blades could conceivably shatter his spine) took him to 7ft 1in. and first place in the recent US Olympic trials.

Fosbury defends his style as being scientifically superior. "I've studied physics and engineering," he explains, "and jumping my way, I am less likely to hit the bar with my head, arms or legs."

For almost a century, the emphasis in the high jump has been on the method of bar clearance. An Irish-American named Mike Sweeney jumped 6ft 5⅝in. in 1895 with a modified scissors clearance known as the Eastern Cut-off, in which he tried to look through his own legs in mid-air. Then George Horine, clearing the bar on his side, jumped 6ft 7in. in 1912; his technique was named the Western Roll—because he was a West Coast American, as opposed to Sweeney, an East Coast American.

In the Thirties, the Straddle was introduced, where the jumper goes over with his stomach to the bar in the style used by all today's best jumpers—except Dick Fosbury. *July 14 1968*

PS. Like Hemery, Dick Fosbury won an Olympic gold medal in Mexico, where he jumped 7ft 4¼in.

The complicated business of just standing still

As the 1978-9 England tourists prepared for their Ashes campaign in Australia, the batting form of their captain was giving rise to concern...

by Robin Marlar

England's cricket captain Mike Brearley was one night last month to be found at the Old Gate House on top of Highgate Hill in London. He had gone to give a gracious thank you to the publican for help with his benefit. On the bar, visible to the point of being compulsive, was a jar of pontoon tickets at 10p a time. Each jar could, all being well, yield him £55: this was the ninth on that bar, and by the time the England players are celebrating New Year's Eve in Australia, there will be few tickets left in the 12th jar.

But we had not met to discuss the rights and wrongs of the benefit system. Instead, it was another stage in a dialogue about coaching which had begun earlier in the summer.

When a cricketer is in a bad trot, no one is as affected as the player himself. Escape is his only thought. But how? In the end he may disappear, like a pole vaulter in a pit of cushions, buried under the advice of well-wishers, qualified or not.

Even the average professional batsman has to find his daily bread at Himalaya level. There the Everest peak is halfway out of this world. Attaining it periodically is a motivation greater than money. At these heights the tuner is fine indeed: there is a wide but by no means obvious difference between the man who can be relied upon to plant the flag at the very top and the competent operator among the lower camps.

The hardest problems to solve, for players and coaches alike, are how to help someone wallowing like a buffalo in the Ganges back to an existence in the land of mystery and among performers at that height; how to lift the very good so that if they are not one of the natural greats they can perform in their sport as if they were.

Brearley took a lot of advice from well-meaning critics during the summer, myself included. I urged him to talk to Ted Dexter. He did. The advice given was to stand still, pick the bat up straight and avoid the early pick-up. Keen observers noticed that Brearley took this advice, albeit only marginally, and thereafter began to make some runs. His previous inability to do so raised the basic question of coaching at the highest level: in the event of a prolonged and serious loss of form, should change be a clean-cut break with the past, a dramatic change, or should it be a gradual, minimal change in the hitherto successful formula?

The suggestion that Brearley should pick the bat up early came originally from Tiger Smith, who now, at 92, is England's oldest Test cricketer, in an attempt to cure Brearley's self-confessed habit of falling to the offside, over-balancing in effect, so that onside strokes became impossible. Normally, a batsman of Brearley's years—he's 36—is leaving middle-age and entering full maturity. This is a time for final alterations in technique, for a return to the basic stance epitomised by the others—Bradman excepted.

When in doubt, there is no substitute for the classic stance. Brearley's change of technique in the summer of 1978 was marginal: so was the improvement in his scoring. His agony of runlessness, the reconciliation of mental and physical demands, represents just one of the problems which confront the man who would attempt to be a coach at the highest level. The problems are daunting. Several top players feel the need to seek advice: few of their peers have the courage to offer it. *October 15 1978*

W. G. Grace. W.G. stood like this, bat lifted and left toe raised. Photographs of the Grand Old Man from the bowler's end indicate a huge gap between bat and pad. It is hard to reconcile such a gap with an adequate defence against the ball cutting back from the off.

Jack Hobbs. What stance could be more calm, yet alert? Hobbs had one fast-bowling combination to face which carved itself into cricketing history—McDonald and Gregory on the tour of Australia in 1920-21. Notice that there is no bat handle visible above the top hand.

Peter May. The traditional stance for the young and green player: ideally equipped to play strokes on the offside because the front foot is advanced towards the offside, thus condemning him to restricted movement on the onside. Which error May overcame in his maturity.

Mike Brearley. Both feet are on the ground, which indicates that the movement of the bat is ahead of the delivery during the bowler's approach. Here we see the gap between the hands. This means that his bat is used for protection—of person and wicket—rather than for assault. Only with both hands together at the top of the handle can there be a full swing.

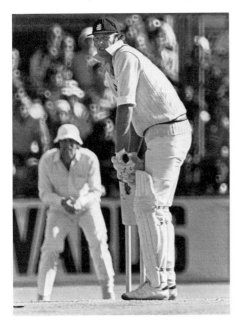

Tony Greig. The upright stance of a man taller than the rest. Notice the inches of bat handle above the top hand—more difficult to spot because of the raising of the bat, and the angle at which it is held. Stance apart, Greig could lay no real claim to be ranked with the others in this group.

Greg Chappell. A classic batsman in the Australian mould. The comparatively sharp angle between thigh and back throws the weight to the offside, and by doing so enables him, in my opinion, to be equally efficient on the onside—the Australian trademark.

Inside track

Jaw Jaw

Blah, blah, blah, blah. That's the sound of Britain's sports administrators talking about the provision of sports facilities for the people of Britain. They include Denis Howell, Minister of Sport, Sir Robin Brook, chairman of the Sports Council, Peter Lawson, general secretary of the Central Council of Physical Recreation.

All these worthies have pontificated time and again about opening up existing facilities belonging to schools, colleges, universities, the services and industry, that they are drastically under-used, and that, in the current economic climate with capital outlay severely restricted, the deprived public should have access as of right.

It's been said so often that it's almost a cliche, but progress has been abysmally slow. Meanwhile money has been found for the expansion of Lilleshall, building a skating rink in Manchester, opening a Centre of Excellence in Leeds next year. Fine for the elite, but we ignore the base of the pyramid at our peril.

All the high-flown phrase-making about aiming seriously at success in the Moscow 1980 Olympics is a nonsense if participation at grassroots level is impaired. The government leaves the responsibility for access to facilities to local authorities. The Government says it cannot legislate to make it compulsory.

Well, if the Government can order local authorities to cut their budgets, it can legislate to open up facilities to the paying public. Anything less now is a dereliction of duty. *November 14 1976*

PS. Since 1976 there have been no significant improvements made. In fact, it was established that the Department of Education and the Science was the stumbling block, impervious to appeals for a radical increase in community access.

● Olympic quote of 1972: "My premier," said Ho Jun Li, North Korea's small-bore rifle prone gold medallist, "advised me to imagine that I was shooting at the enemies of my country." *December 31 1972*

● No marks for guessing the only nation which allowed its unmarried men and women to sleep together at the European Championship village. The proof of the pudding is in the eating, and the tally on Sweden's official scoreboard at week's end was one medal, a silver in the all-rounders' event, the decathlon. *August 22 1971*

EXMOOR   SHETLAND   WELSH MOUNTAIN   HIGHLAND   DALE

The indulgent parents' guide to choosing a pony

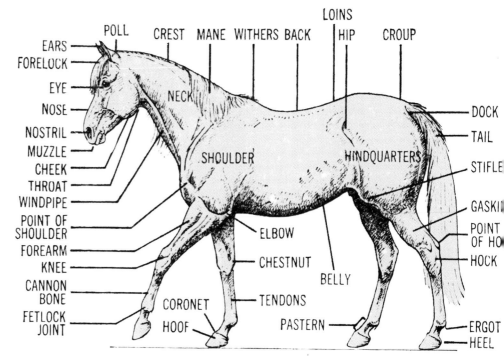

More than a million and a half people, at the latest estimate, ride for pleasure in Britain. A great proportion of them are children, and from them will come our future international riders. Many own their own pony, and the number who do so is increasing every year.

A pony, though deceptively small and furry, like a family dog, is in fact a scaled-down, more intelligent horse. He is a gregarious, gentle and somewhat nervous animal, with no great reasoning power but with an excellent memory which he uses cleverly.

A pony is greedy, and tends to over-eat in spring and summer. He needs a constant supply of fresh water and a fair amount of room to live and graze in (though unless there are real objections to riding a beast with a wet coat in bad weather, he does not need to be stabled); he needs his shoes removed and refitted every month or six weeks. But the cost and upkeep are not as high as might be imagined.

There are many books about the care of ponies, and on equipping, training and riding them, but for anyone with the space and the time to contemplate adding a large new member to the family the trickiest art is the most important of all—how do I go about buying one?

Note: this introduction to the pony was compiled in April 1973, and the prices quoted will inevitably have risen with inflation.

by Caroline Silver
Drawings by Christine Bousfield

Are you sure that you can cope with one?

● Don't buy a pony unless the child really wants one and understands that it will have to take on the daily responsibility of looking after it, regardless of the weather (if you don't get this clear at the start, you will probably end up looking after the pony yourself).

Ask yourself these questions:

Can you afford it (£100–£200 a year)?
Where will you keep it?
Has the child enough time (up to two hours a day)?
Is your area safe enough for riding (is there a lot of traffic), and varied enough to make riding every day enjoyable?
Are there other children to ride with (much more fun)?
Is there someone to look after it when you are on holiday?
Does the child fully understand the practical problems? Do you?

What kind should you think about buying?

● Within reason, let the child choose. It is important that the child likes the pony.
● Before looking at ponies for sale, decide abstractly what you want so that you aren't tempted by charming, but unsuitable, ponies.
● Get a pony about a hand (4in—hands are measured from the withers) too big. The child will grow into it soon enough, and out of it far too quickly. If you want to show it, remember the 12.2, 13.2, and 14.2 hands height limits for classes. A 12.3 pony, no matter how good a jumper, won't win jumping contests (but could be a bargain fox-hunter).

Ask yourself these questions:

What do you want to use the pony for?
How good a rider is the child?
What is the maximum you are willing to pay?

FELL   NEW FOREST   DARTMOOR   CONNEMARA

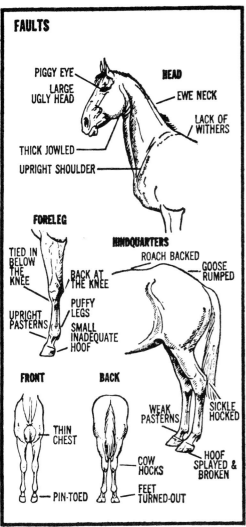

FAULTS

PIGGY EYE
LARGE UGLY HEAD
HEAD
EWE NECK
LACK OF WITHERS
THICK JOWLED
UPRIGHT SHOULDER

FORELEG
HINDQUARTERS
TIED IN BELOW THE KNEE
ROACH BACKED
GOOSE RUMPED
BACK AT THE KNEE
UPRIGHT PASTERNS
PUFFY LEGS
SMALL INADEQUATE HOOF

FRONT
BACK
THIN CHEST
WEAK PASTERNS
SICKLE HOCKED
COW HOCKS
HOOF SPLAYED & BROKEN
PIN-TOED
FEET TURNED-OUT

● A pony is an athlete, and should look like one. Compare the illustrations of faults (*above*) with the illustration (*above left*) of a nicely balanced pony. Here are some points to look for:

Head: small, alert, and proudly held. A pony with a large, heavy head is heavy on the reins.

Eyes: large and intelligent. Kind ponies have kindly eyes. Piggy little eyes reveal piggy little natures.

Withers: prominent, and back not too fat, otherwise the saddle will slip forwards or sideways.

Legs: smooth and cool to the touch. A pony whose legs are scarred or bumpy, if not actually unsound, will certainly be careless. Have him trotted towards you and away. If his feet swing out sideways, or alternatively if he almost crosses them over, avoid him. Don't buy him if he shuffles.

Pasterns: strong and springy. If nearly vertical ("upright") they will get jarred trotting on roads.

Feet: round and neat. If they are splayed, uneven, split, or cracked—especially if cracked from the top of the hoof down—don't have him.

Colour: immaterial. There is no such thing as a bad colour.

COST

Between £100 and £200. Don't economise if you don't have to: it's always worth paying a bit extra for your peace of mind.

HOW TO BUY IT

1. Buy a pony you know and like from a friend who has outgrown it.
2. Buy from a reputable dealer (one who's been in business for some time in the same locality). Tell him what you want and your price, so that he can find you a pony (if he hasn't got one in stock) that may be suitable. Try it out and buy it "subject to veterinary examination," so that if your vet objects to it you can send it back. And always choose a vet yourself, a member of the British Equine Association (you don't want a poultry vet): fee about £7. Try also to get a week's trial, but do not expect it—if *you* were selling a good pony, would you lend it to a stranger who might do it harm?
3. Buy your favourite pony at the local riding stable. This is a possible mistake, because you know him only as a hard-working member of a herd (ponies behave better in company). By himself and lightly worked, he might be a little brute.
4. Advertisements. May mean travelling miles, only to find that what the advertisement thinks is a beauty is, in your opinion, a wretch. Shipping the pony home can cost £20.
5. Sales. Avoid these—no opportunity to test the pony.

HOW TO TRY IT

Ask to see it caught—you don't want a pony who is difficult to catch. Have it walked and trotted past you, towards you and away from you, to see if it carries itself well, if it has nice springy strides and if its action is straight. Saddle it up yourself to see if it is well-behaved. Mount it and walk, trot and canter it. Put it over a small jump. Test it in traffic (safer to lead it, in case it fails).

... AND A WORD ABOUT CLOTHING

Never mind aesthetics—essentials are warmth, footwear that won't stick in the stirrups, leg covering thick enough to prevent painful rubbing by the stirrup leathers and a crash hat. If the hat is to be effective, it must be on the head at the moment of impact. My personal preference is for the kind of crash helmet used at Badminton—strapped on by a safety harness under the chin and, having no peak, difficult to knock off.

DON'T ☐ *Settle for a difficult pony. There are lots of nice ones.* ☐ *Buy a pony that isn't safe in traffic.* ☐ *Buy a pony under four. People say : "It will grow up with the kids." It won't : it will get worse. Young ponies require expert riders.* ☐ *Reject a pony over 12 because of its age. Provided it's healthy, an experienced old pony is a fine teacher.*

DO ☐ *When you first buy it, give it time to settle down. Moving is traumatic for a pony. Until it knows you and comes to meet you, leave a head-collar on it in the field with 12in. of rope attached. This will make it easier to catch.*

A master to the very fingertips — the all-embracing hands of Gordon Banks

A critical survey of the two greatest assets of England's—perhaps the world's—greatest post-war goalkeeper.

by Hunter Davies

He was sitting in the boardroom at Stoke, splaying out his hands on the table as if they weren't his but offerings on a fish slab. He apologised and said they weren't pretty. They just happen to be his livelihood.

He's wrong. As hands go, they are pretty. They're smooth and white, well cared for, well scrubbed. They're not big and hairy like Pat Jennings's, nor big and bony like Bonetti's. They're just ordinary, medium-sized, white-collar hands.

Laid out to rest, white palms up, they were almost feminine, soft from their daily bath. Then he held them in the air and Paul Trevillion, who'd been drawing and photographing them, almost averted his eyes. You could now see that almost every finger had been mangled. At least three were deformed, with bulging, obscene joints. And when he clenched his left fist one knuckle was missing. They may be his livelihood now. But in middle age his hands are clearly destined for arthritis.

He went over the geography, reeling off the battles and the breaks, from his worst one, a broken right wrist way back in his Leicester days during a friendly which kept him out for eight weeks, to his latest one during the summer in South Africa when he broke and dislocated his thumb. He was doing a four-week guest appearance for Hellenic. It happened in the first week, diving at someone's feet. The bone was sticking out and they appealed to the crowd for a doctor to shove it back in.

The missing knuckle (from the back of the little finger of his left hand) is a mystery. He first noticed it had gone about three years ago. "It must have been a collision or a kick. All they ever say is 'Can you play?' and if you say yes, you're straight back. Afterwards, unless it's a break or a dislocation, you forget about it. That's why they're so crooked. You play with many injuries which don't get a chance to heal properly."

In describing his best saves, he was much more explicit, remembering every move and every player involved. The save from the Pele header in Mexico he had to put first, not just because it is famous throughout the football world, but because it came at a time, with about 20 minutes gone, when England's morale could have been seriously deflated.

It was noticeable, with injuries and saves, that his right hand has done most. He's basically right-handed, always writing with his right hand, but he can use both—he plays snooker with his left, cuts bread with his left and uses a spoon with his left.

He didn't particularly want to be a goalkeeper. "You know what it's like as a kid. You take turns for one goal each because no one will go in. I found I did it well and quite enjoyed it so I got stuck with it." He got his first bad injury while playing with Chesterfield's A team—a fractured right elbow. He was in hospital for a week and they put a screw in it. "I suppose it's dissolved by now."

Being the last line of defence, whose mistakes can never be rectified the way a forward's can, is always a psychological problem for a goalie.

Banks still feels it, despite all these years at the top ("I'm 32 by the way. Put that down"). In all practice matches, five-a-sides in the gym or on the training pitch, even with the England squad, he never plays in goal but rushes around like an idiot, playing midfield and striker at the same time.

It's rare, in any sport, to find the Number One so universally acclaimed, inside and outside the business. You almost fear he's just the World's Number One in Britain, with every other country having its own World's Number One, till you look at the cuttings and see what Eusebio and Pele and the rest have said about him, all of them drooling.

Pele, of course, couldn't believe that Mexico save. Alan Mullery swears he heard Pele shouting "Goal!" as he waved his hands in the air. "I'm just as bad," says Banks. "When I see it repeated on the telly I look at myself and say it's not on. He won't save that. I don't know how I did."

November 7 1971

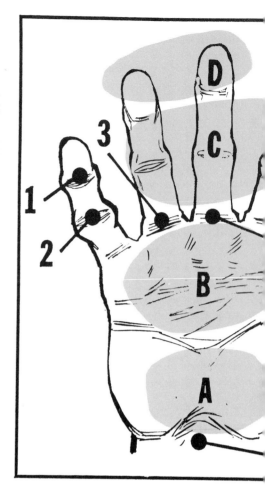

● **THE INJURIES**

1. Top joint little finger of the right hand: broken in the kick-around before a League match at Newcastle three years ago. In holding a practice shot from teammate Peter Dobing he trapped his little finger between the ball and the hard ground. Banks played the game despite the pain (score: 1–1).

2. Lower joint little finger: broken in a League match three years ago. Kicked while going down to an attacker's feet to take the ball. Little finger in splints. Out for six weeks.

3. Dislocated finger: kicked by an opponent in League match.

4. Dislocated finger: misjudged a hard high ball while playing at Leicester some years ago. The ball landed on top of his fingers.

5. Lower thumb: broken and dislocated this summer in South Africa while playing for Hellenic. Dived at opponent's feet. Out for three weeks.

6. Wrist: broken during Leicester days against Northampton Town in a friendly. Dived for a hard ball and fell awkwardly. Worst injury so far. Out for eight weeks.

7. Thumb, left hand: torn ligaments and dislocation after collision.

8. Third finger: broken bottom joint in collision.

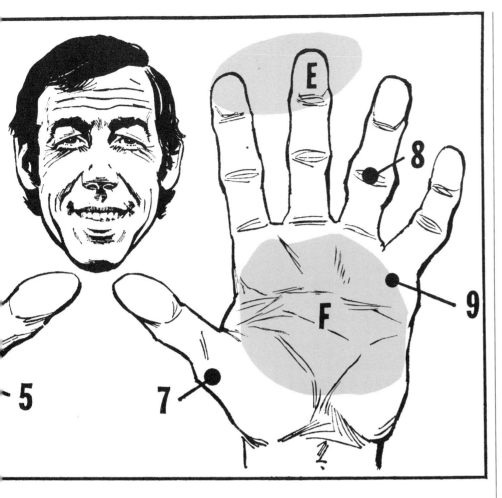

Cold Tip

Followers of the *Sunday Times* middle-age fitness campaign who haven't read about, or heard of, the unfortunate experience of the male American who carried on regardless of minus eight degrees centigrade weather, please read on. The poor man's frostbite plight was brought to the notice of the New England Journal of Medicine by Melvin Hershkowitz MD of the New Jersey Medical Center.

We quote: "From 7.00 to 7.25pm the jog was routine. At 7.25pm the jogger noted an unpleasant painful burning sensation at the penile tip. From 7.25 to 7.30pm this discomfort became more intense, the pain increasing with each stride as the exercise neared its end." So the guy got home, and "immediate therapy was begun." He divested himself of trousers etc., and "in a straddled standing position, the patient created a cradle for rapid rewarming by covering the penile tip with one cupped palm. Response was rapid and complete . . .

"Side effects: at 7.50pm the patient's wife returned from a local shopping trip, and observed him during the treatment procedure. She saw him standing, legs apart, in the bedroom, nude below the waist, holding the tip of his penis in his right hand, turning the pages of the New England Journal of Medicine with his left. Spouse's observation of therapy produced rapid onset of numerous, varied and severe side effects (personal communication)."

Like a trouper the man just wrapped more warmly and carried on jogging. Moral: protect the pudenda at all costs.
February 20 1977

● The cheap way to watch Henley, a friend tells us, is to row in it, badly. His club, by entering the eight-oared event, was given enclosure badges for the crew, coxswain and five spare boat-movers, plus three car park tickets—in effect, £73 worth of tickets and prestige. For this they spent ten guineas for the team entrance fee. So who cares if they lost on the first day? *July 6 1969*

9. Little finger: no knuckle left. Banks says it just disappeared about three years ago. Can't remember which match.

● **THE GREAT SAVES**

A. Pele: World Cup, Mexico, 1970. His most famous save. Pele himself thought it was in and even shouted "Goal!" Banks got the lower palm of his right hand to it and knocked it up and over.

B. George Best: League match against Manchester United at Stoke, 1969. Best was clean through when Banks advanced from his goal and saved Best's low hard shot with the middle of his right palm.

C. Francis Lee: League match last season at Manchester City. Lee free kick, saved with the bridge of the three fingers of right hand.

D. Wyn Davies: header, three years ago in League match against Newcastle at Stoke. Davies headed high ball from close range. Tipped over bar with the finger tips of his right hand.

E. Martin Peters: header, last season at Spurs. Tipped over bar with fingertips of his left hand.

F. Bobby Charlton: a Charlton thunderbolt from inside the box during League match at Stoke, 1969. Stopped with the palm of his left hand.

Crouch, throw, twist, serve, spin — how to shoot a sitting duck

In the autumn of 1970 a Japanese table tennis team invaded England. They won by 6 matches to 1 in London, 4 matches to 3 in Exeter, 5 matches to 2 in Birmingham, 5 matches to 2 in Thornaby-on-Tees, then flew out to Germany to continue their tour. One of the team was Shigeo Itoh, the reigning world men's singles champion, who introduced what looked like an unanswerable combination of short service and dauntingly fast forehand.

by Dudley Doust

Shigeo Itoh (below) and his fellow Japanese came to England last week and, after they left, there was little doubt why they were the table tennis champions of the world.

The best player in Japan's 3-man, 2-woman team is Itoh, 25. He is thought by many to be the fastest-moving player in the game, and, surely, is the one with the most deadly kill. Chester Barnes, Britain's No. 2, says: "I've never seen a ball hit so hard," and until Thursday Itoh seemed invincible.

Itoh's kill is with the forehand and, to favour it, he stands at the corner of the table, leaving the entire playing surface open to his right-hand side. Moreover, his cunning serve sets up this merciless slam. He serves it with such a trembling top-spin that his rival's return pops back, fat as a duck, for Itoh to kill. Denis Neale, Britain's No. 1, says: "There's no time for a go at the ball."

Neale returned Itoh's serve not only too high but suicidally deep and in London he was thrashed by the Japanese 18–21 and 11–21. Barnes, watching, learned and three days later played Itoh in Birmingham. "My idea was to return his serve just over the net," Barnes said later, "and stop him swinging. It messed him up, didn't it?" On his own part, Barnes served short and once the rallies got going he often scored by jamming the ball far wide of Itoh's forehand. Barnes beat the champion, 21–15 and 21–13.

Japan's cunning extended to doubles, where, before putting the ball into play, the server signalled beneath the table to his partner the nature of the depth and spin of the forthcoming serve: extended forefinger, crooked forefinger, extended little finger, crooked little finger, the fist. "And once the Japs find a weakness," says Neale, "they play to it—*every single shot.*"

Itoh graduated with an economics degree and now works for a table tennis equipment manufacturer. He runs 10 kilometres and spends three hours either at the practice table or in a gymnasium each day. So supple is he, in fact, that he can slide into a splits and touch his forehead to the floor. Itoh defends his world title next April in Tokyo against, among others, the two brightest names in the game these days: Communist China's Chuang Tse-tung, and a long-haired boy named Barnes   *October 25 1970*

PS. Itoh was beaten in the men's singles final in Tokyo in 1971 by Sweden's Stellan Bengtsson.

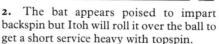

1. Itoh crouches, his bat below the table surface, then throws up the ball with his flat left hand and twists on his back leg.

2. The bat appears poised to impart backspin but Itoh will roll it over the ball to get a short service heavy with topspin.

3. Opponents see hope in the wide open spaces on Itoh's forehand. But the twisting top spin makes a low return difficult.

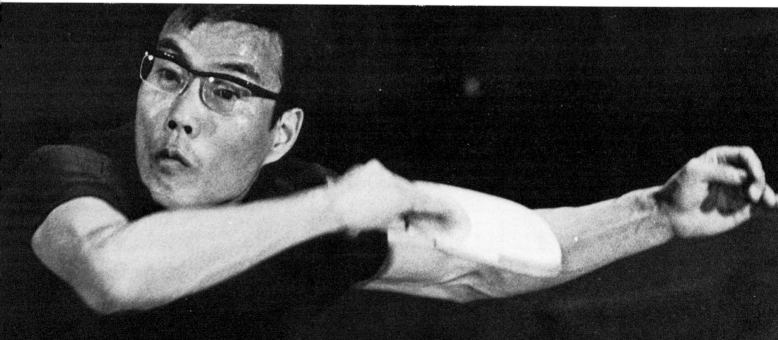

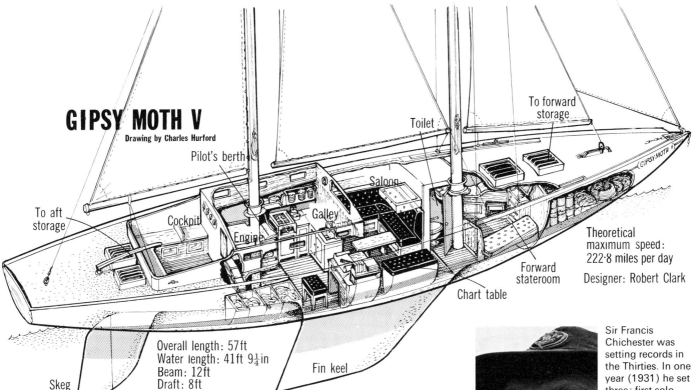

GIPSY MOTH V
Drawing by Charles Hurford

Pilot's berth

Toilet

To forward storage

To aft storage

Cockpit

Engine

Galley

Saloon

Theoretical maximum speed: 222·8 miles per day

Forward stateroom

Designer: Robert Clark

Chart table

Skeg rudder

Fin keel

Overall length: 57ft
Water length: 41ft 9¼in
Beam: 12ft
Draft: 8ft
Weight: 29 tons

Sir Francis aims to coax Gipsy Moth V into doing what no boat has ever done before

by John Lovesey

There are few objectives in sport which compare with the four-minute mile for mathematical symmetry and physical elusiveness. But at 69, Sir Francis Chichester has discovered one, and in its pursuit he will this week set sail from Plymouth, where he completed his circumnavigation in 1967.

His destination will be Bissau in Portuguese Guinea, and from that strange place he plans to set out from the Geba estuary during the first week in January for San Juan del Norte in Nicaragua, Central America. By his own calculation the distance, provided he backs up into the estuary for 55 miles, adds up to 4,003⅙ miles. His objective is to sail single-handed 200 miles a day, completing his voyage in 20 days.

Chichester's own speed record was set in 1967 during his round-the-world voyage, when he notched 1,408 miles during an eighty-day run to average 176 miles a day. That was in Gipsy Moth IV, designed by John Illingworth and a boat with which Chichester eventually expressed some disen-

chantment. "If I'd pressed it to its limit in the Southern Ocean, it would have turned over," he said.

The theoretical maximum speed of Gipsy Moth IV was 208.3 miles a day, while that of his new yacht is 222.8 miles a day. "No boat," Chichester said, looking round the cabin of Gipsy Moth V, "has ever done it."

Gipsy Moth V was basically conceived during a sail taken by Chichester in Sir Thomas Lipton with its designer Robert Clark, who also designed Chichester's 1960 Transatlantic winner, Gipsy Moth III.

"As soon as I saw it," said Chichester, "I wanted one like it. Clark drew out a plan on the back of an envelope and he never changed it a scrap. "It is a similar design to Intrepid (the successful America's Cup defender) with a fin keel, and skeg and rudder dish, like a big dinghy really." Chichester tapped the floor of the cabin with his foot. "There's really no bilge here at all."

The hull is so flattened off that the 7½-ton keel is simply bolted on. It is in shape rather like a dinghy's centreboard. She is rigged as a staysail ketch, her sails designed for downwind sailing rather than beating.

Sir Francis Chichester was setting records in the Thirties. In one year (1931) he set three: first solo flight in a seaplane from New Zealand to Japan, first to navigate over sea by sextant observation alone from New Zealand to Lord Howe Island, and first solo flight from New Zealand to Australia.

The main staysail, for example, is fastened in a conventional fashion on a track running up the mast, but is not fastened on to the main boom except by the clew at the end. This makes Chichester's yacht less efficient than a normally-rigged yacht for on-the-wind sailing because it is more difficult to tighten in the belly of the sail, but efficient for off-the-wind sailing.

To cram on maximum power, the yacht also has a main topsail to fill in the gap between the main and mizzen. "He's chancing his arm quite a bit, trying to get 200 miles a day," one expert at Buckler's Hard remarked, "but he might do it, provided he gets strong winds." *December 13 1970*

PS. This proved the last complete voyage Sir Francis made. Although he did not sail 4,000 miles in 20 days, he did set a record by sailing over 1,000 miles in five days. He died in 1972.

Curbing the bouncer: a case for revising cricket's woolly law

The technique of removing stubborn late-order batsmen no longer includes the fast, intimidatory short-pitched delivery. This ball, bowled during England's defeat of Pakistan at Edgaston, led directly to the designation of "non-recognised batsmen" and, incidentally, to the widespread use of protective helmets.

by Robin Marlar

The number of statements about last Monday's Iqbal Qasim incident in the first Test shows the care that modern managers have for the game and its players. Their motives are usually right, as they were in wanting more money for players in the pre-Packer days, and in seeking to increase the overs bowled per hour, and in wanting to limit the worldwide increase in *persistent* short-pitched bowling.

The superb picture here by Patrick Eagar shows the menace; the lonely Pakistani left-hander Qasim (1) is reeling from a hit in the mouth from the England fast bowler, Bob Willis (4), who has gone round the wicket so that he can get a better sight of the stumps. At first slip is his captain, Mike Brearley (2), whose responsibility for preventing bouncers being bowled at non-recognised batsmen is clearly laid down. With his hand behind his back is umpire Palmer (5), who cannot be excused from his responsibility for implementing the regulations on the grounds that there is a convention that umpires in their first few Tests should be seen and not heard.

Standing beside Palmer is Sadiq (3)

the non-striker, wearing one of the helmets batsmen have been forced to adopt because legislators and umpires have persistently failed to give them adequate protection.

My sympathies are wholly with the victim, but my understanding goes to Willis and Brearley because the present regulation imposed on the players represents bad law.

There seems no justification for protecting non-recognised batsmen from the occasional bouncer. In the old days tail-enders gave the ball some width if they couldn't cope. The sending in of a nightwatchman to block is a tactic designed to save wickets. Most nightwatchmen go off duty at dawn, but in cricket they become stubborn daytime defenders, drawing pace from both pitch and bowler, as Qasim was doing. A legitimate tactic against such defence is the occasional (never persistent) use of the bouncer. Furthermore, is it right that a fast bowler who may be a non-recognised batsman shall never be given a taste of his own medicine in the form of a bouncer? That, in my opinion, is an absurd proposition: not cricket.

Cricket, Brearley says, is a hard game. The blood flowed down Alfred Mynn's legs in the days before pads. I hate to see helmets, but rather them than support for regulations which unjustifiably binds Test captains and their fast bowlers.

That said, no one could be hotter than I in condemning *persistent* short-pitched bowling. Here the regulation is better: no more than three bouncers in two overs, though it might be better still if it said two in three: the ball is a surprise delivery, and not one intended to kill or maim. Tony Greig's published notion that cricket can be sold in the United States on "blood and bouncers" may yet be tested: if that is the approach of circus cricket, the sooner the great divide is dug between that and Test cricket the better.

To be fair to the Test and County Cricket Board, it has got this part of the regulations right in theory. Unfortunately, it is just not being implemented, either in our own cricket or, more especially, in the West Indies, where four short-pitched balls an over was the normal thing last winter. Years ago bouncers were bowled as a surprise, but 50 per cent of them were harmless because bowlers had not learned to control them. Now they have, and hence the outbreak of helmets. *June 11 1978*

The protagonists: Iqbal Qasim (1), Mike Brearley (2), Sadiq Mohammad (3), Bob Willis (4), umpire Ken Palmer (5).

wrong way

right way

right way

It's tricky — skiing down a red carpet

When Prince Charles took a late spring skiing holiday in Isola, he perhaps did not expect to come under the scrutiny of the authors of *The Sunday Times* book *We Learned to Ski*—Brian Jackman, Harold Evans and Mark Ottaway. These were their comments:

Prince Charles wears the right kind of skis and clothes and looks good—but otherwise he is just like other beginners. For example, in the first picture he is on the move, but not so sure he wants to be. When running straight downhill the skier should have his body advanced much more than Prince Charles has. If the weight is on the tails of the skis, the tips shoot forward at greater speed. The effect is like having a rug pulled from under your feet. On a slightly steeper slope, Prince Charles would be sure to fall in this position. The diagram shows the right and wrong way.

In the second picture the stiff upper lip is not enough. The posture is not too bad, but it should be more aggressive, leaning forward as in the diagram.

Prince Charles's skis are open in the third picture at an angle (a stem) which is a good way to learn to turn, but beginners, fearful of the slope, lean into the hill, put the weight on the wrong ski and find turning very difficult. This is exactly the fault Prince Charles is making.

Conclusion: Prince Charles is obviously going to get a lot of fun out of ski-ing. A Smiley on his back suggests he has the right attitude: To Hell with style. I'm enjoying myself. *May 1 1977*

Inside track

Gold Diggers of '76

Act I: (Enter Brian Glanville, our football correspondent, seeking 10-minute interviews with European soccer superstars, Johan Cruyff and Franz Beckenbauer, for a Thames TV documentary): "How much?"

Cor Coster, Cruyff's father-in-law agent: "£1,000."

(Collapse of Glanville, who thought he'd heard it all.)

Act II: Glanville to Beckenbauer: "How much?"

Beckenbauer: "Give my fee, whatever it is, to charity. And you and your director and crew of five, come and lunch with me."

(Glanville, after seeing the polished German pay a £50 bill, leaves stage singing "You'll Never Walk Alone.")

August 15 1976

The vital ingredients for a British challenge in Europe's richest race

The excitement of horse racing has always lain in the emotions generated by anticipation of the result and the good or bad fortune experienced afterwards. But the aesthetic pleasure derives from the extent of the human's ability to control the raw power of the animal.

by Brough Scott

Geoff Lewis and Mill Reef are a near perfect blending of skills, and when they appear this afternoon at Longchamp for Europe's greatest race, the £100,000 Prix de l'Arc de Triomphe, it will be the coming together of two rarely surpassed talents; a man at the pinnacle of his profession and a horse that happens once in a jockey's lifetime, if that. Lewis will know as soon as he sees Mill Reef whether their chances are good or already doomed.

On the two occasions Mill Reef has been beaten, he has looked a smaller horse, like a man, says Lewis, with a stomach ache. But when he is on form, Mill Reef strides out with a grace and length that belies his small size and makes him today's favourite.

"Going to the start," says Lewis, "I always grab him a little because you don't want him to take off with you . . . at the finish I have to shorten up a bit to make him really concentrate . . . he's got this little habit of poking his old head out—asking you for more rein. He starts very fast, then it's up to them to take it off me—after all they know he is the fastest horse in the race. I don't believe in any fancy business in a race like this—you take risks on horses who can't win otherwise." *October 3 1971*

PS. Mill Reef won the 1971 Prix de l'Arc de Triomphe by three lengths from the top French filly, Pistol Packer.

Lewis plans to make Mill Reef's effort early in the straight, coming out gradually so as not to unbalance the horse. "If everything's okay, it will take a furlong before I've got them. That should leave me a furlong and a quarter to be in front . . . should be about right."

Today's Arc race compares to the athlete's mile (1). Mill Reef would be a good miler, but an even better half-miler than others. Lewis says it will be fatal for others to wait behind him. A nine-handicap golfer, Lewis adds that big-race nerves centre on the hands (2). "You can get the yips, just as in golf. You must master yourself, or your hands start to pump the horse up too early." On the other hand (3), if Lewis pulls hard, Mill Reef just cannot stay. "It's like a car running over-revved," he says. To prevent this he has developed a uniquely effective method of slipping the reins (dotted line) three or four inches to give more play on the mouth.

Skilful amateurs and slugging pros: a communist takeover

The erosion of traditional, indeed elementary, skills in British professional boxing is largely the result of commercial pressures. But there is an argument which says it need never have happened.

by John Lovesey
Drawings by Paul Trevillion

In recent years one of the most disillusioning aspects of British professional boxing has been the lessening of appreciation of skill as a direct result of a concentration on bigger and clumsy fighters. Indeed, the art of feinting, drawing and counterpunching is basically a lost and disregarded art in this country's professional boxing.

By contrast, in communist countries such as Russia, Poland and Hungary, lobbies against boxing in the mid-Fifties, produced an obsession with technique. The result is they have become the repositories of the craft and this month, a British audience had a rare chance to glimpse this when a Russian team beat England.

Soviet boxing, at its best, is clearly a game of chess with muscles, played by fighters who are notable for their all-round athleticism as well as boxing skills (some of which are illustrated right as they might appear against the West's pros), which is boxing as it should be. The emphasis in amateur boxing, of course, is not so much on power as the number of scoring blows struck over nine minutes. But the evidence of the communist boxers' mastery is in their defensive as well as attacking techniques and their unmarked faces.

The professional field contends that fighting over three rounds is a world apart from fighting over the longer professional distances. The argument discounts the fact that skill can be constant and that only the training and pacing need be different. Hungary's Laszlo Papp, who turned professional after winning gold medals at three consecutive Olympic Games—1948, 1952 and 1956—effectively proved this. As a pro, Papp thrashed everyone in sight in Western Europe and became the European professional middleweight champion—at 36. *November 12 1972*

oteoteotototeoteotototeototeoteotototeototeototeotototeototeototeototeototeotototeototeototeototeototeototeotot

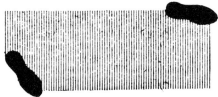

PYRAMID BASE. A style used by most boxers from communist countries. With one foot off-set from the other, placed well apart and firmly planted, the body is held decidedly sideways to the opponent, thus presenting a minimal target. From this fundamental position a long, leading left is deployed, keeping the opponent an off-putting distance away, and yet feeling him out, drawing him, diverting him and finally throwing him off balance in order to go forward and score with counterpunches. By comparison, too many of our own amateurs have concentrated on the professional style depicted here.

BURSTS. Communist boxers disdain flashy wasteful combinations beloved of professionals and instead use economic, straight, short bursts to build up points. They come forward quickly and back out fast, manoeuvring both straight on and laterally in relation to their opponent.

SHIFT AND HIT. A classic ploy taught to communist fighters. From an orthodox stance, they shift forward to the right but score with a swinging left hook. The ploy was used notably, for example, by Russia's Vladimir Jengi- barian, who won the light-welterweight gold medal in the 1956 Olympics and has been acclaimed by professionals as well as amateurs as one of the greatest fighters to emerge since the war.

DOOR SLAM. The right side is transferred round the firm line formed by the left side of the body which acts as the hinge to the movement. The right is delivered like a door slamming, generating far more velocity than such a punch delivered from a square-on position.

UPPERCUT. A less orthodox style, the gloves are held very low, like Muhammad Ali, and counterpunches and blows are thrown from whichever position the boxer's hands happen to be in. Thus the uppercut illustrated here is delivered in a great curve with a great suppleness of the shoulder.

SWAY BACK. The firm wide platform formed by the feet, and the concentration, as part of their training, on suppleness of the lower back and hip joints, allows communist boxers to sway back or to the side to avoid many punches with great facility. It is a style, however, preached as heresy among the pros and only Muhammad Ali has successfully got away with it.

PICTURE FILE

Most sport takes place outside the big arenas, much of it far off the beaten track. Young Jeremy Hibble from Bradford once badly lacked strength and self-confidence; now he's British junior white water champion. "To be good," he says, "you've got to know water, but mostly you've got to know yourself." Sportsmen and women everywhere know that feeling, as they find reward in the so-called "minority" sports. In fact, these sports are pursued by the majority.

Saturday morning on the river. One of the great club rowing days, celebrated in the Head of the River race: a time race, over a 4¼-mile course, for a great procession of some 400 crews, from mighty Leander to Midland Bank III.

Saturday afternoon in the tub. These are antique hip baths; the changing rooms are in the long-established Thames Hare and Hounds Club; and these runners have been contesting the Oxford-Cambridge match. But the principle of aching, muddy limbs being soaked in hot water is universal.

Sunday morning on the road. The start point is "electric light pole No. 12, two miles south of Ringwood"; the man on the mark is Ken Jones, a 52-year-old Nottinghamshire teacher; the event is the Veterans 50-mile time-trial championship.

Paul Svehlik chose to deploy his natural sporting ability and his powerful 14-stone physique in hockey, and the England team had good reason to be grateful. Svehlik's exploitation of the penalty corner was almost lethal.

On a South London back lawn, one Englishman advances on another, *shinai* raised. The sport being practised is the ancient Japanese martial art of kendo.

The English and the Scots have their football, the Welsh have their rugby. The Irish have their own game, here demonstrated at Wembley by a Limerick man and a Kilkenny man. This game of sticks-and-stones is called hurling.

Alone in a tunnel of water, an expert surfer rides the inside of a long, long wave—at 35 mph—into Maaloea Beach in the Hawaiian Islands.

Alone in the air, a ski-glider drifts through the Swiss Alps. In an age which has rediscovered the balloon and developed the glider, the freedom of wings has now been added to the freedom of skis. The Swiss call the apparatus Ski-Icarus.

Alone on the river, an angler stalks his prey. On the Kennet the mayfly are hatching by the million, for once in the year the trout are going mad, and the angler means not to miss his chance. He will end the day with his best catch of the season.

The woman ruling the table tennis table is Jill Hammersley, a Surrey housewife, whose victory in the 1976 English championship, against a Swedish opponent, occupied just 22 minutes.

The woman commanding the road is Jane Colebrook, whose European indoor 800m title in 1977 proved what could be done in lonely Lincolnshire, aided by a mother who on winter nights lights the way with a torch and in summer loyally comes along just for company.

Index

Authors', photographers' and artists' names are in *italics*
★ Indicates the inclusion of illustrations

Picture credits

To Michael
Christmas 1979
love
Greg + Jane